MINT CHOCOLATE

1

MAMI ORIKASA

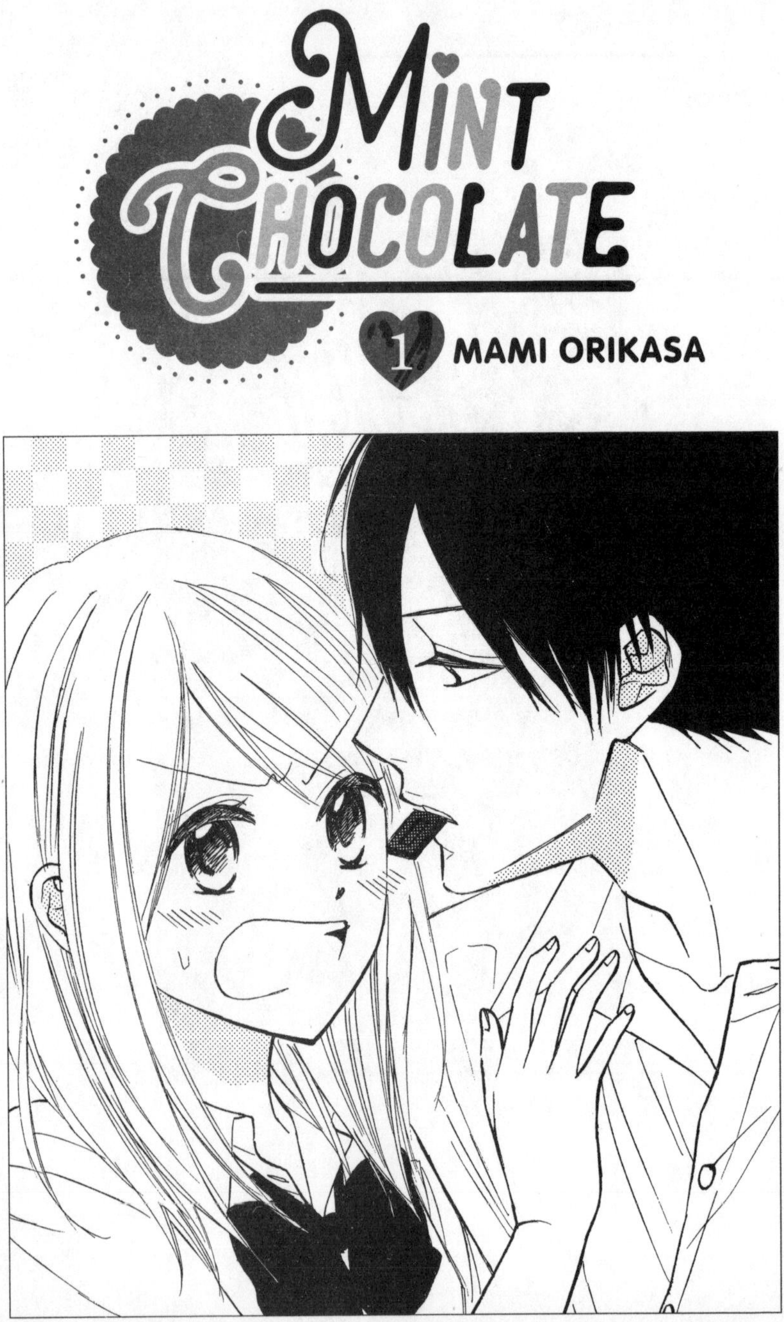

Mint Chocolate

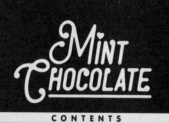

CONTENTS

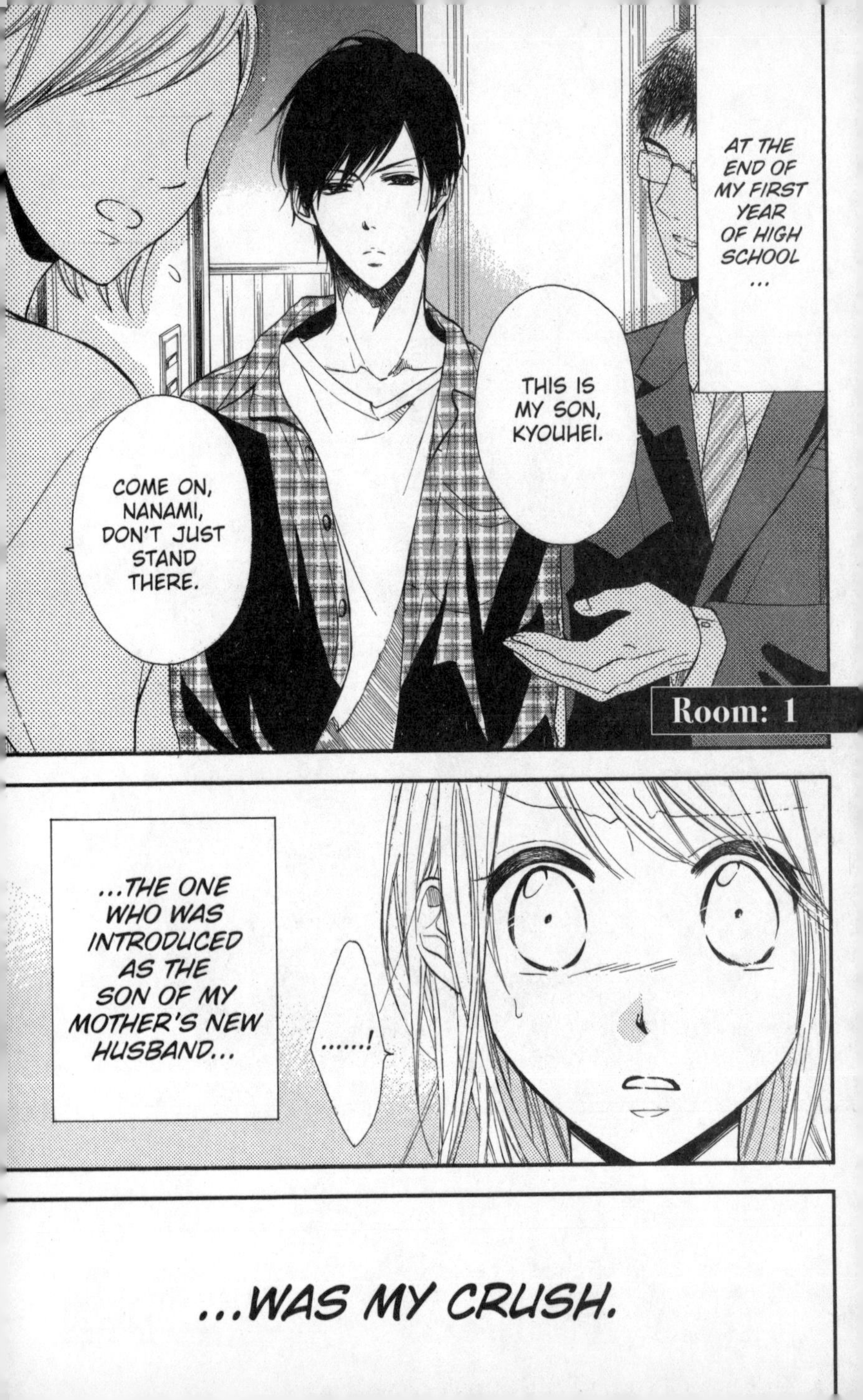
AT THE END OF MY FIRST YEAR OF HIGH SCHOOL...
THIS IS MY SON, KYOUHEI.
COME ON, NANAMI, DON'T JUST STAND THERE.
Room: 1
......!
...THE ONE WHO WAS INTRODUCED AS THE SON OF MY MOTHER'S NEW HUSBAND...
...WAS MY CRUSH.

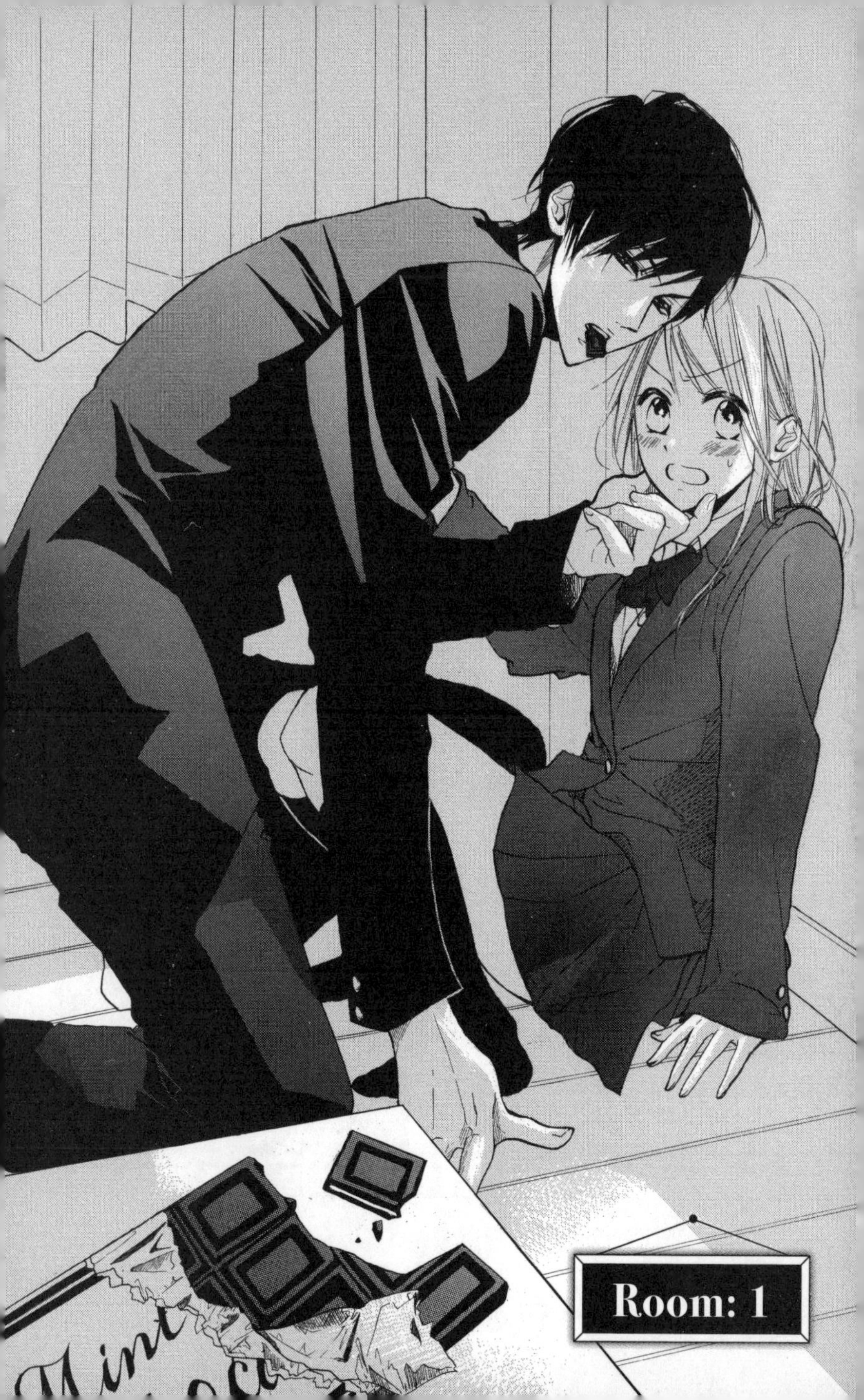
Room: 1
Mint

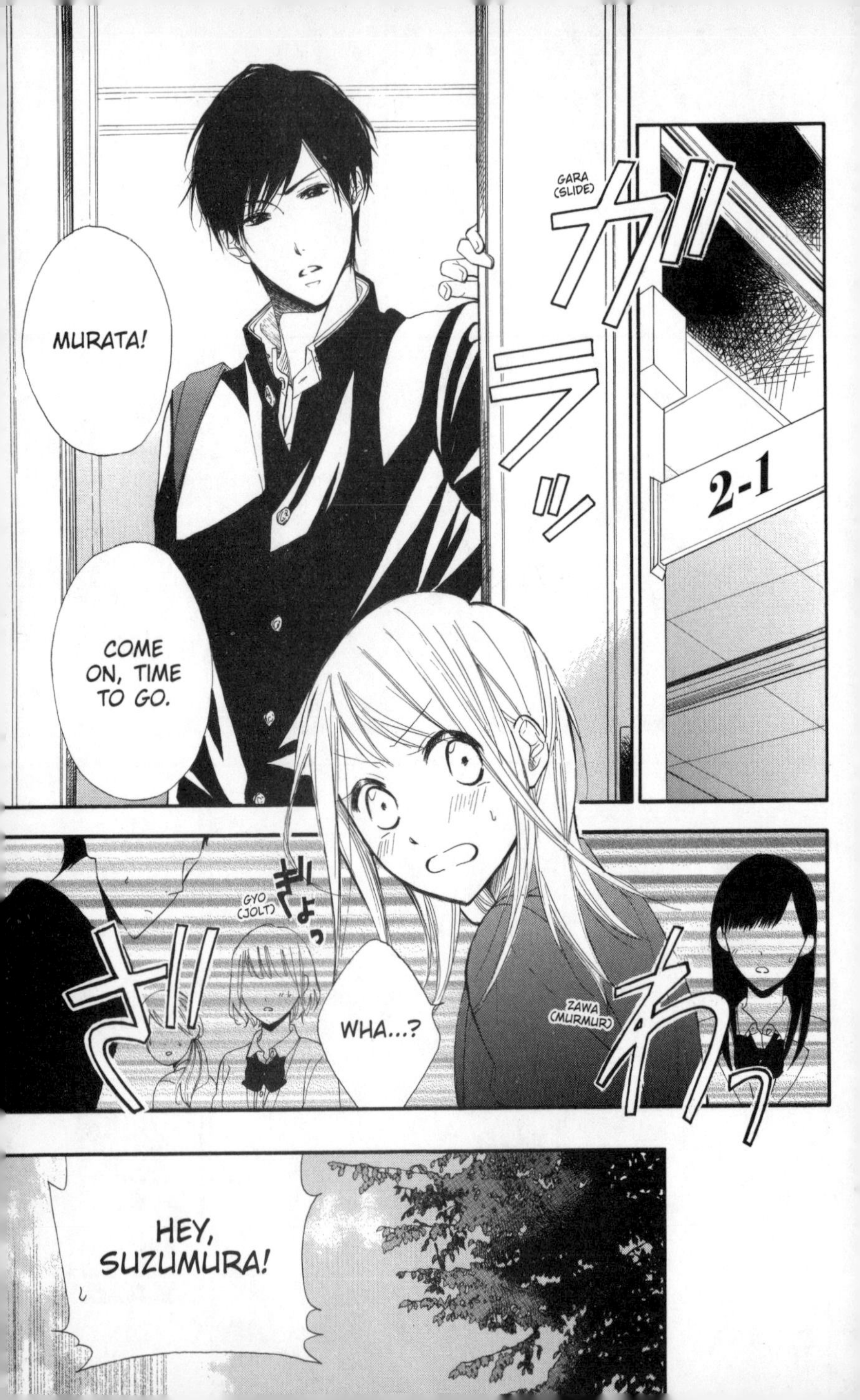
ガラッ
GARA (SLIDE)
2-1
MURATA!
COME ON, TIME TO GO.
わっ
ZAWA (MURMUR)
WHA...?
ぎょっ
GYO (JOLT)
ざ
HEY, SUZUMURA!

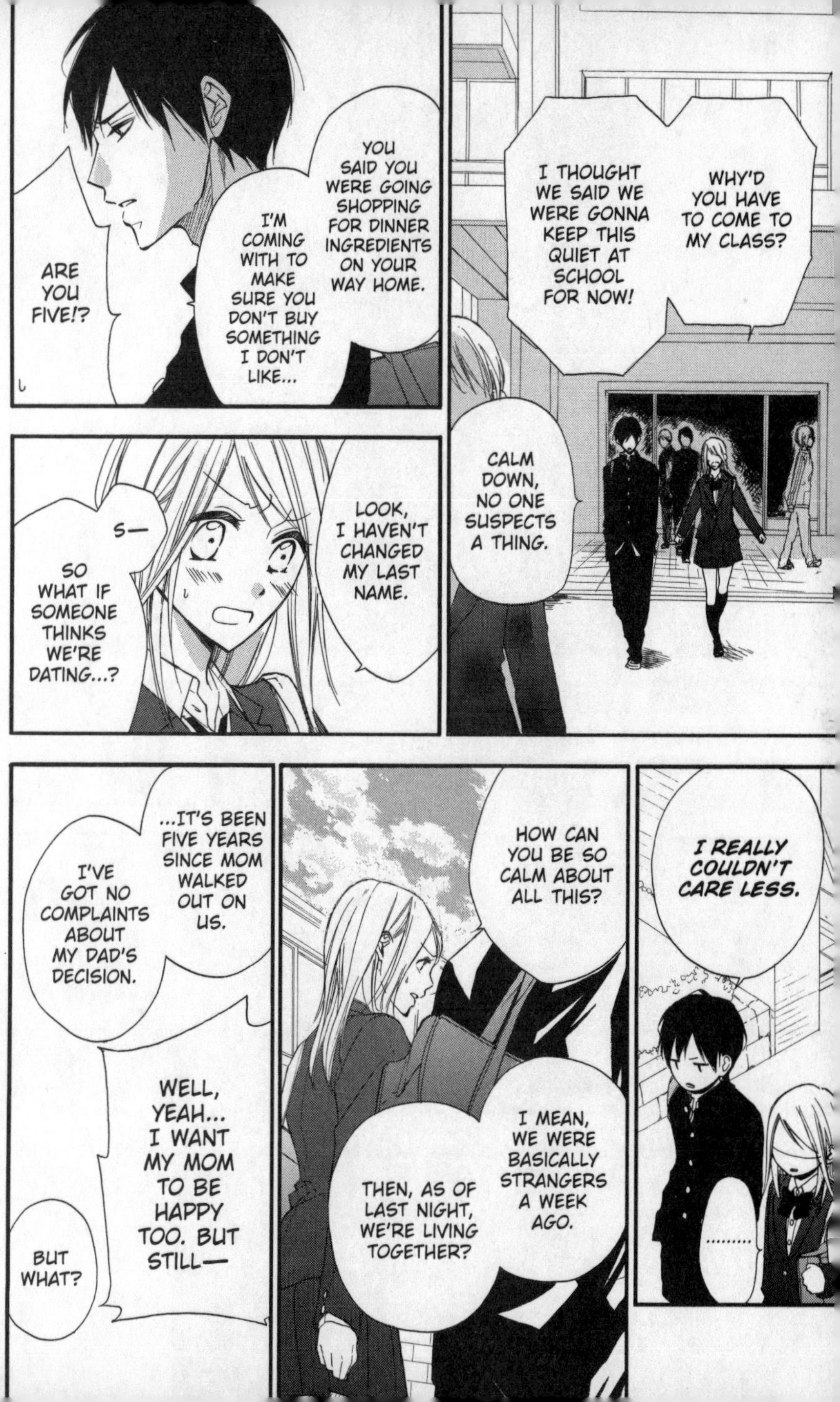
WHY'D YOU HAVE TO COME TO MY CLASS?
I THOUGHT WE SAID WE WERE GONNA KEEP THIS QUIET AT SCHOOL FOR NOW!
CALM DOWN, NO ONE SUSPECTS A THING.
YOU SAID YOU WERE GOING SHOPPING FOR DINNER INGREDIENTS ON YOUR WAY HOME.
I'M COMING WITH TO MAKE SURE YOU DON'T BUY SOMETHING I DON'T LIKE...
ARE YOU FIVE!?
LOOK, I HAVEN'T CHANGED MY LAST NAME.
S—
SO WHAT IF SOMEONE THINKS WE'RE DATING...?
I REALLY COULDN'T CARE LESS.
....
HOW CAN YOU BE SO CALM ABOUT ALL THIS?
I MEAN, WE WERE BASICALLY STRANGERS A WEEK AGO.
THEN, AS OF LAST NIGHT, WE'RE LIVING TOGETHER?
...IT'S BEEN FIVE YEARS SINCE MOM WALKED OUT ON US.
I'VE GOT NO COMPLAINTS ABOUT MY DAD'S DECISION.
WELL, YEAH... I WANT MY MOM TO BE HAPPY TOO. BUT STILL—
BUT WHAT?

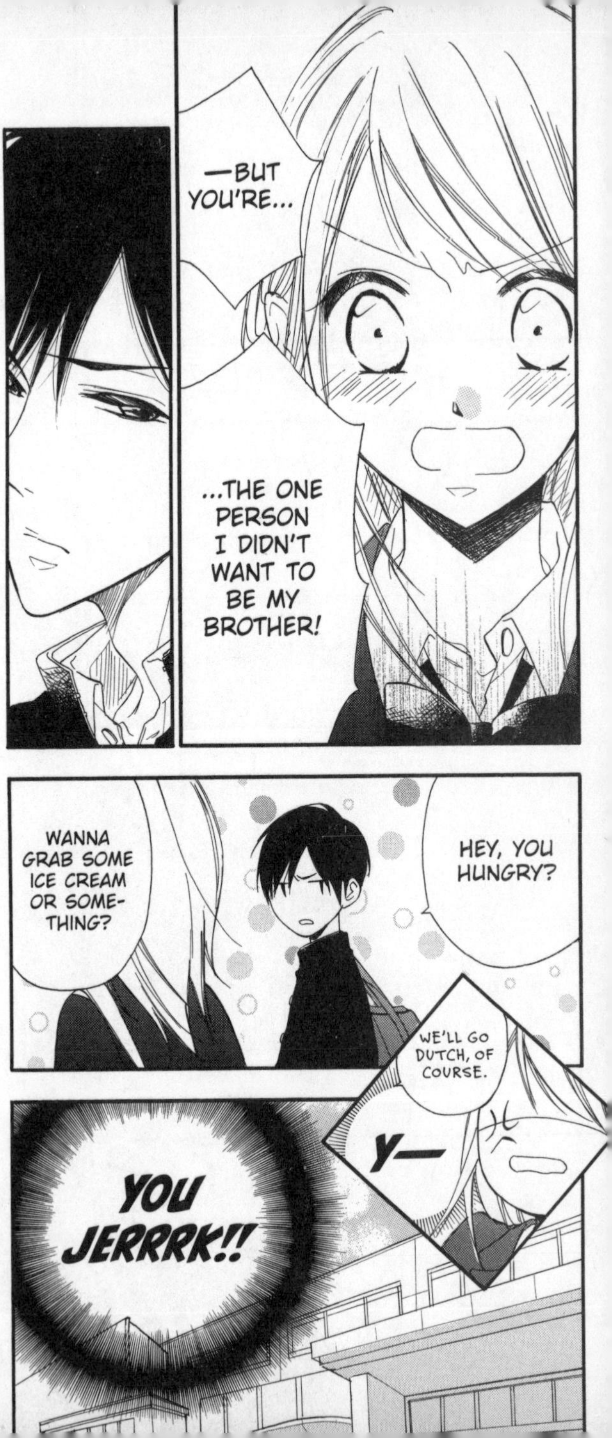
—BUT YOU'RE...
...THE ONE PERSON I DIDN'T WANT TO BE MY BROTHER!
HEY, YOU HUNGRY?
WANNA GRAB SOME ICE CREAM OR SOME-THING?
WE'LL GO DUTCH, OF COURSE.
Y—
YOU JERRRK!!

AUTHOR'S GREETING.

HELLO. NICE TO MEET YOU. I'M MAMI ORIKASA.

THANK YOU FOR PICKING UP THE FIRST VOLUME OF MY FIRST SERIES.

BY THE TIME THIS VOLUME HIT THE SHELVES, I HAD ALREADY BEEN DRAWING THESE KIDS OF MINE FOR OVER TWO YEARS!

I'M INCREDIBLY GRATEFUL THAT THIS WORK—WHICH BEGAN AS A ONE-SHOT—LED TO THIS COLLECTED VOLUME.

SOME PARTS MAY BE A BIT ROUGH AROUND THE EDGES, BUT I HOPE YOU ENJOY IT NONETHELESS.

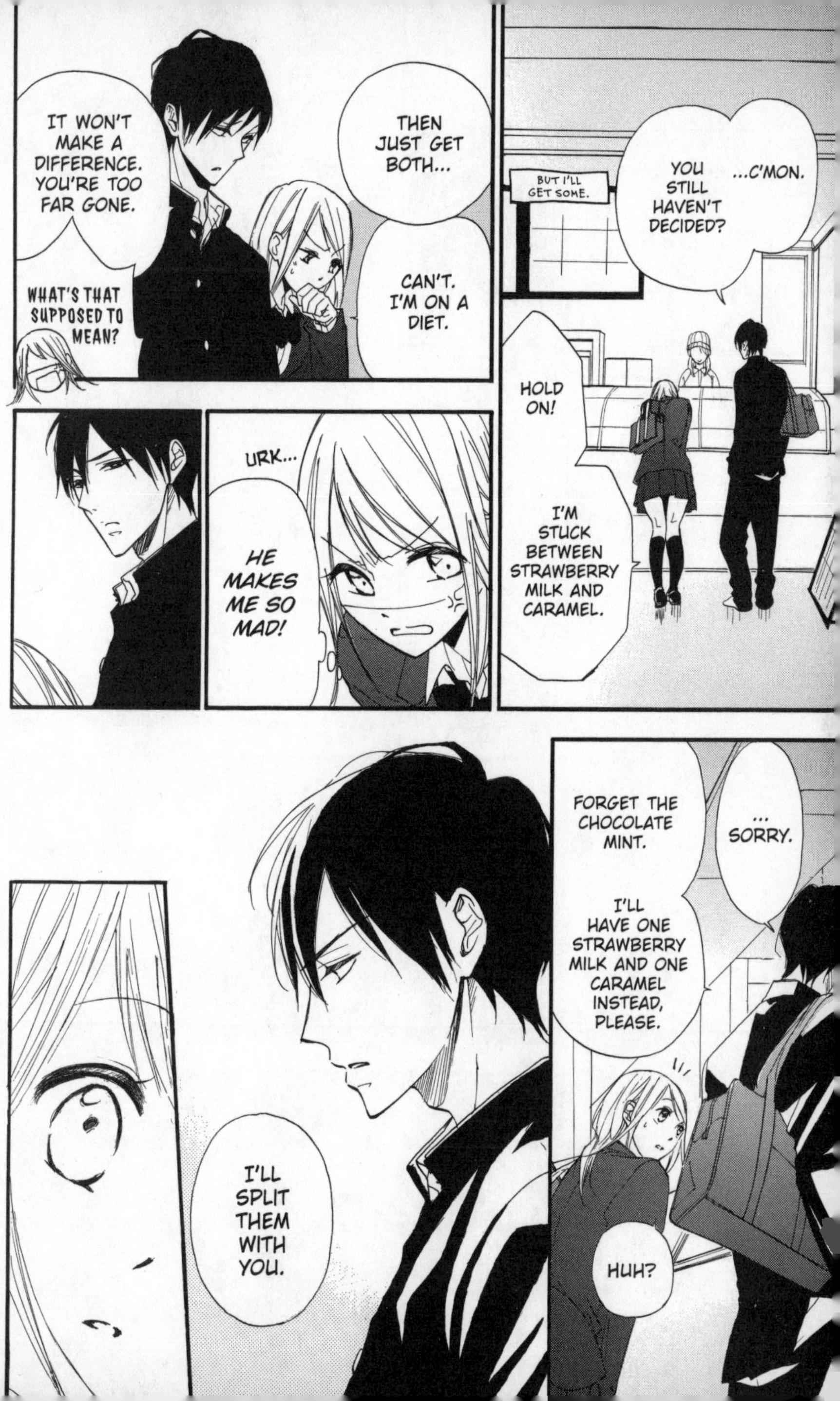
...C'MON.
YOU STILL HAVEN'T DECIDED?
BUT I'LL GET SOME.
HOLD ON!
I'M STUCK BETWEEN STRAWBERRY MILK AND CARAMEL.
THEN JUST GET BOTH...
CAN'T. I'M ON A DIET.
IT WON'T MAKE A DIFFERENCE. YOU'RE TOO FAR GONE.
WHAT'S THAT SUPPOSED TO MEAN?
URK...
HE MAKES ME SO MAD!
... SORRY.
FORGET THE CHOCOLATE MINT.
I'LL HAVE ONE STRAWBERRY MILK AND ONE CARAMEL INSTEAD, PLEASE.
HUH?
I'LL SPLIT THEM WITH YOU.

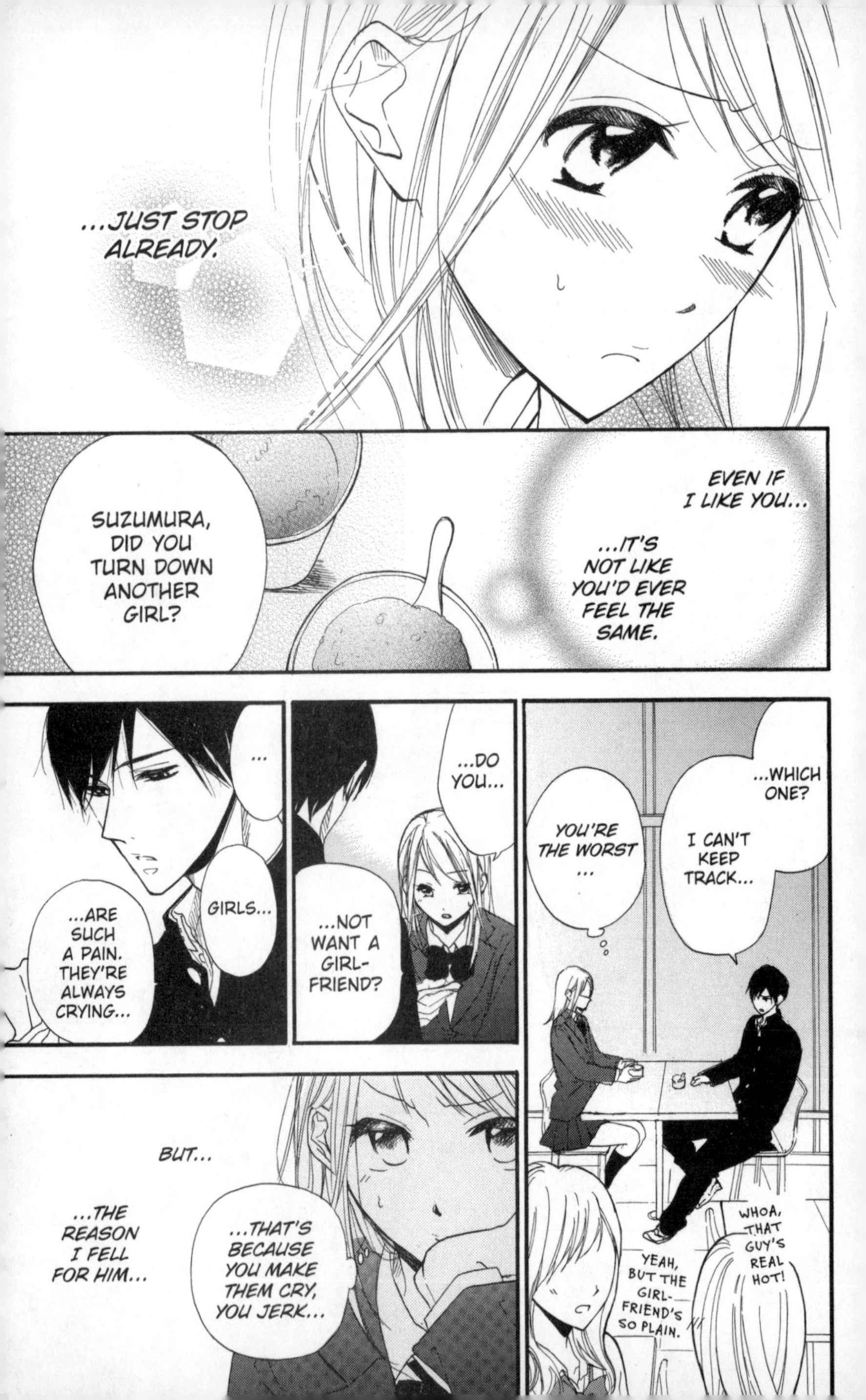
...JUST STOP ALREADY.
EVEN IF I LIKE YOU...
...IT'S NOT LIKE YOU'D EVER FEEL THE SAME.
SUZUMURA, DID YOU TURN DOWN ANOTHER GIRL?
...WHICH ONE?
I CAN'T KEEP TRACK...
YOU'RE THE WORST ...
WHOA, THAT GUY'S REAL HOT!
YEAH, BUT THE GIRL-FRIEND'S SO PLAIN.
...DO YOU...
...NOT WANT A GIRL-FRIEND?
...
GIRLS...
...ARE SUCH A PAIN. THEY'RE ALWAYS CRYING...
...THAT'S BECAUSE YOU MAKE THEM CRY, YOU JERK...
BUT...
...THE REASON I FELL FOR HIM...

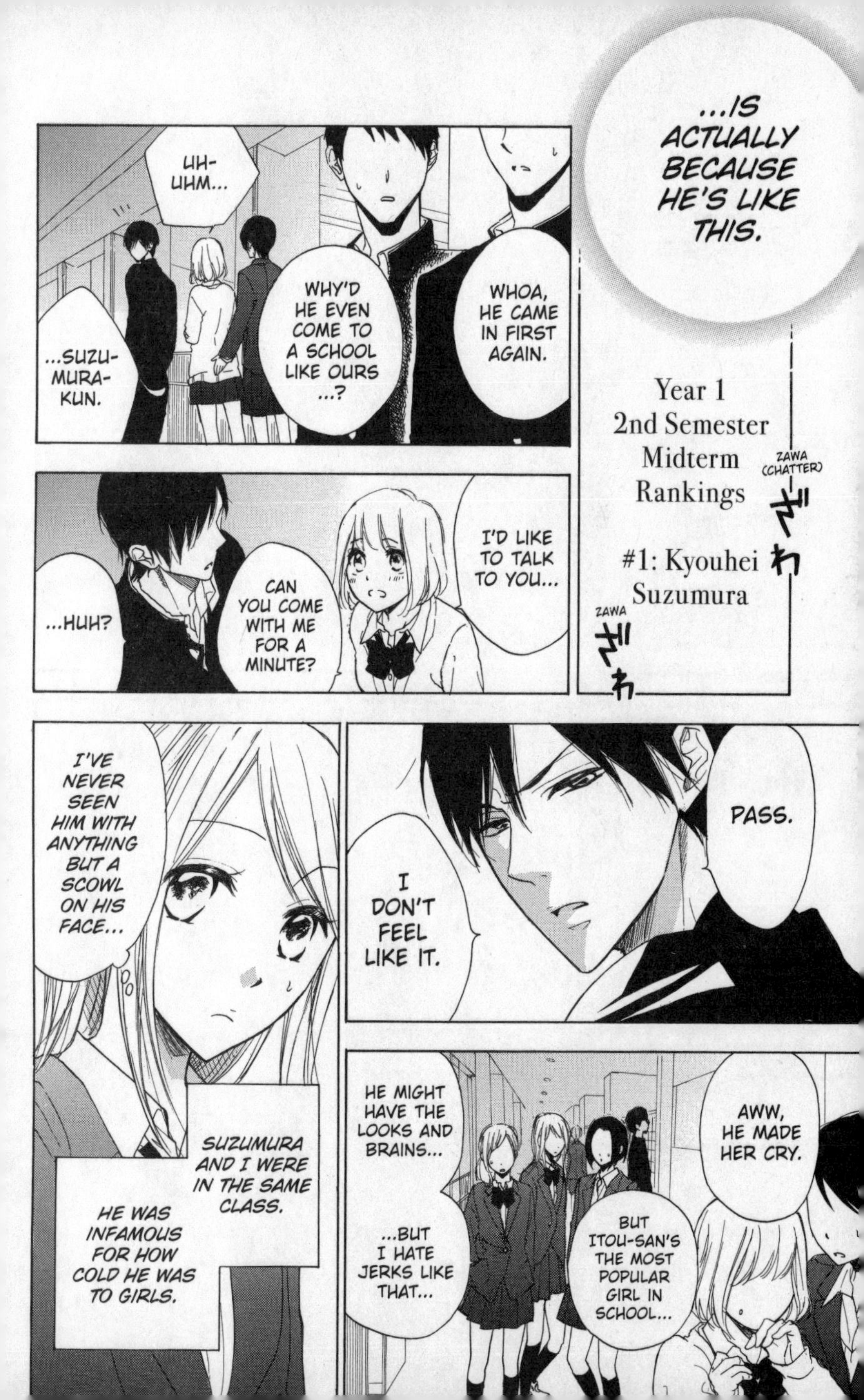
...IS ACTUALLY BECAUSE HE'S LIKE THIS.
Year 1 2nd Semester Midterm Rankings
#1: Kyouhei Suzumura
ZAWA (CHATTER) ざわ
ZAWA ざわ
WHOA, HE CAME IN FIRST AGAIN.
WHY'D HE EVEN COME TO A SCHOOL LIKE OURS ...?
UH-UHM...
...SUZU-MURA-KUN.
I'D LIKE TO TALK TO YOU...
CAN YOU COME WITH ME FOR A MINUTE?
...HUH?
PASS.
I DON'T FEEL LIKE IT.
AWW, HE MADE HER CRY.
HE MIGHT HAVE THE LOOKS AND BRAINS...
BUT ITOU-SAN'S THE MOST POPULAR GIRL IN SCHOOL...
...BUT I HATE JERKS LIKE THAT...
I'VE NEVER SEEN HIM WITH ANYTHING BUT A SCOWL ON HIS FACE...
SUZUMURA AND I WERE IN THE SAME CLASS.
HE WAS INFAMOUS FOR HOW COLD HE WAS TO GIRLS.

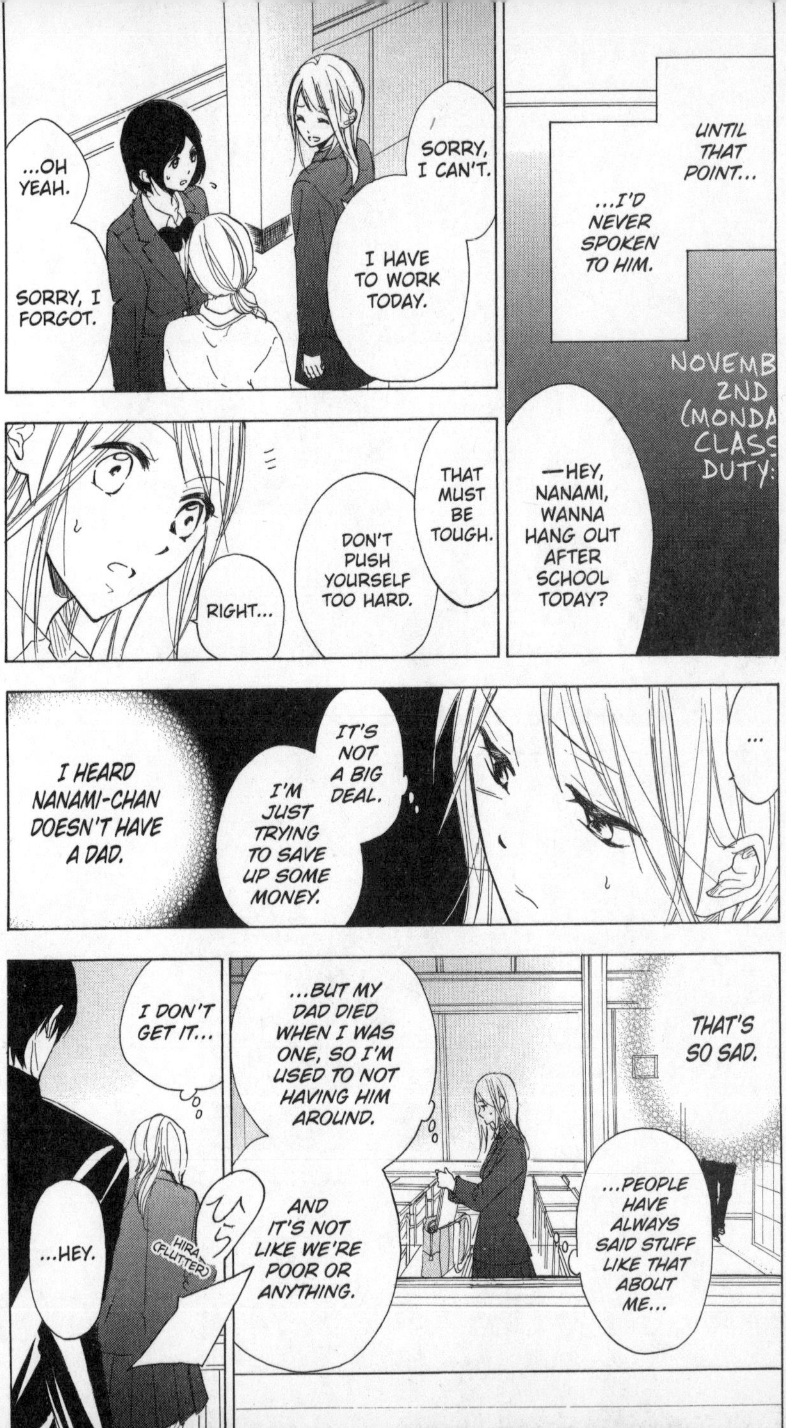

UNTIL THAT POINT...
...I'D NEVER SPOKEN TO HIM.
NOVEMB
2ND
(MONDA
CLASS
DUTY:
—HEY, NANAMI, WANNA HANG OUT AFTER SCHOOL TODAY?
SORRY, I CAN'T.
I HAVE TO WORK TODAY.
...OH YEAH.
SORRY, I FORGOT.
THAT MUST BE TOUGH.
DON'T PUSH YOURSELF TOO HARD.
RIGHT...
...
IT'S NOT A BIG DEAL.
I'M JUST TRYING TO SAVE UP SOME MONEY.
I HEARD NANAMI-CHAN DOESN'T HAVE A DAD.
THAT'S SO SAD.
...PEOPLE HAVE ALWAYS SAID STUFF LIKE THAT ABOUT ME...
...BUT MY DAD DIED WHEN I WAS ONE, SO I'M USED TO NOT HAVING HIM AROUND.
AND IT'S NOT LIKE WE'RE POOR OR ANYTHING.
I DON'T GET IT...
ひら
HIRA (FLUTTER)
...HEY.

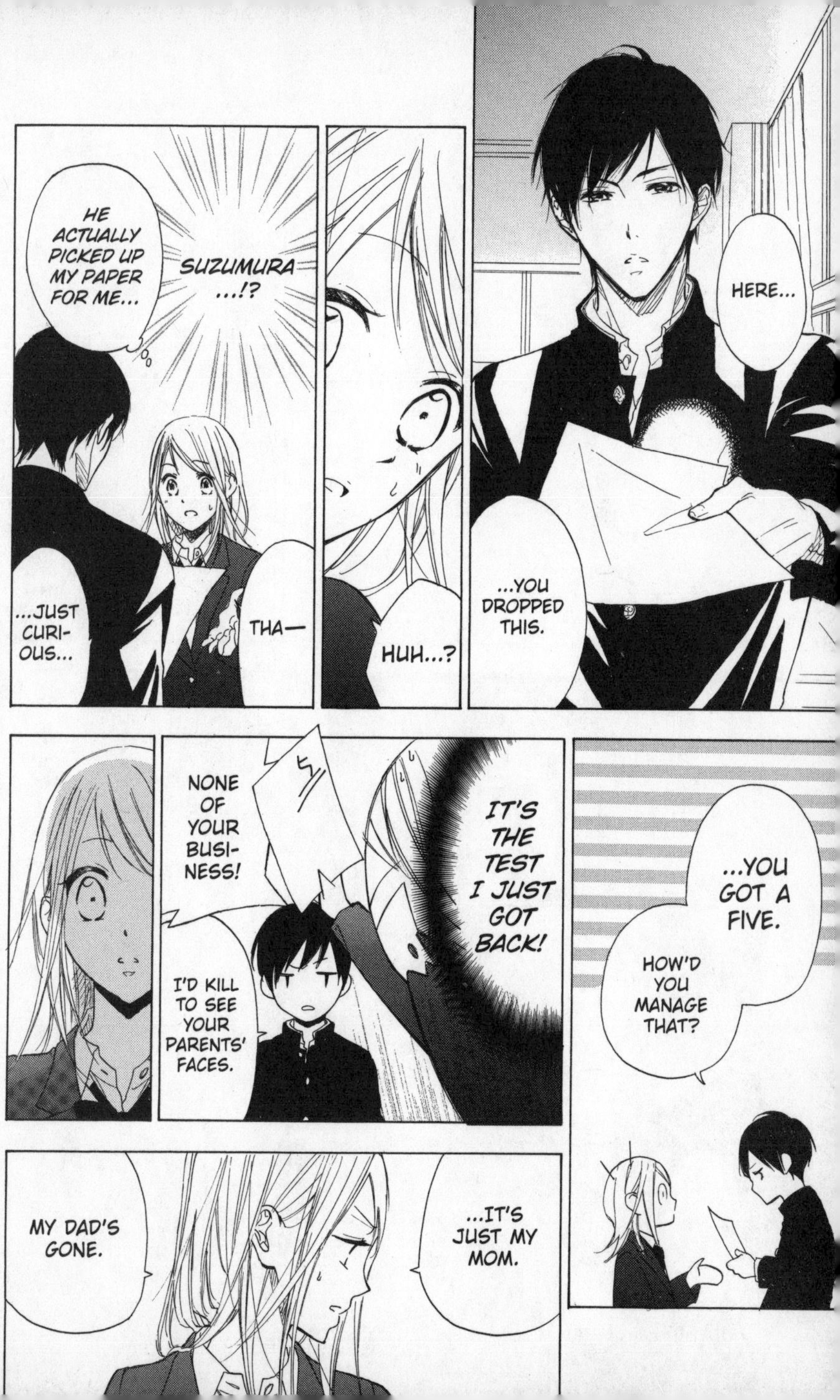
HERE...
...YOU DROPPED THIS.
HUH...?
SUZUMURA ...!?
HE ACTUALLY PICKED UP MY PAPER FOR ME...
THA—
...JUST CURIOUS...
...YOU GOT A FIVE.
HOW'D YOU MANAGE THAT?
IT'S THE TEST I JUST GOT BACK!
NONE OF YOUR BUSINESS!
I'D KILL TO SEE YOUR PARENTS' FACES.
...IT'S JUST MY MOM.
MY DAD'S GONE.

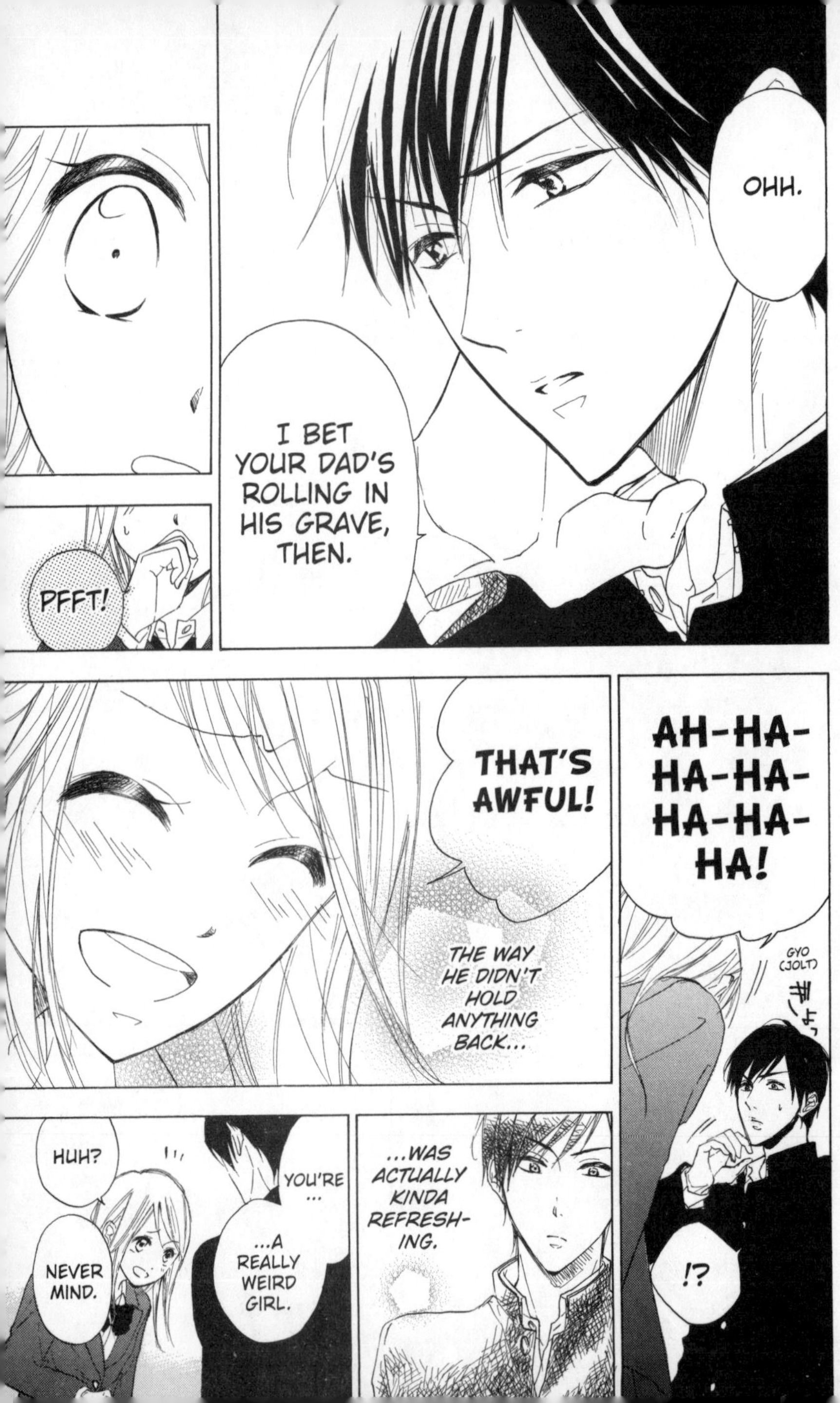

OHH.
I BET YOUR DAD'S ROLLING IN HIS GRAVE, THEN.
PFFT!
AH-HA-HA-HA-HA-HA-HA!
GYO (JOLT)
ぎょっ
!?
THAT'S AWFUL!
THE WAY HE DIDN'T HOLD ANYTHING BACK...
...WAS ACTUALLY KINDA REFRESH-ING.
YOU'RE ...
...A REALLY WEIRD GIRL.
HUH?
NEVER MIND.

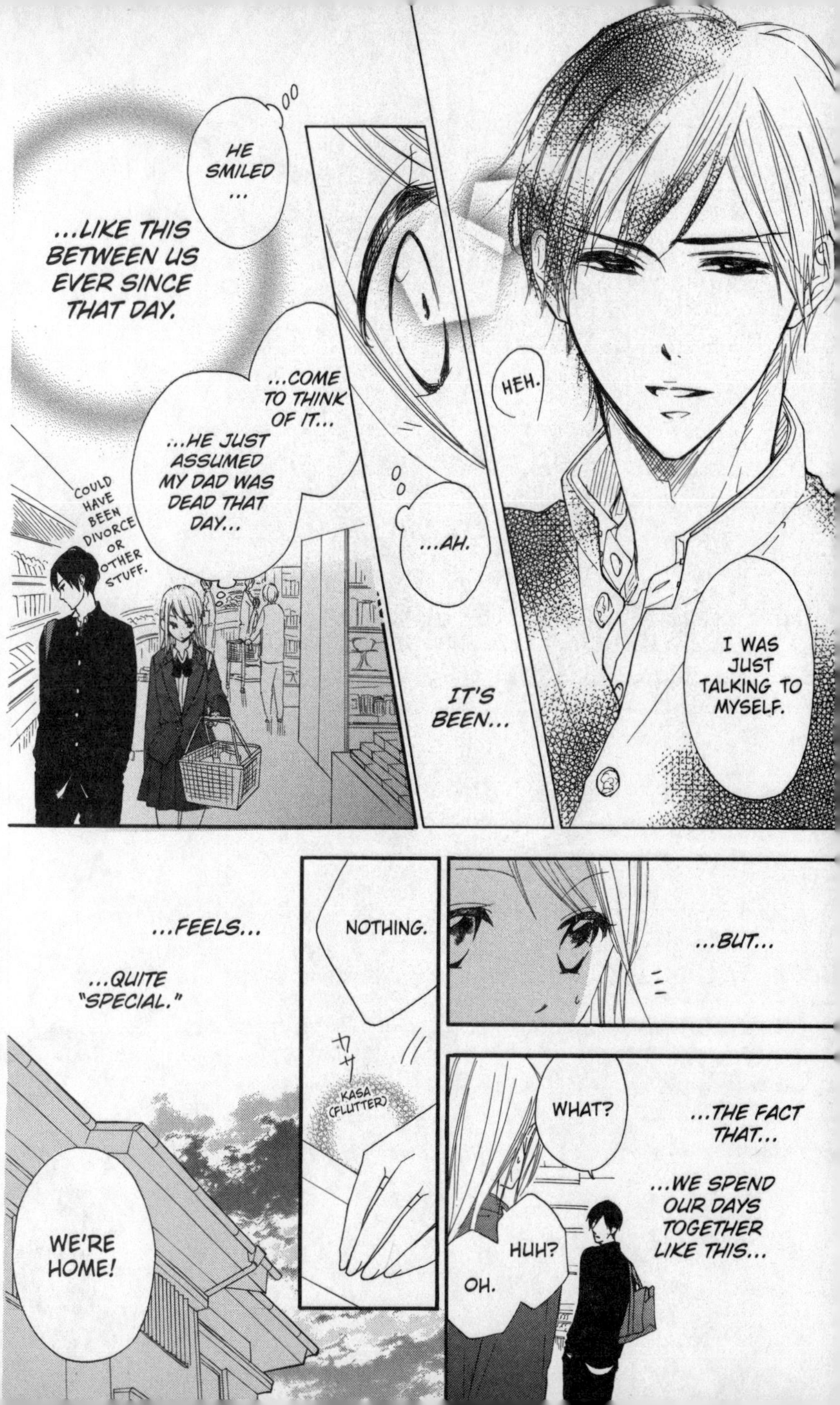
HEH.
I WAS JUST TALKING TO MYSELF.
IT'S BEEN...
...AH.
HE SMILED ...
...LIKE THIS BETWEEN US EVER SINCE THAT DAY.
...COME TO THINK OF IT...
...HE JUST ASSUMED MY DAD WAS DEAD THAT DAY...
COULD HAVE BEEN DIVORCE OR OTHER STUFF.
...BUT...
...THE FACT THAT...
WHAT?
...WE SPEND OUR DAYS TOGETHER LIKE THIS...
HUH?
OH.
NOTHING.
カサ
KASA (FLUTTER)
...FEELS...
...QUITE "SPECIAL."
WE'RE HOME!

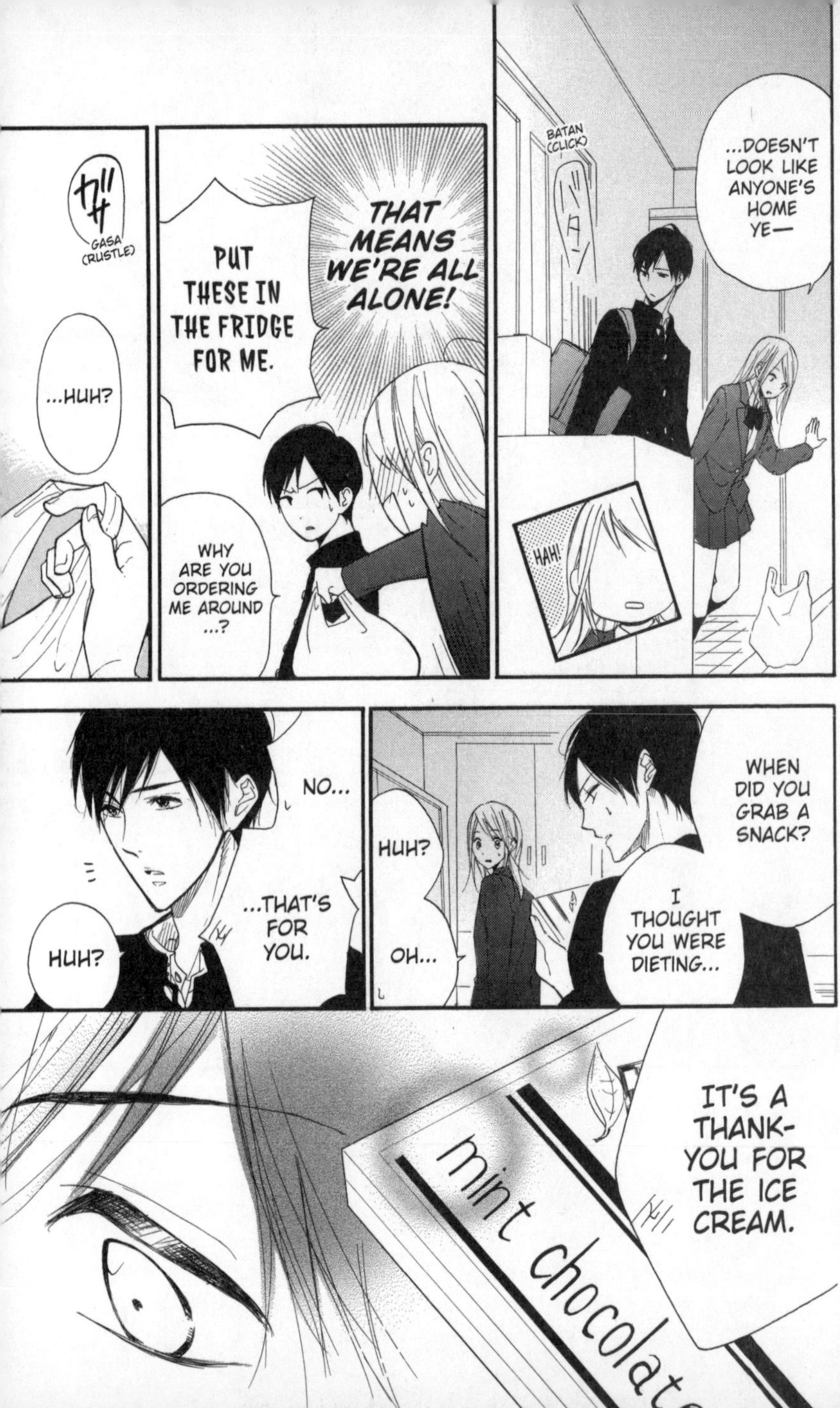
...DOESN'T LOOK LIKE ANYONE'S HOME YE—
BATAN (CLICK)
HAH!
THAT MEANS WE'RE ALL ALONE!
PUT THESE IN THE FRIDGE FOR ME.
WHY ARE YOU ORDERING ME AROUND ...?
GASA (RUSTLE)
...HUH?
WHEN DID YOU GRAB A SNACK?
I THOUGHT YOU WERE DIETING...
HUH?
OH...
NO...
...THAT'S FOR YOU.
HUH?
IT'S A THANK-YOU FOR THE ICE CREAM.
mint chocolat

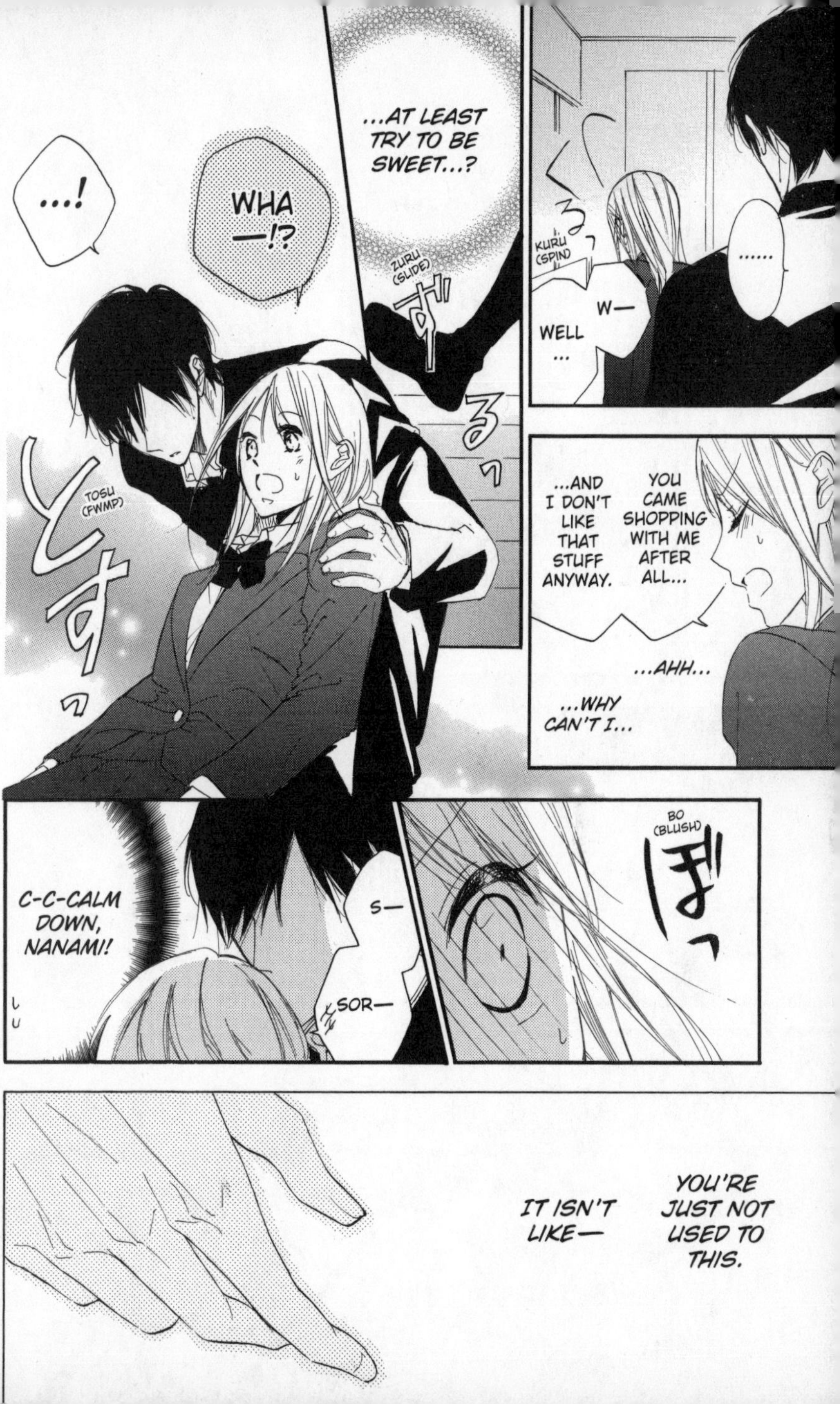
......
KURU (SPIN)
W— WELL ...
YOU CAME SHOPPING WITH ME AFTER ALL...
...AND I DON'T LIKE THAT STUFF ANYWAY.
...AHH...
...WHY CAN'T I...
...AT LEAST TRY TO BE SWEET...?
ZURU (SLIDE)
WHA —!?
...!
TOSU (FWMP)
BO (BLUSH)
S—
SOR—
C-C-CALM DOWN, NANAMI!
YOU'RE JUST NOT USED TO THIS.
IT ISN'T LIKE—

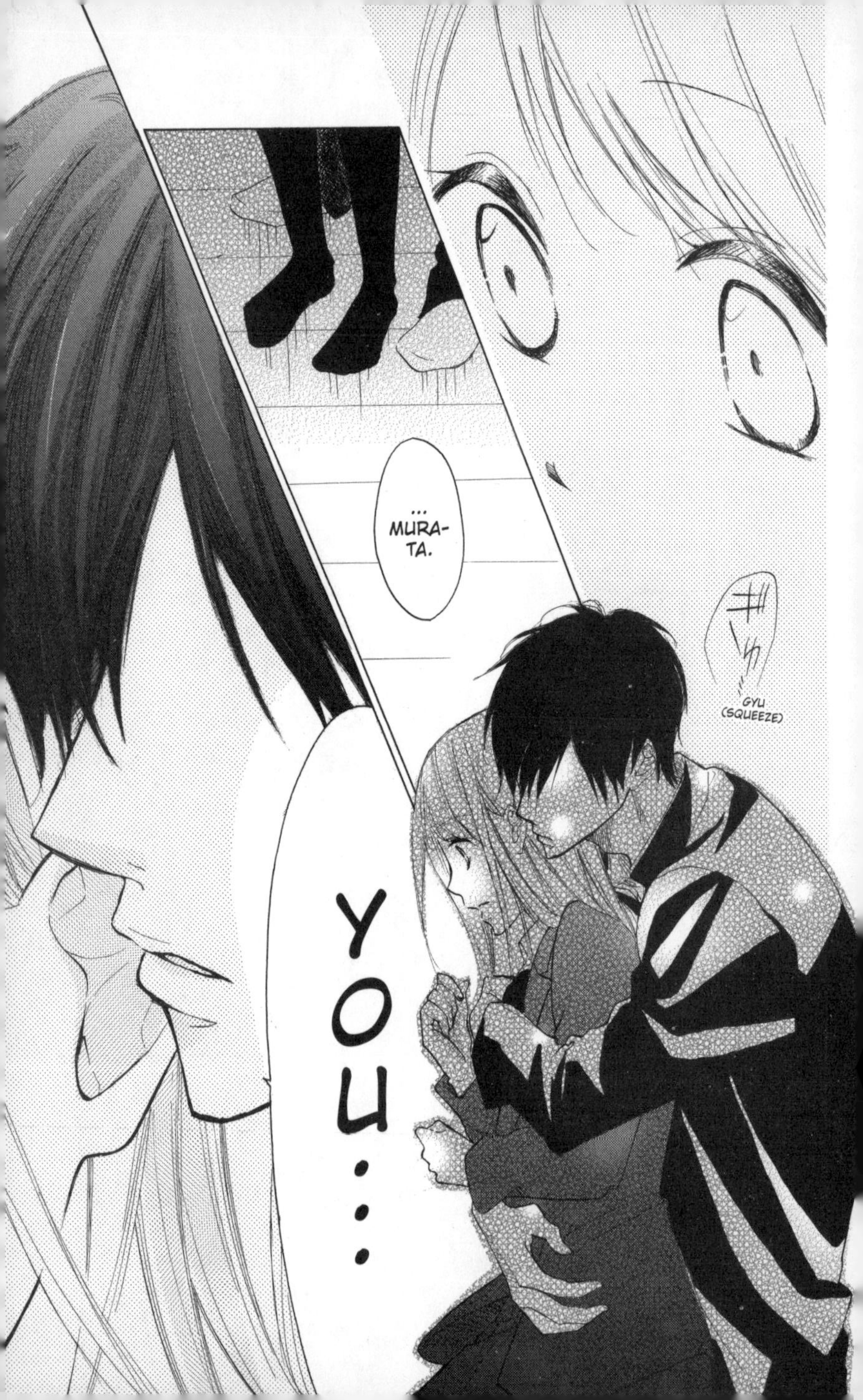
...MURA-TA.
GYU (SQUEEZE)
YOU...

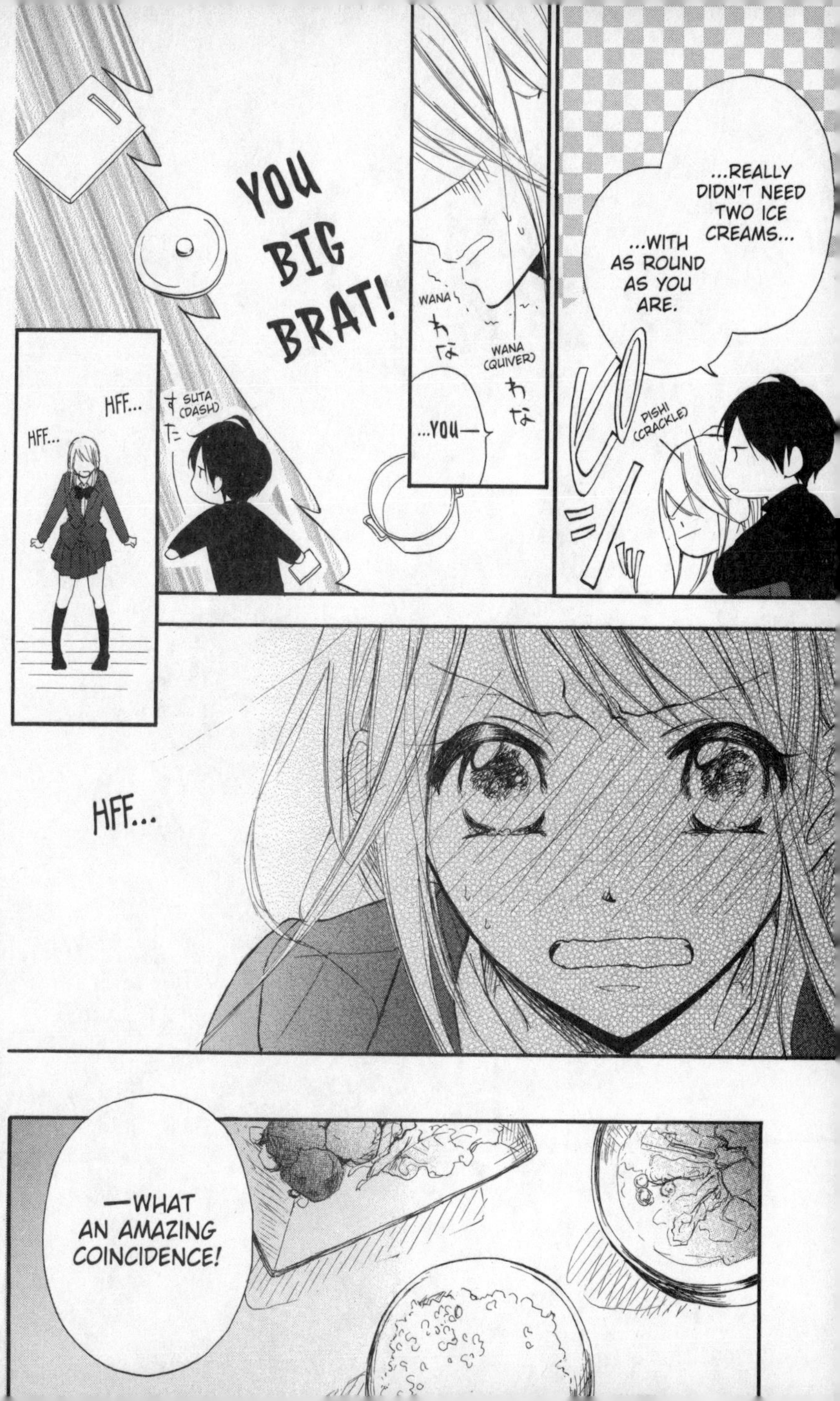
...REALLY DIDN'T NEED TWO ICE CREAMS...
...WITH AS ROUND AS YOU ARE.
PISHI (CRACKLE)
WANA わな
WANA (QUIVER) わな
...YOU—
YOU BIG BRAT!
すた SUTA (DASH)
HFF...
HFF...
HFF...
—WHAT AN AMAZING COINCIDENCE!

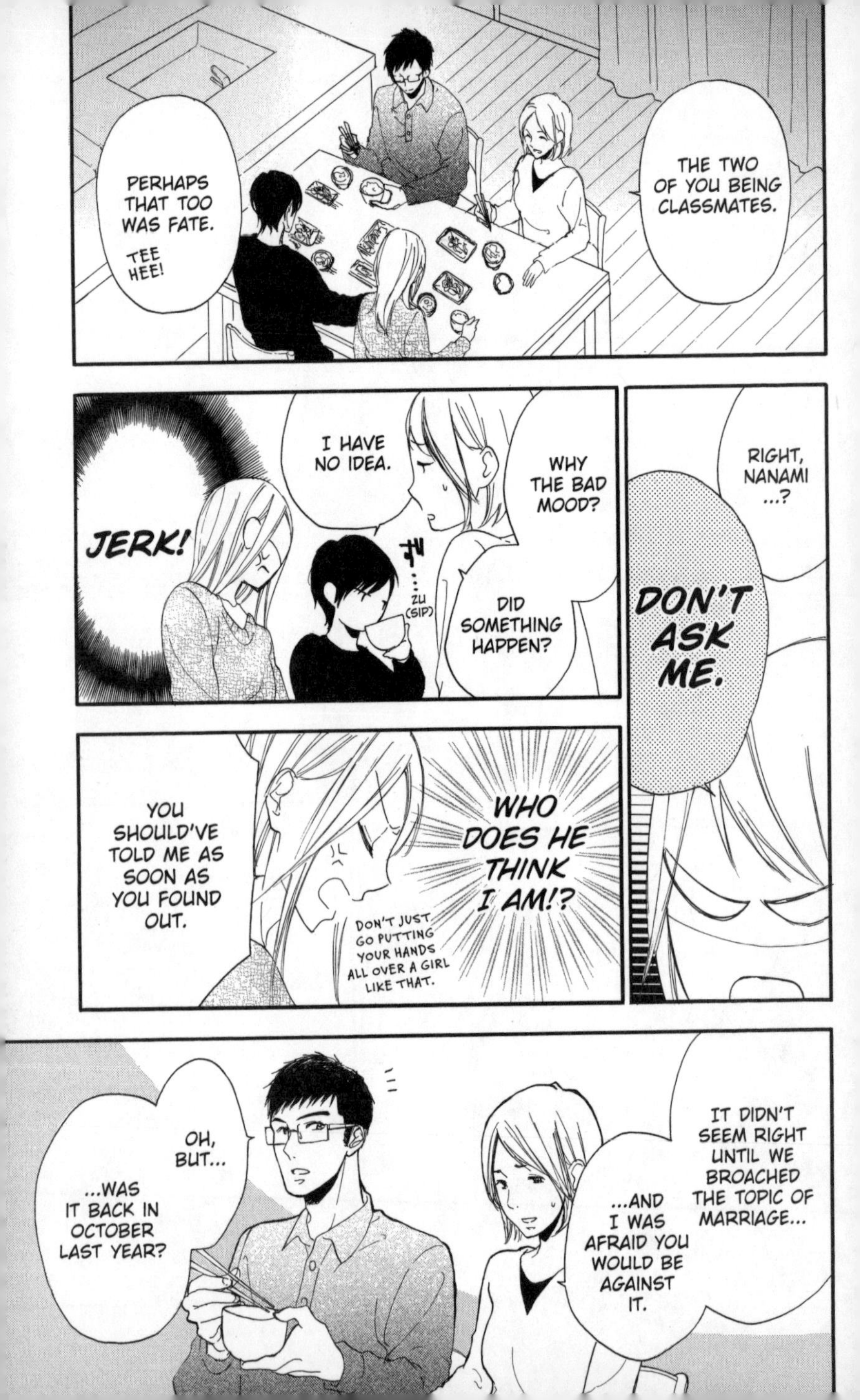
THE TWO OF YOU BEING CLASSMATES.
PERHAPS THAT TOO WAS FATE.
TEE HEE!
RIGHT, NANAMI ...?
DON'T ASK ME.
WHY THE BAD MOOD?
DID SOMETHING HAPPEN?
I HAVE NO IDEA.
ZU (SIP)
JERK!
WHO DOES HE THINK I AM!?
DON'T JUST GO PUTTING YOUR HANDS ALL OVER A GIRL LIKE THAT.
YOU SHOULD'VE TOLD ME AS SOON AS YOU FOUND OUT.
IT DIDN'T SEEM RIGHT UNTIL WE BROACHED THE TOPIC OF MARRIAGE...
...AND I WAS AFRAID YOU WOULD BE AGAINST IT.
OH, BUT...
...WAS IT BACK IN OCTOBER LAST YEAR?

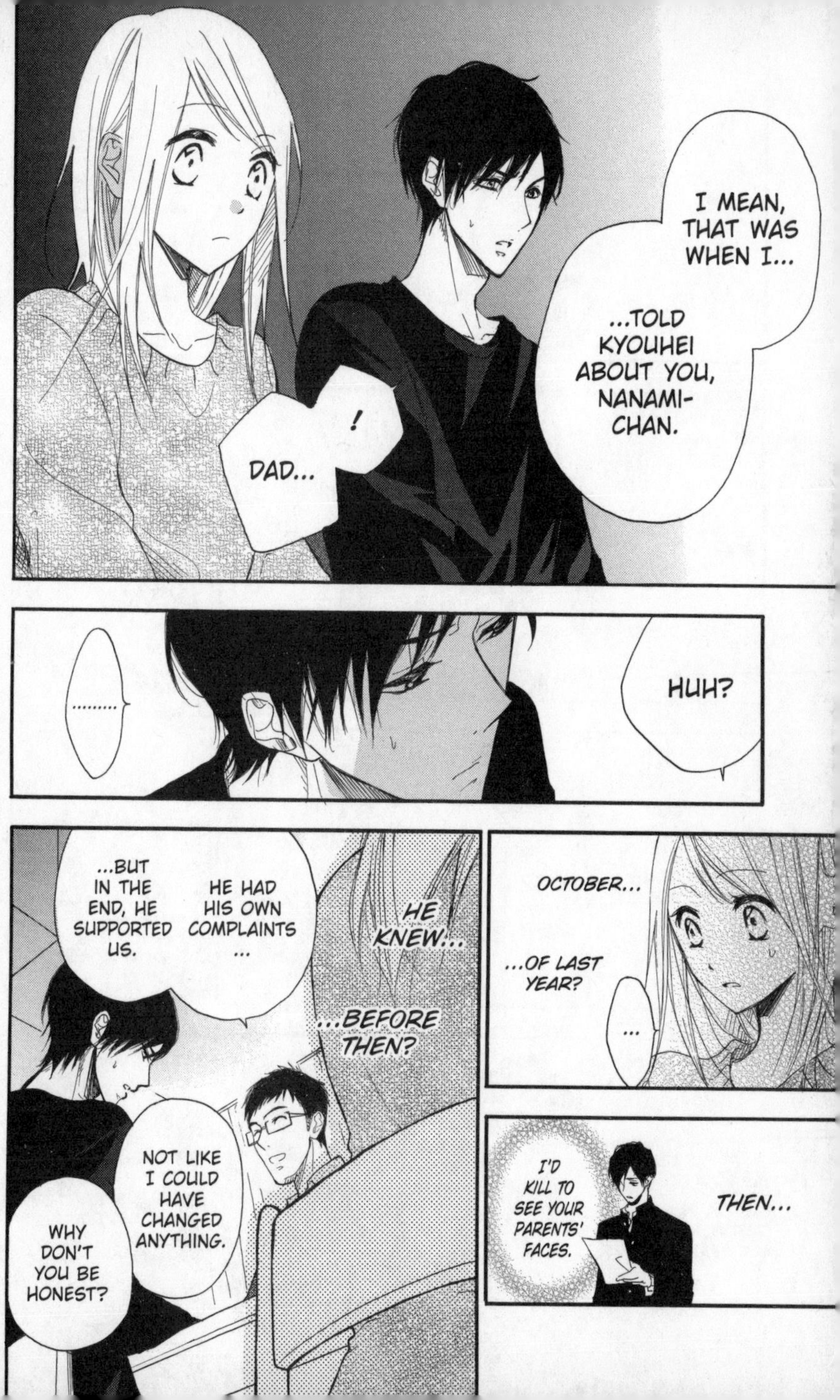
I MEAN, THAT WAS WHEN I...
...TOLD KYOUHEI ABOUT YOU, NANAMI-CHAN.
! DAD...
HUH?
....
OCTOBER...
...OF LAST YEAR?
...
THEN...
I'D KILL TO SEE YOUR PARENTS' FACES.
HE KNEW...
...BEFORE THEN?
HE HAD HIS OWN COMPLAINTS...
...BUT IN THE END, HE SUPPORTED US.
NOT LIKE I COULD HAVE CHANGED ANYTHING.
WHY DON'T YOU BE HONEST?

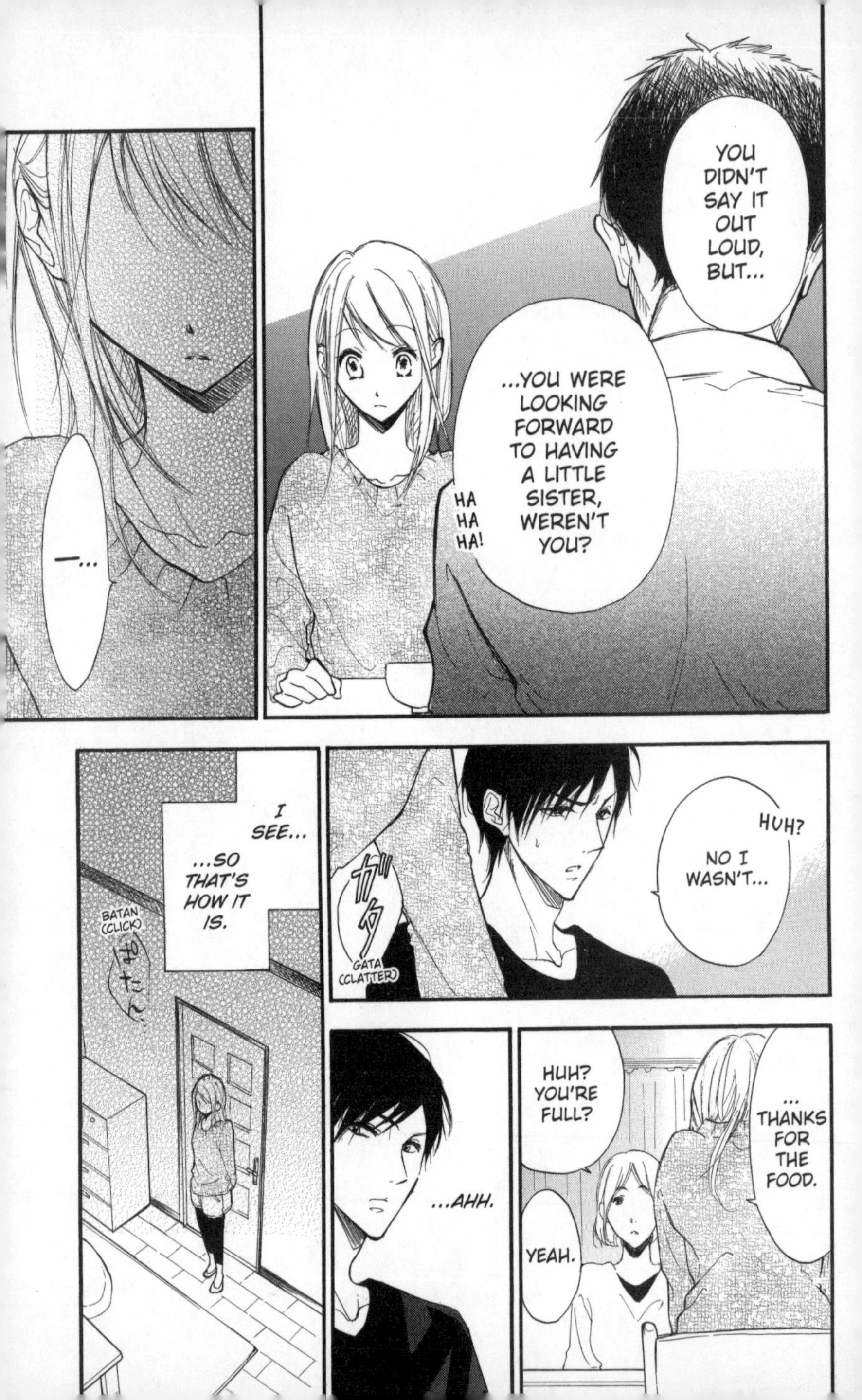
YOU DIDN'T SAY IT OUT LOUD, BUT...
...YOU WERE LOOKING FORWARD TO HAVING A LITTLE SISTER, WEREN'T YOU?
HA HA HA!
—...
HUH? NO I WASN'T...
ガタ
GATA (CLATTER)
... THANKS FOR THE FOOD.
HUH? YOU'RE FULL?
YEAH.
...AHH.
I SEE...
...SO THAT'S HOW IT IS.
BATAN (CLICK)
ぱたん

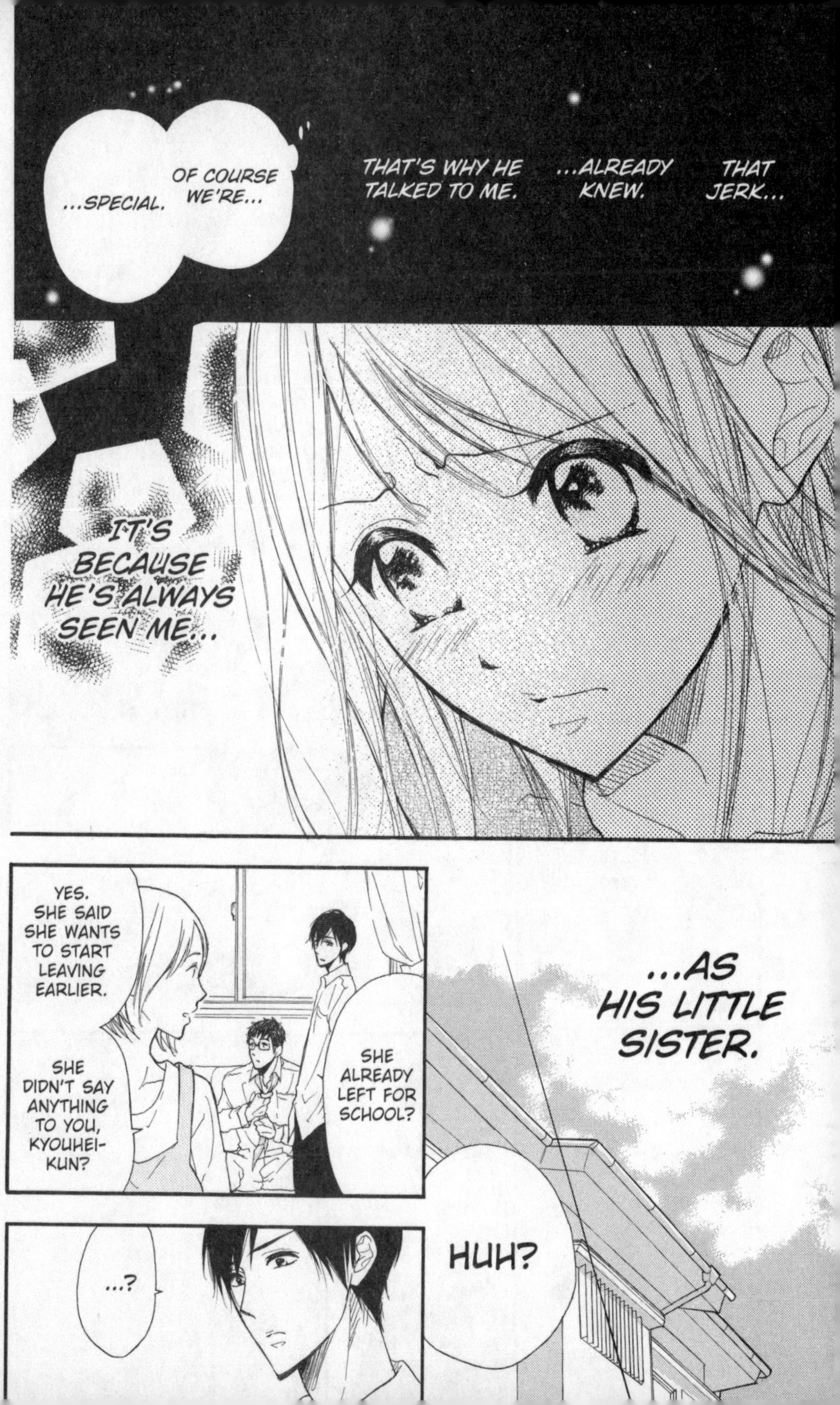
THAT JERK...
...ALREADY KNEW.
THAT'S WHY HE TALKED TO ME.
OF COURSE WE'RE...
...SPECIAL.
IT'S BECAUSE HE'S ALWAYS SEEN ME...
...AS HIS LITTLE SISTER.
HUH?
SHE ALREADY LEFT FOR SCHOOL?
YES. SHE SAID SHE WANTS TO START LEAVING EARLIER.
SHE DIDN'T SAY ANYTHING TO YOU, KYOUHEI-KUN?
...?

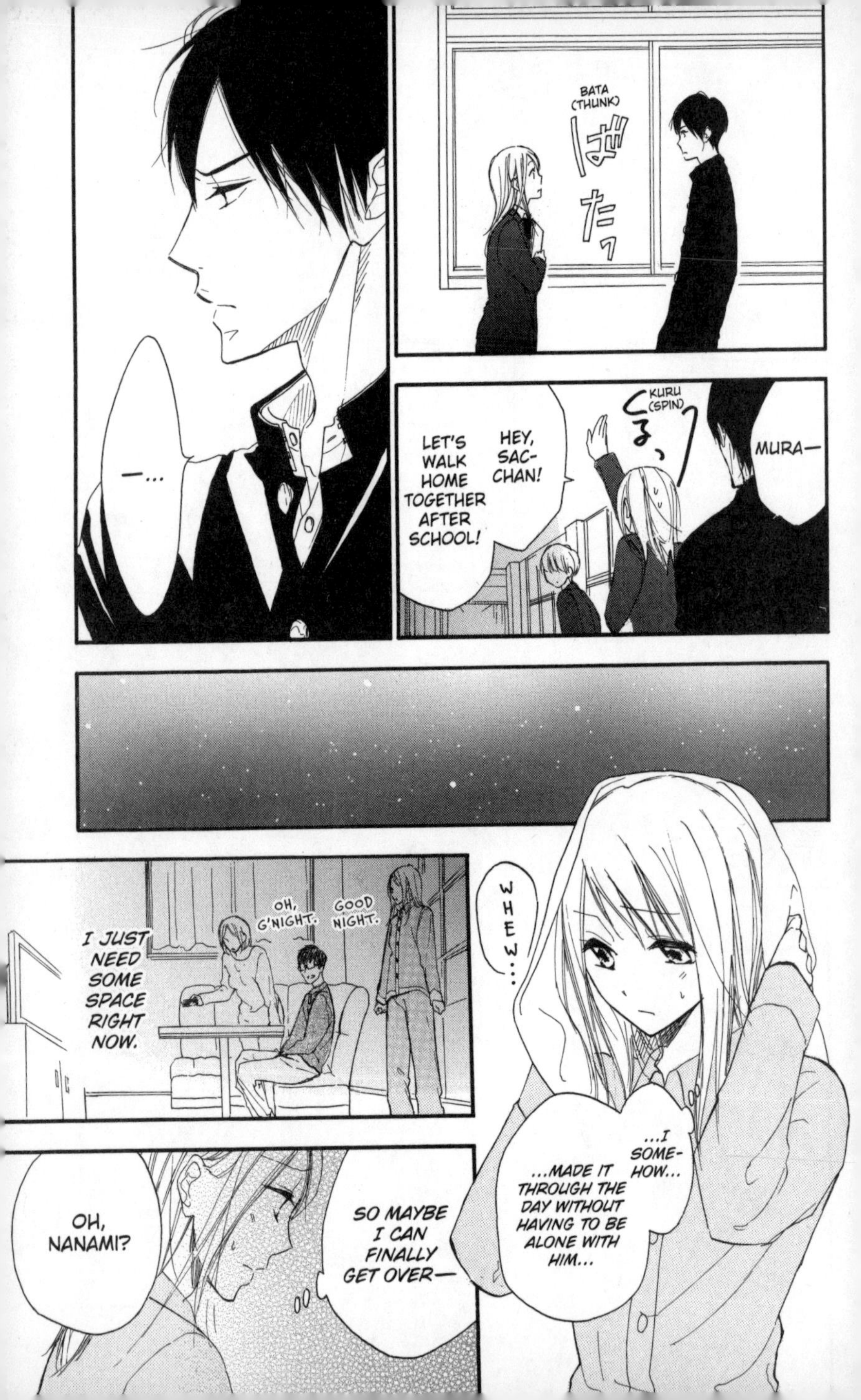
BATA (THUNK)
ばたっ
KURU (SPIN)
くるっ
MURA—
HEY, SAC-CHAN!
LET'S WALK HOME TOGETHER AFTER SCHOOL!
—...
WHEW...
...I SOMEHOW...
...MADE IT THROUGH THE DAY WITHOUT HAVING TO BE ALONE WITH HIM...
GOOD NIGHT.
OH, G'NIGHT.
I JUST NEED SOME SPACE RIGHT NOW.
SO MAYBE I CAN FINALLY GET OVER—
OH, NANAMI?

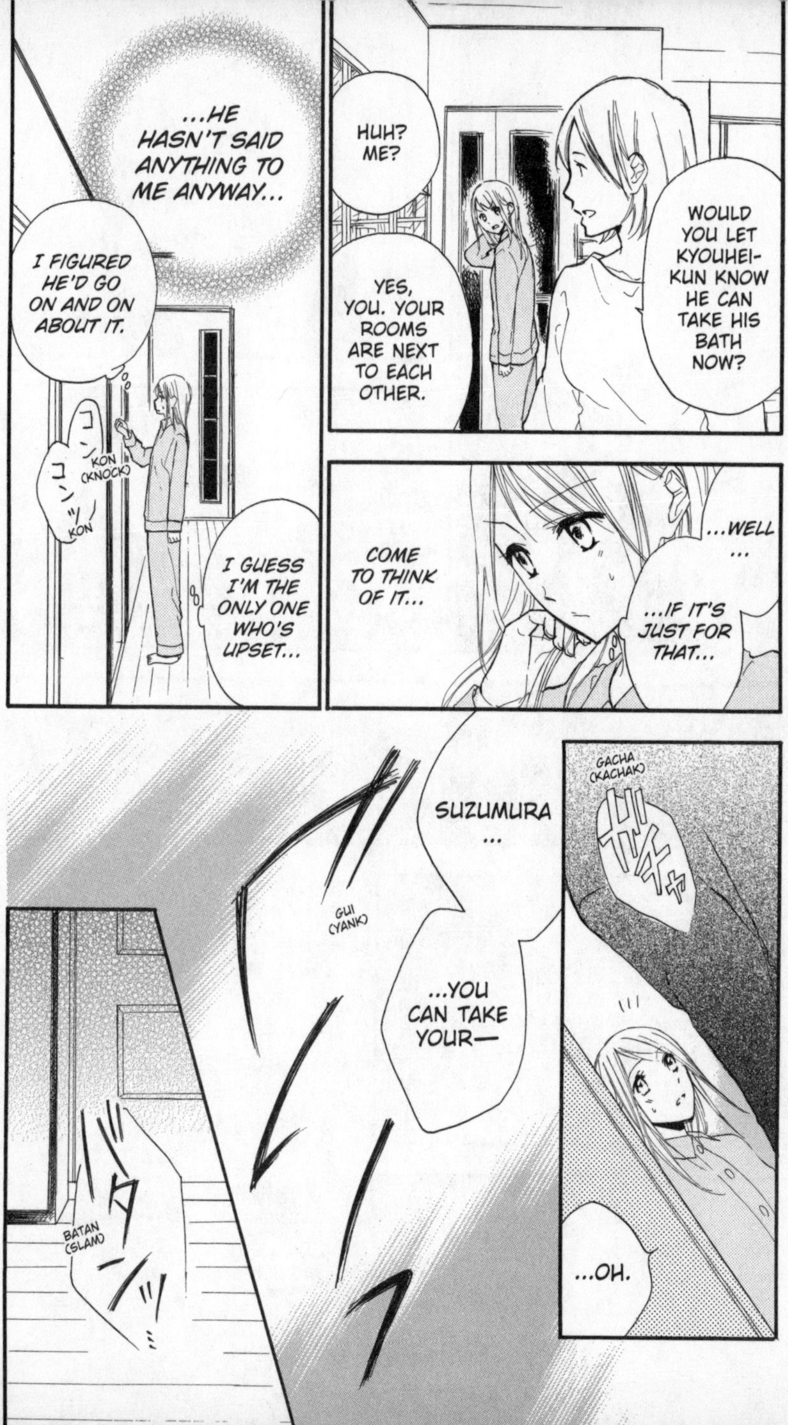
WOULD YOU LET KYOUHEI-KUN KNOW HE CAN TAKE HIS BATH NOW?
HUH? ME?
YES, YOU. YOUR ROOMS ARE NEXT TO EACH OTHER.
...WELL...
...IF IT'S JUST FOR THAT...
COME TO THINK OF IT...
...HE HASN'T SAID ANYTHING TO ME ANYWAY...
I FIGURED HE'D GO ON AND ON ABOUT IT.
KON (KNOCK)
KON
I GUESS I'M THE ONLY ONE WHO'S UPSET...
GACHA (KACHAK)
...OH.
SUZUMURA...
GUI (YANK)
...YOU CAN TAKE YOUR—
BATAN (SLAM)

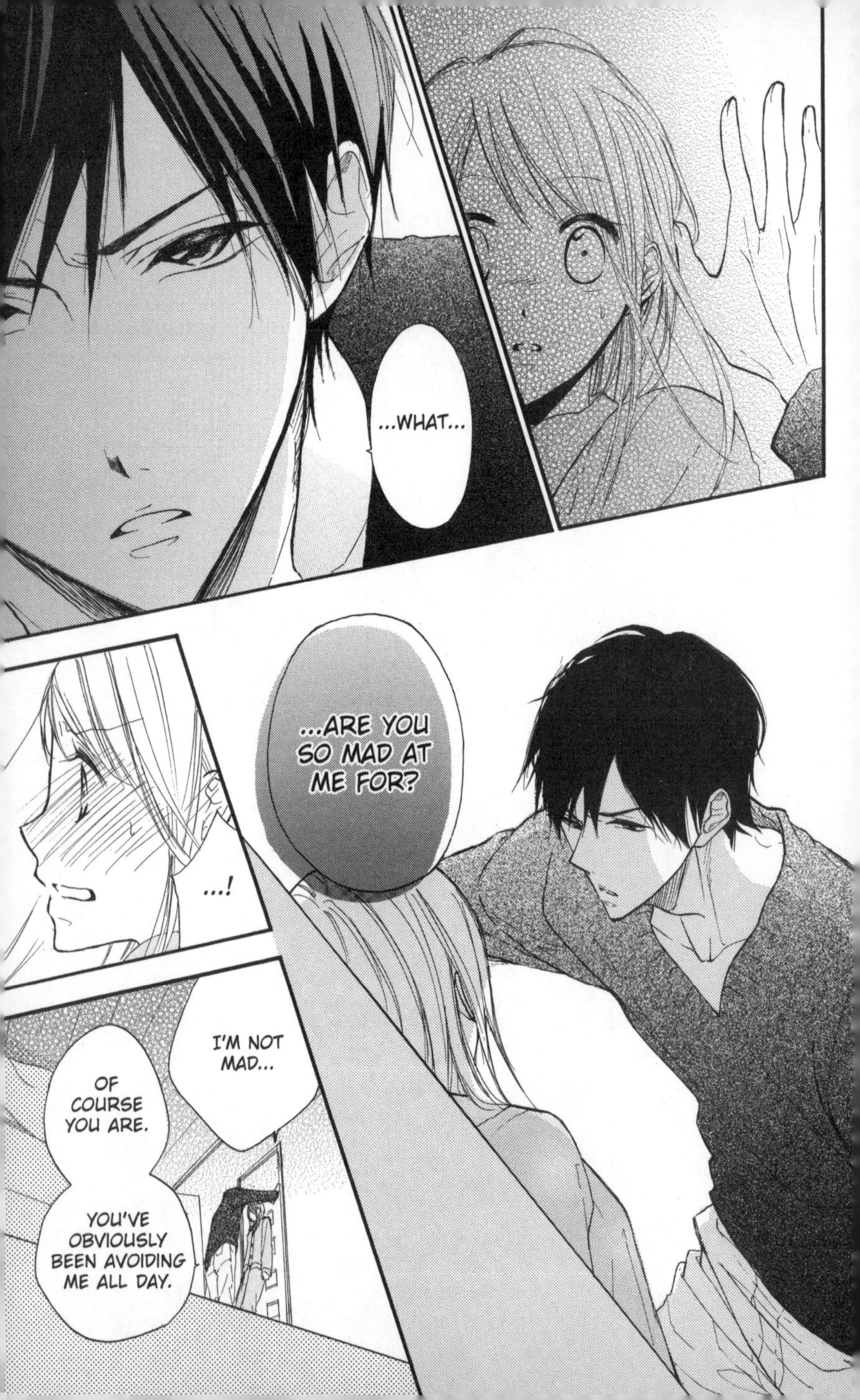
...WHAT...
...ARE YOU SO MAD AT ME FOR?
...!
I'M NOT MAD...
OF COURSE YOU ARE.
YOU'VE OBVIOUSLY BEEN AVOIDING ME ALL DAY.

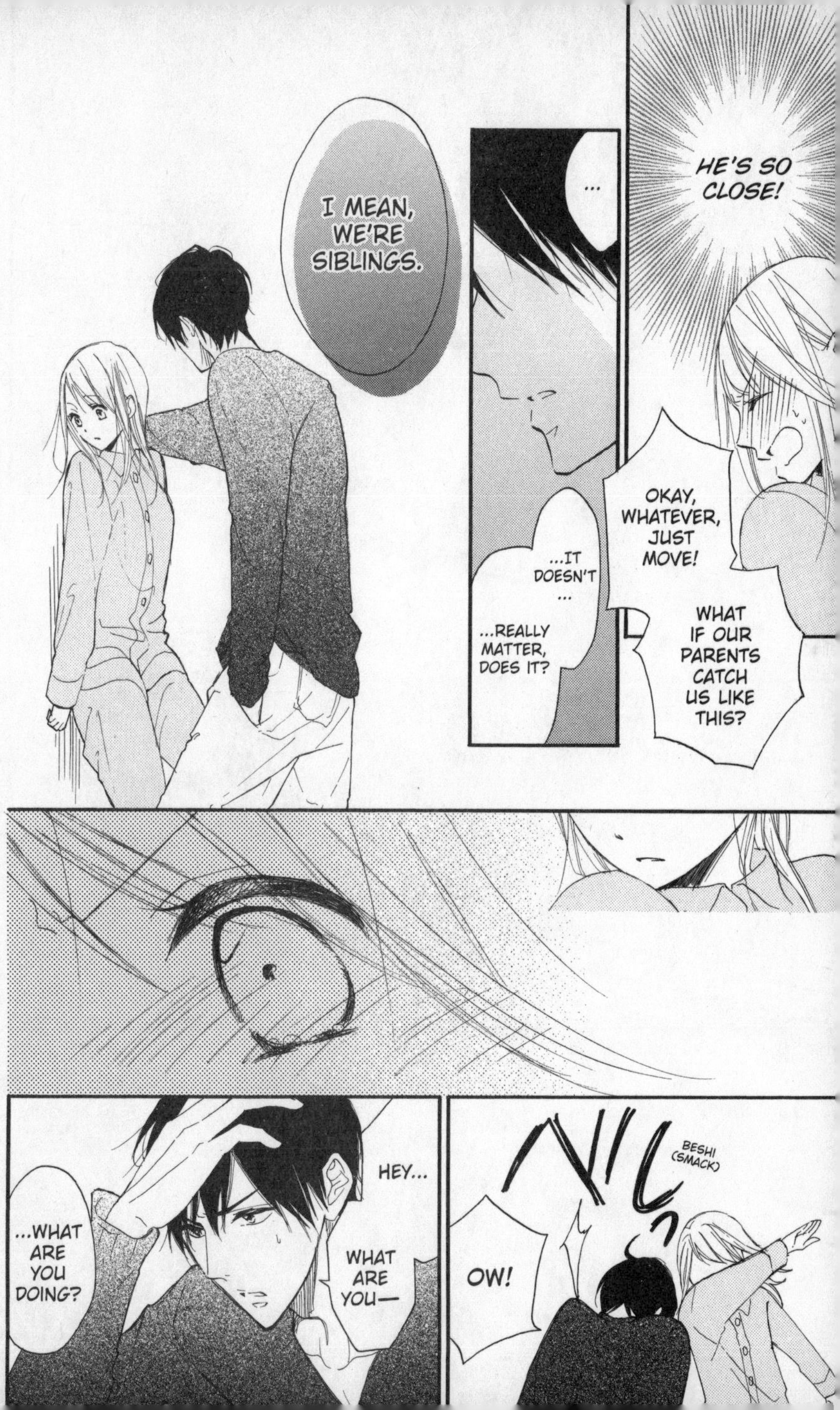
HE'S SO CLOSE!
OKAY, WHATEVER, JUST MOVE!
WHAT IF OUR PARENTS CATCH US LIKE THIS?
...
...IT DOESN'T ...
...REALLY MATTER, DOES IT?
I MEAN, WE'RE SIBLINGS.
BESHI (SMACK)
OW!
HEY...
WHAT ARE YOU—
...WHAT ARE YOU DOING?

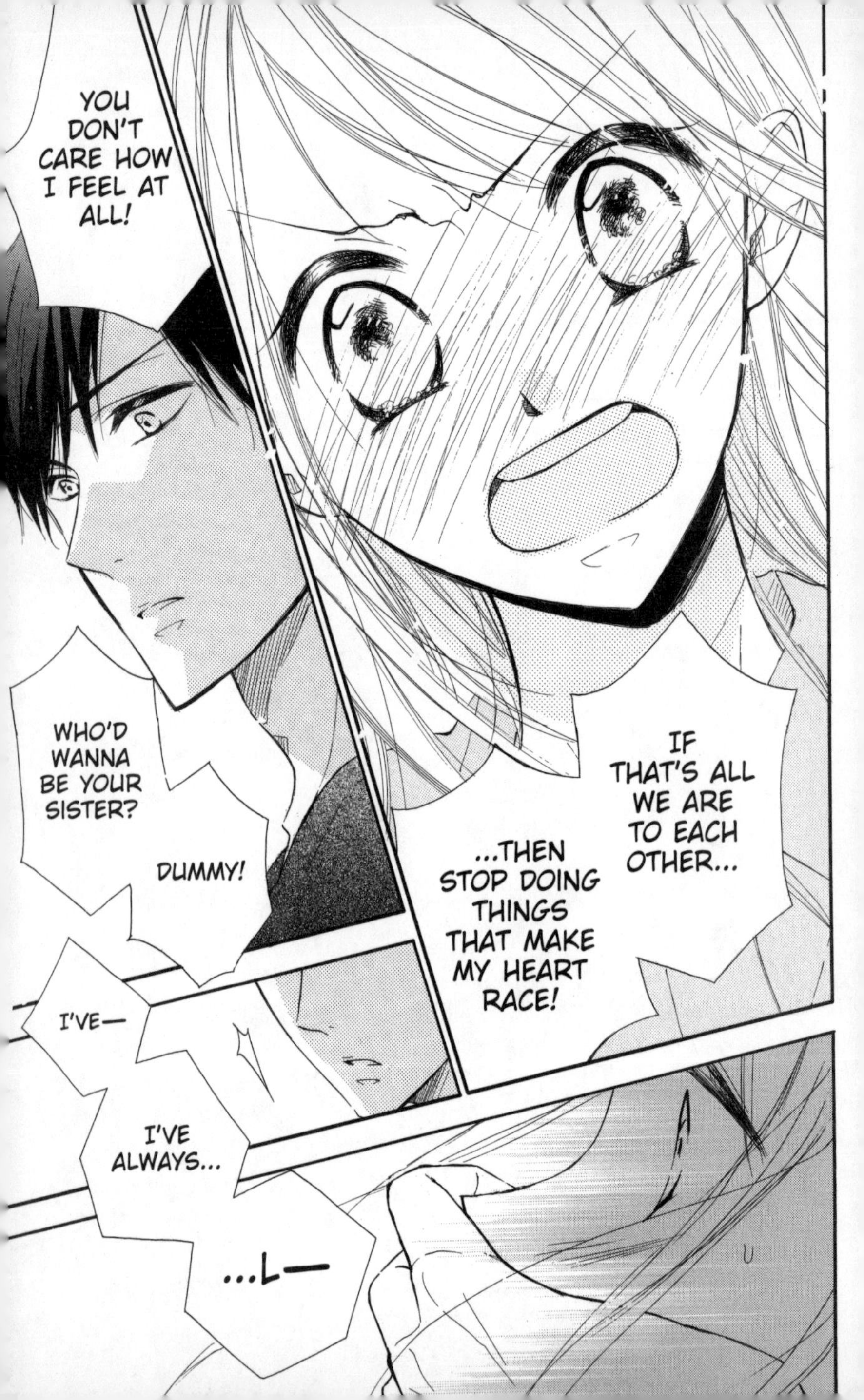
IF THAT'S ALL WE ARE TO EACH OTHER...
...THEN STOP DOING THINGS THAT MAKE MY HEART RACE!
YOU DON'T CARE HOW I FEEL AT ALL!
WHO'D WANNA BE YOUR SISTER?
DUMMY!
I'VE—
I'VE ALWAYS...
...L—

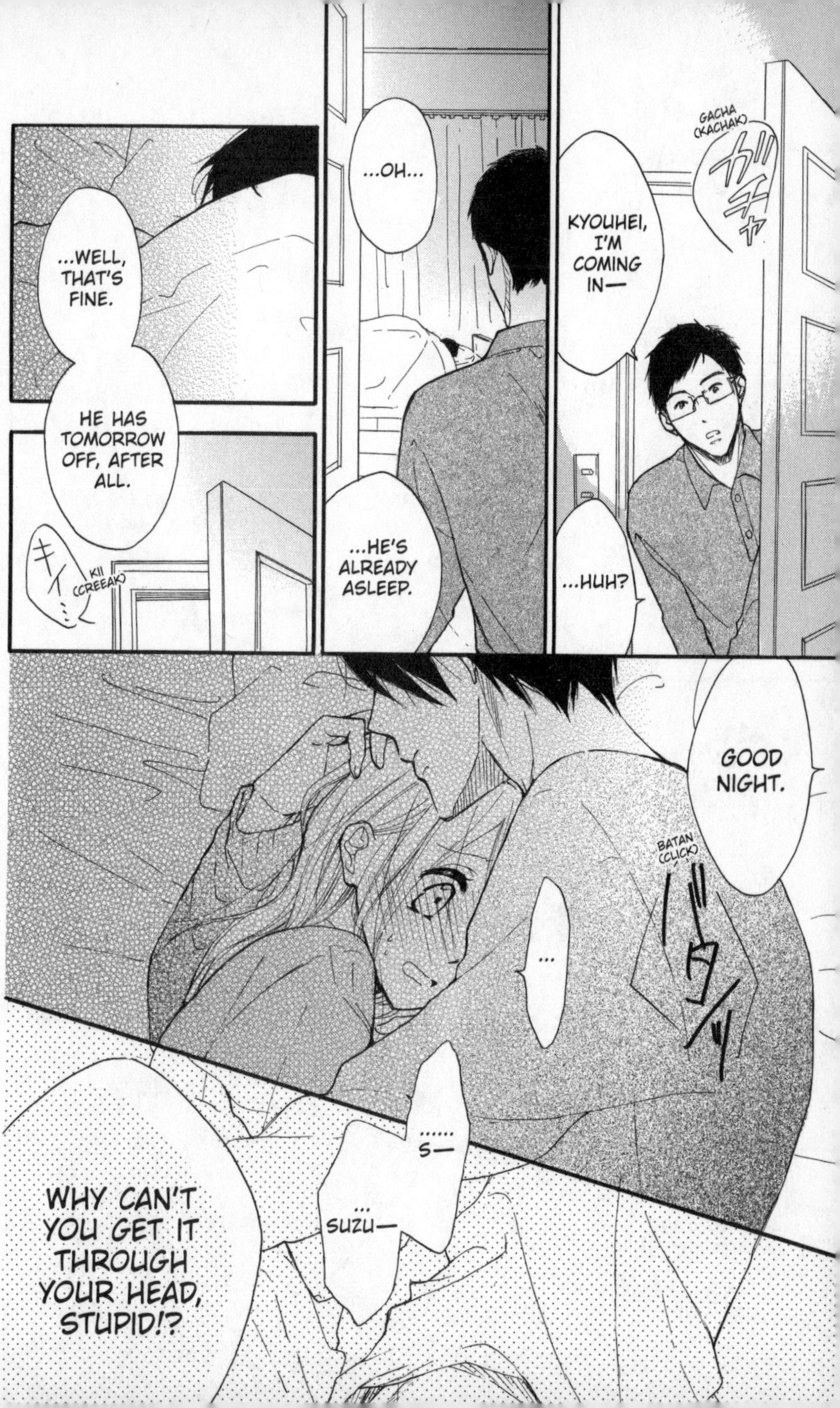
GACHA (KACHAK)
KYOUHEI, I'M COMING IN—
...HUH?
...OH...
...HE'S ALREADY ASLEEP.
...WELL, THAT'S FINE.
HE HAS TOMORROW OFF, AFTER ALL.
KII (CREEAK)
GOOD NIGHT.
BATAN (CLICK)
...
...... S—
... SUZU—
WHY CAN'T YOU GET IT THROUGH YOUR HEAD, STUPID!?

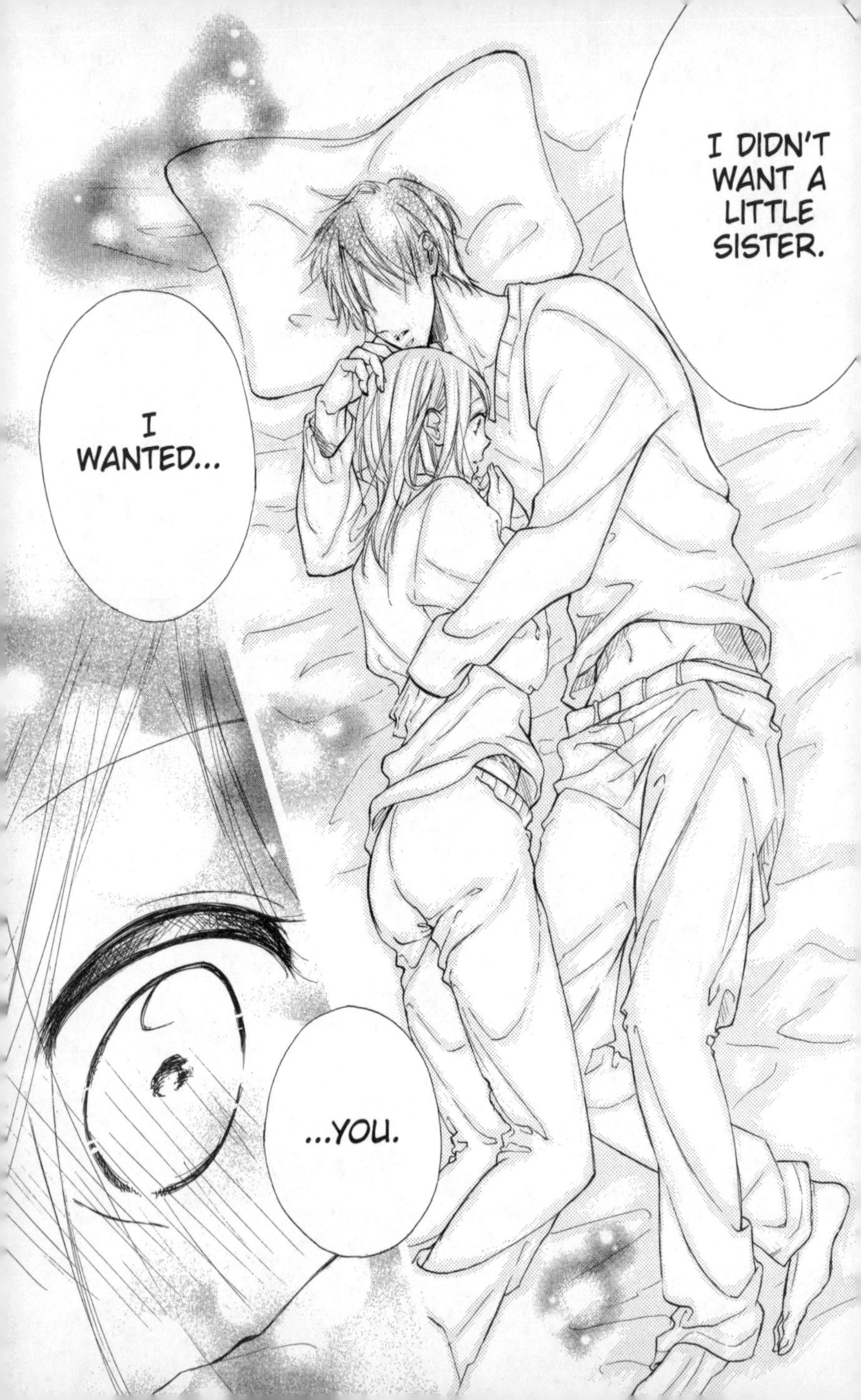
I DIDN'T WANT A LITTLE SISTER.
I WANTED...
...YOU.

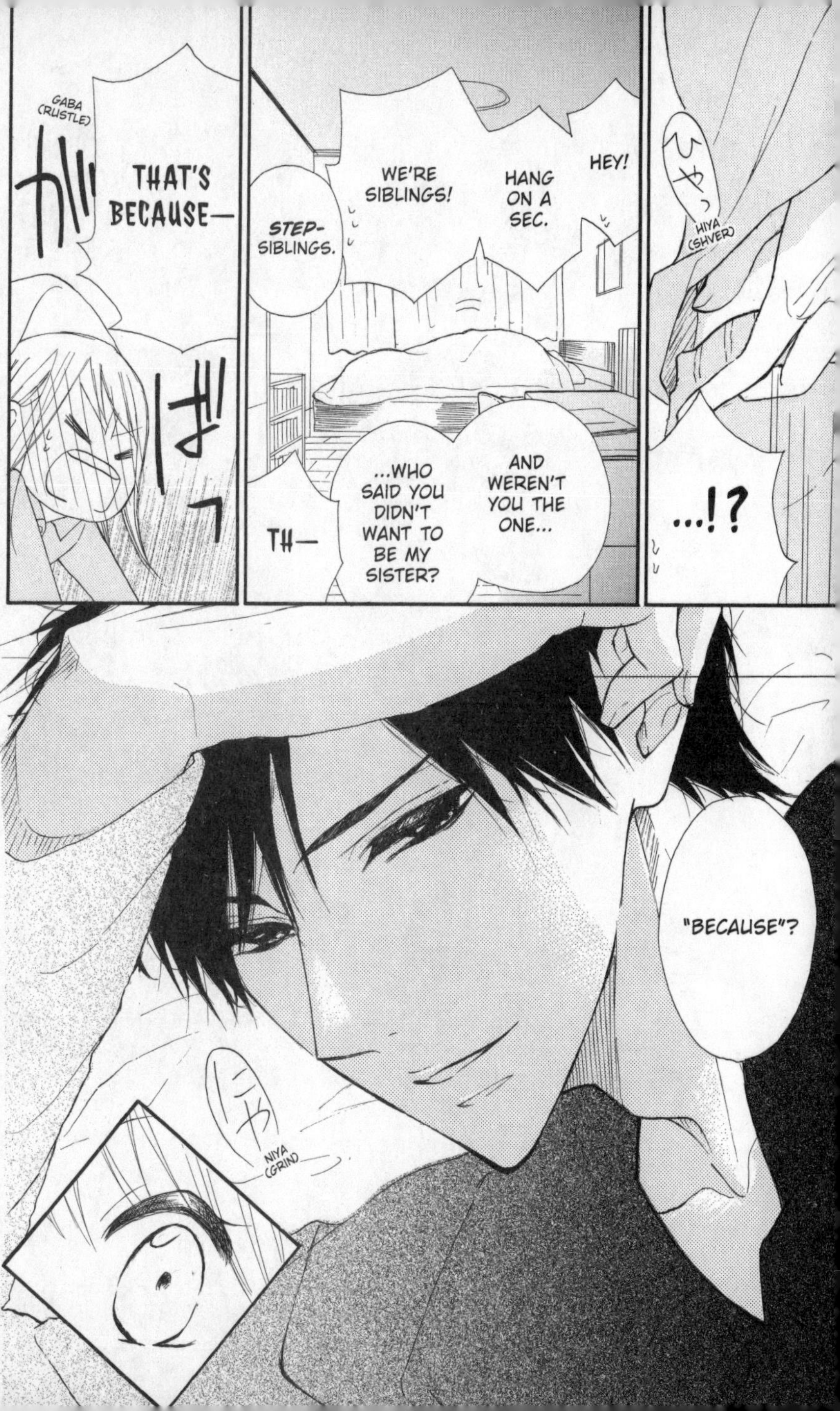
HIYA (SHVER)
...!?
HEY!
HANG ON A SEC.
WE'RE SIBLINGS!
STEP-SIBLINGS.
AND WEREN'T YOU THE ONE...
...WHO SAID YOU DIDN'T WANT TO BE MY SISTER?
TH—
GABA (RUSTLE)
THAT'S BECAUSE—
"BECAUSE"?
NIYA (GRIN)

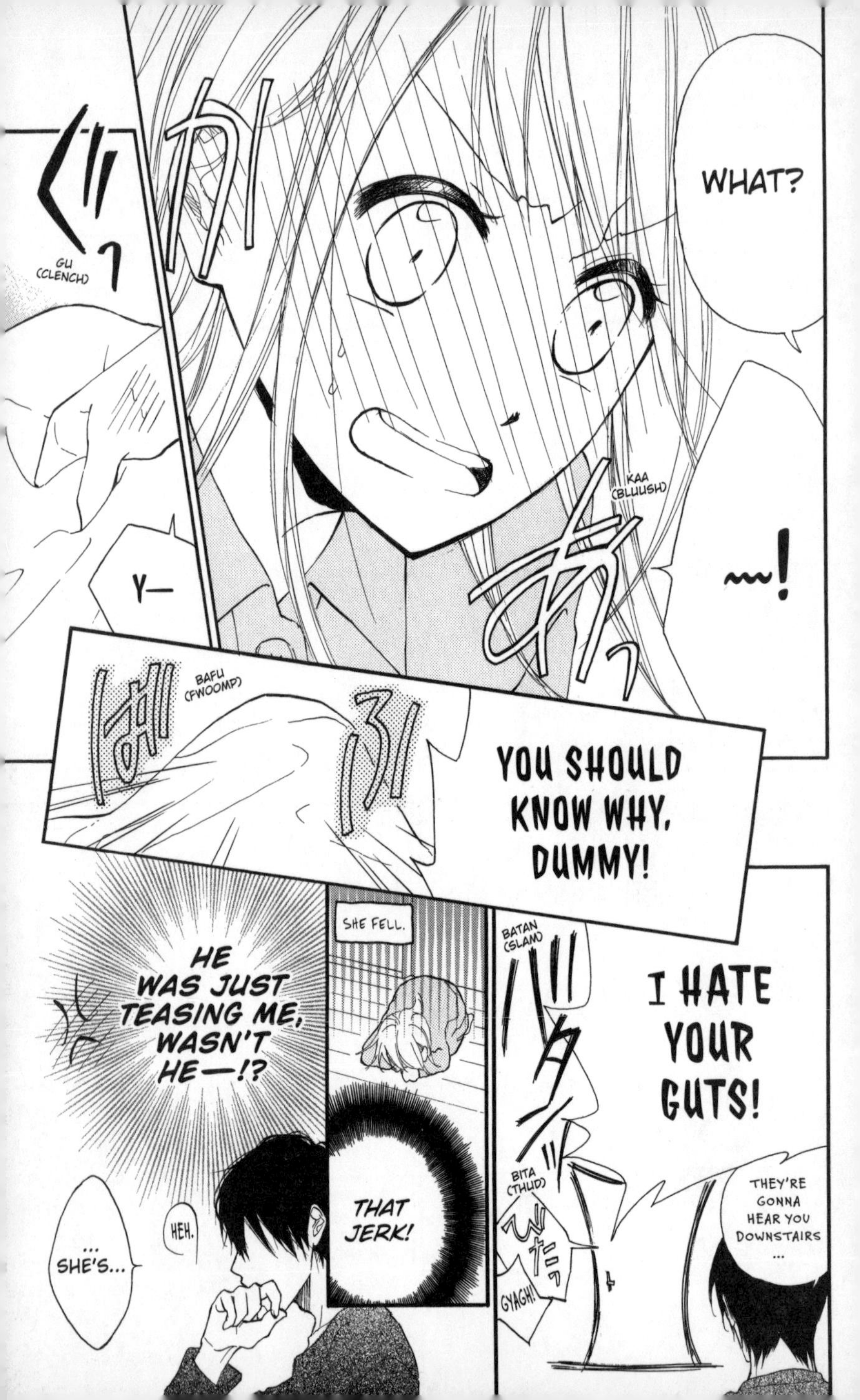
WHAT?
KAA (BLUUSH)
~~!
GU (CLENCH)
Y—
BAFU (FWOOMP)
YOU SHOULD KNOW WHY, DUMMY!
I HATE YOUR GUTS!
BATAN (SLAM)
BITA (THUD)
GYAGH!
THEY'RE GONNA HEAR YOU DOWNSTAIRS ...
SHE FELL.
THAT JERK!
HE WAS JUST TEASING ME, WASN'T HE—!?
HEH.
... SHE'S...

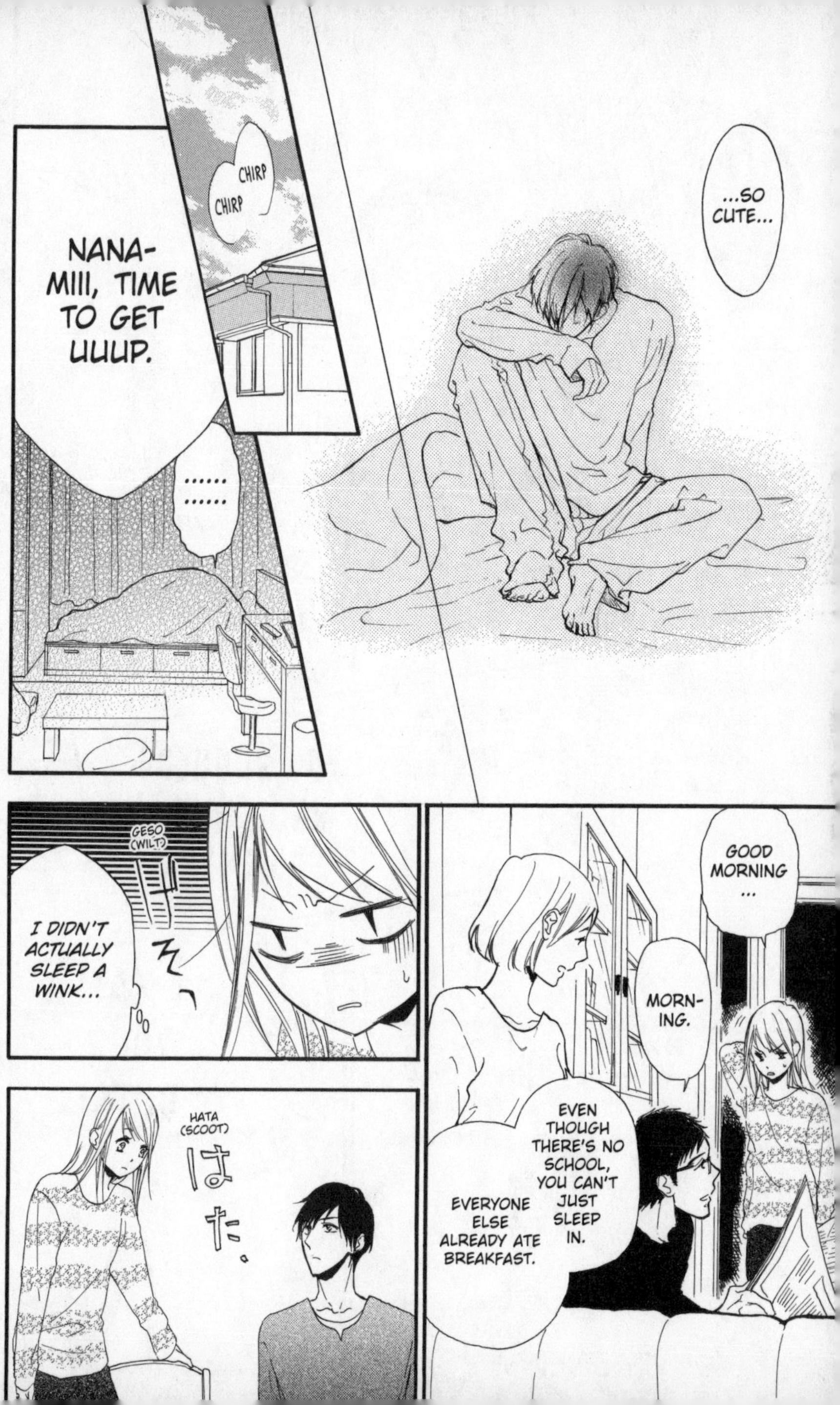
...SO CUTE...
CHIRP
CHIRP
NANA-MIII, TIME TO GET UUUP.
......
......
GOOD MORNING...
MORN-ING.
EVEN THOUGH THERE'S NO SCHOOL, YOU CAN'T JUST SLEEP IN.
EVERYONE ELSE ALREADY ATE BREAKFAST.
GESO (WILT)
I DIDN'T ACTUALLY SLEEP A WINK...
HATA (SCOOT)
はた。

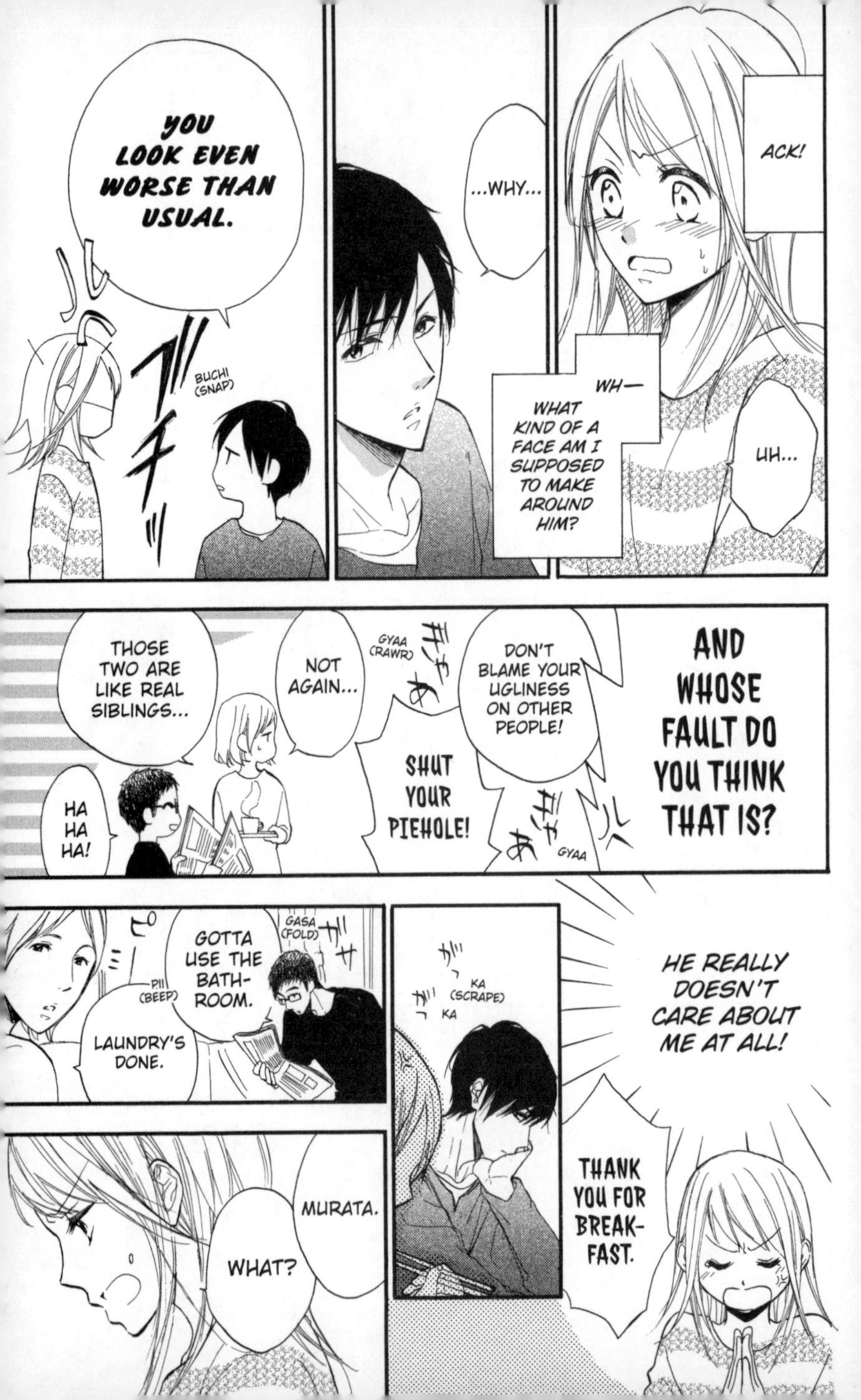
ACK!
UH...
WH—
WHAT KIND OF A FACE AM I SUPPOSED TO MAKE AROUND HIM?
...WHY...
YOU LOOK EVEN WORSE THAN USUAL.
BUCHI (SNAP)
AND WHOSE FAULT DO YOU THINK THAT IS?
DON'T BLAME YOUR UGLINESS ON OTHER PEOPLE!
GYAA
GYAA (RAWR)
SHUT YOUR PIEHOLE!
NOT AGAIN...
THOSE TWO ARE LIKE REAL SIBLINGS...
HA HA HA!
KA (SCRAPE)
KA
HE REALLY DOESN'T CARE ABOUT ME AT ALL!
THANK YOU FOR BREAKFAST.
GASA (FOLD)
GOTTA USE THE BATHROOM.
PII (BEEP)
LAUNDRY'S DONE.
MURATA.
WHAT?

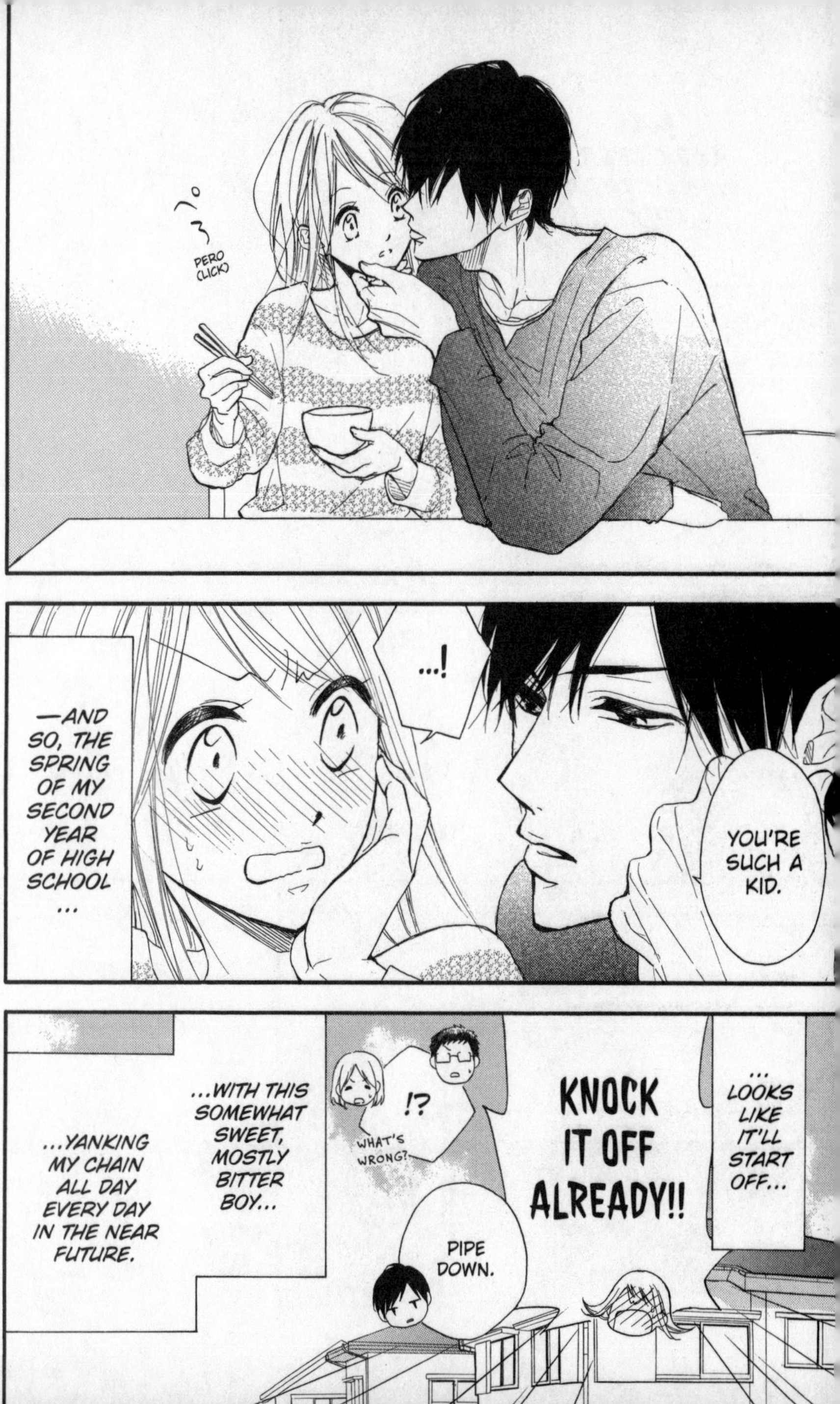
PERO (LICK)
YOU'RE SUCH A KID.
...!
—AND SO, THE SPRING OF MY SECOND YEAR OF HIGH SCHOOL...
...LOOKS LIKE IT'LL START OFF...
KNOCK IT OFF ALREADY!!
!?
WHAT'S WRONG?
PIPE DOWN.
...WITH THIS SOMEWHAT SWEET, MOSTLY BITTER BOY...
...YANKING MY CHAIN ALL DAY EVERY DAY IN THE NEAR FUTURE.

Room: 2

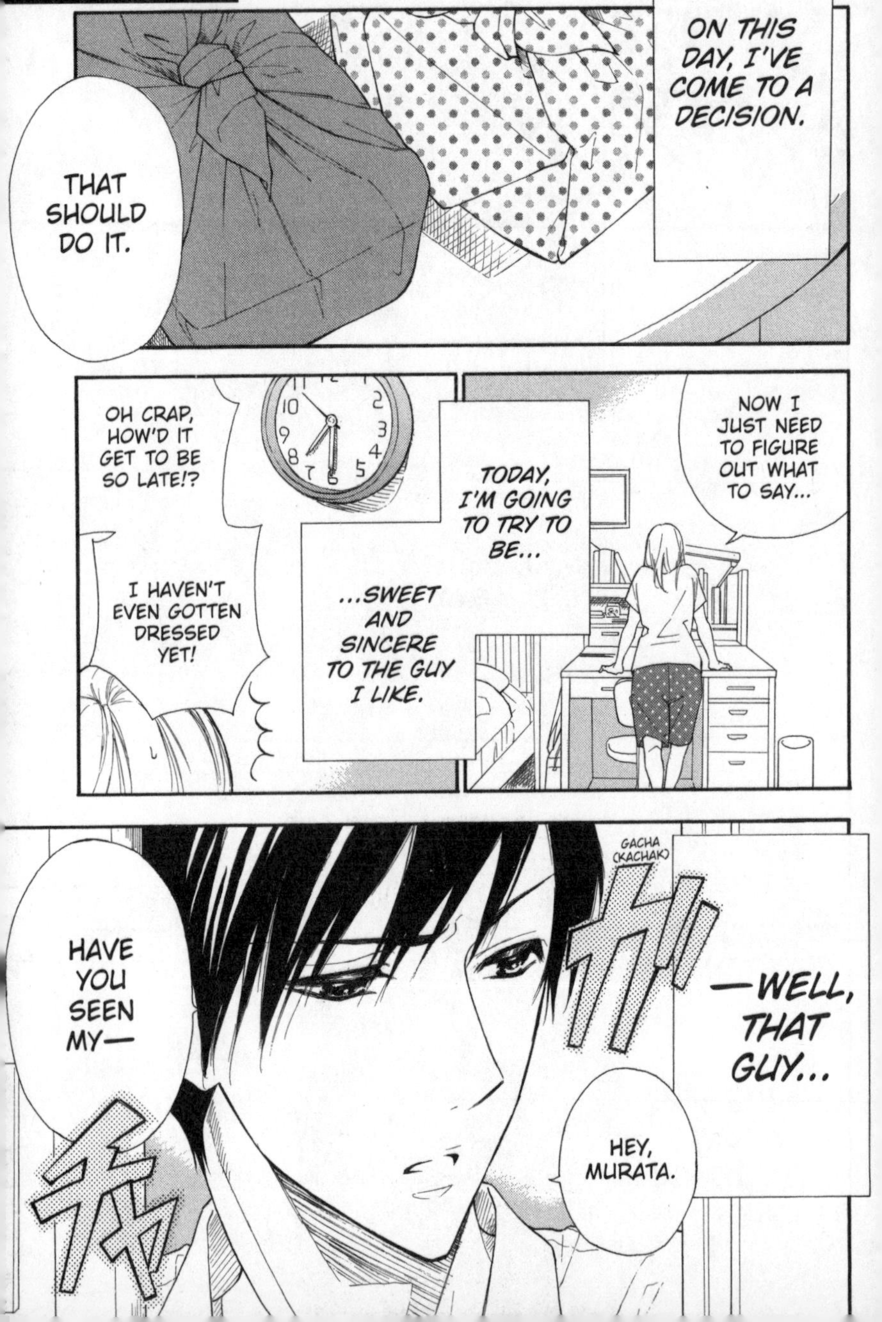
ON THIS DAY, I'VE COME TO A DECISION.
THAT SHOULD DO IT.
NOW I JUST NEED TO FIGURE OUT WHAT TO SAY...
TODAY, I'M GOING TO TRY TO BE...
...SWEET AND SINCERE TO THE GUY I LIKE.
OH CRAP, HOW'D IT GET TO BE SO LATE!?
I HAVEN'T EVEN GOTTEN DRESSED YET!
GACHA (KACHAK)
—WELL, THAT GUY...
HEY, MURATA.
HAVE YOU SEEN MY—

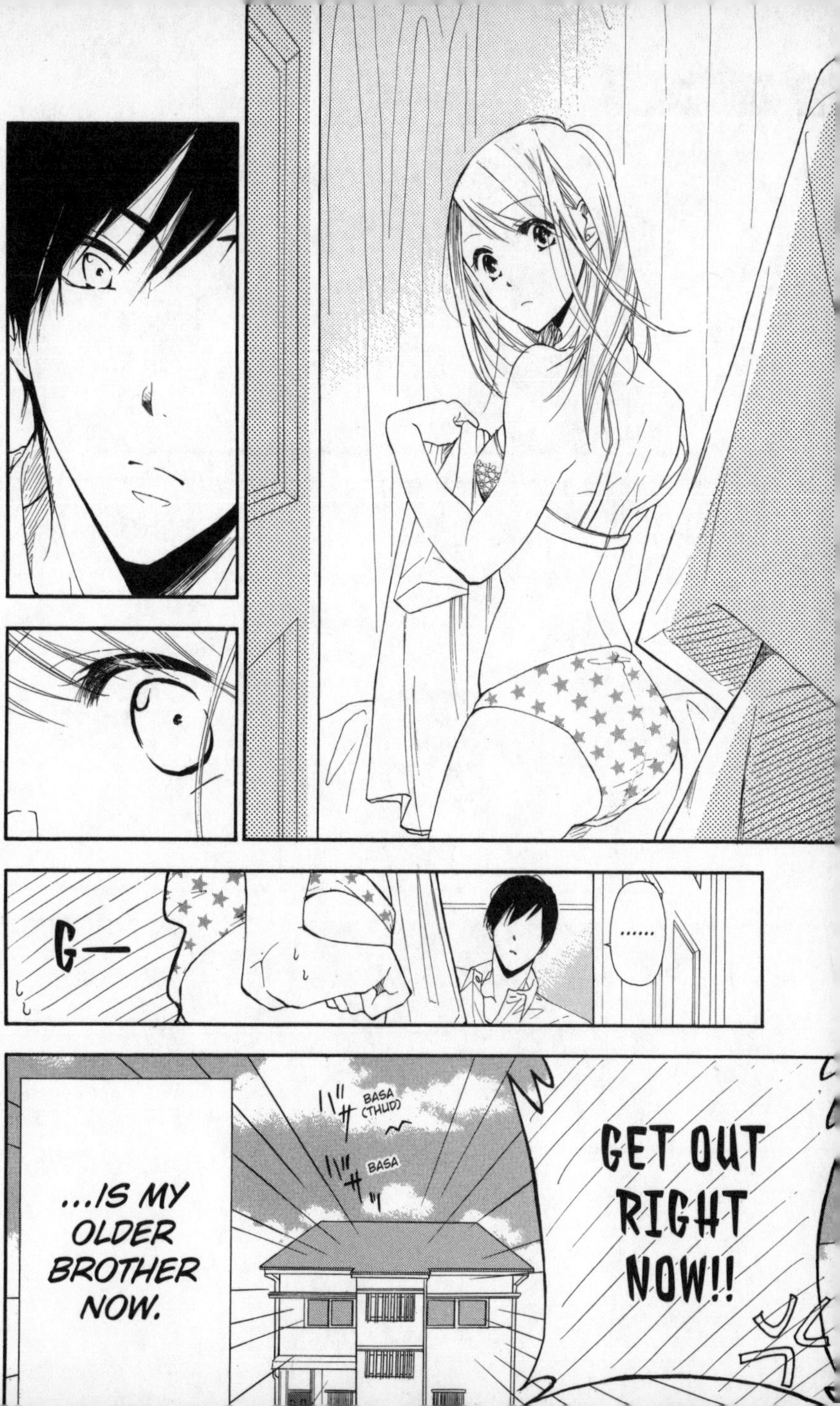

......
G—
GET OUT RIGHT NOW!!
BASA (THUD)
BASA
...IS MY OLDER BROTHER NOW.

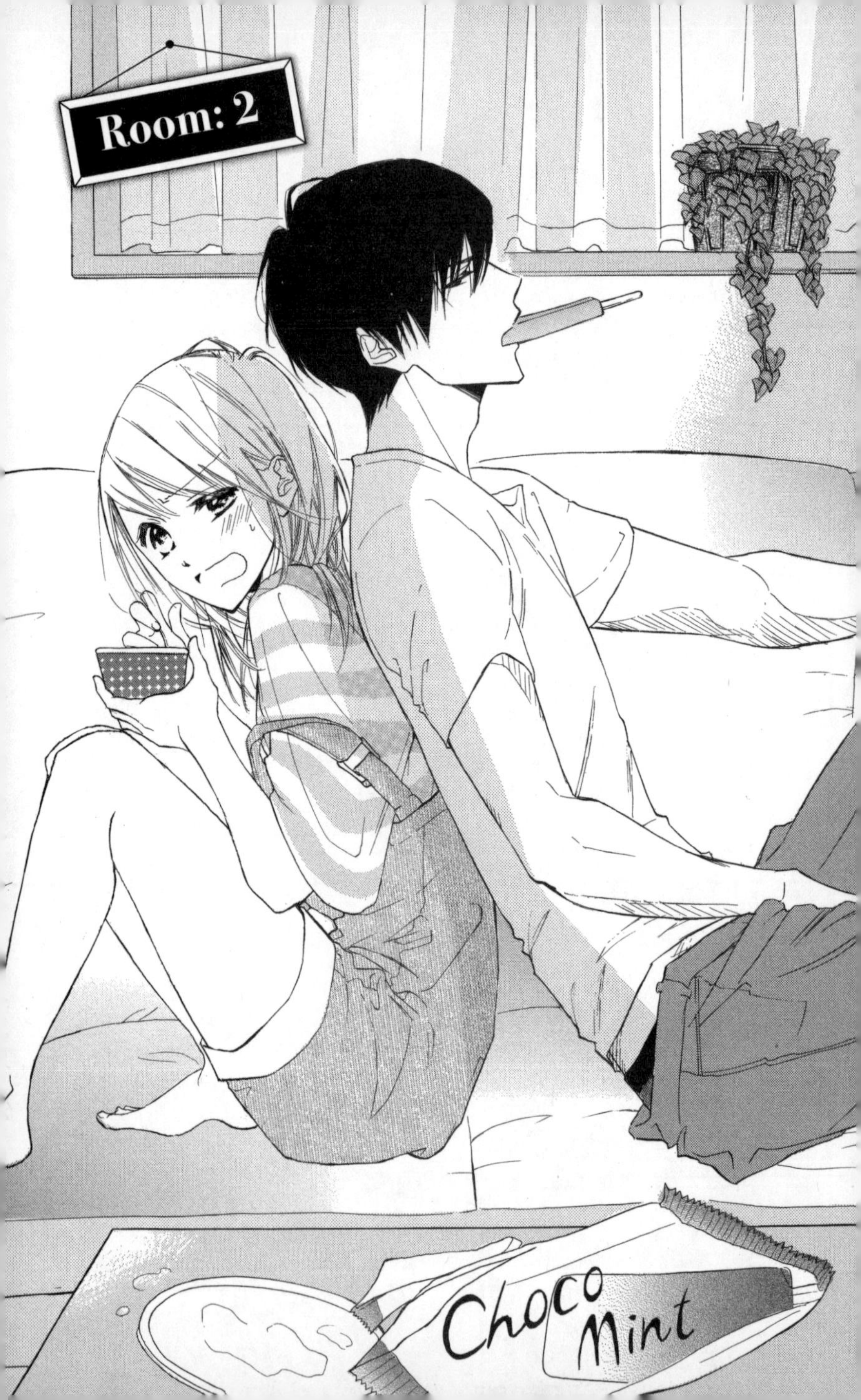
Room: 2
Choco Mint

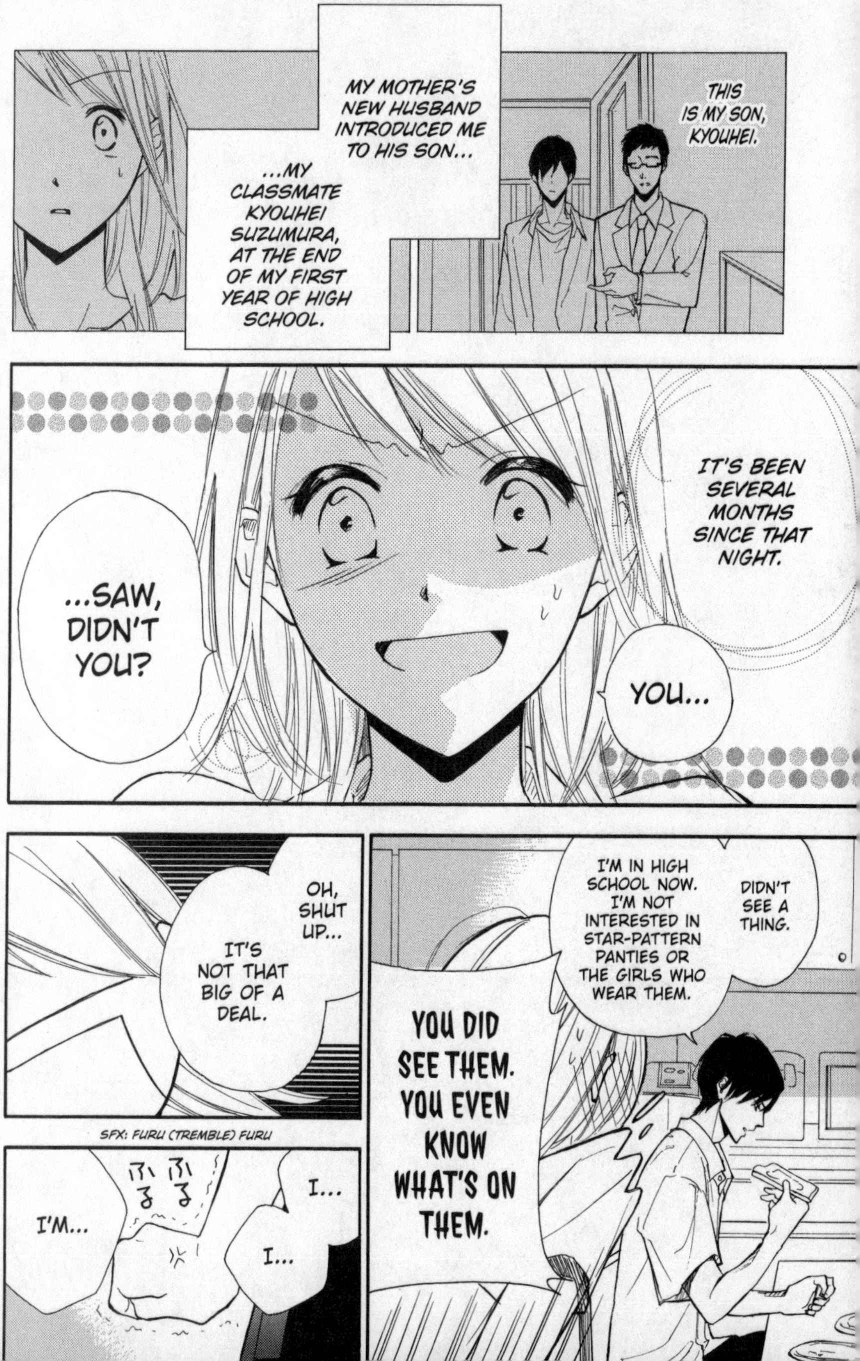
THIS IS MY SON, KYOUHEI.
MY MOTHER'S NEW HUSBAND INTRODUCED ME TO HIS SON...
...MY CLASSMATE KYOUHEI SUZUMURA, AT THE END OF MY FIRST YEAR OF HIGH SCHOOL.
IT'S BEEN SEVERAL MONTHS SINCE THAT NIGHT.
YOU...
...SAW, DIDN'T YOU?
DIDN'T SEE A THING.
I'M IN HIGH SCHOOL NOW. I'M NOT INTERESTED IN STAR-PATTERN PANTIES OR THE GIRLS WHO WEAR THEM.
YOU DID SEE THEM. YOU EVEN KNOW WHAT'S ON THEM.
OH, SHUT UP...
IT'S NOT THAT BIG OF A DEAL.
SFX: FURU (TREMBLE) FURU
ふるふる
I...
I...
I'M...

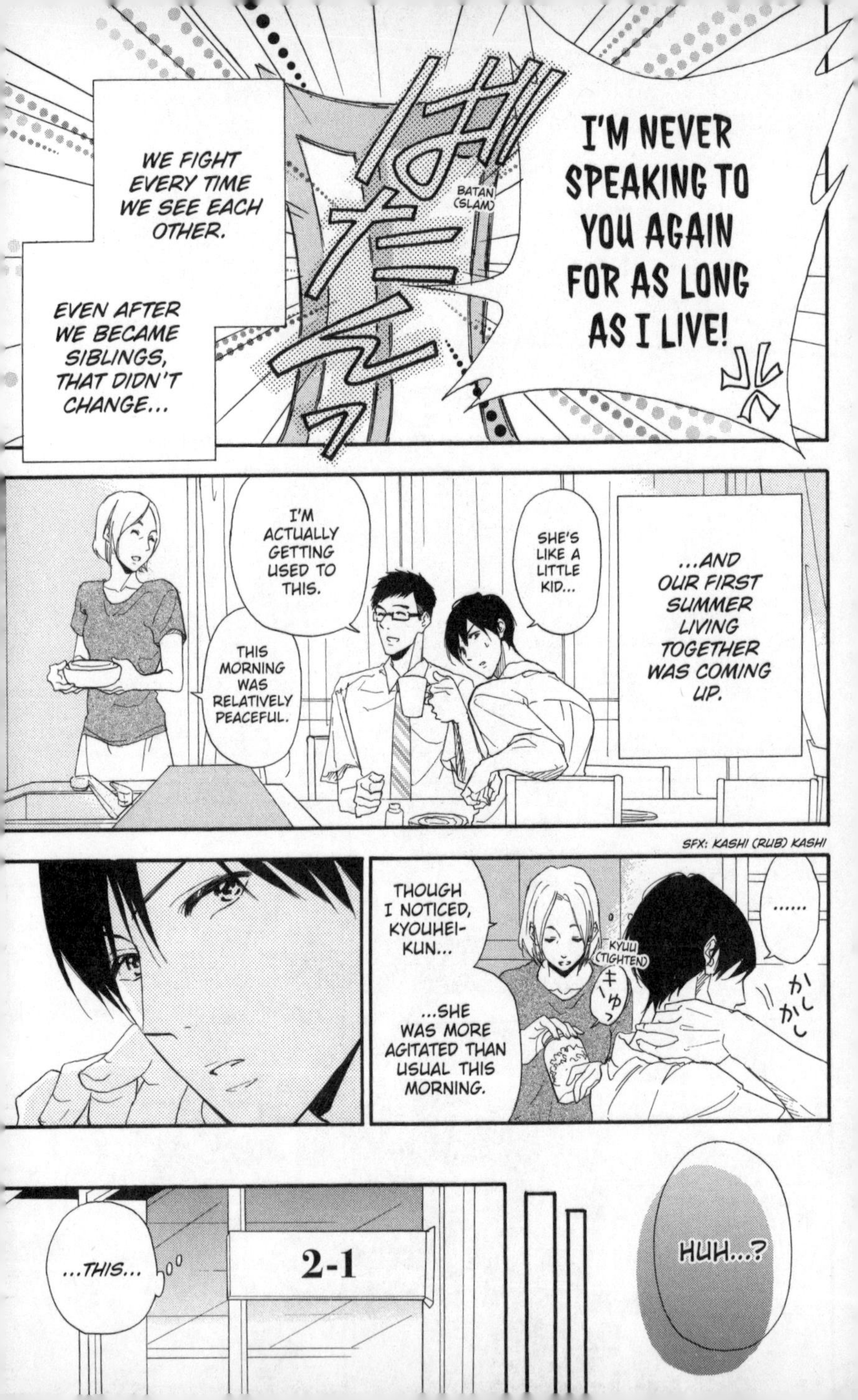
I'M NEVER SPEAKING TO YOU AGAIN FOR AS LONG AS I LIVE!
BATAN (SLAM)
WE FIGHT EVERY TIME WE SEE EACH OTHER.
EVEN AFTER WE BECAME SIBLINGS, THAT DIDN'T CHANGE...
...AND OUR FIRST SUMMER LIVING TOGETHER WAS COMING UP.
SHE'S LIKE A LITTLE KID...
I'M ACTUALLY GETTING USED TO THIS.
THIS MORNING WAS RELATIVELY PEACEFUL.
SFX: KASHI (RUB) KASHI
......
KYUU (TIGHTEN)
THOUGH I NOTICED, KYOUHEI-KUN...
...SHE WAS MORE AGITATED THAN USUAL THIS MORNING.
HUH...?
2-1
...THIS...

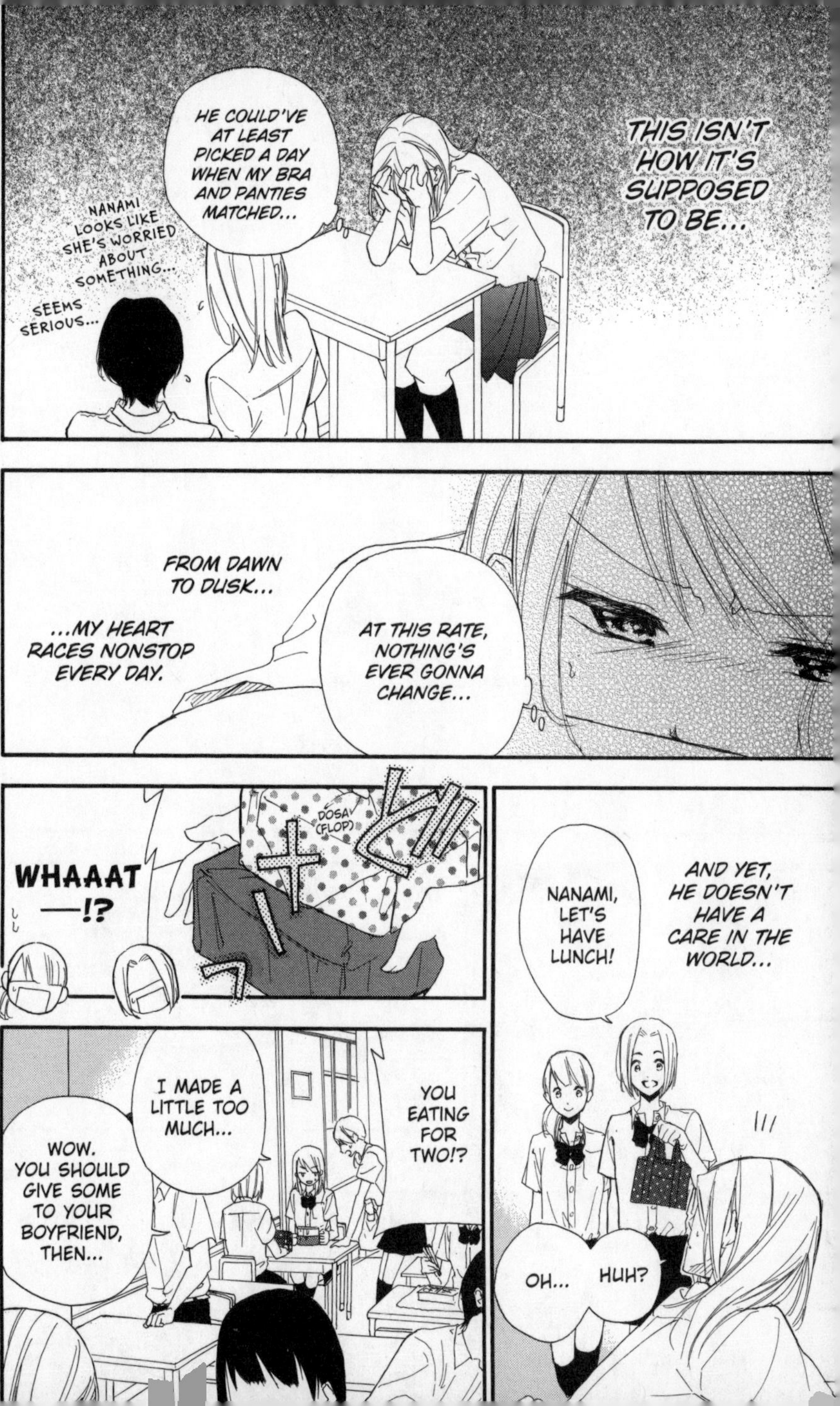
THIS ISN'T HOW IT'S SUPPOSED TO BE...
HE COULD'VE AT LEAST PICKED A DAY WHEN MY BRA AND PANTIES MATCHED...
NANAMI LOOKS LIKE SHE'S WORRIED ABOUT SOMETHING...
SEEMS SERIOUS...
FROM DAWN TO DUSK...
...MY HEART RACES NONSTOP EVERY DAY.
AT THIS RATE, NOTHING'S EVER GONNA CHANGE...
AND YET, HE DOESN'T HAVE A CARE IN THE WORLD...
NANAMI, LET'S HAVE LUNCH!
HUH?
OH...
DOSA (FLOP)
WHAAAT—!?
YOU EATING FOR TWO!?
I MADE A LITTLE TOO MUCH...
WOW. YOU SHOULD GIVE SOME TO YOUR BOYFRIEND, THEN...

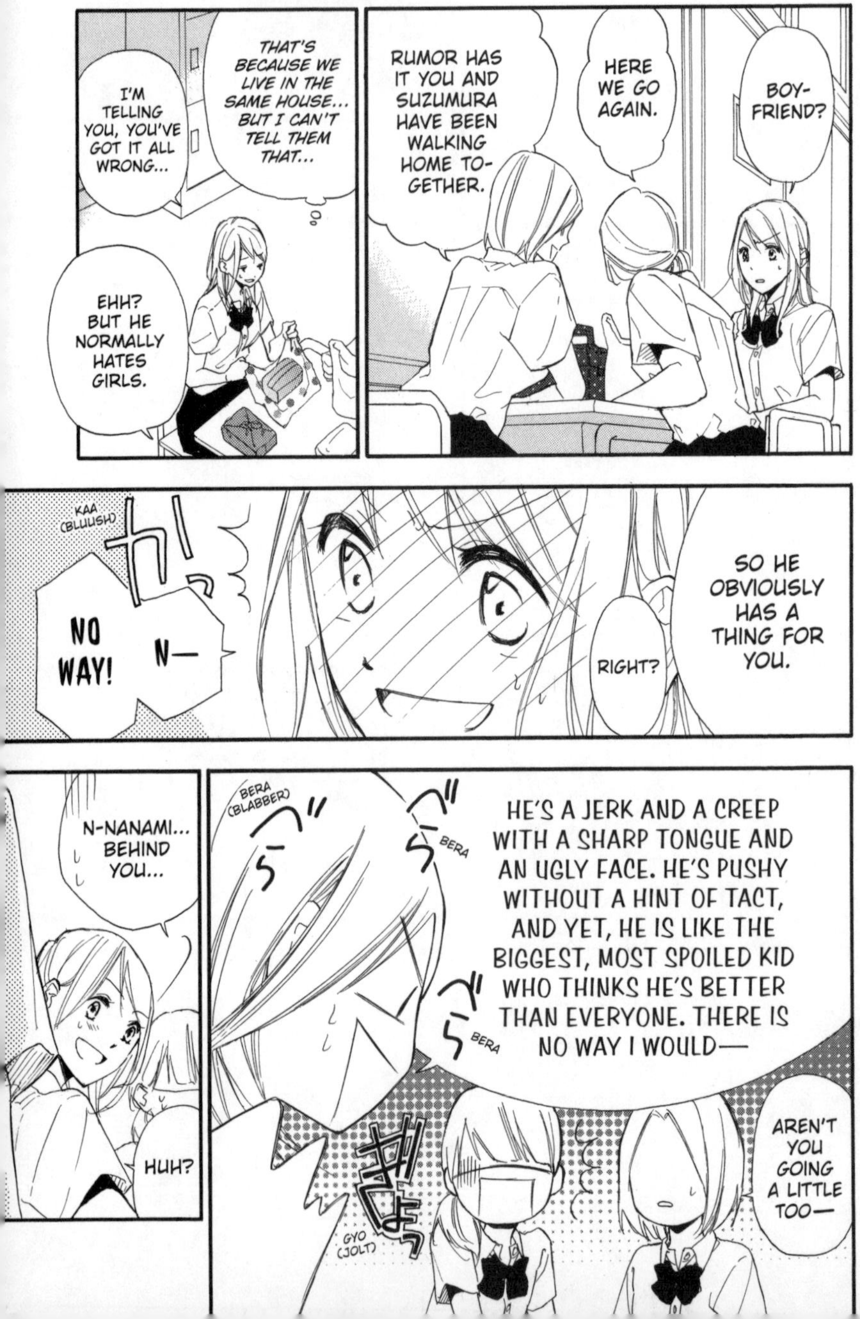
BOY-FRIEND?
HERE WE GO AGAIN.
RUMOR HAS IT YOU AND SUZUMURA HAVE BEEN WALKING HOME TO-GETHER.
I'M TELLING YOU, YOU'VE GOT IT ALL WRONG...
THAT'S BECAUSE WE LIVE IN THE SAME HOUSE... BUT I CAN'T TELL THEM THAT...
EHH? BUT HE NORMALLY HATES GIRLS.
SO HE OBVIOUSLY HAS A THING FOR YOU.
RIGHT?
KAA (BLUUSH)
N—
NO WAY!
BERA (BLABBER)
BERA
HE'S A JERK AND A CREEP WITH A SHARP TONGUE AND AN UGLY FACE. HE'S PUSHY WITHOUT A HINT OF TACT, AND YET, HE IS LIKE THE BIGGEST, MOST SPOILED KID WHO THINKS HE'S BETTER THAN EVERYONE. THERE IS NO WAY I WOULD—
BERA
AREN'T YOU GOING A LITTLE TOO—
GYO (JOLT)
N-NANAMI... BEHIND YOU...
HUH?

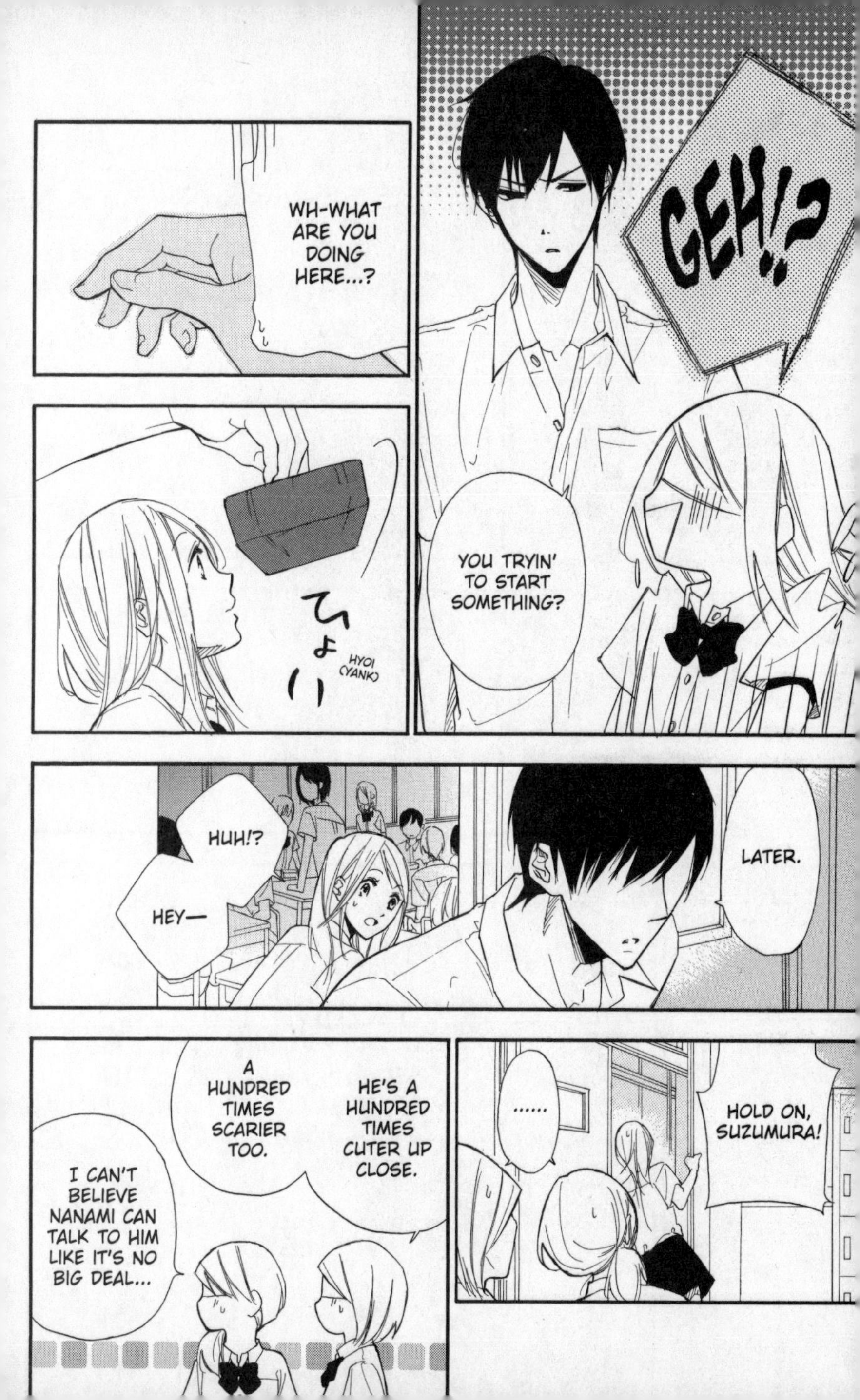
GEH!?
YOU TRYIN' TO START SOMETHING?
WH-WHAT ARE YOU DOING HERE...?
ひょい
HYOI (YANK)
LATER.
HUH!?
HEY—
HOLD ON, SUZUMURA!
......
HE'S A HUNDRED TIMES CUTER UP CLOSE.
A HUNDRED TIMES SCARIER TOO.
I CAN'T BELIEVE NANAMI CAN TALK TO HIM LIKE IT'S NO BIG DEAL...

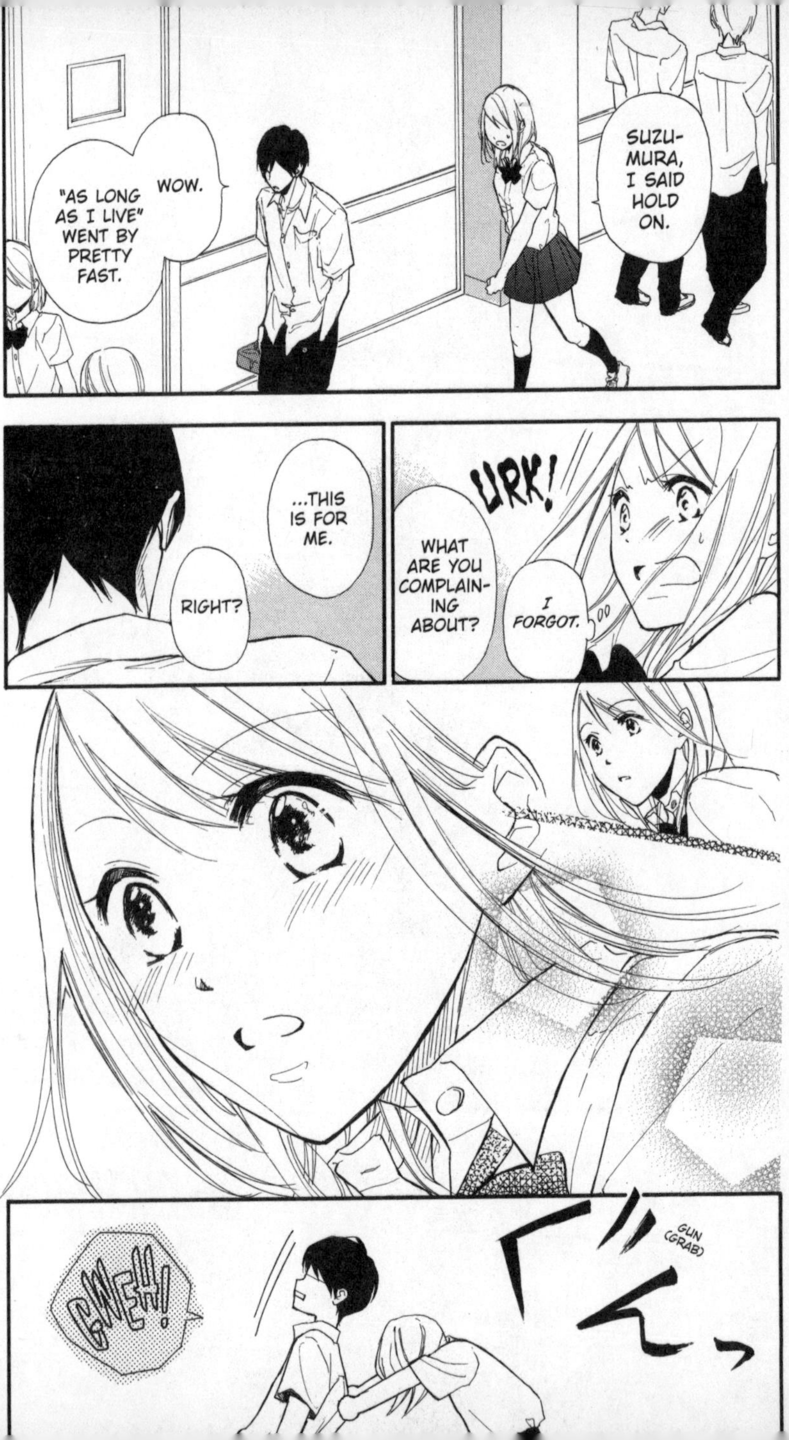
SUZU-MURA, I SAID HOLD ON.
WOW.
"AS LONG AS I LIVE" WENT BY PRETTY FAST.
URK!
I FORGOT.
WHAT ARE YOU COMPLAINING ABOUT?
...THIS IS FOR ME.
RIGHT?
GUN (GRAB)
GWEH!

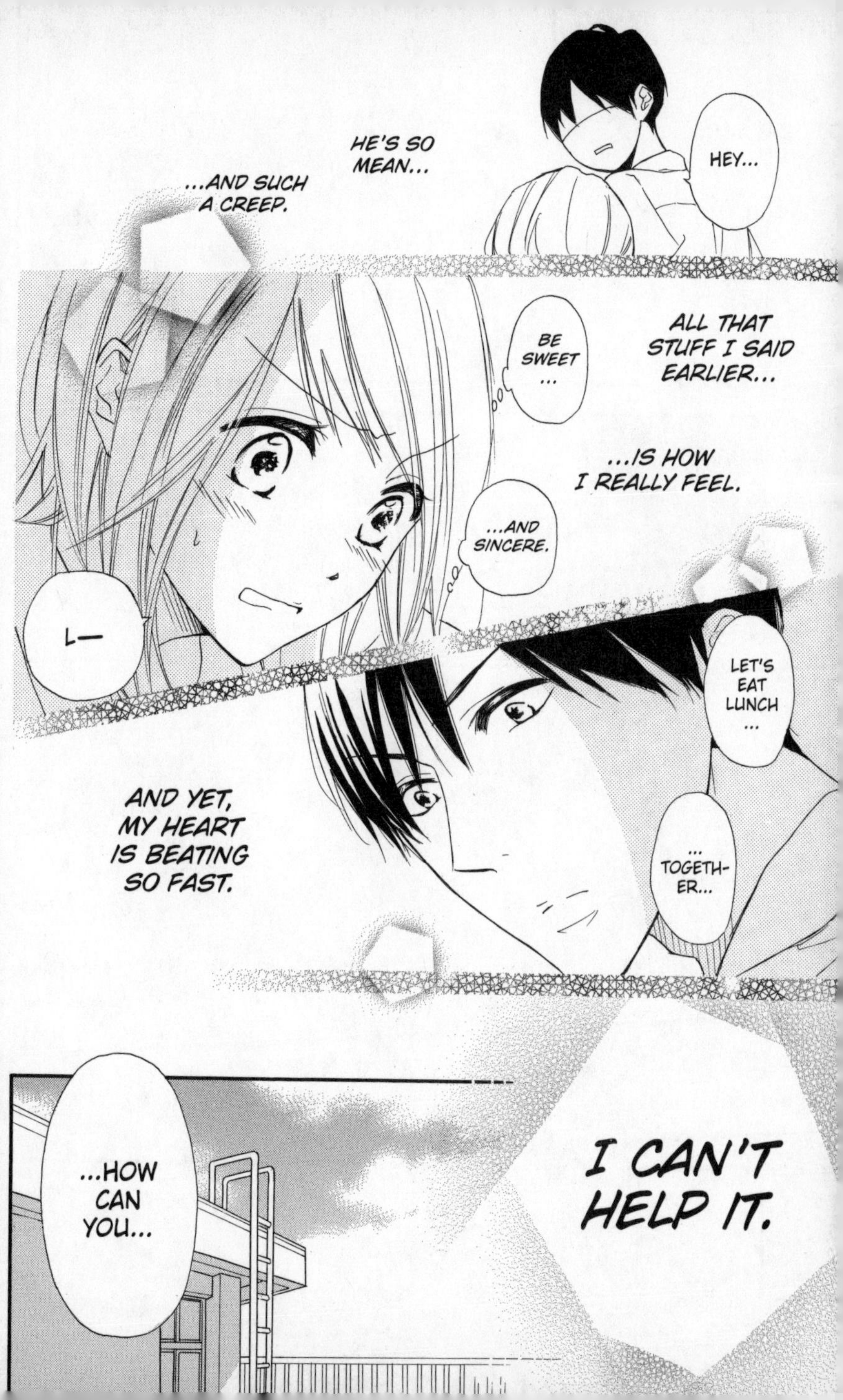
HEY...
HE'S SO MEAN...
...AND SUCH A CREEP.
ALL THAT STUFF I SAID EARLIER...
BE SWEET...
...IS HOW I REALLY FEEL.
...AND SINCERE.
L—
LET'S EAT LUNCH...
...TOGETHER...
AND YET, MY HEART IS BEATING SO FAST.
I CAN'T HELP IT.
...HOW CAN YOU...

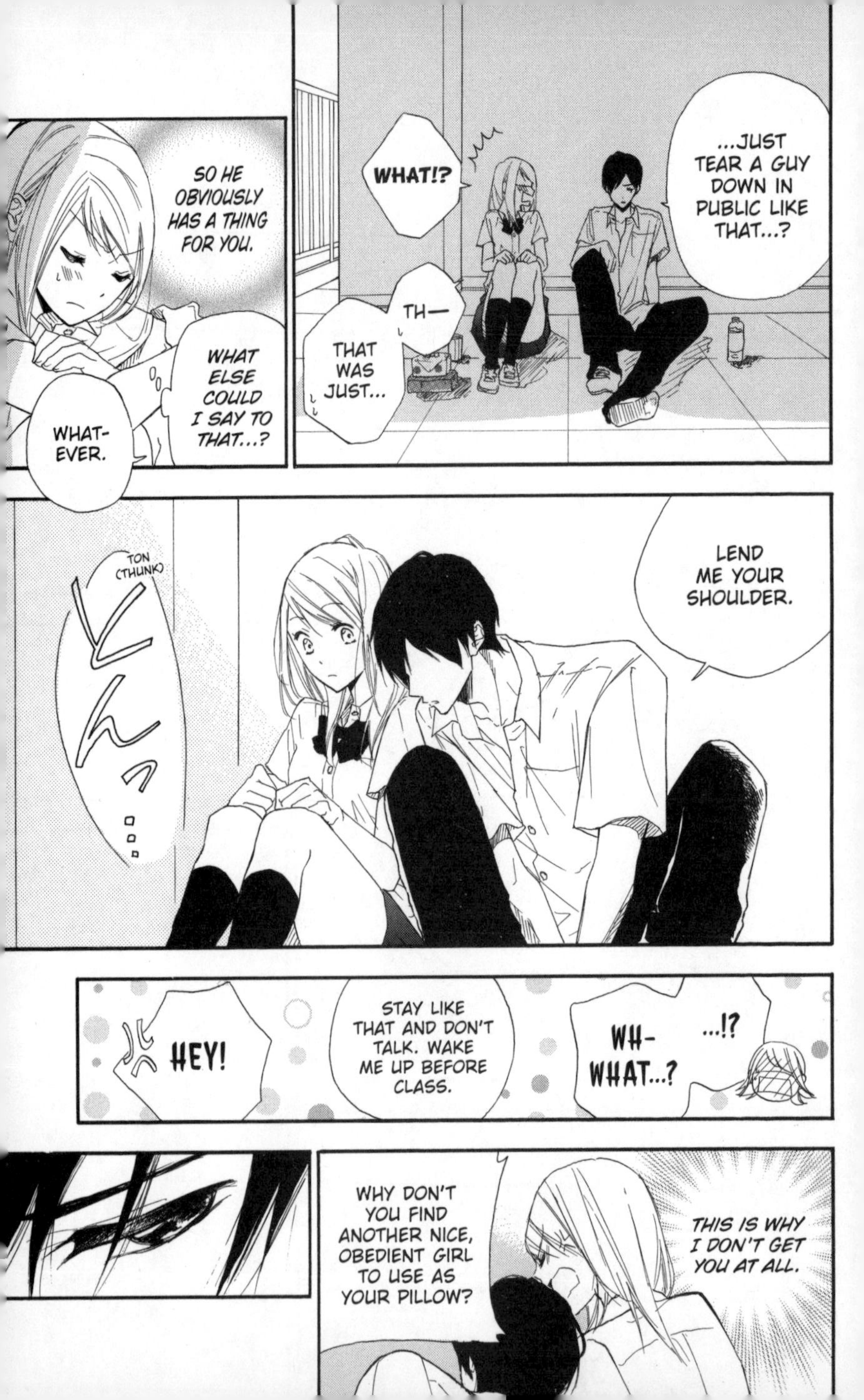
...JUST TEAR A GUY DOWN IN PUBLIC LIKE THAT...?
WHAT!?
TH—
THAT WAS JUST...
SO HE OBVIOUSLY HAS A THING FOR YOU.
WHAT ELSE COULD I SAY TO THAT...?
WHAT-EVER.
LEND ME YOUR SHOULDER.
TON (THUNK)
...!?
WH- WHAT...?
STAY LIKE THAT AND DON'T TALK. WAKE ME UP BEFORE CLASS.
HEY!
THIS IS WHY I DON'T GET YOU AT ALL.
WHY DON'T YOU FIND ANOTHER NICE, OBEDIENT GIRL TO USE AS YOUR PILLOW?

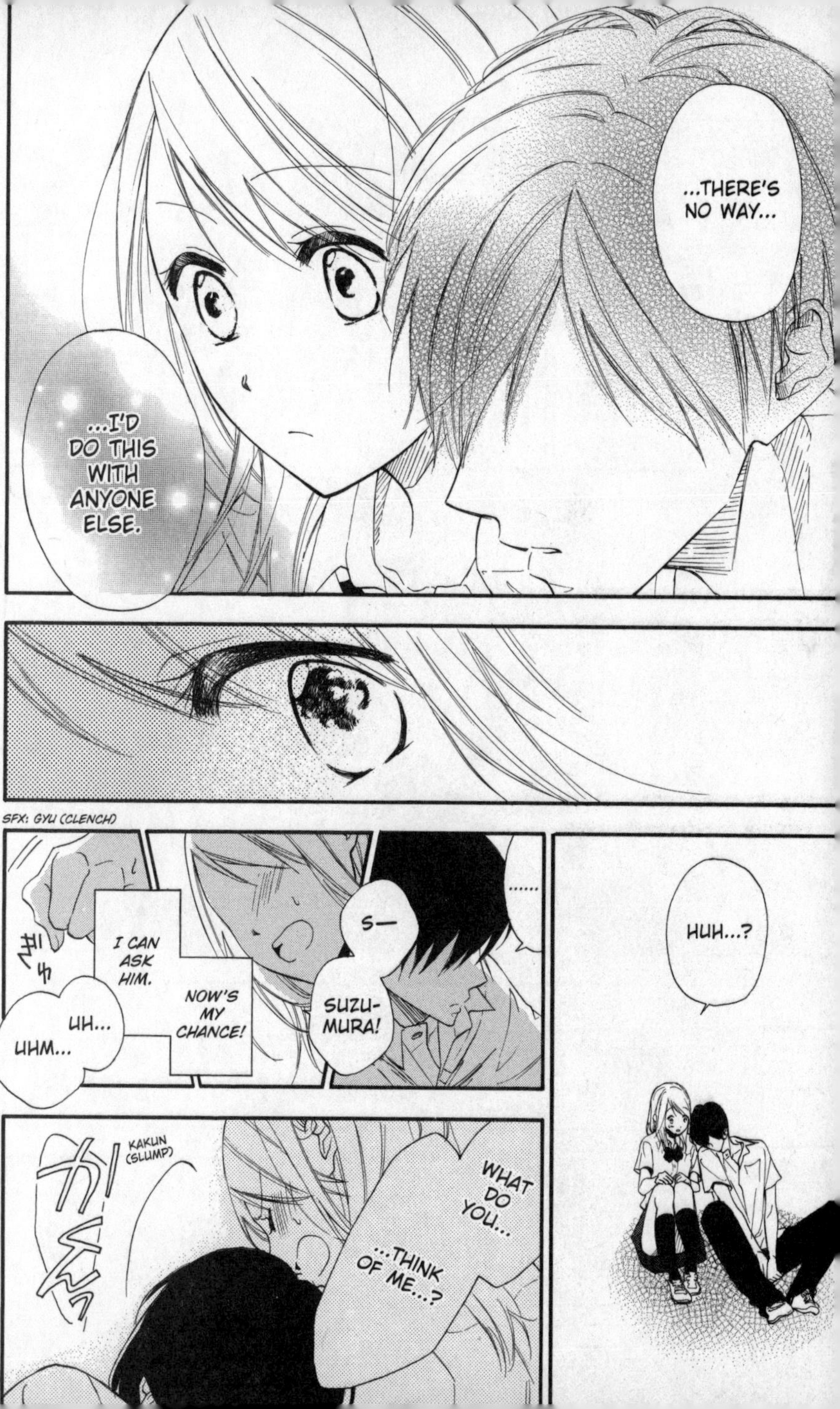
...THERE'S NO WAY...
...I'D DO THIS WITH ANYONE ELSE.
SFX: GYU (CLENCH)
HUH...?
......
S—
SUZU-MURA!
I CAN ASK HIM.
NOW'S MY CHANCE!
UH... UHM...
WHAT DO YOU...
...THINK OF ME...?
KAKUN (SLUMP)

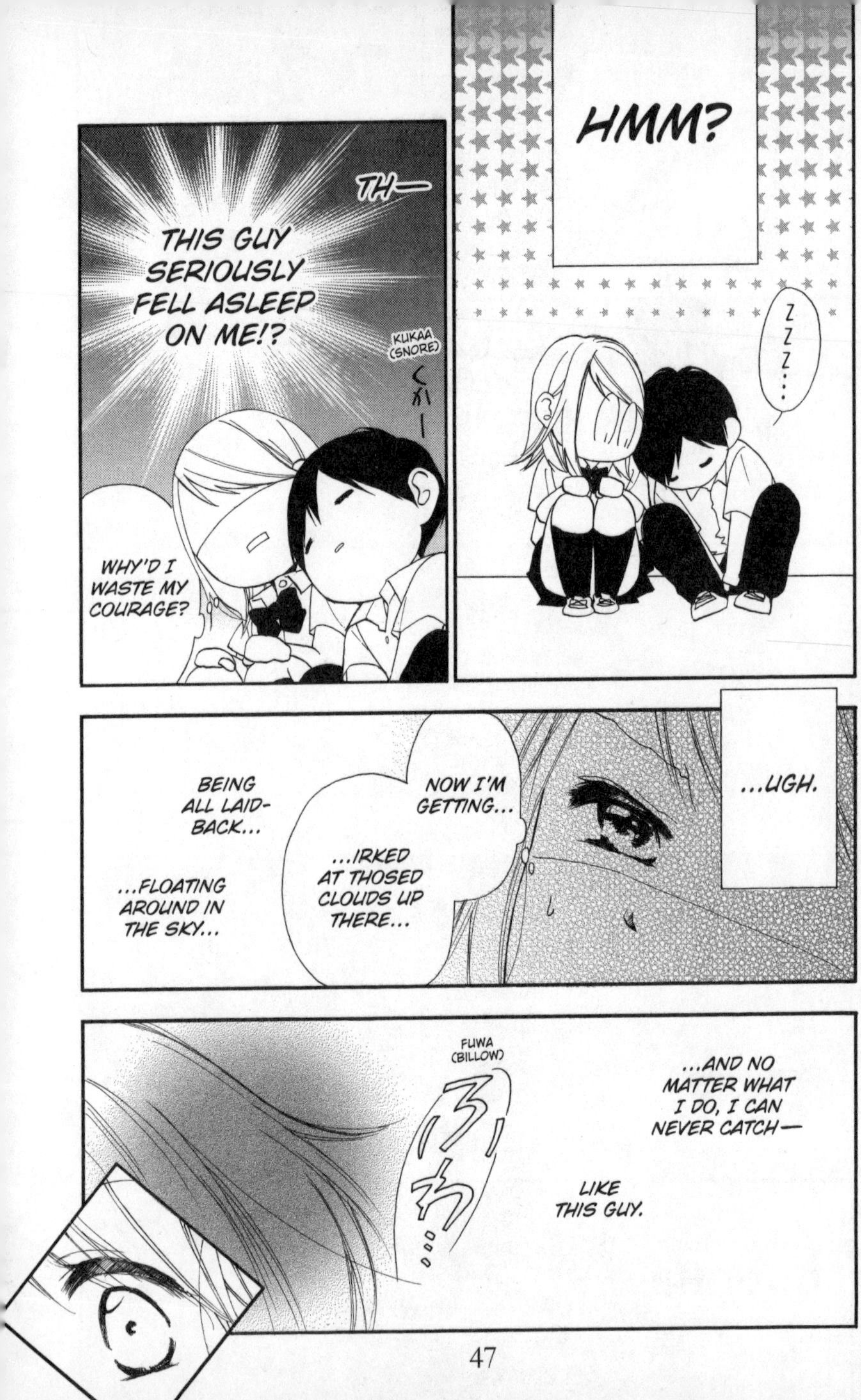
HMM?
ZZZ...
TH—
THIS GUY SERIOUSLY FELL ASLEEP ON ME!?
KUKAA (SNORE)
くかー
WHY'D I WASTE MY COURAGE?
...UGH.
NOW I'M GETTING...
...IRKED AT THOSED CLOUDS UP THERE...
BEING ALL LAID-BACK...
...FLOATING AROUND IN THE SKY...
...AND NO MATTER WHAT I DO, I CAN NEVER CATCH—
LIKE THIS GUY.
FUWA (BILLOW)
ふわ...

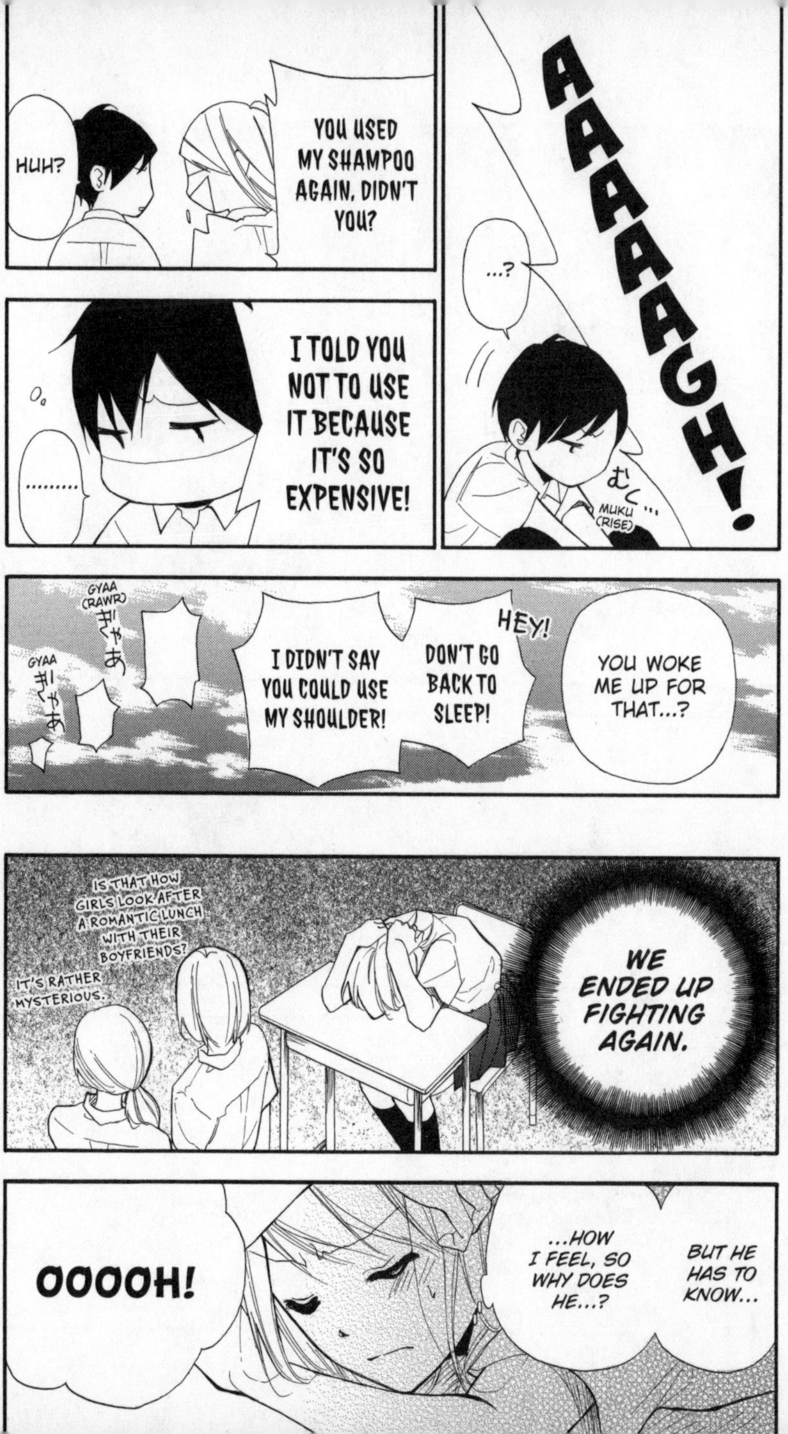
AAAAAAGH!
...?
むく...
MUKU (RISE)
YOU USED MY SHAMPOO AGAIN, DIDN'T YOU?
HUH?
I TOLD YOU NOT TO USE IT BECAUSE IT'S SO EXPENSIVE!
Oa
....
YOU WOKE ME UP FOR THAT...?
HEY!
DON'T GO BACK TO SLEEP!
I DIDN'T SAY YOU COULD USE MY SHOULDER!
ぎゃあ
GYAA (RAWR)
ぎゃあ
GYAA
WE ENDED UP FIGHTING AGAIN.
IS THAT HOW GIRLS LOOK AFTER A ROMANTIC LUNCH WITH THEIR BOYFRIENDS?
IT'S RATHER MYSTERIOUS.
BUT HE HAS TO KNOW...
...HOW I FEEL, SO WHY DOES HE...?
OOOOH!

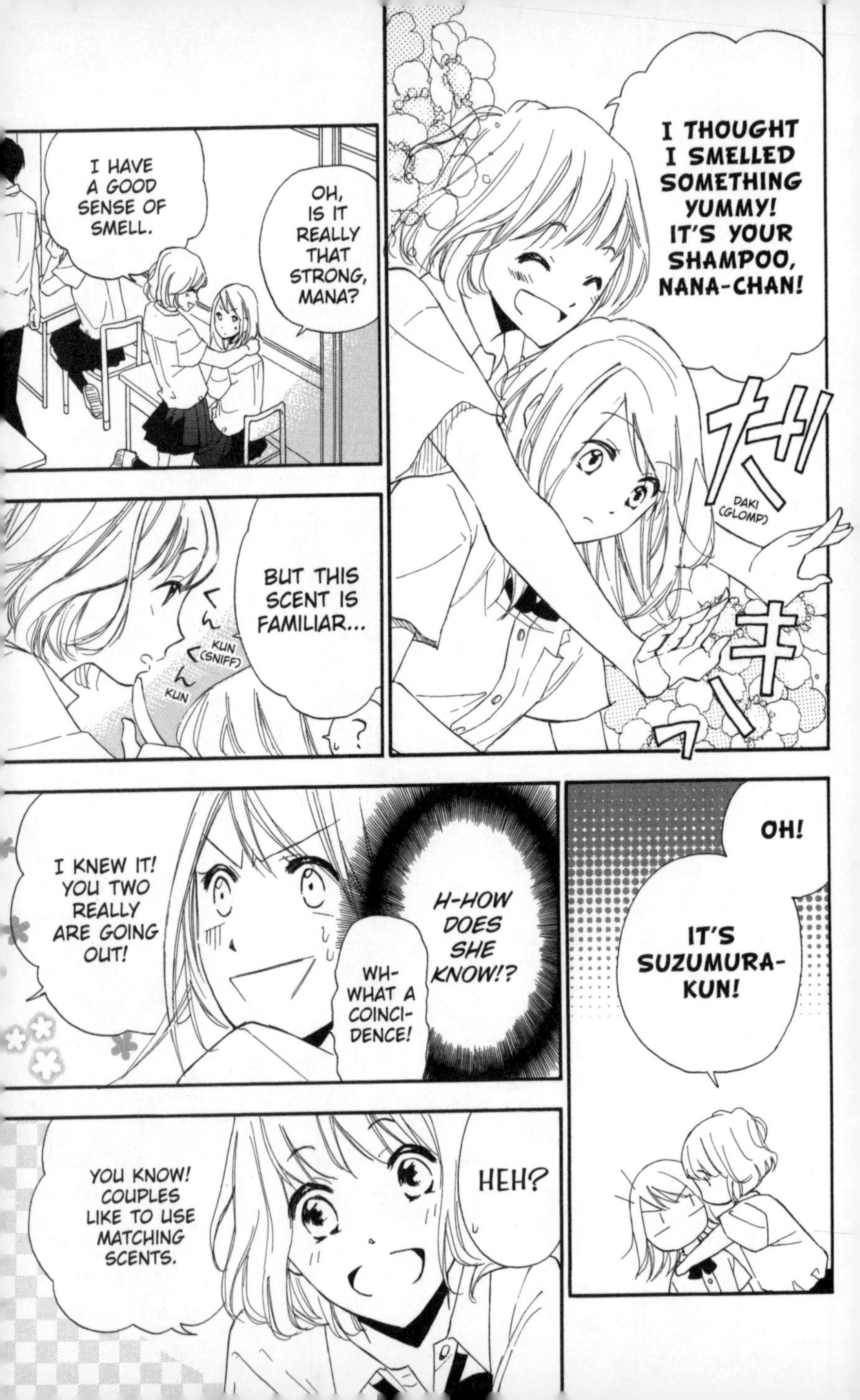
I THOUGHT I SMELLED SOMETHING YUMMY! IT'S YOUR SHAMPOO, NANA-CHAN!
DAKI (GLOMP)
OH, IS IT REALLY THAT STRONG, MANA?
I HAVE A GOOD SENSE OF SMELL.
BUT THIS SCENT IS FAMILIAR...
KUN (SNIFF)
KUN
OH!
IT'S SUZUMURA-KUN!
H-HOW DOES SHE KNOW!?
WH-WHAT A COINCIDENCE!
I KNEW IT! YOU TWO REALLY ARE GOING OUT!
HEH?
YOU KNOW! COUPLES LIKE TO USE MATCHING SCENTS.

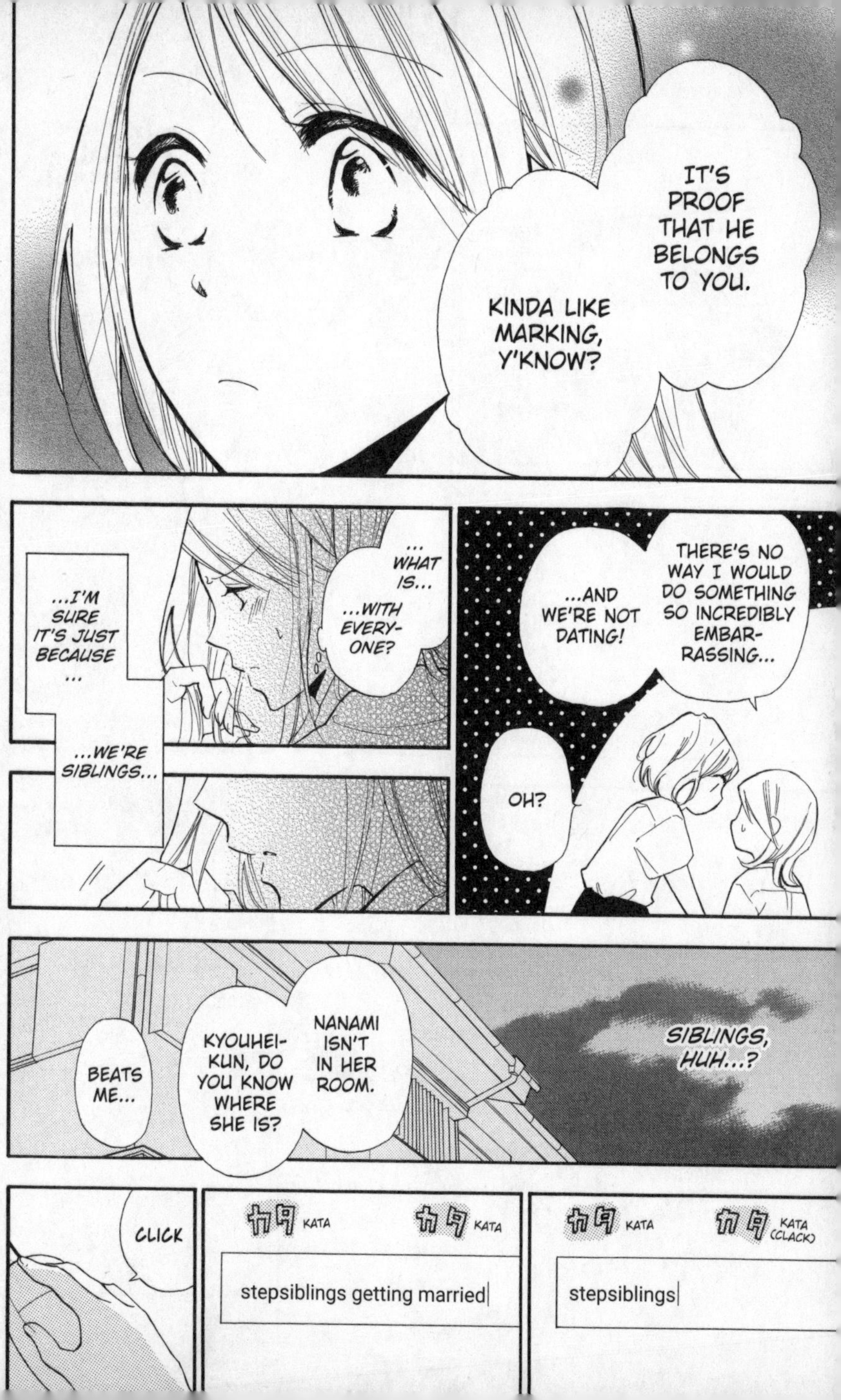
IT'S PROOF THAT HE BELONGS TO YOU.
KINDA LIKE MARKING, Y'KNOW?
THERE'S NO WAY I WOULD DO SOMETHING SO INCREDIBLY EMBARRASSING...
...AND WE'RE NOT DATING!
OH?
...WHAT IS...
...WITH EVERYONE?
...I'M SURE IT'S JUST BECAUSE...
...WE'RE SIBLINGS...
SIBLINGS, HUH...?
NANAMI ISN'T IN HER ROOM.
KYOUHEI-KUN, DO YOU KNOW WHERE SHE IS?
BEATS ME...
カタ KATA
カタ KATA (CLACK)
stepsiblings
カタ KATA
カタ KATA
stepsiblings getting married
CLICK

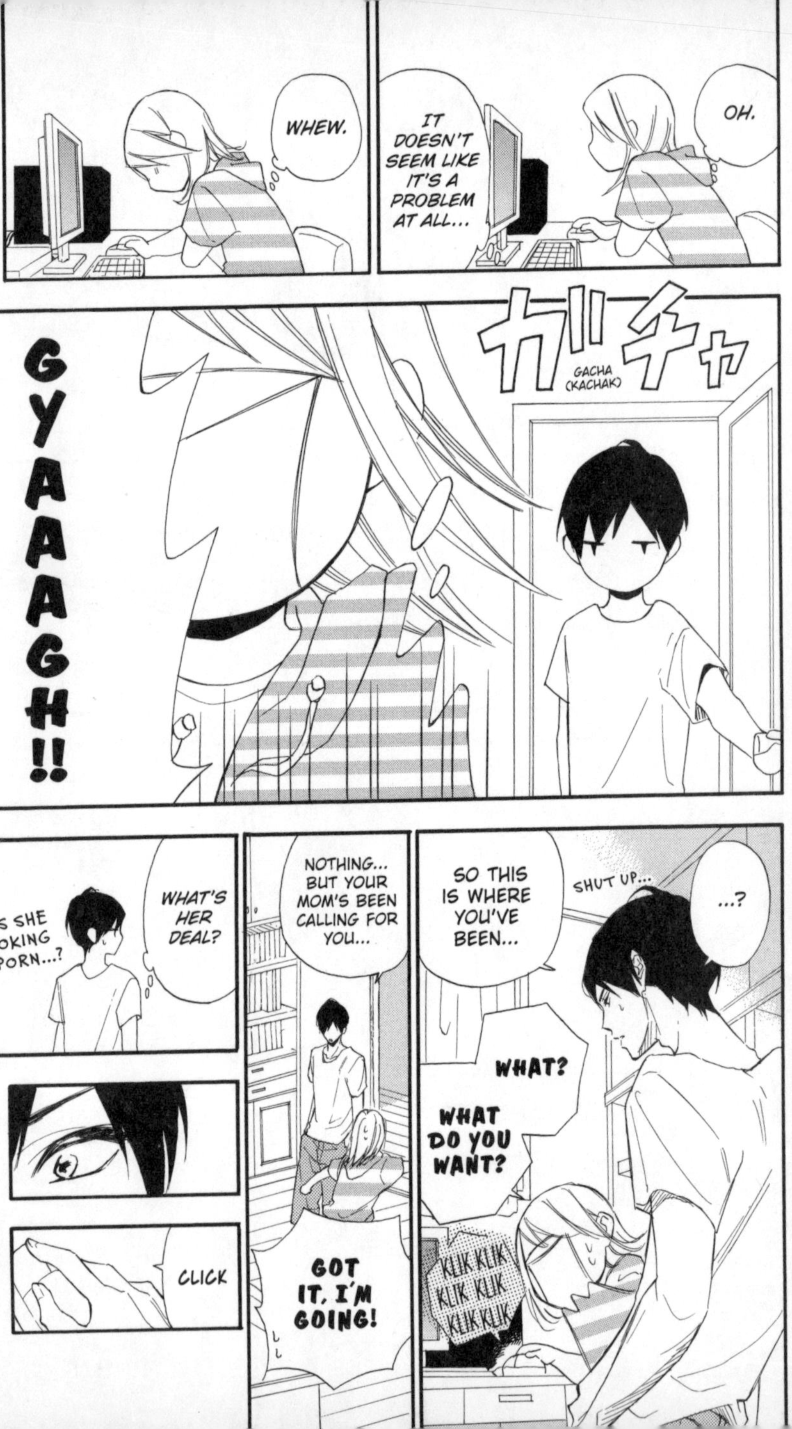
OH.
IT DOESN'T SEEM LIKE IT'S A PROBLEM AT ALL...
WHEW.
カチャ
GACHA (KACHAK)
GYAAAGH!!
...?
SHUT UP...
SO THIS IS WHERE YOU'VE BEEN...
WHAT?
WHAT DO YOU WANT?
KLIK KLIK KLIK KLIK KLIK KLIK
NOTHING... BUT YOUR MOM'S BEEN CALLING FOR YOU...
GOT IT, I'M GOING!
WHAT'S HER DEAL?
WAS SHE LOOKING AT PORN...?
CLICK

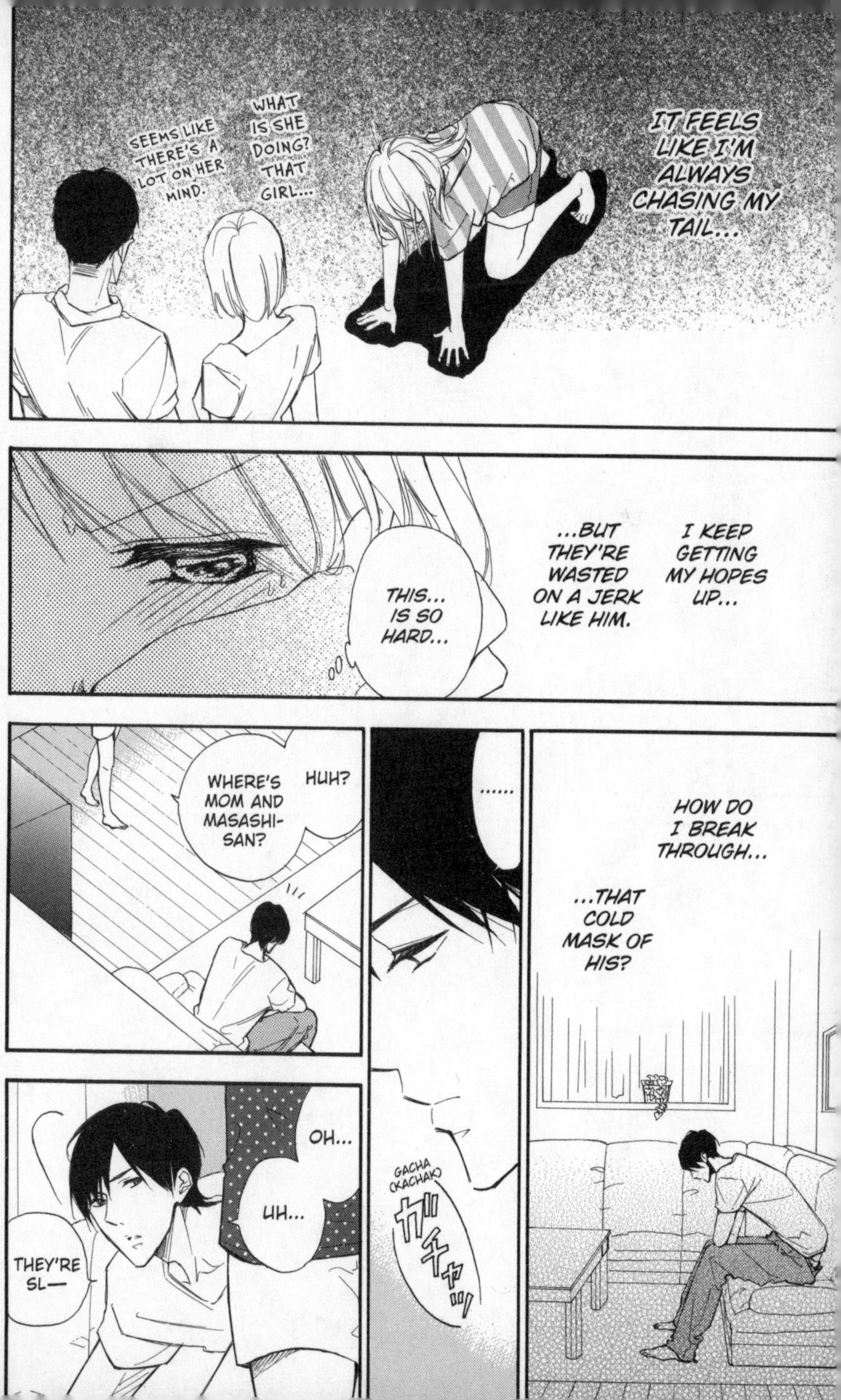
IT FEELS LIKE I'M ALWAYS CHASING MY TAIL...
WHAT IS SHE DOING? THAT GIRL...
SEEMS LIKE THERE'S A LOT ON HER MIND.
I KEEP GETTING MY HOPES UP...
...BUT THEY'RE WASTED ON A JERK LIKE HIM.
THIS... IS SO HARD...
HOW DO I BREAK THROUGH...
...THAT COLD MASK OF HIS?
......
GACHA (KACHAK)
ガチャッ
HUH?
WHERE'S MOM AND MASASHI-SAN?
OH...
UH...
THEY'RE SL—

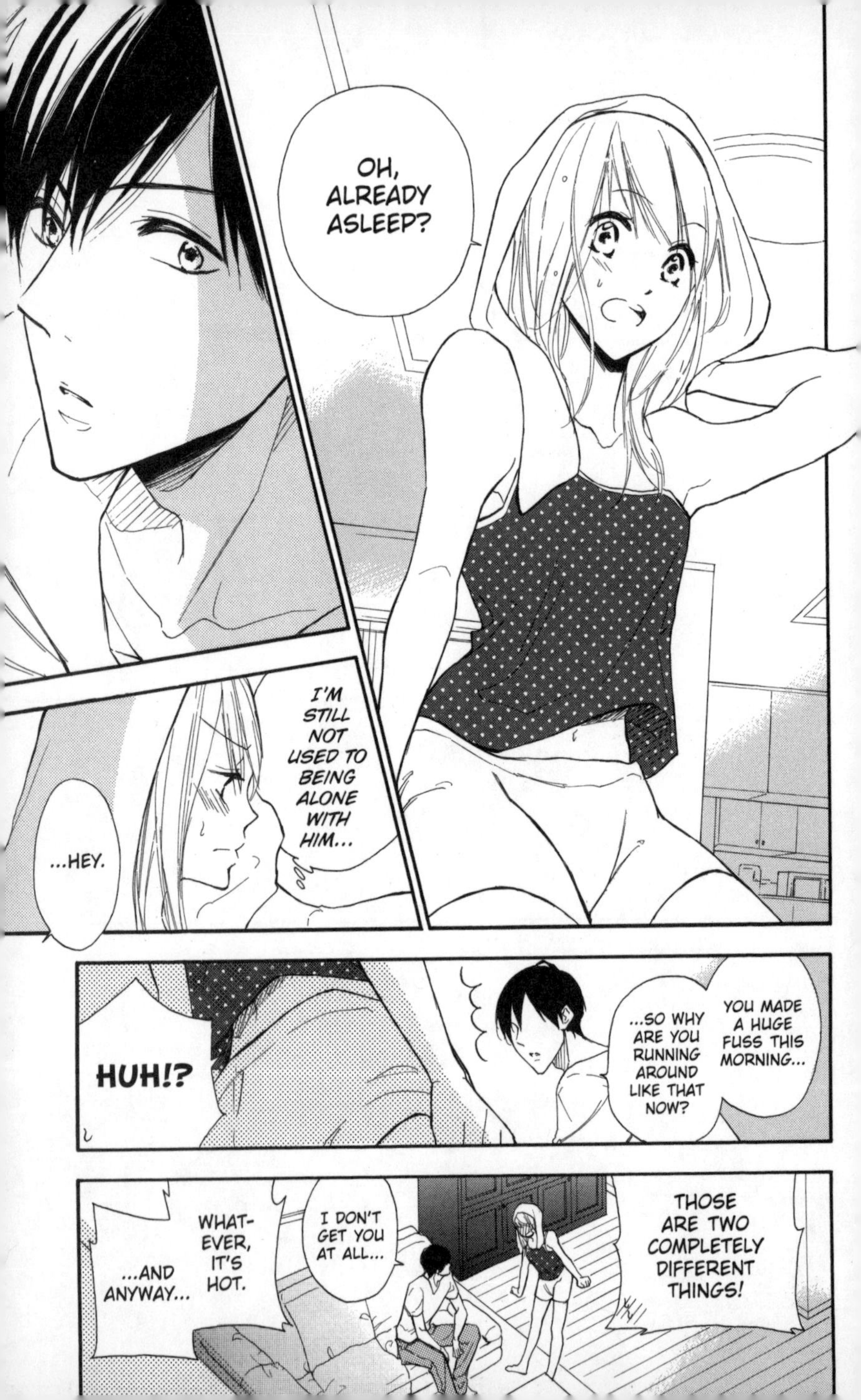
OH, ALREADY ASLEEP?
I'M STILL NOT USED TO BEING ALONE WITH HIM...
...HEY.
YOU MADE A HUGE FUSS THIS MORNING...
...SO WHY ARE YOU RUNNING AROUND LIKE THAT NOW?
HUH!?
THOSE ARE TWO COMPLETELY DIFFERENT THINGS!
I DON'T GET YOU AT ALL...
WHAT-EVER, IT'S HOT.
...AND ANYWAY...

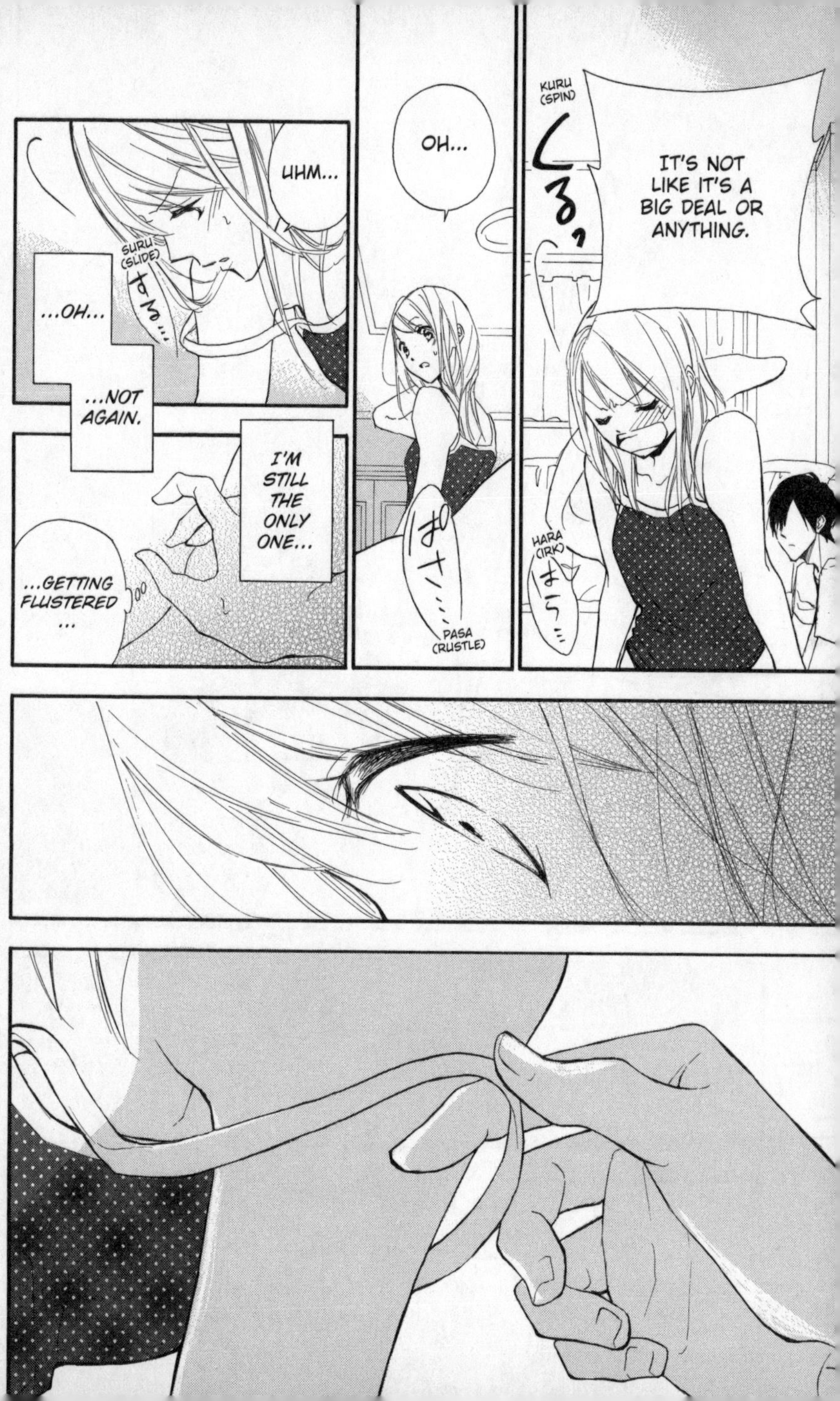
KURU (SPIN)
くるっ
IT'S NOT LIKE IT'S A BIG DEAL OR ANYTHING.
HARA (IRK)
はら…
OH...
ぱさ…
PASA (RUSTLE)
UHM...
SURU (SLIDE)
する…
...OH...
...NOT AGAIN.
I'M STILL THE ONLY ONE...
...GETTING FLUSTERED ...

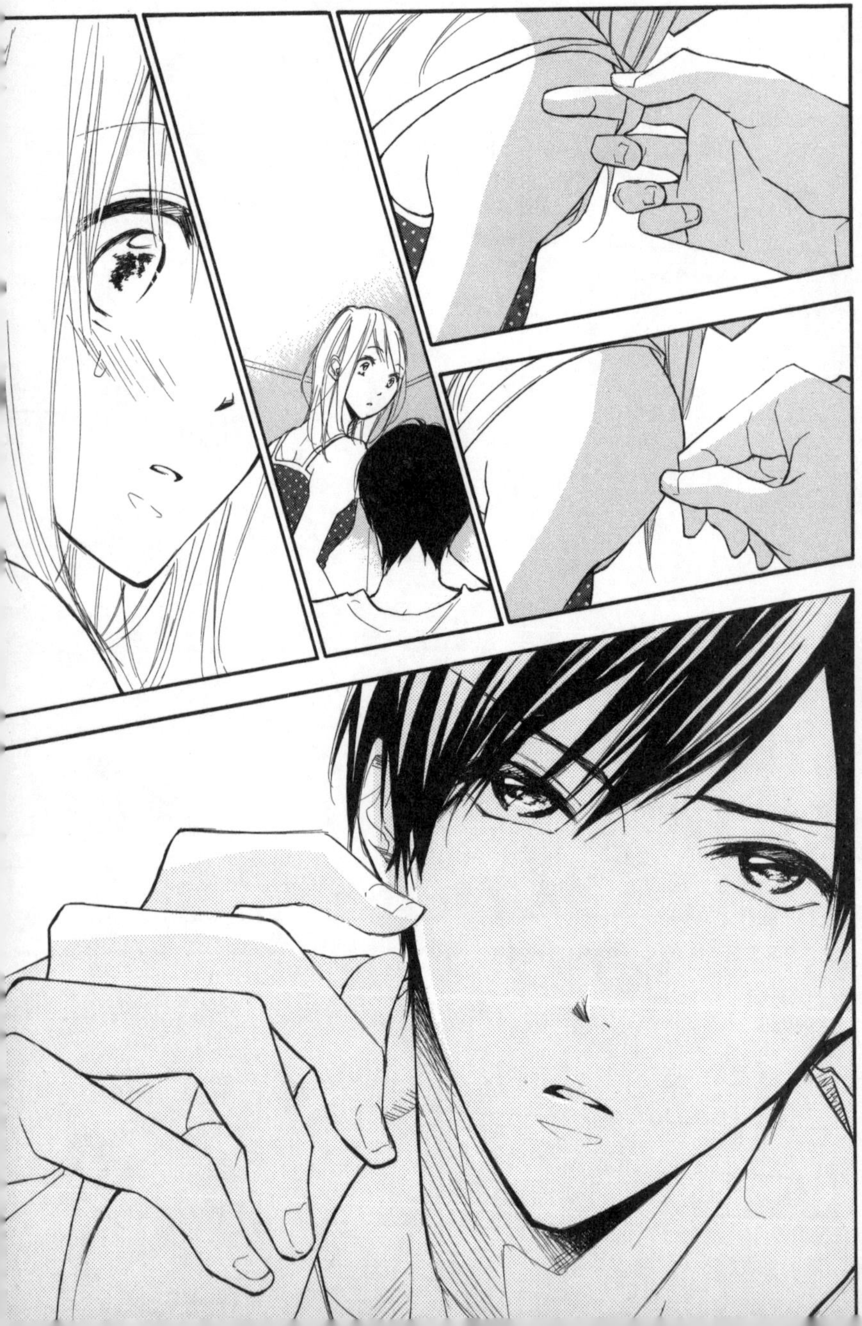

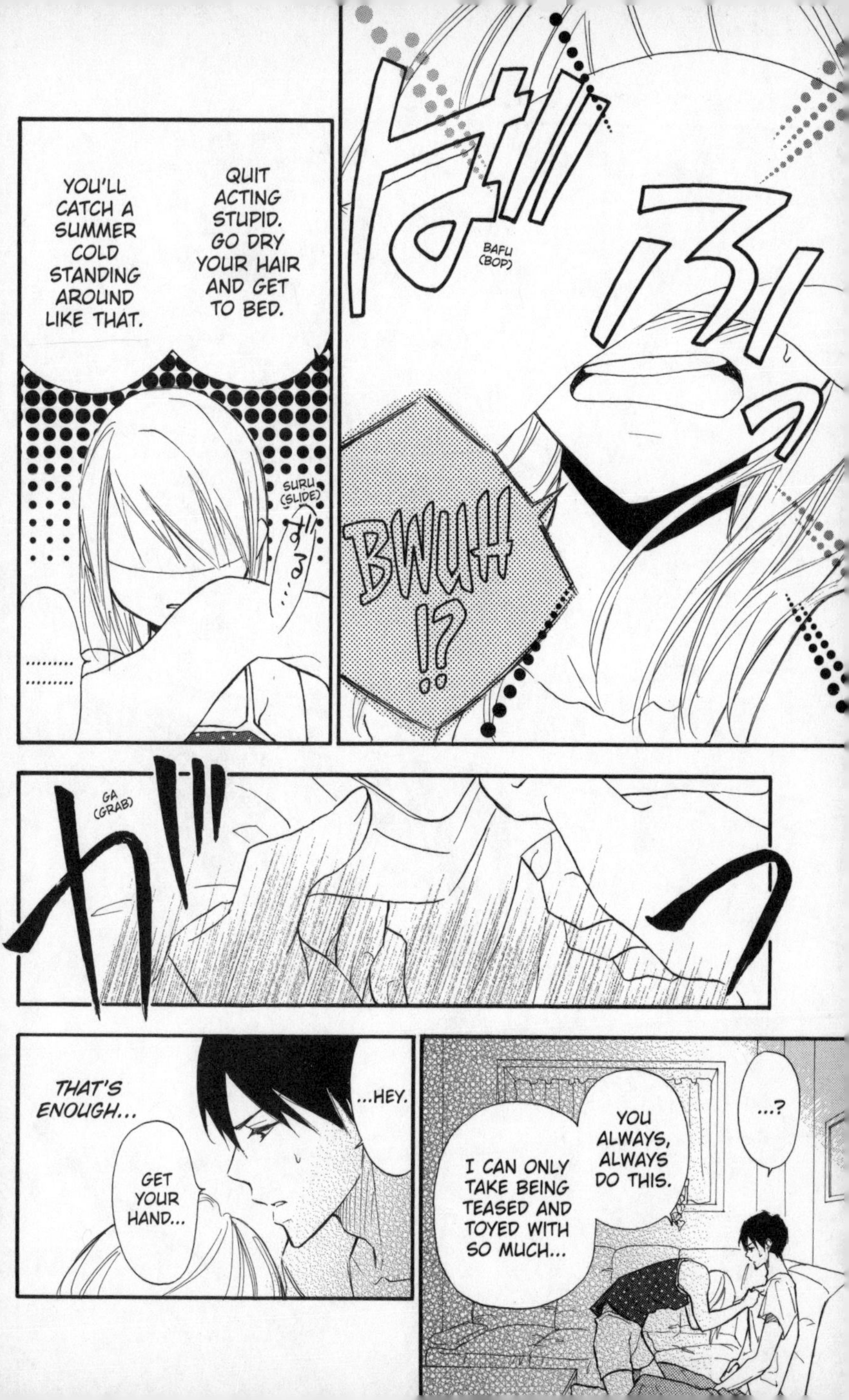

ばふっ
BAFU (BOP)
BWUH !?
QUIT ACTING STUPID. GO DRY YOUR HAIR AND GET TO BED.
YOU'LL CATCH A SUMMER COLD STANDING AROUND LIKE THAT.
SURU (SLIDE)
....
....
ガッ
GA (GRAB)
...?
YOU ALWAYS, ALWAYS DO THIS.
I CAN ONLY TAKE BEING TEASED AND TOYED WITH SO MUCH...
...HEY.
THAT'S ENOUGH...
GET YOUR HAND...

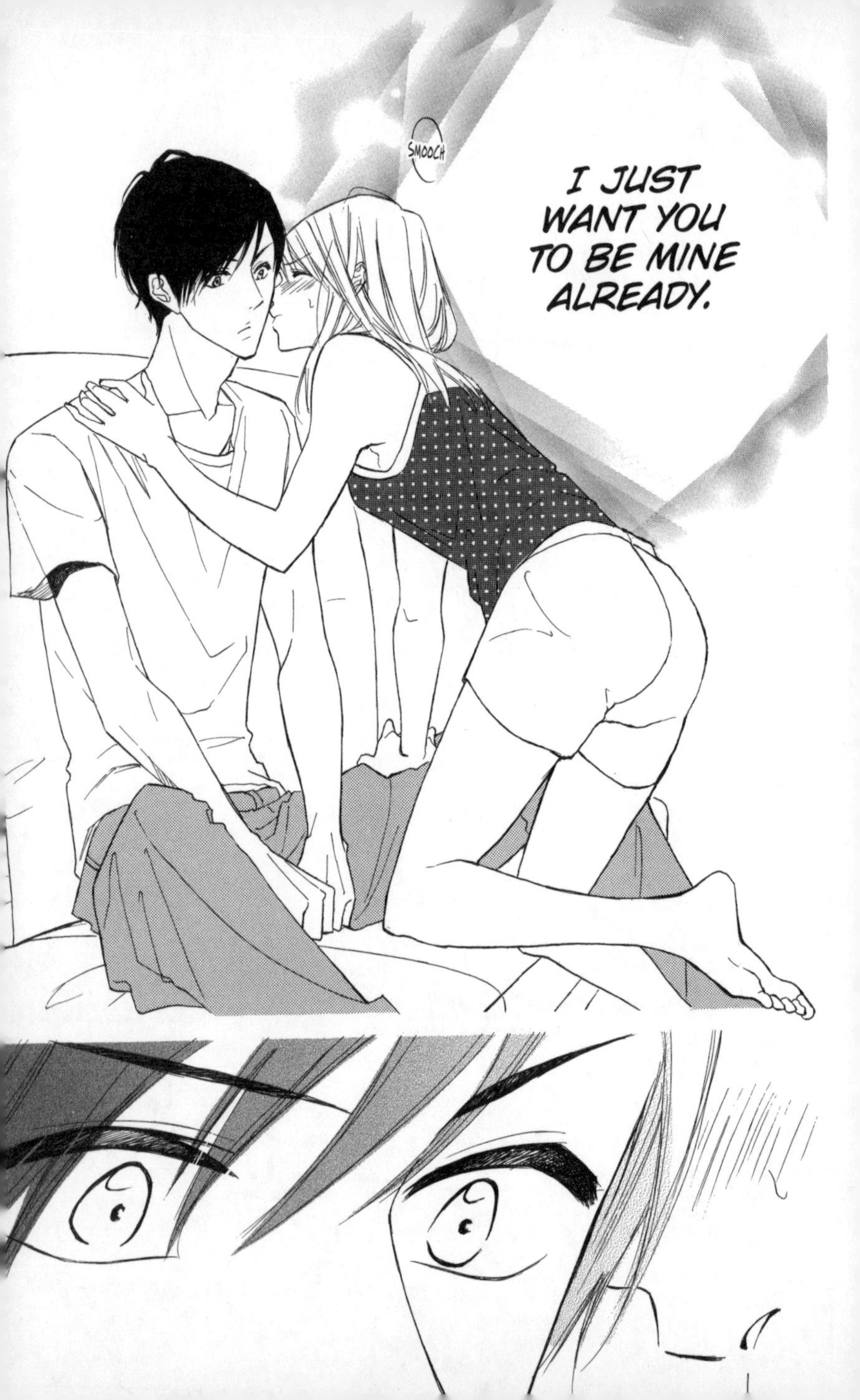
I JUST WANT YOU TO BE MINE ALREADY.
SMOOCH

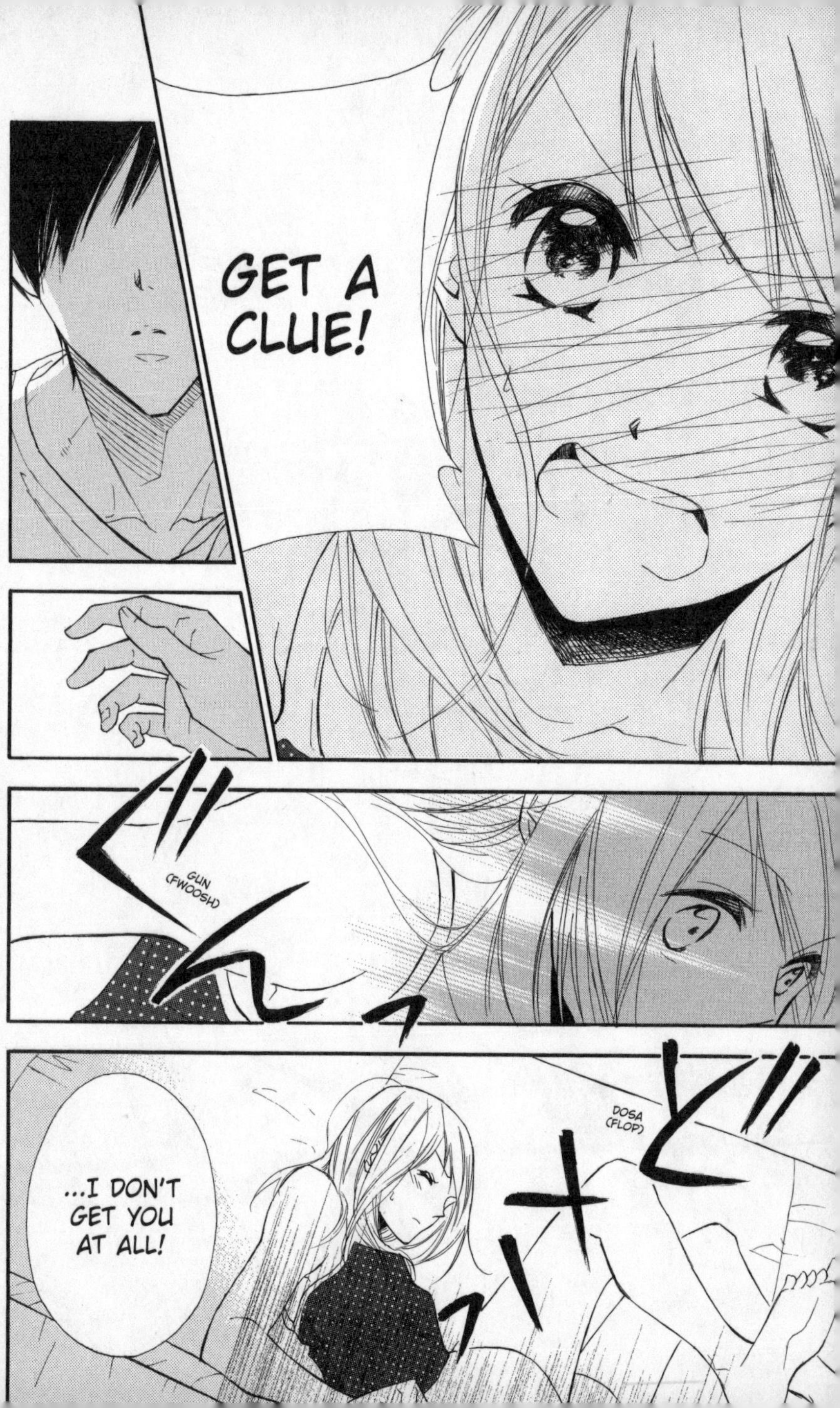
GET A CLUE!
GUN (FWOOSH)
DOSA (FLOP)
...I DON'T GET YOU AT ALL!

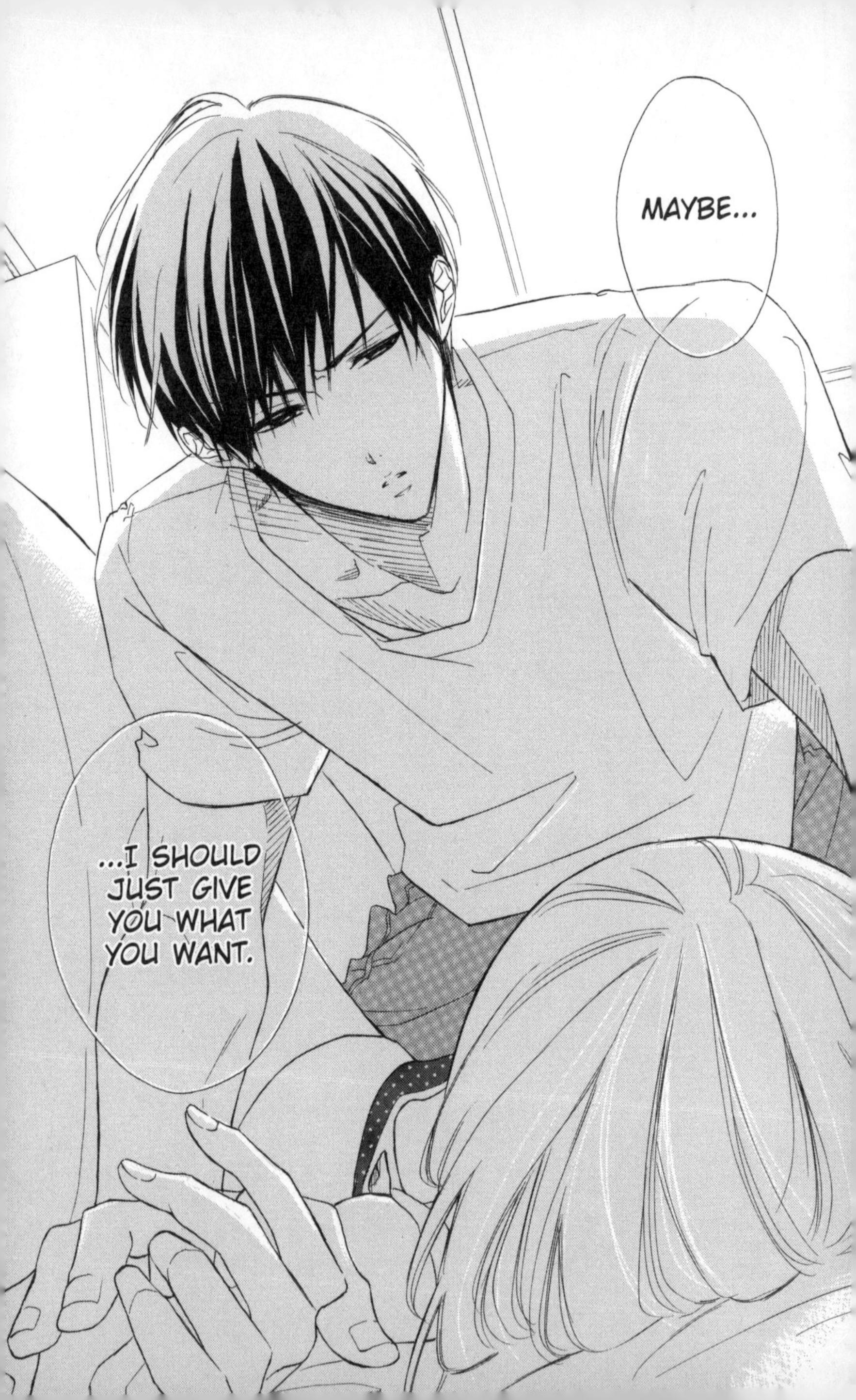
MAYBE...
...I SHOULD JUST GIVE YOU WHAT YOU WANT.

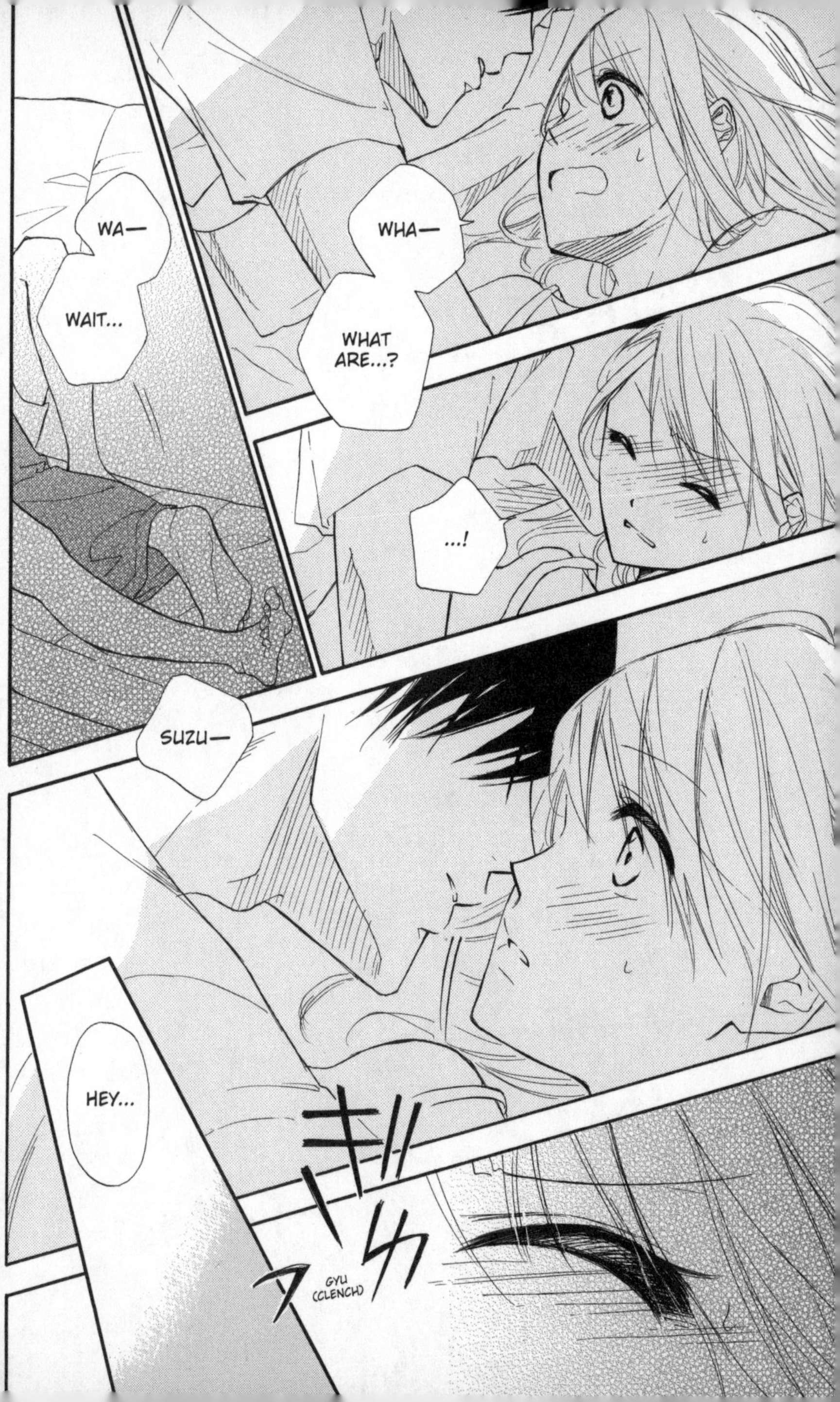
WHA—
WHAT ARE...?
...!
WA—
WAIT...
SUZU—
ギュッ
GYU (CLENCH)
HEY...

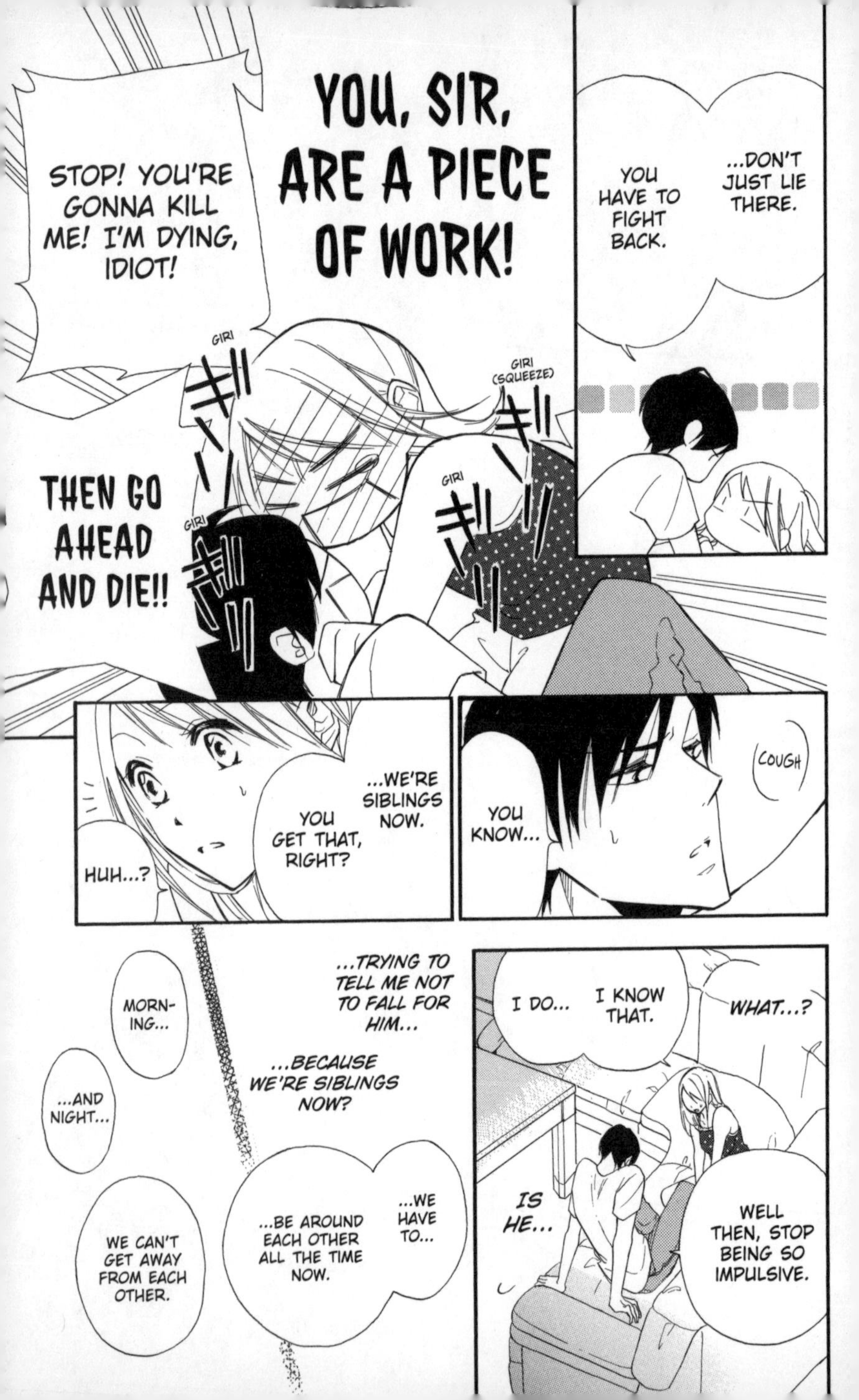
...DON'T JUST LIE THERE.
YOU HAVE TO FIGHT BACK.
YOU, SIR, ARE A PIECE OF WORK!
STOP! YOU'RE GONNA KILL ME! I'M DYING, IDIOT!
GIRI (SQUEEZE)
GIRI
GIRI
GIRI
THEN GO AHEAD AND DIE!!
COUGH
YOU KNOW...
...WE'RE SIBLINGS NOW.
YOU GET THAT, RIGHT?
HUH...?
WHAT...?
I KNOW THAT.
I DO...
WELL THEN, STOP BEING SO IMPULSIVE.
IS HE...
...TRYING TO TELL ME NOT TO FALL FOR HIM...
...BECAUSE WE'RE SIBLINGS NOW?
MORNING...
...AND NIGHT...
...WE HAVE TO...
...BE AROUND EACH OTHER ALL THE TIME NOW.
WE CAN'T GET AWAY FROM EACH OTHER.

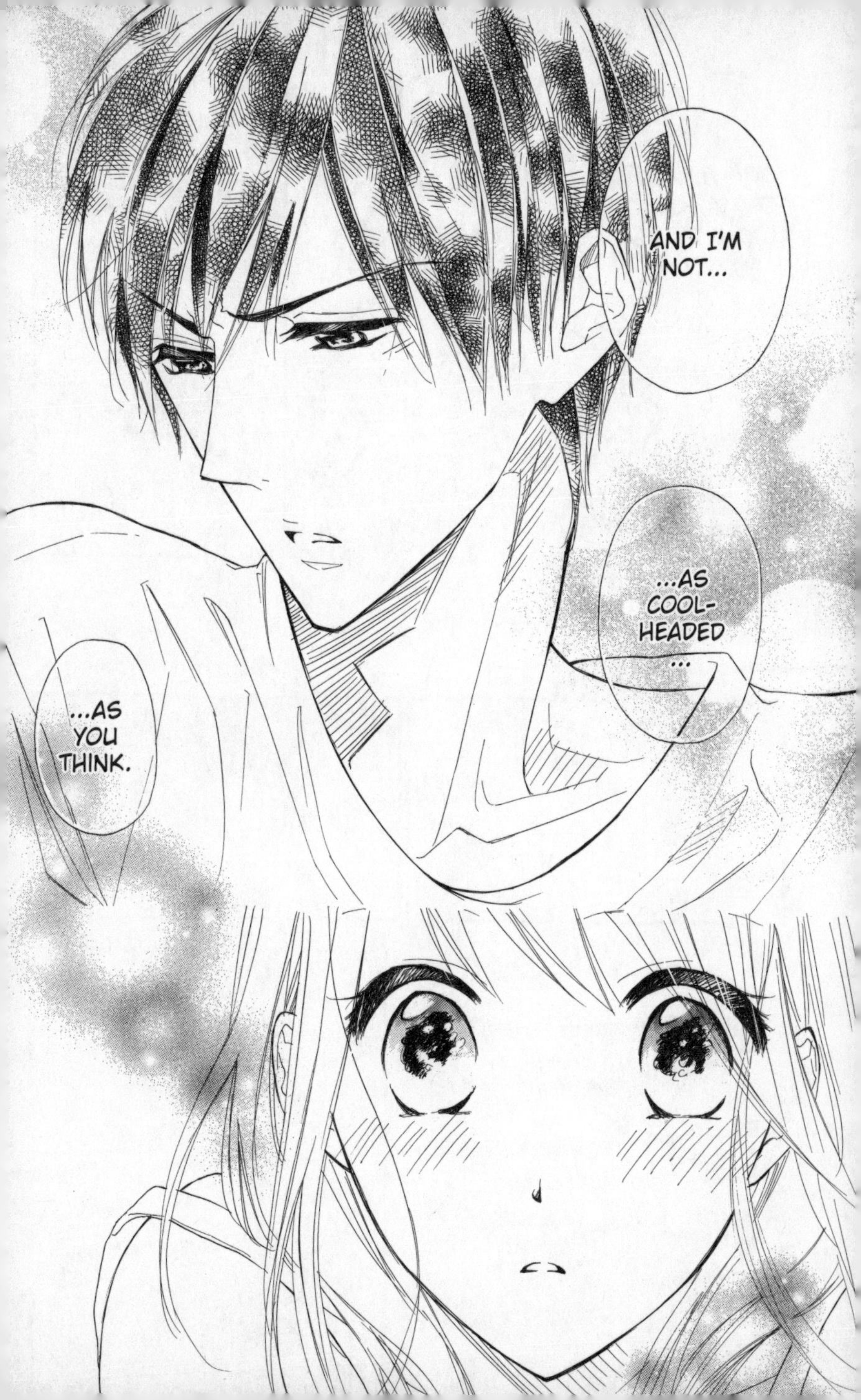
AND I'M NOT...
...AS COOL-HEADED ...
...AS YOU THINK.

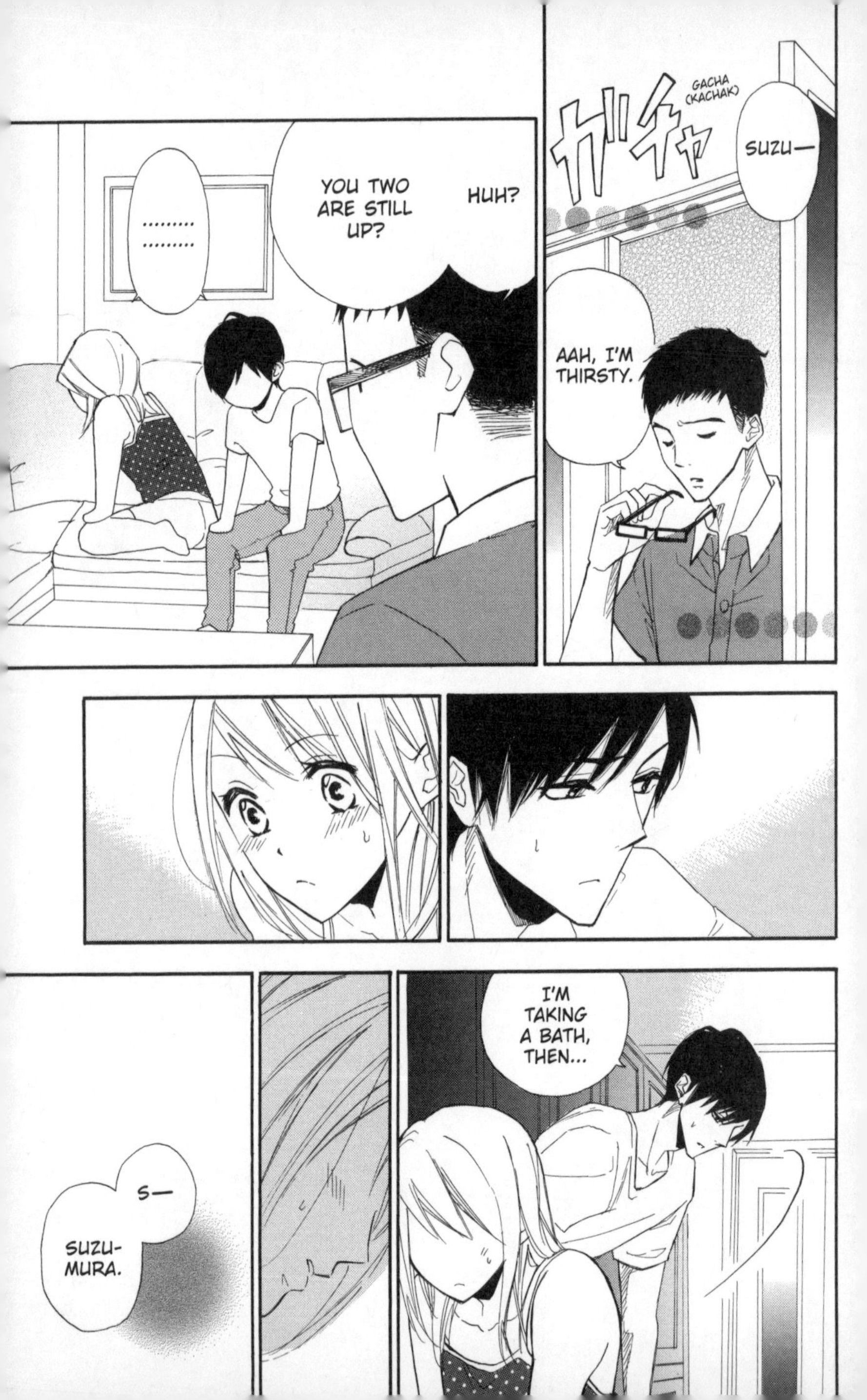

ガチャ
GACHA (KACHAK)
SUZU—
AAH, I'M THIRSTY.
HUH?
YOU TWO ARE STILL UP?
....
....
I'M TAKING A BATH, THEN...
S—
SUZU-MURA.

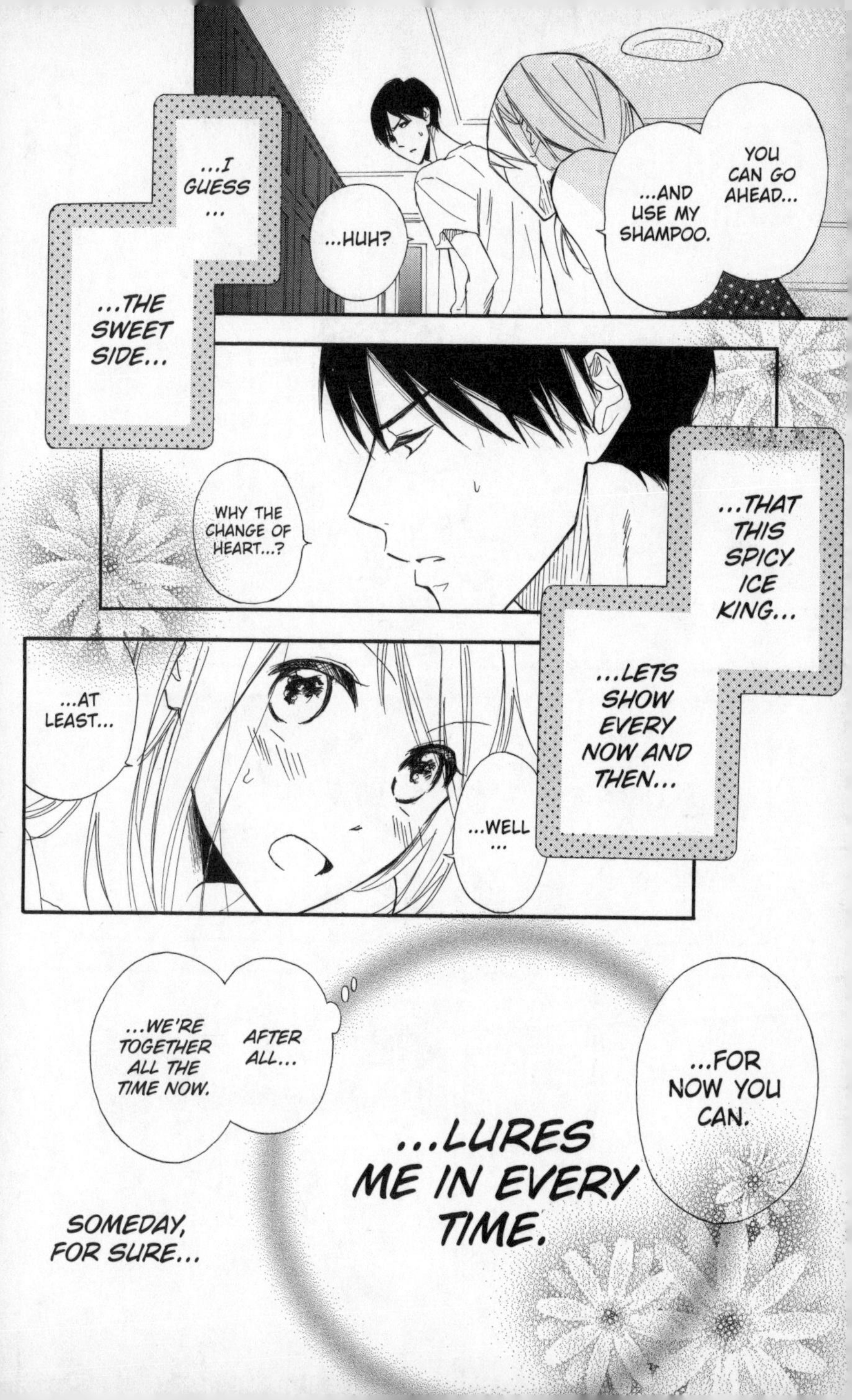
YOU CAN GO AHEAD...
...AND USE MY SHAMPOO.
...HUH?
...I GUESS...
...THAT THIS SPICY ICE KING...
WHY THE CHANGE OF HEART...?
...THE SWEET SIDE...
...LETS SHOW EVERY NOW AND THEN...
...WELL...
...AT LEAST...
...FOR NOW YOU CAN.
...LURES ME IN EVERY TIME.
AFTER ALL...
...WE'RE TOGETHER ALL THE TIME NOW.
SOMEDAY, FOR SURE...

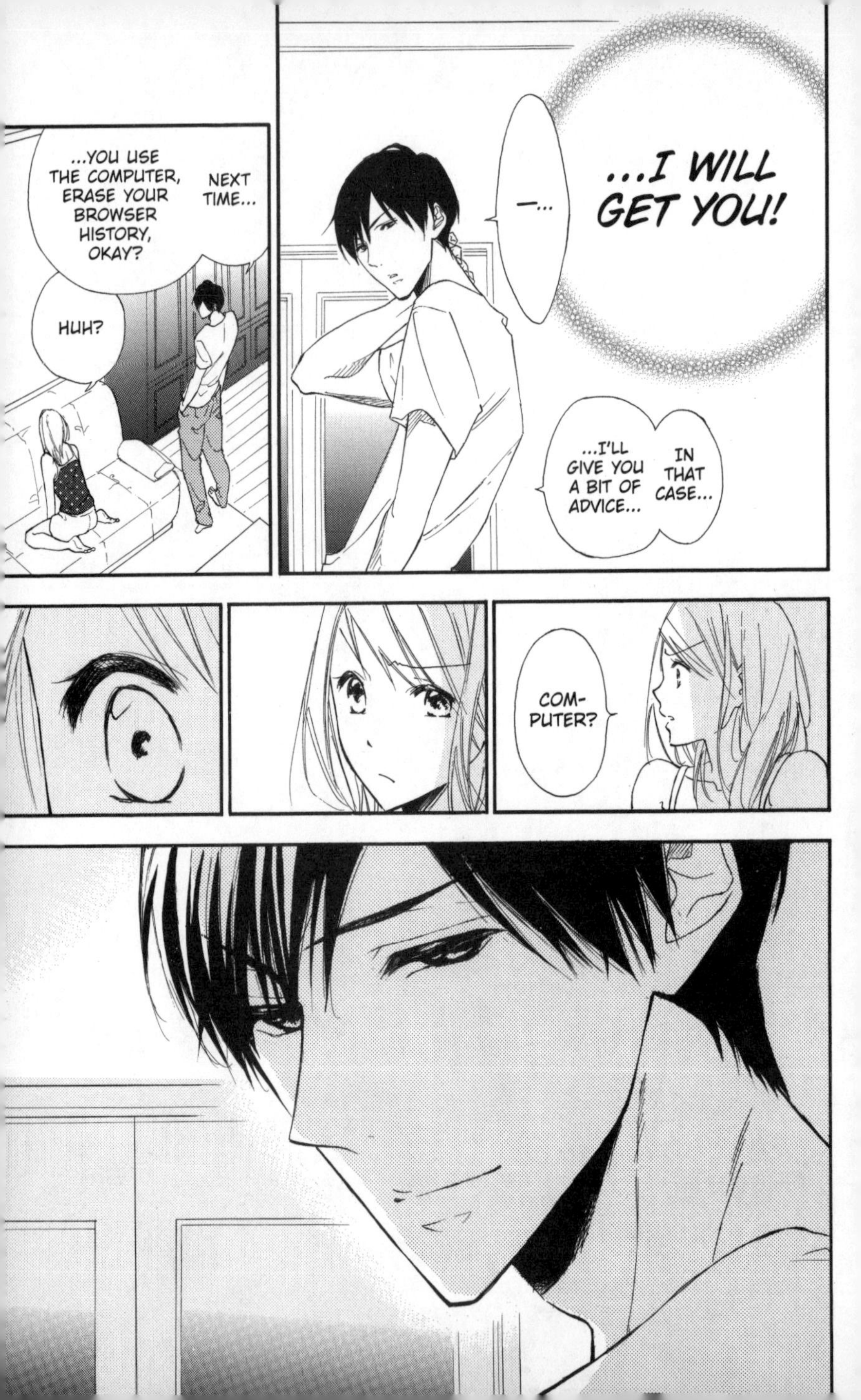
...I WILL GET YOU!
—...
IN THAT CASE...
...I'LL GIVE YOU A BIT OF ADVICE...
NEXT TIME...
...YOU USE THE COMPUTER, ERASE YOUR BROWSER HISTORY, OKAY?
HUH?
COM-PUTER?

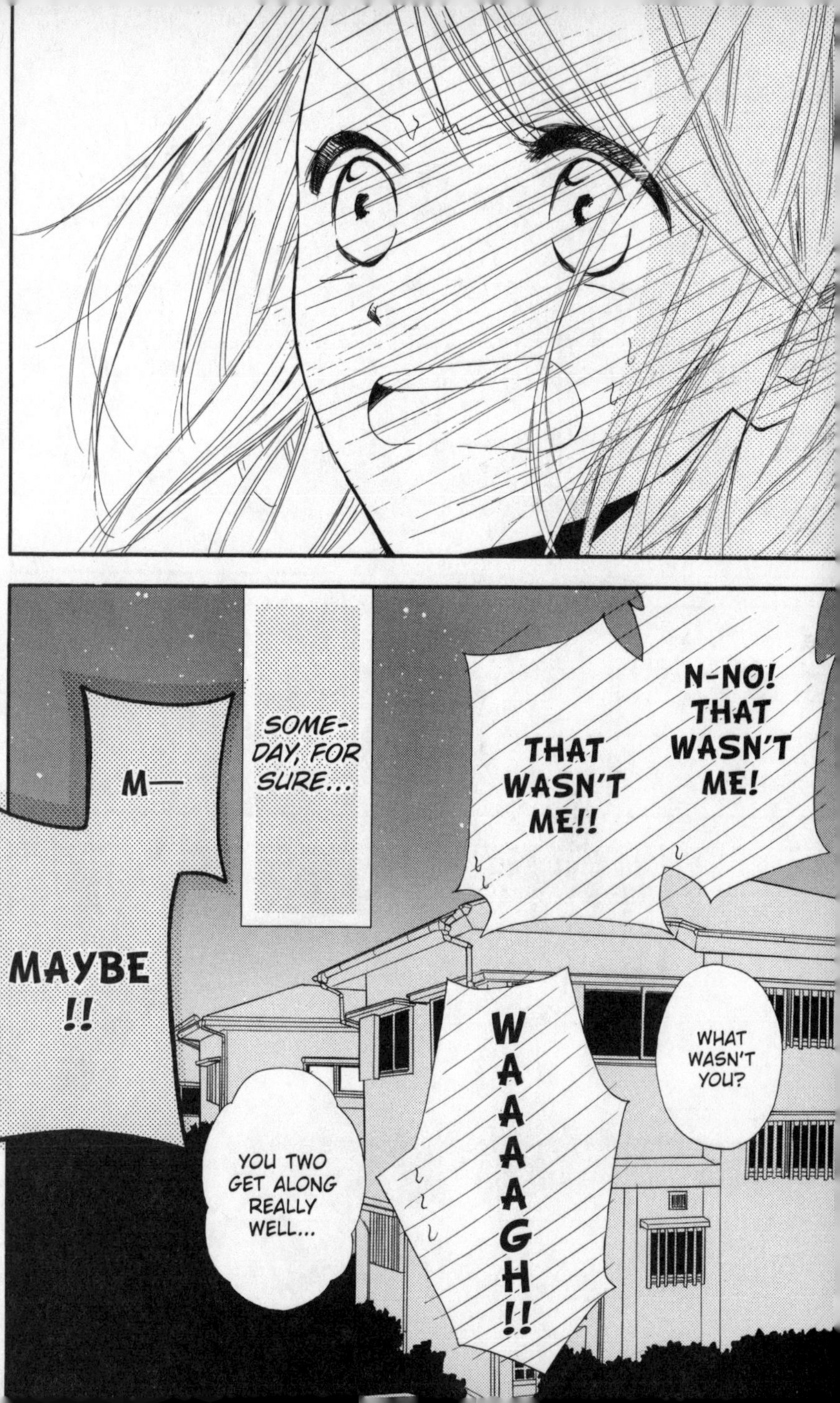
N-NO! THAT WASN'T ME!
THAT WASN'T ME!!
SOME-DAY, FOR SURE...
M—
MAYBE !!
WHAT WASN'T YOU?
WAAAAAGH!!
YOU TWO GET ALONG REALLY WELL...

Room: 3

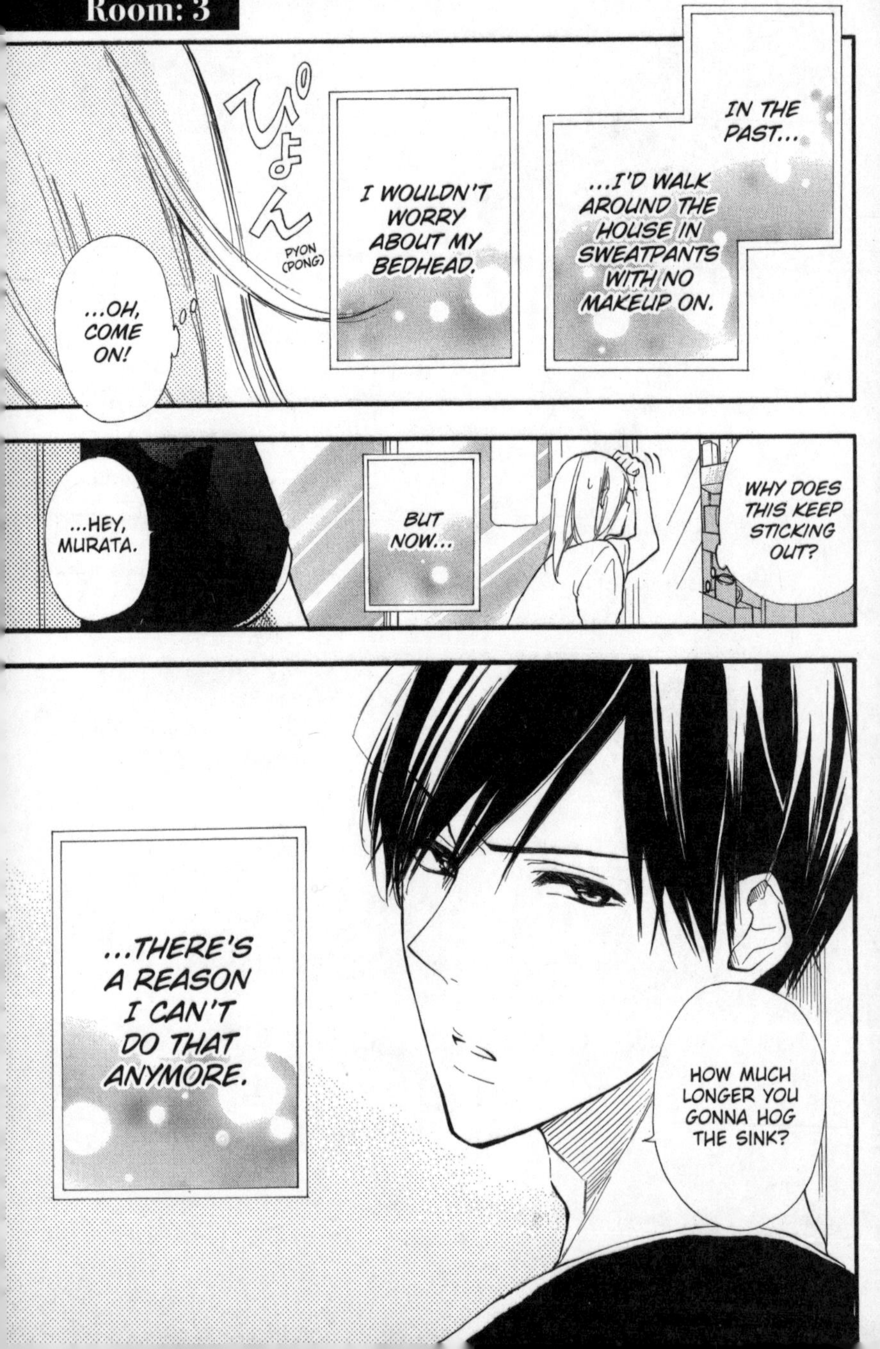
IN THE PAST...
...I'D WALK AROUND THE HOUSE IN SWEATPANTS WITH NO MAKEUP ON.
I WOULDN'T WORRY ABOUT MY BEDHEAD.
ぴょん
PYON (PONG)
...OH, COME ON!
WHY DOES THIS KEEP STICKING OUT?
BUT NOW...
...HEY, MURATA.
...THERE'S A REASON I CAN'T DO THAT ANYMORE.
HOW MUCH LONGER YOU GONNA HOG THE SINK?

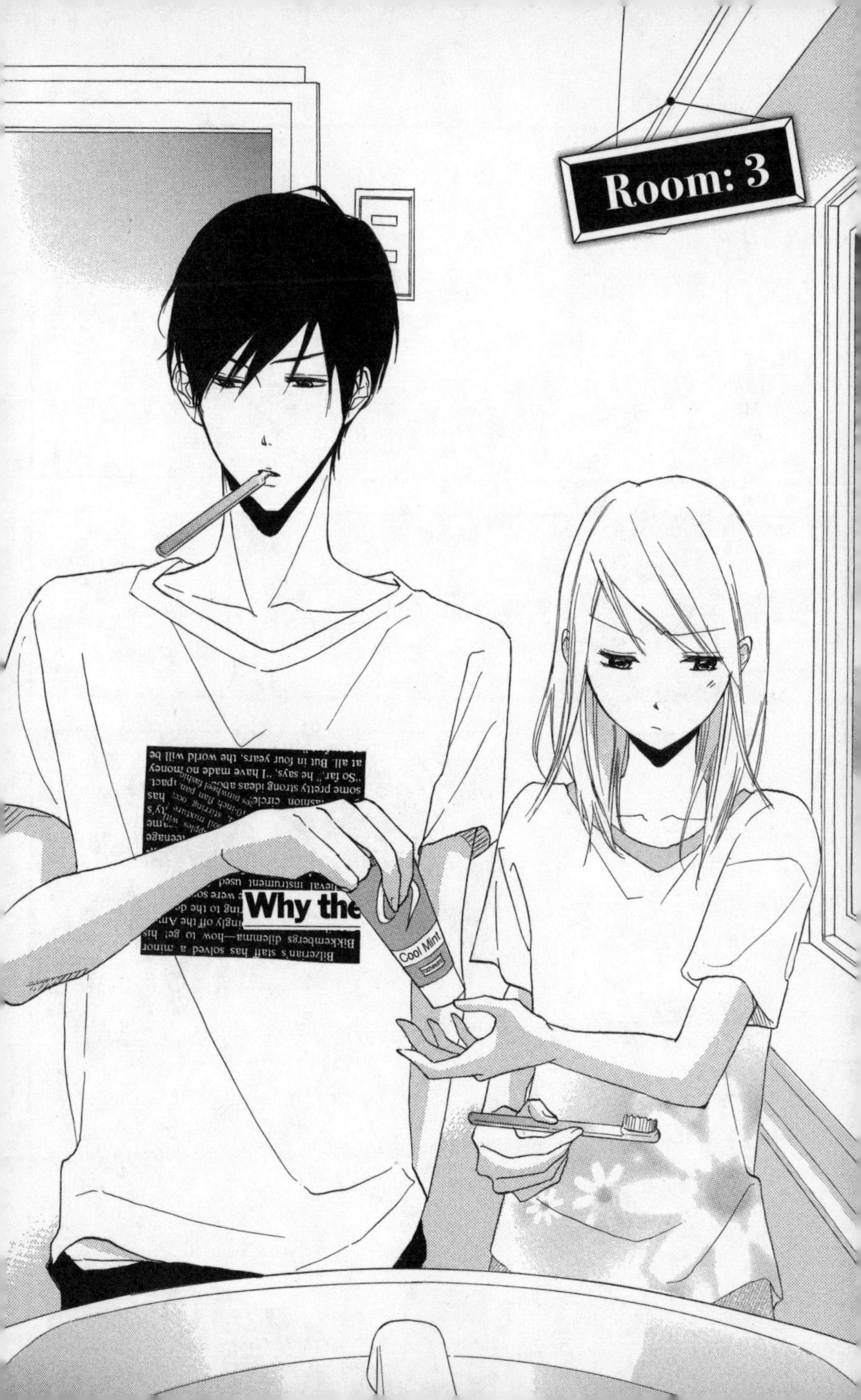
Room: 3
Why the
Cool Mint

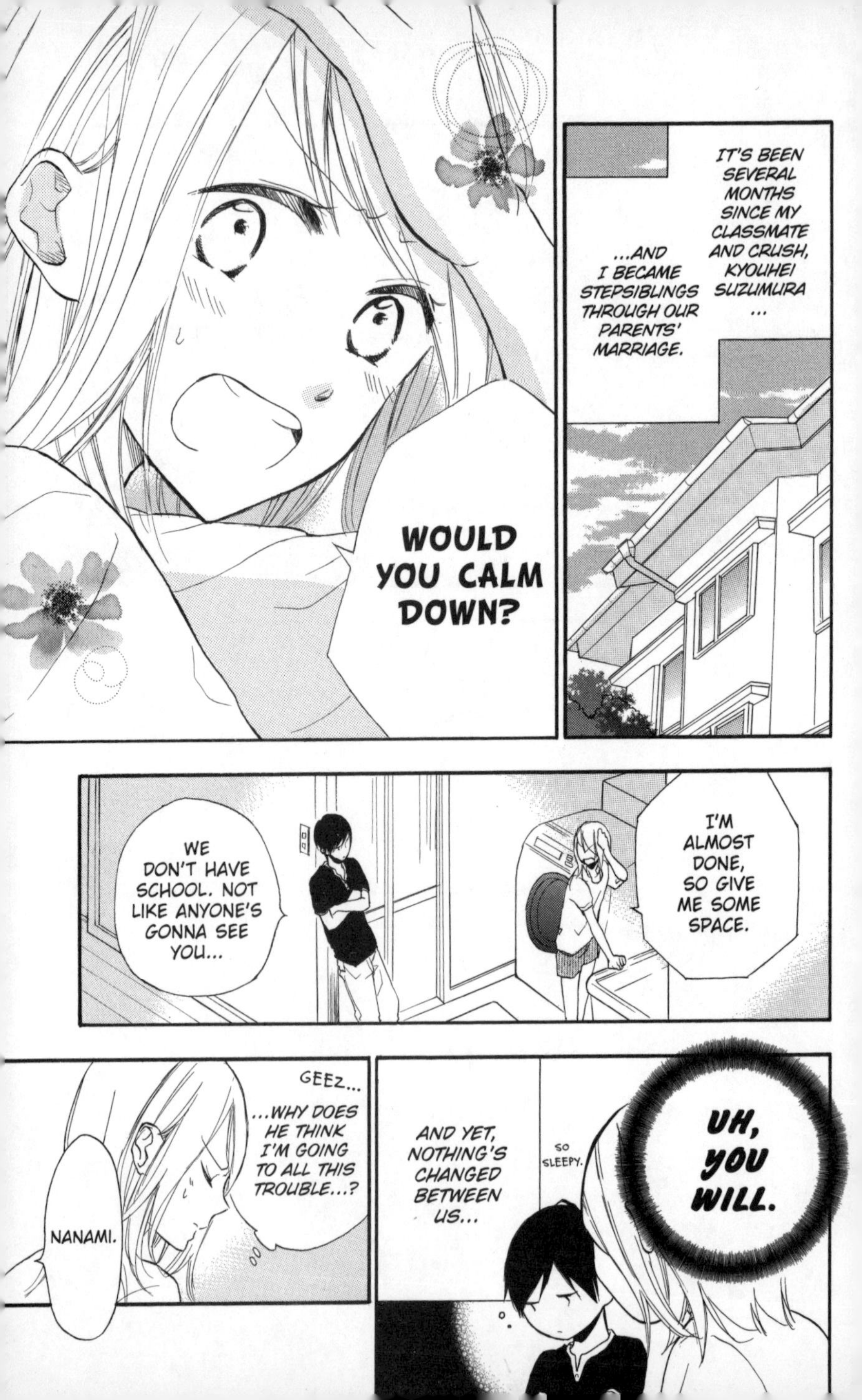
IT'S BEEN SEVERAL MONTHS SINCE MY CLASSMATE AND CRUSH, KYOUHEI SUZUMURA ...
...AND I BECAME STEPSIBLINGS THROUGH OUR PARENTS' MARRIAGE.
WOULD YOU CALM DOWN?
I'M ALMOST DONE, SO GIVE ME SOME SPACE.
WE DON'T HAVE SCHOOL. NOT LIKE ANYONE'S GONNA SEE YOU...
UH, YOU WILL.
SO SLEEPY.
AND YET, NOTHING'S CHANGED BETWEEN US...
GEEZ...
...WHY DOES HE THINK I'M GOING TO ALL THIS TROUBLE...?
NANAMI.

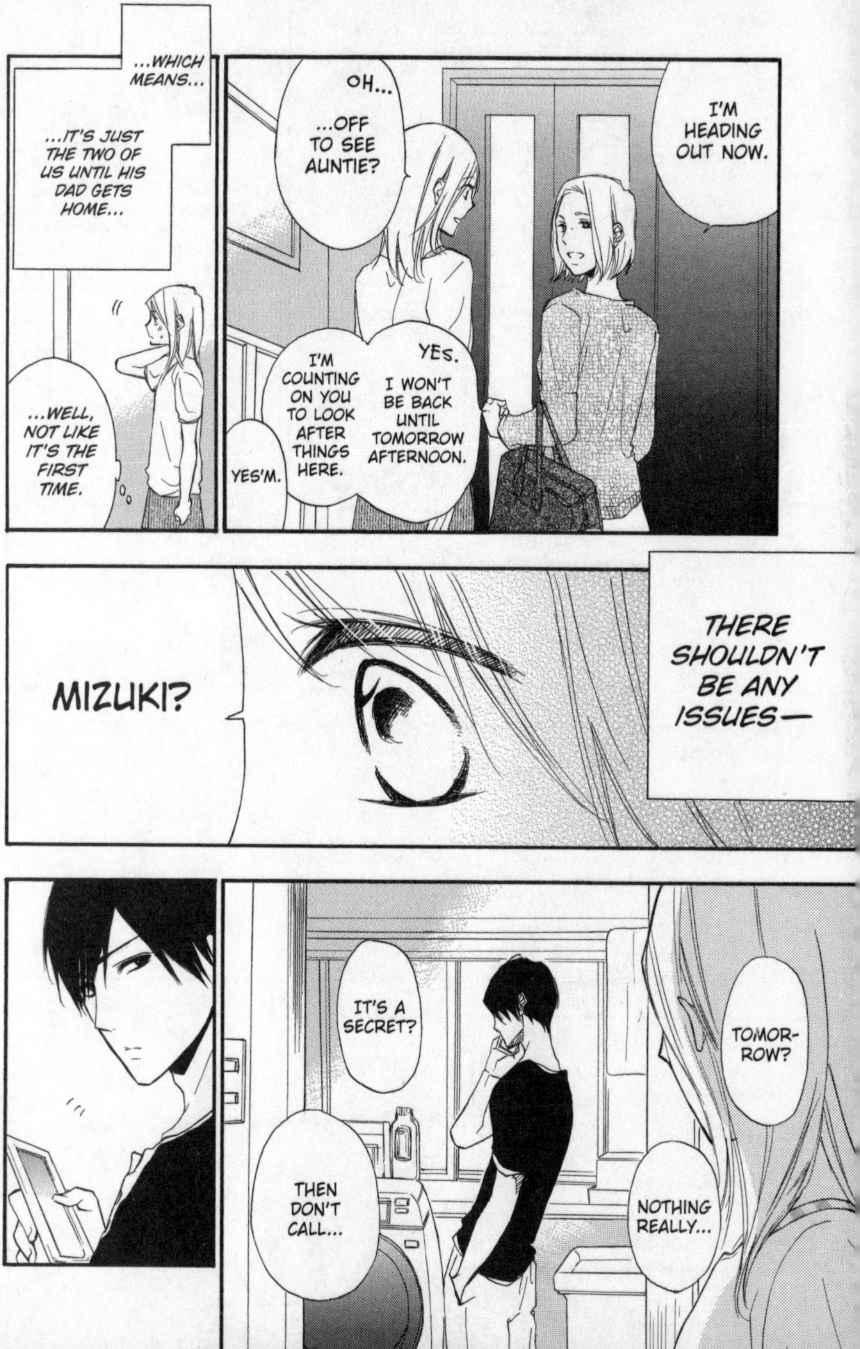
I'M HEADING OUT NOW.
OH... ...OFF TO SEE AUNTIE?
YES. I WON'T BE BACK UNTIL TOMORROW AFTERNOON.
I'M COUNTING ON YOU TO LOOK AFTER THINGS HERE.
YES'M.
...WHICH MEANS...
...IT'S JUST THE TWO OF US UNTIL HIS DAD GETS HOME...
...WELL, NOT LIKE IT'S THE FIRST TIME.
THERE SHOULDN'T BE ANY ISSUES—
MIZUKI?
TOMOR-ROW?
NOTHING REALLY...
IT'S A SECRET?
THEN DON'T CALL...

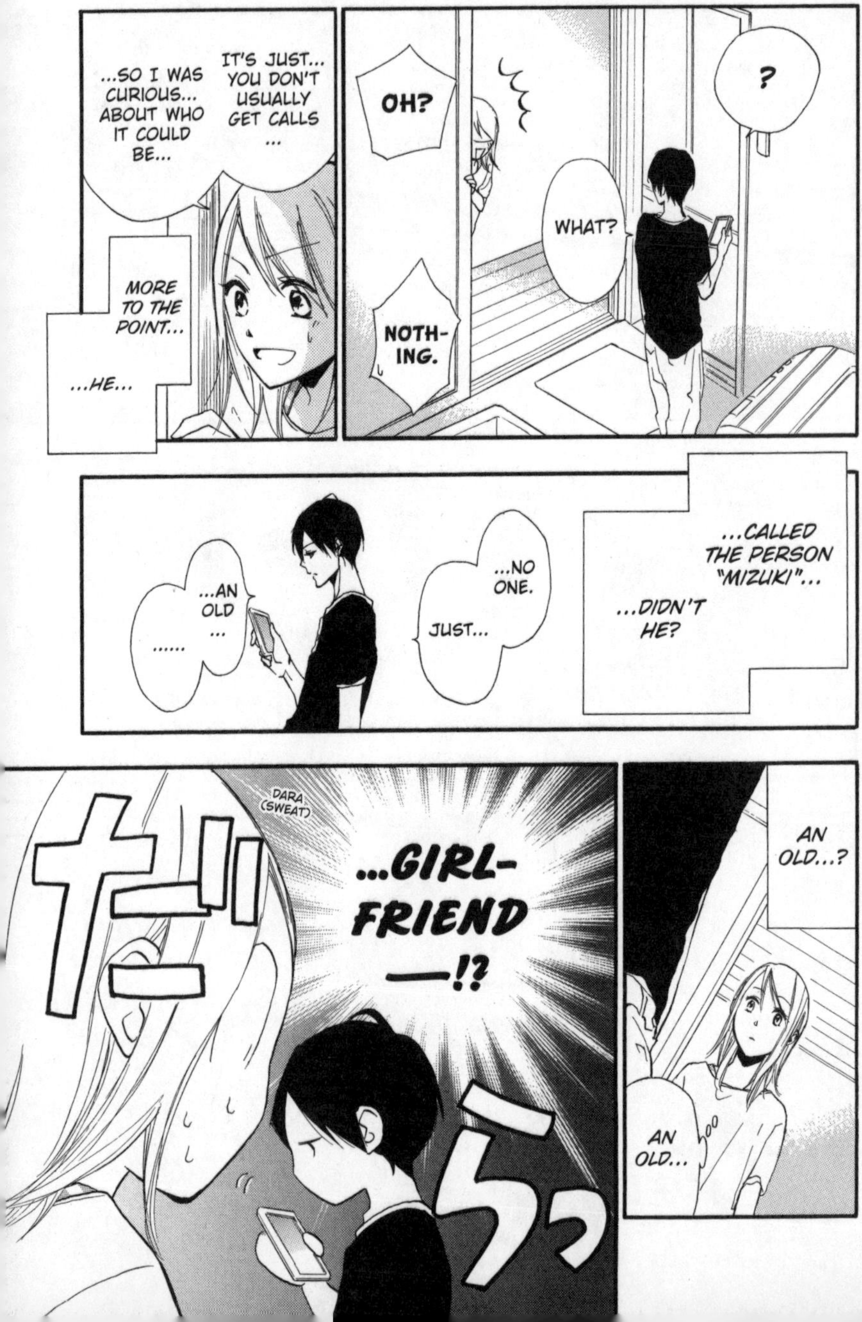
?
OH?
WHAT?
NOTH-ING.
IT'S JUST... YOU DON'T USUALLY GET CALLS ...
...SO I WAS CURIOUS... ABOUT WHO IT COULD BE...
MORE TO THE POINT...
...HE...
...CALLED THE PERSON "MIZUKI"...
...DIDN'T HE?
...NO ONE.
JUST...
...AN OLD ...
......
AN OLD...?
AN OLD...
DARA (SWEAT)
...GIRL-FRIEND—!?

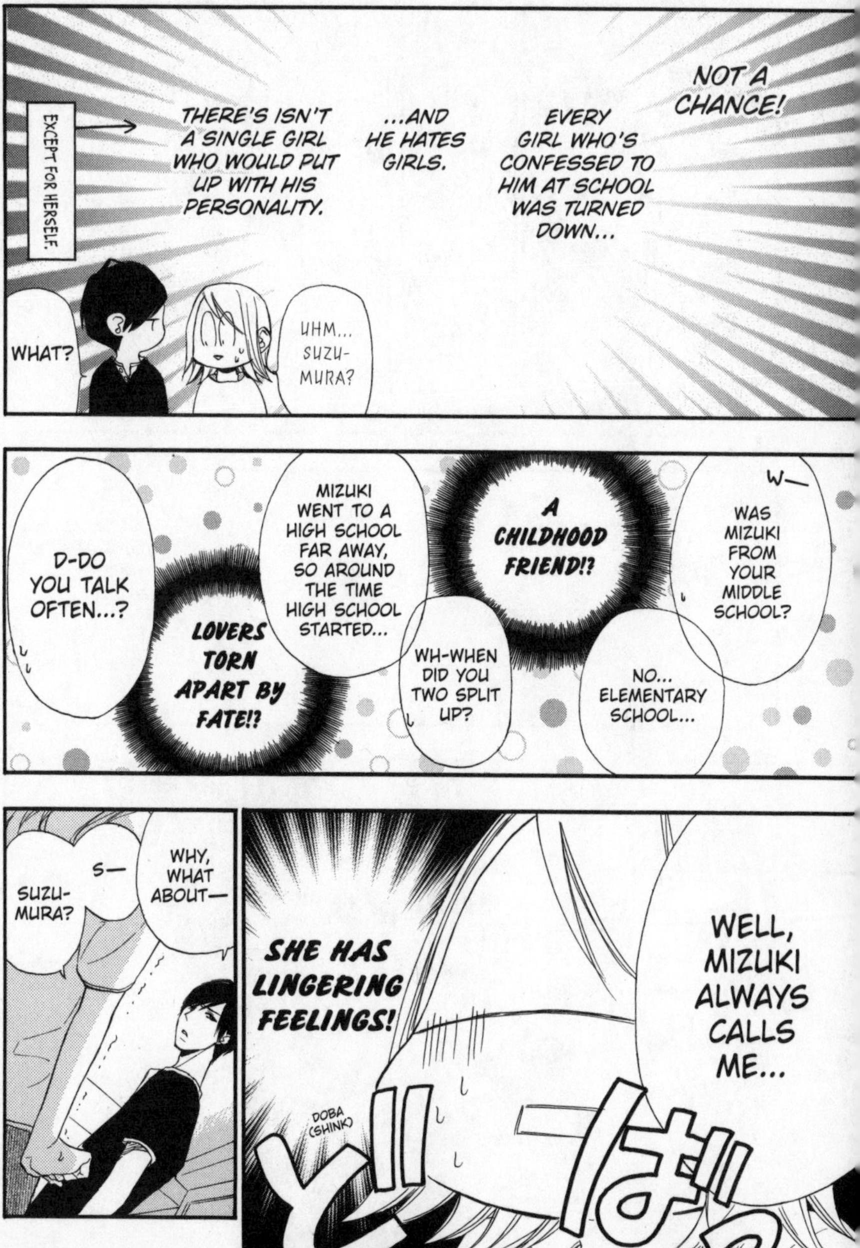
NOT A CHANCE!
EVERY GIRL WHO'S CONFESSED TO HIM AT SCHOOL WAS TURNED DOWN...
...AND HE HATES GIRLS.
THERE'S ISN'T A SINGLE GIRL WHO WOULD PUT UP WITH HIS PERSONALITY.
EXCEPT FOR HERSELF.
UHM... SUZU-MURA?
WHAT?
W—
WAS MIZUKI FROM YOUR MIDDLE SCHOOL?
NO... ELEMENTARY SCHOOL...
A CHILDHOOD FRIEND!?
WH-WHEN DID YOU TWO SPLIT UP?
MIZUKI WENT TO A HIGH SCHOOL FAR AWAY, SO AROUND THE TIME HIGH SCHOOL STARTED...
LOVERS TORN APART BY FATE!?
D-DO YOU TALK OFTEN...?
WELL, MIZUKI ALWAYS CALLS ME...
SHE HAS LINGERING FEELINGS!
DOBA (SHINK)
WHY, WHAT ABOUT—
S—
SUZU-MURA?

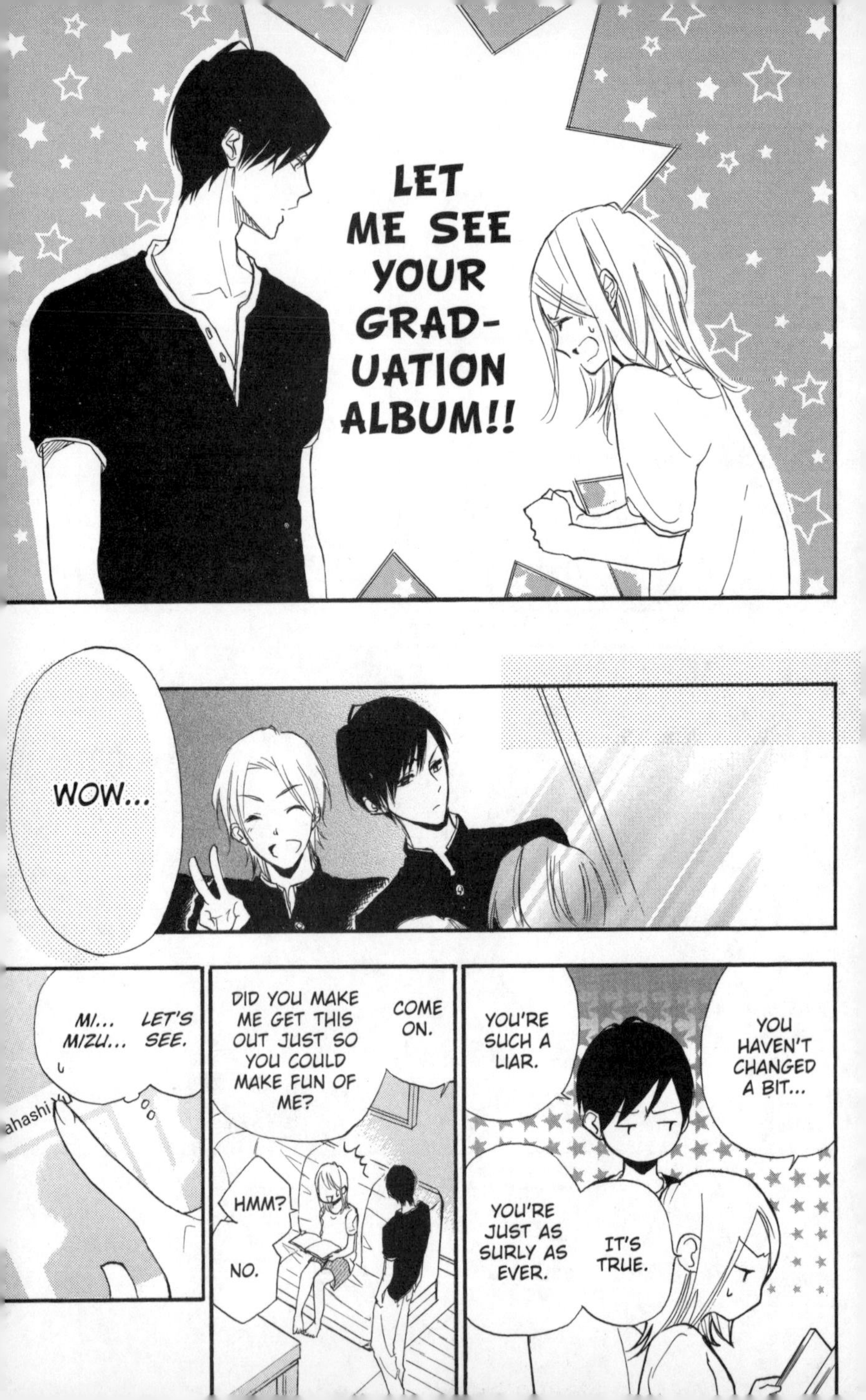
LET ME SEE YOUR GRADUATION ALBUM!!
WOW...
YOU HAVEN'T CHANGED A BIT...
YOU'RE SUCH A LIAR.
IT'S TRUE.
YOU'RE JUST AS SURLY AS EVER.
COME ON.
DID YOU MAKE ME GET THIS OUT JUST SO YOU COULD MAKE FUN OF ME?
HMM?
NO.
LET'S SEE.
MI... MIZU...

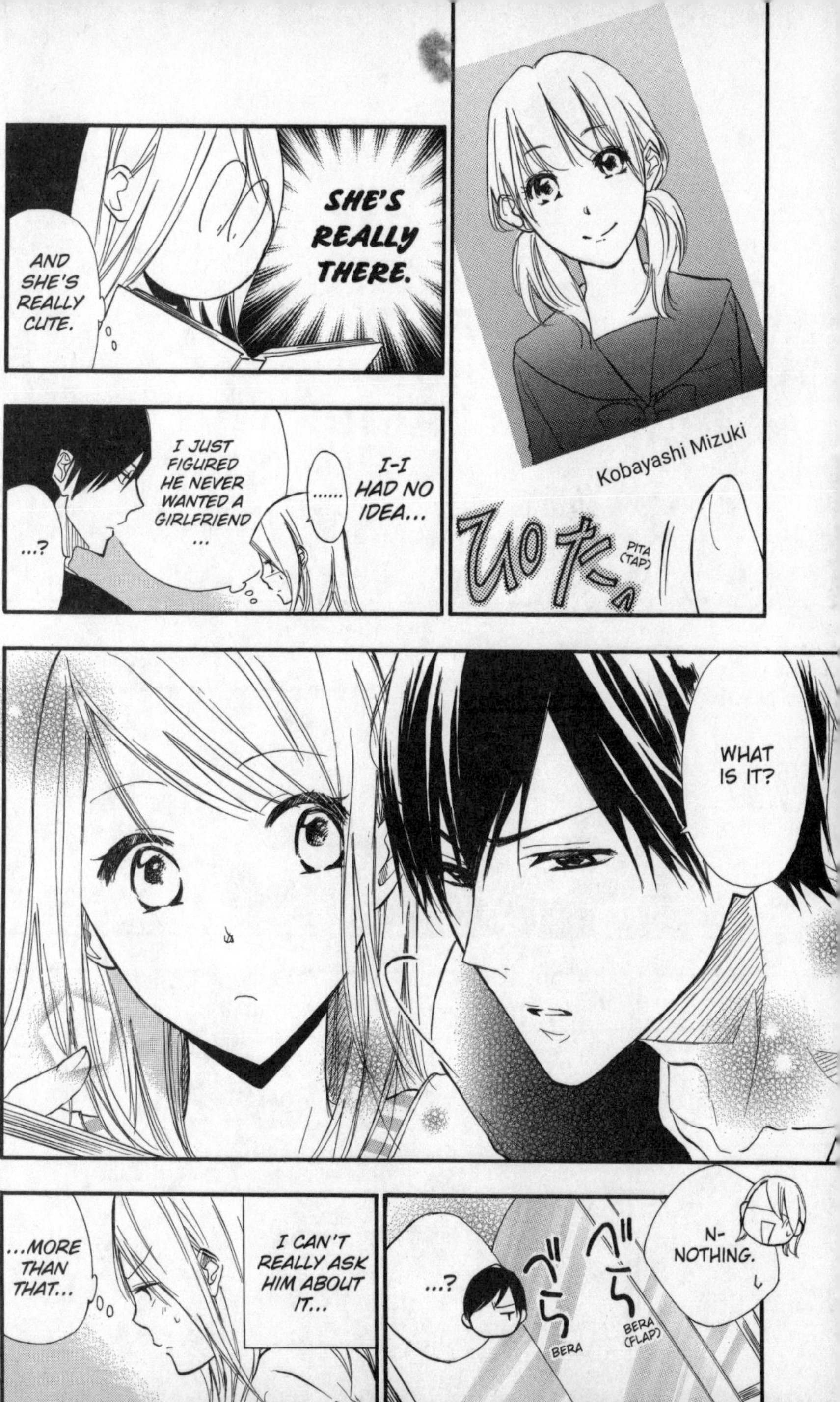
Kobayashi Mizuki
PITA (TAP)
SHE'S REALLY THERE.
AND SHE'S REALLY CUTE.
I-I HAD NO IDEA...
......
I JUST FIGURED HE NEVER WANTED A GIRLFRIEND ...
...?
WHAT IS IT?
N-NOTHING.
BERA (FLAP)
BERA
...?
I CAN'T REALLY ASK HIM ABOUT IT...
...MORE THAN THAT...

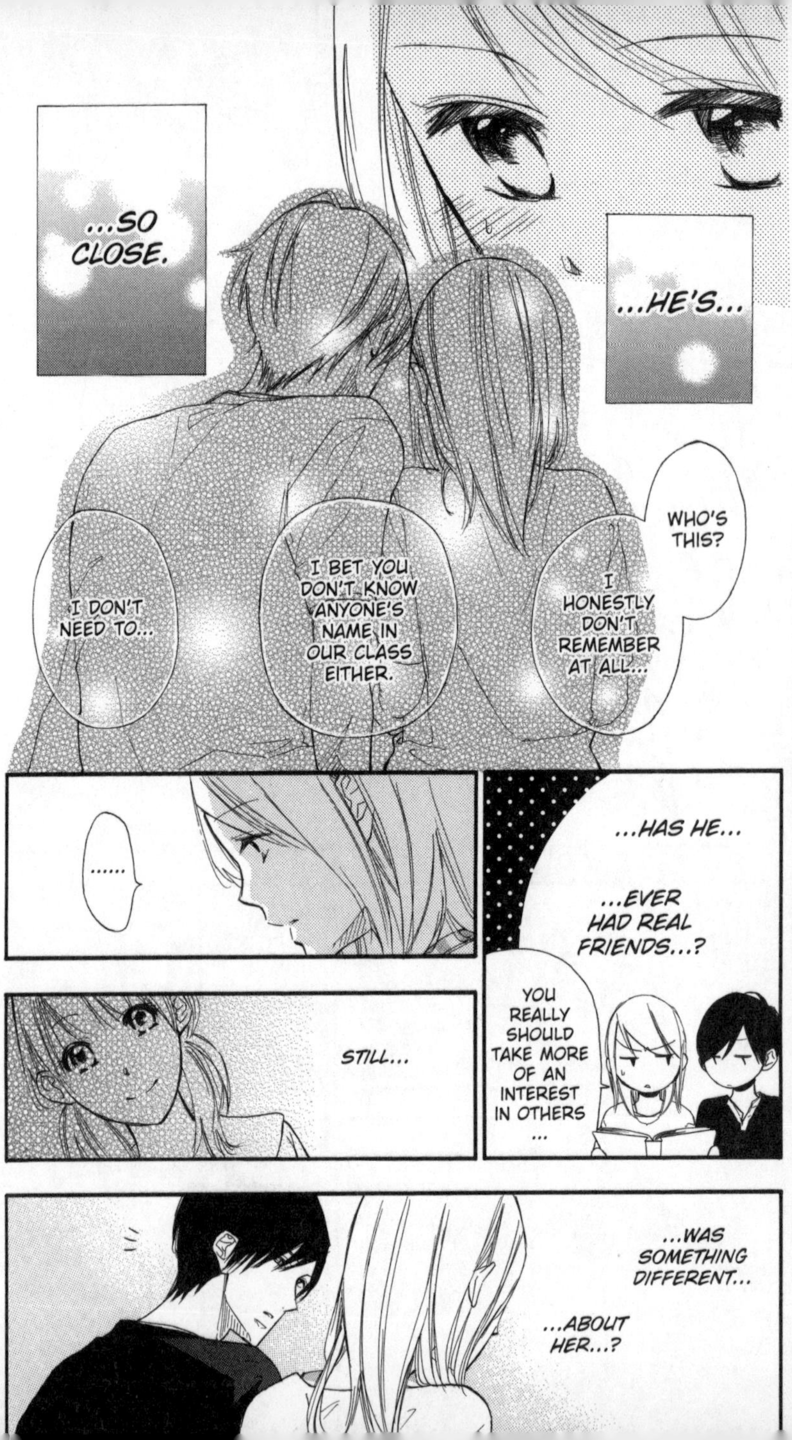
...HE'S...
...SO CLOSE.
WHO'S THIS?
I HONESTLY DON'T REMEMBER AT ALL...
I BET YOU DON'T KNOW ANYONE'S NAME IN OUR CLASS EITHER.
I DON'T NEED TO...
...HAS HE...
...EVER HAD REAL FRIENDS...?
YOU REALLY SHOULD TAKE MORE OF AN INTEREST IN OTHERS ...
......
STILL...
...WAS SOMETHING DIFFERENT...
...ABOUT HER...?

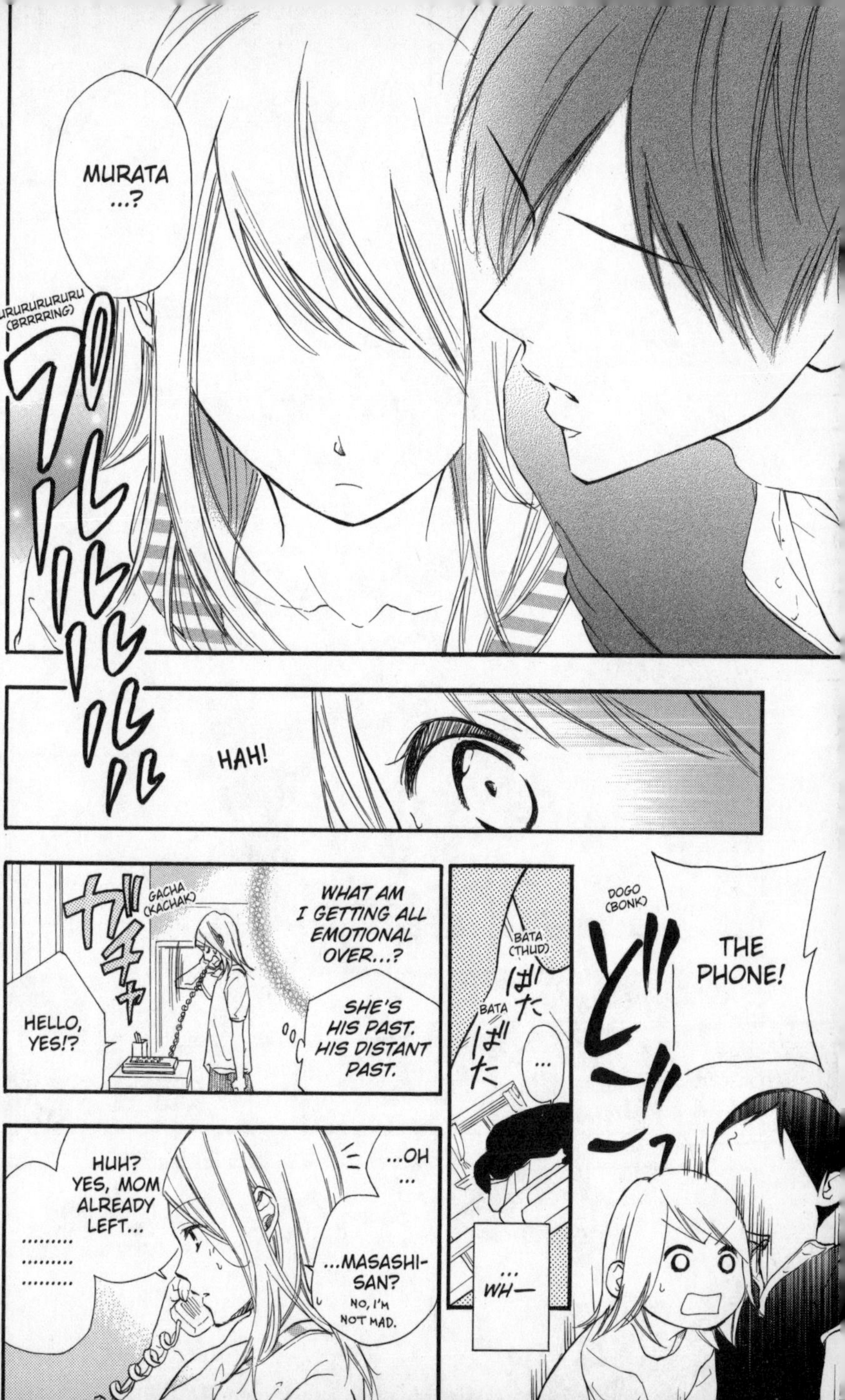
MURATA ...?
PURURURURURU (BRRRRING)
HAH!
DOGO (BONK)
THE PHONE!
BATA (THUD)
BATA
ばた ばた
...
... WH—
WHAT AM I GETTING ALL EMOTIONAL OVER...?
SHE'S HIS PAST. HIS DISTANT PAST.
GACHA (KACHAK)
HELLO, YES!?
...OH ...
...MASASHI-SAN?
NO, I'M NOT MAD.
HUH? YES, MOM ALREADY LEFT...
....

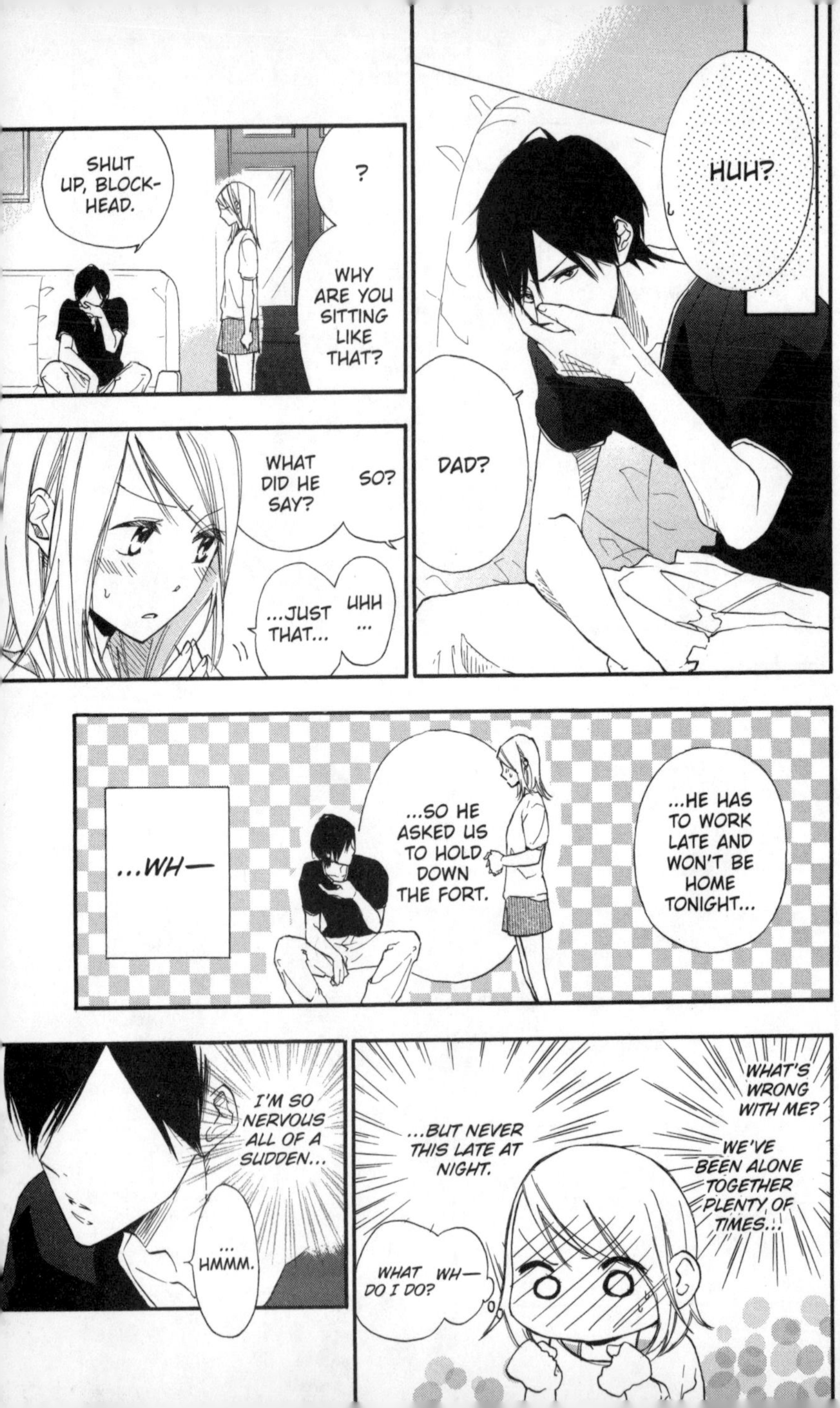
HUH?
DAD?
?
WHY ARE YOU SITTING LIKE THAT?
SHUT UP, BLOCKHEAD.
SO?
WHAT DID HE SAY?
UHH...
...JUST THAT...
...HE HAS TO WORK LATE AND WON'T BE HOME TONIGHT...
...SO HE ASKED US TO HOLD DOWN THE FORT.
...WH—
WHAT'S WRONG WITH ME?
WE'VE BEEN ALONE TOGETHER PLENTY OF TIMES...
...BUT NEVER THIS LATE AT NIGHT.
WH—
WHAT DO I DO?
I'M SO NERVOUS ALL OF A SUDDEN...
... HMMM.

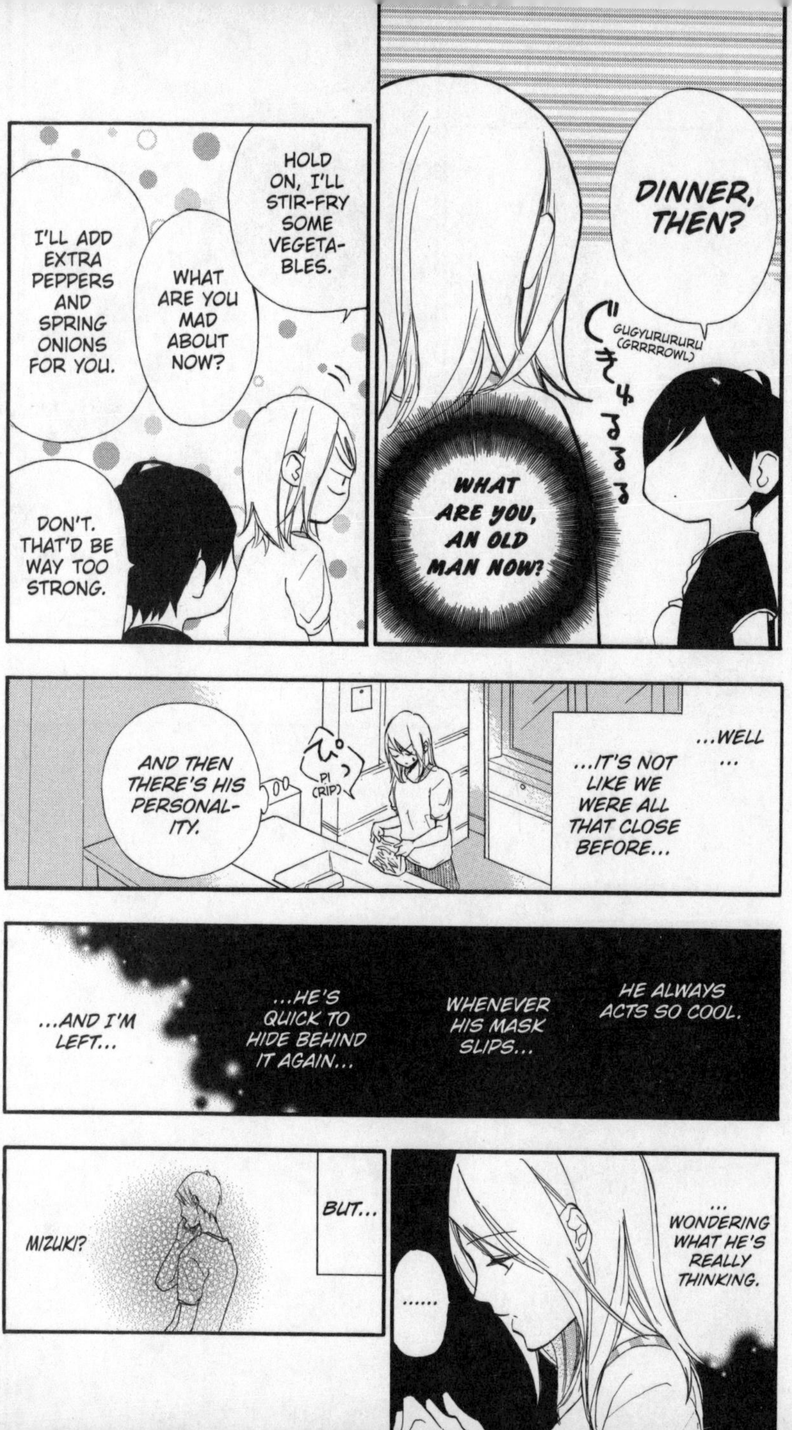
DINNER, THEN?
GUGYURURURU (GRRRROWL)
WHAT ARE YOU, AN OLD MAN NOW?
HOLD ON, I'LL STIR-FRY SOME VEGETA-BLES.
WHAT ARE YOU MAD ABOUT NOW?
I'LL ADD EXTRA PEPPERS AND SPRING ONIONS FOR YOU.
DON'T. THAT'D BE WAY TOO STRONG.
...WELL ...
...IT'S NOT LIKE WE WERE ALL THAT CLOSE BEFORE...
ぴっ
PI (RIP)
AND THEN THERE'S HIS PERSONAL-ITY.
HE ALWAYS ACTS SO COOL.
WHENEVER HIS MASK SLIPS...
...HE'S QUICK TO HIDE BEHIND IT AGAIN...
...AND I'M LEFT...
... WONDERING WHAT HE'S REALLY THINKING.
......
BUT...
MIZUKI?

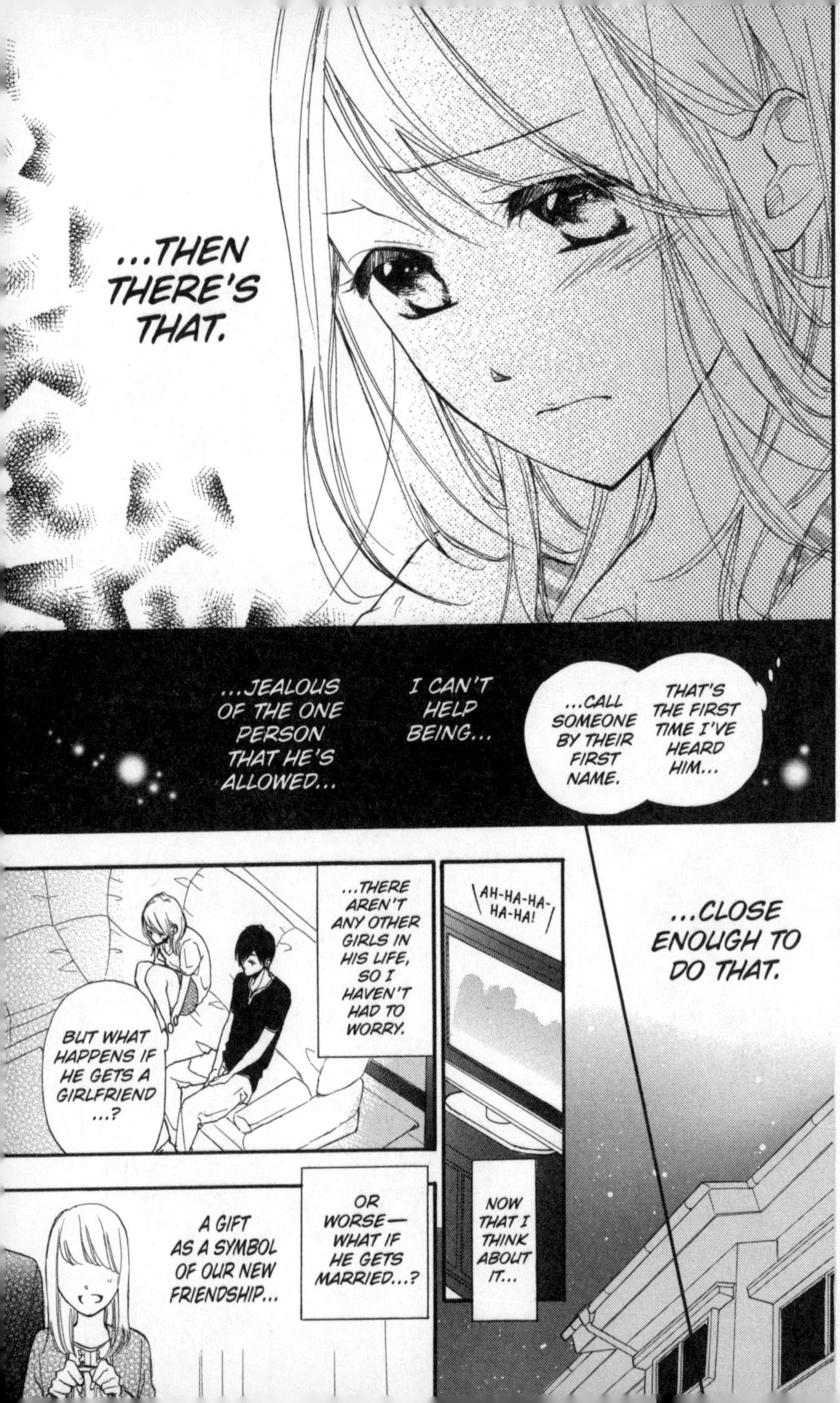
...THEN THERE'S THAT.
THAT'S THE FIRST TIME I'VE HEARD HIM...
...CALL SOMEONE BY THEIR FIRST NAME.
I CAN'T HELP BEING...
...JEALOUS OF THE ONE PERSON THAT HE'S ALLOWED...
...CLOSE ENOUGH TO DO THAT.
NOW THAT I THINK ABOUT IT...
AH-HA-HA-HA-HA!
...THERE AREN'T ANY OTHER GIRLS IN HIS LIFE, SO I HAVEN'T HAD TO WORRY.
BUT WHAT HAPPENS IF HE GETS A GIRLFRIEND ...?
OR WORSE—WHAT IF HE GETS MARRIED...?
A GIFT AS A SYMBOL OF OUR NEW FRIENDSHIP...

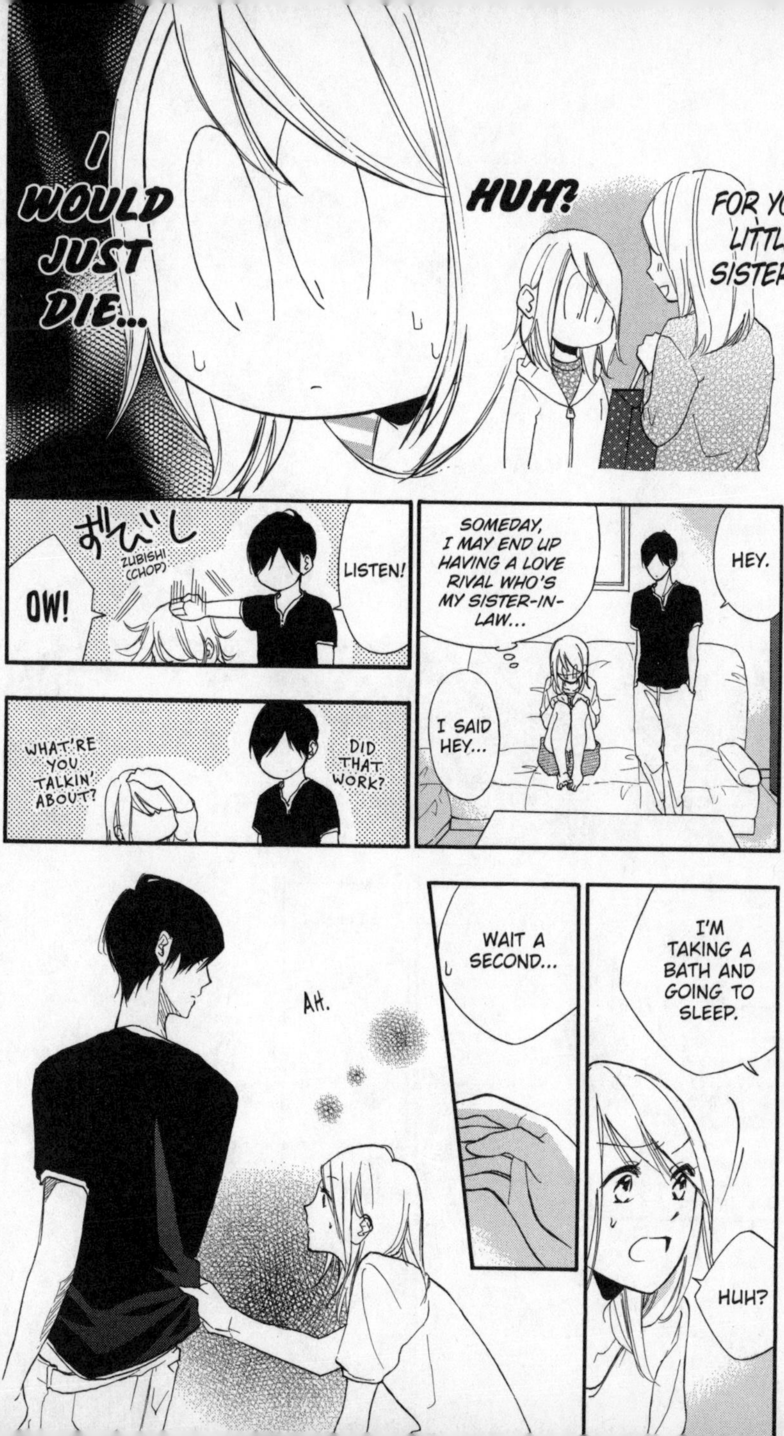
FOR YOU, LITTLE SISTER...
HUH?
I WOULD JUST DIE...
HEY.
SOMEDAY, I MAY END UP HAVING A LOVE RIVAL WHO'S MY SISTER-IN-LAW...
I SAID HEY...
LISTEN!
ずびし
ZUBISHI (CHOP)
OW!
DID THAT WORK?
WHAT'RE YOU TALKIN' ABOUT?
I'M TAKING A BATH AND GOING TO SLEEP.
HUH?
WAIT A SECOND...
AH.

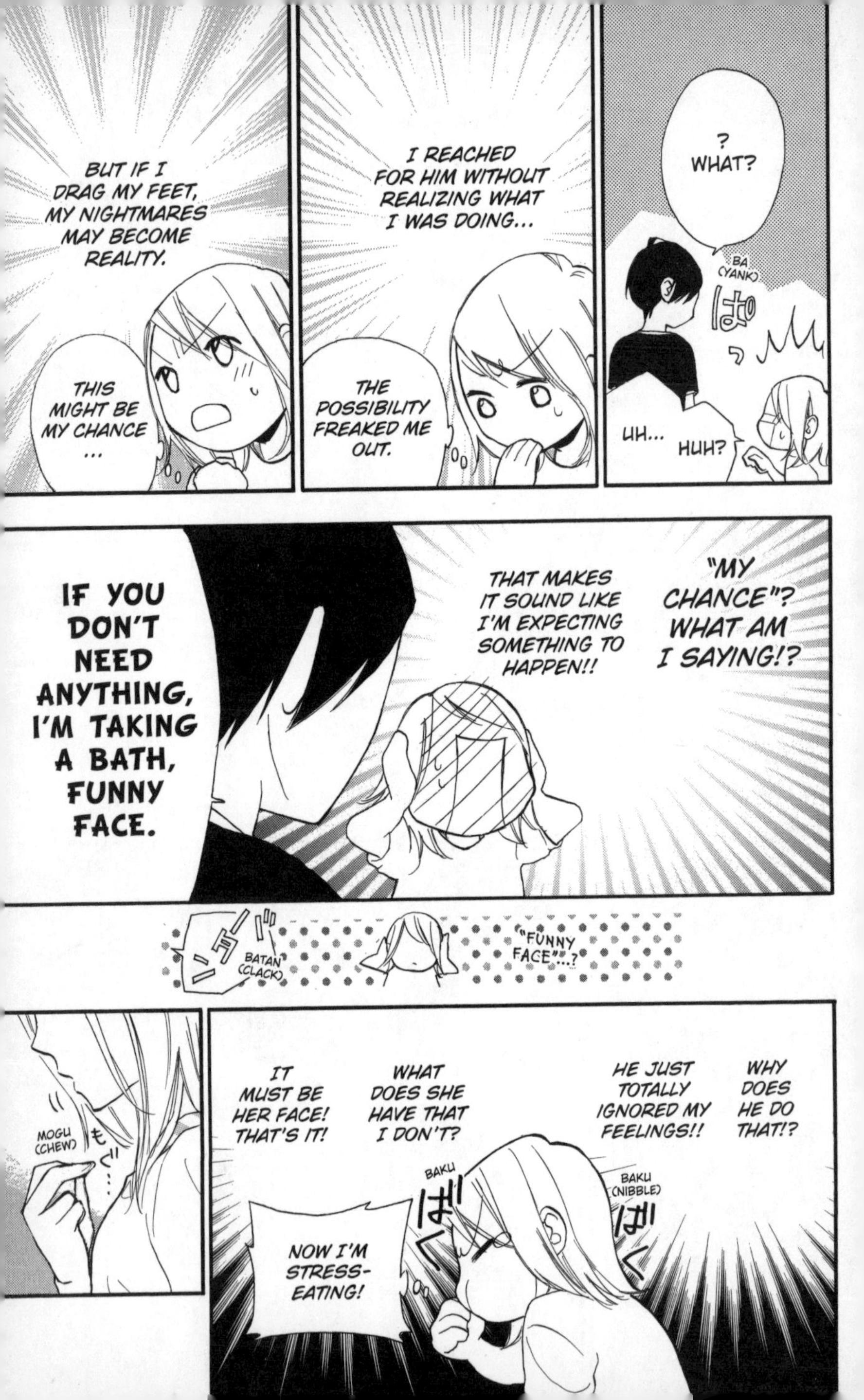
? WHAT?
BA (YANK)
HUH?
UH...
I REACHED FOR HIM WITHOUT REALIZING WHAT I WAS DOING...
THE POSSIBILITY FREAKED ME OUT.
BUT IF I DRAG MY FEET, MY NIGHTMARES MAY BECOME REALITY.
THIS MIGHT BE MY CHANCE...
"MY CHANCE"? WHAT AM I SAYING!?
THAT MAKES IT SOUND LIKE I'M EXPECTING SOMETHING TO HAPPEN!!
IF YOU DON'T NEED ANYTHING, I'M TAKING A BATH, FUNNY FACE.
"FUNNY FACE"...?
BATAN (CLACK)
WHY DOES HE DO THAT!?
HE JUST TOTALLY IGNORED MY FEELINGS!!
WHAT DOES SHE HAVE THAT I DON'T?
IT MUST BE HER FACE! THAT'S IT!
BAKU (NIBBLE)
BAKU
NOW I'M STRESS-EATING!
MOGU (CHEW)

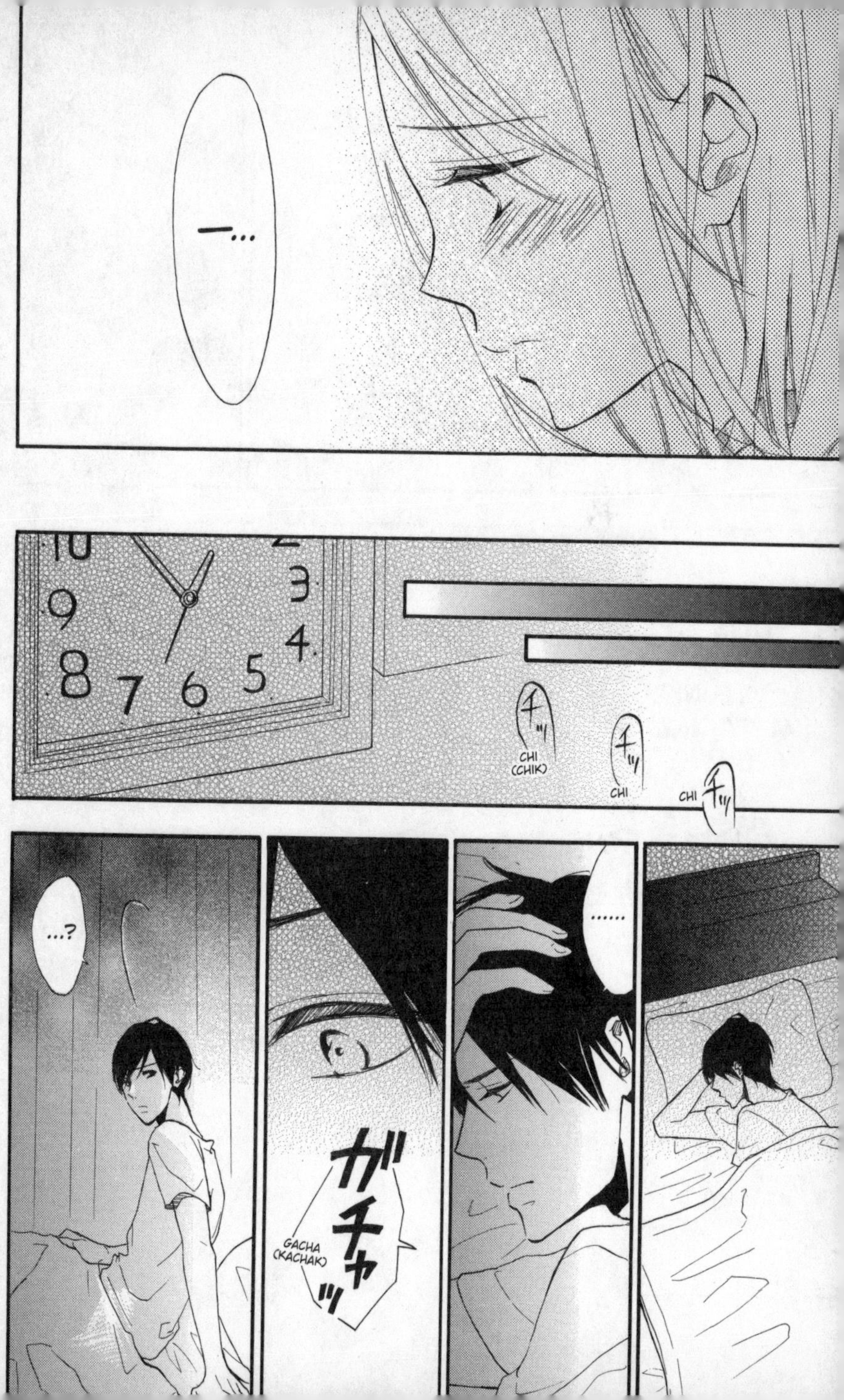
—...
チッ
CHI
チッ
CHI
チッ
CHI
(CHIK)
......
ガチャッ
GACHA
(KACHAK)
...?

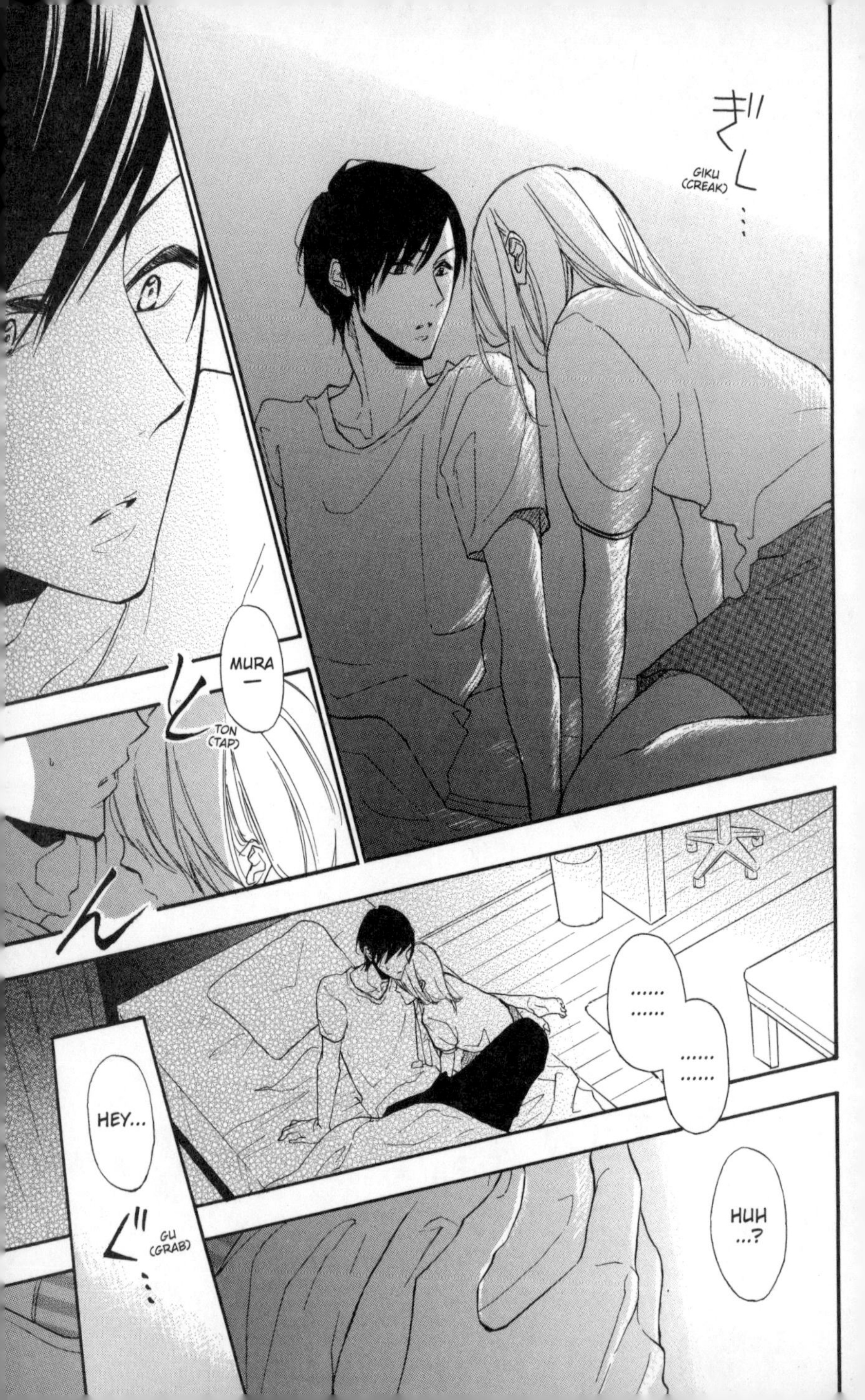
GIKU (CREAK)
MURA—
TON (TAP)
......
......
......
......
HEY...
HUH ...?
GU (GRAB)

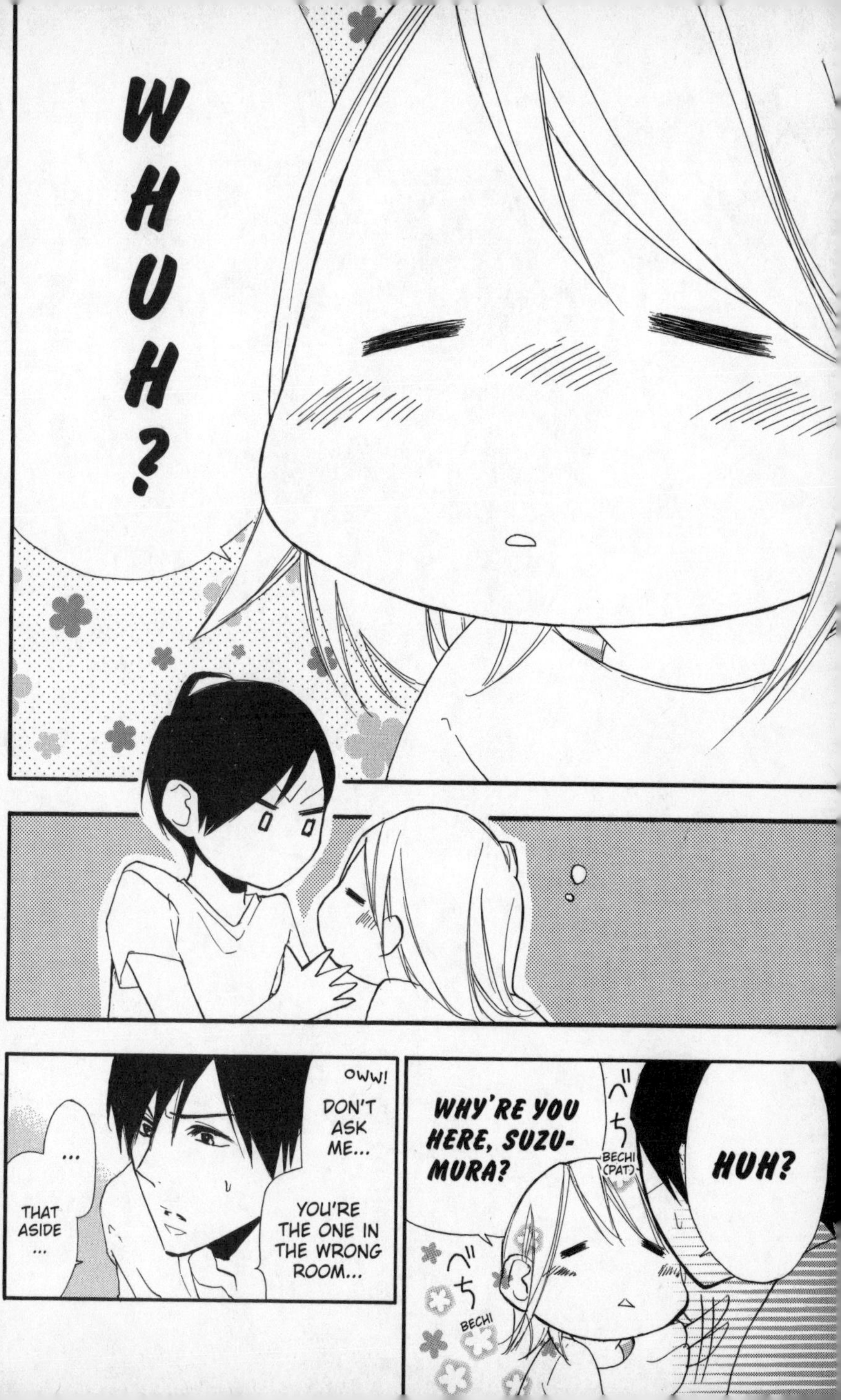
WHHUH?
HUH?
べち
BECHI (PAT)
WHY'RE YOU HERE, SUZU-MURA?
べち
BECHI
OWW!
DON'T ASK ME...
YOU'RE THE ONE IN THE WRONG ROOM...
...
THAT ASIDE...

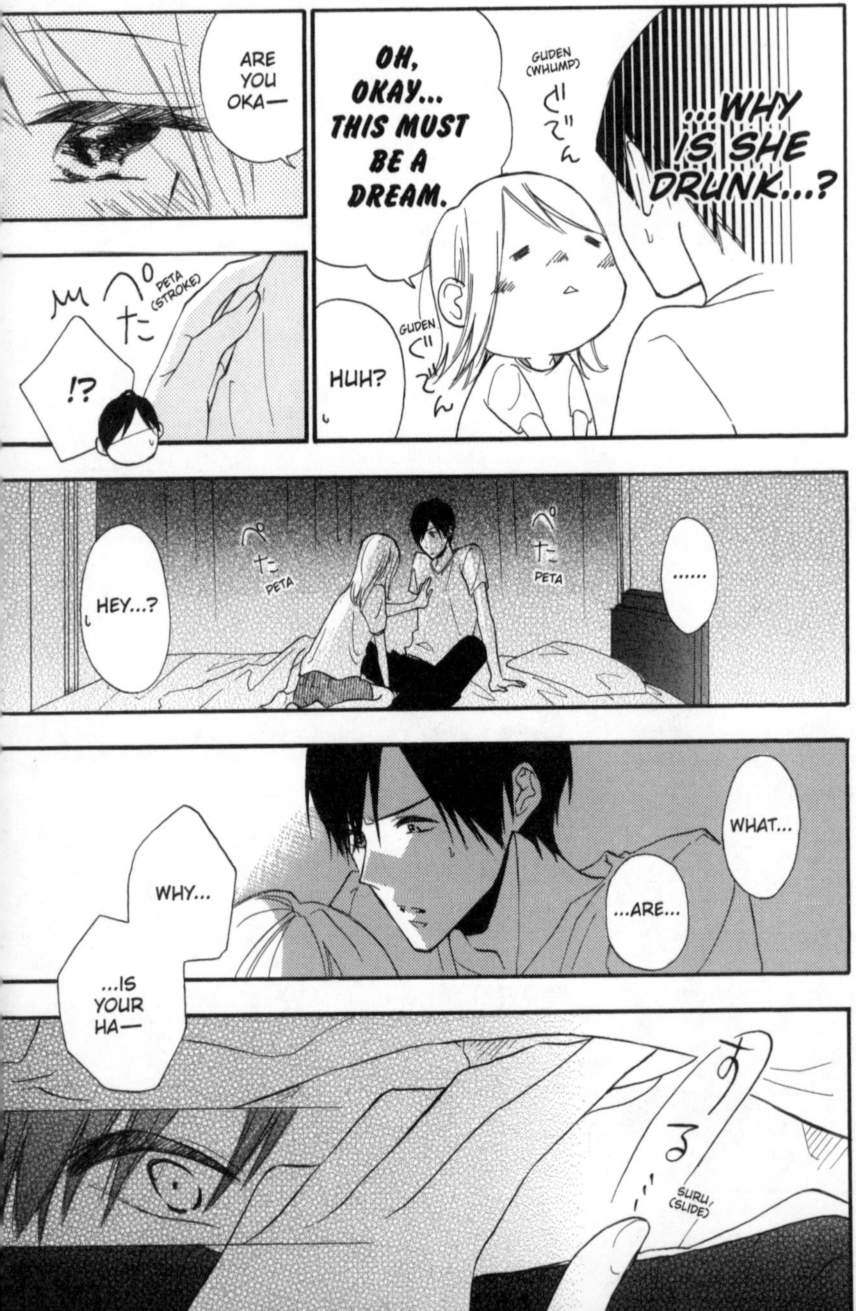
...WHY IS SHE DRUNK...?
GUDEN (WHUMP)
ぐでん
OH, OKAY... THIS MUST BE A DREAM.
GUDEN
ぐでん
HUH?
ARE YOU OKA—
PETA (STROKE)
ぺた
!?
......
PETA
ぺた
ぺた
PETA
HEY...?
WHAT...
...ARE...
WHY...
...IS YOUR HA—
する
SURU (SLIDE)

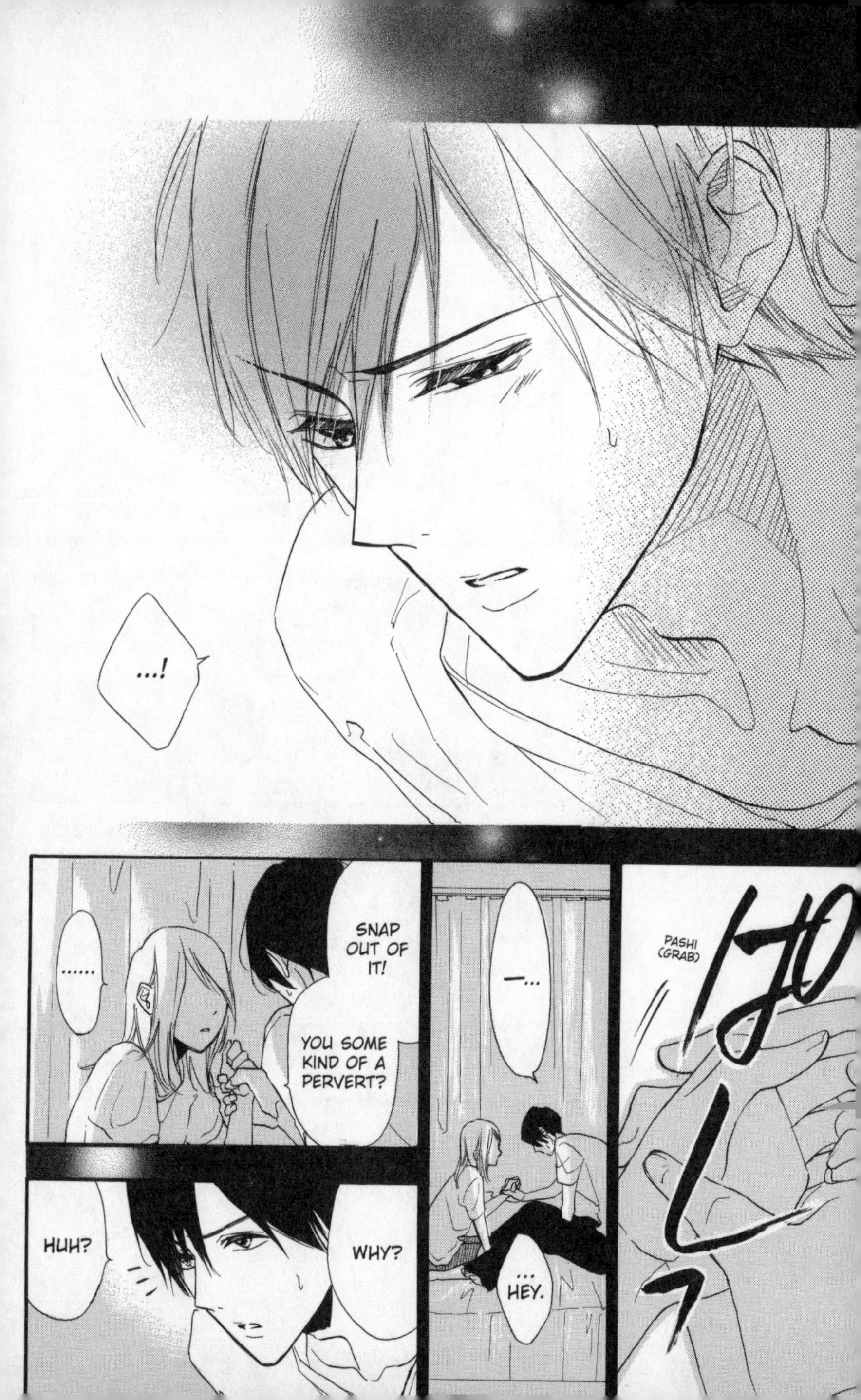
...!
PASHI (GRAB)
—...
... HEY.
SNAP OUT OF IT!
YOU SOME KIND OF A PERVERT?
......
WHY?
HUH?

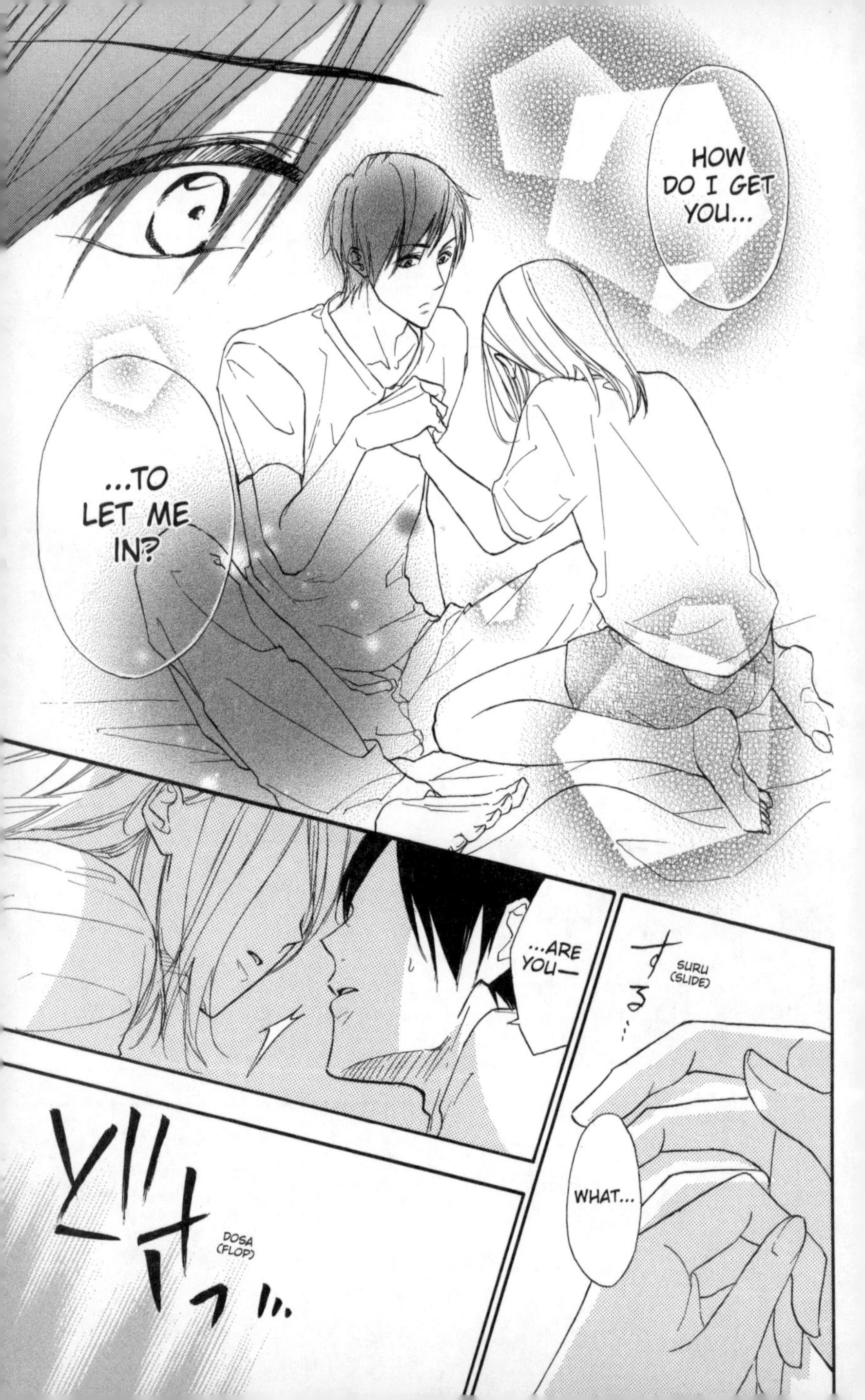
HOW DO I GET YOU...
...TO LET ME IN?
する…
SURU (SLIDE)
WHAT...
...ARE YOU—
ドサッ
DOSA (FLOP)

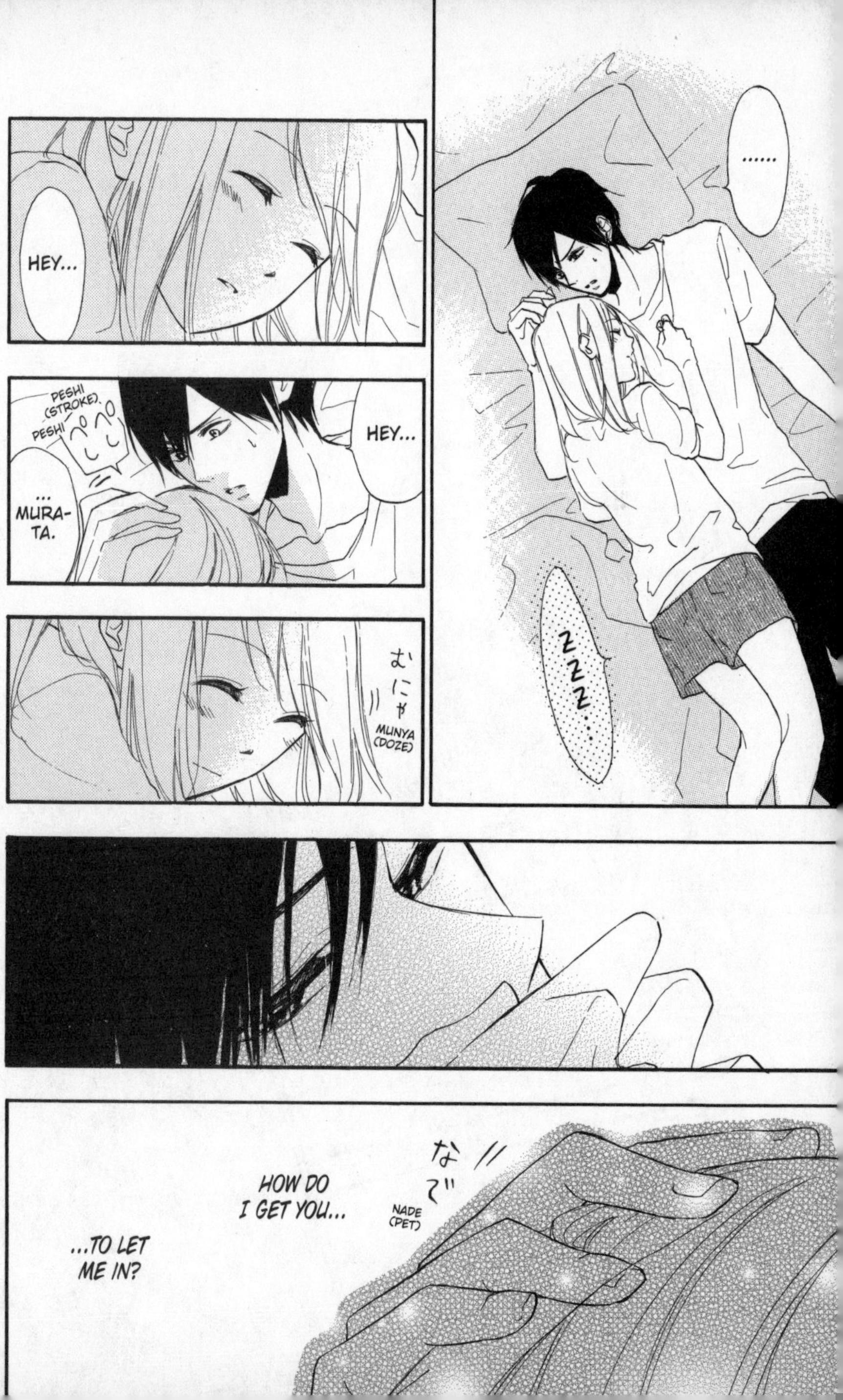
......
ZZZ...
HEY...
HEY...
PESHI (STROKE) PESHI
... MURA-TA.
むにゃ
MUNYA (DOZE)
なで
NADE (PET)
HOW DO I GET YOU...
...TO LET ME IN?

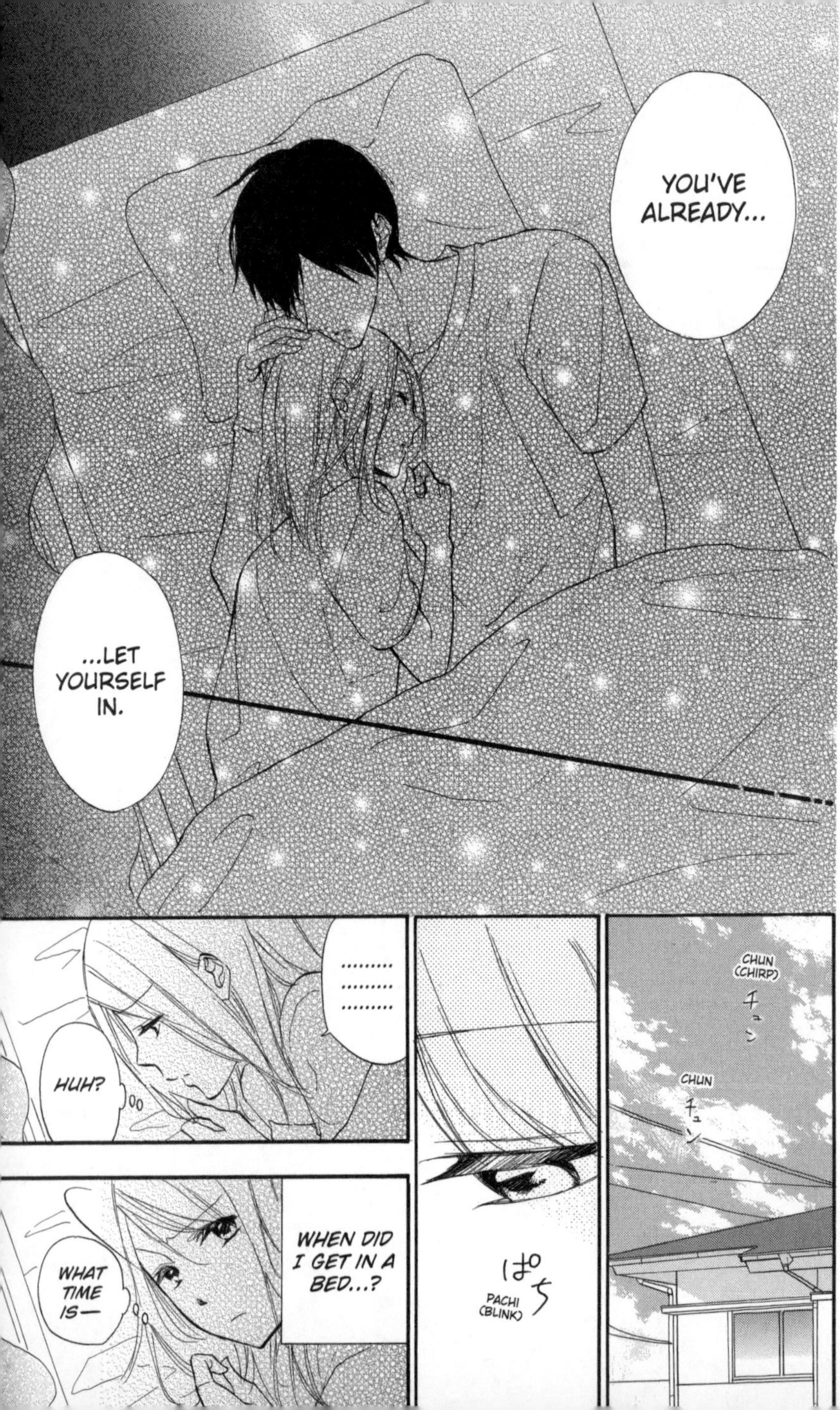
YOU'VE ALREADY...
...LET YOURSELF IN.
CHUN (CHIRP)
チュン
CHUN
チュン
ぱち
PACHI (BLINK)
....
....
....
HUH?
WHEN DID I GET IN A BED...?
WHAT TIME IS—

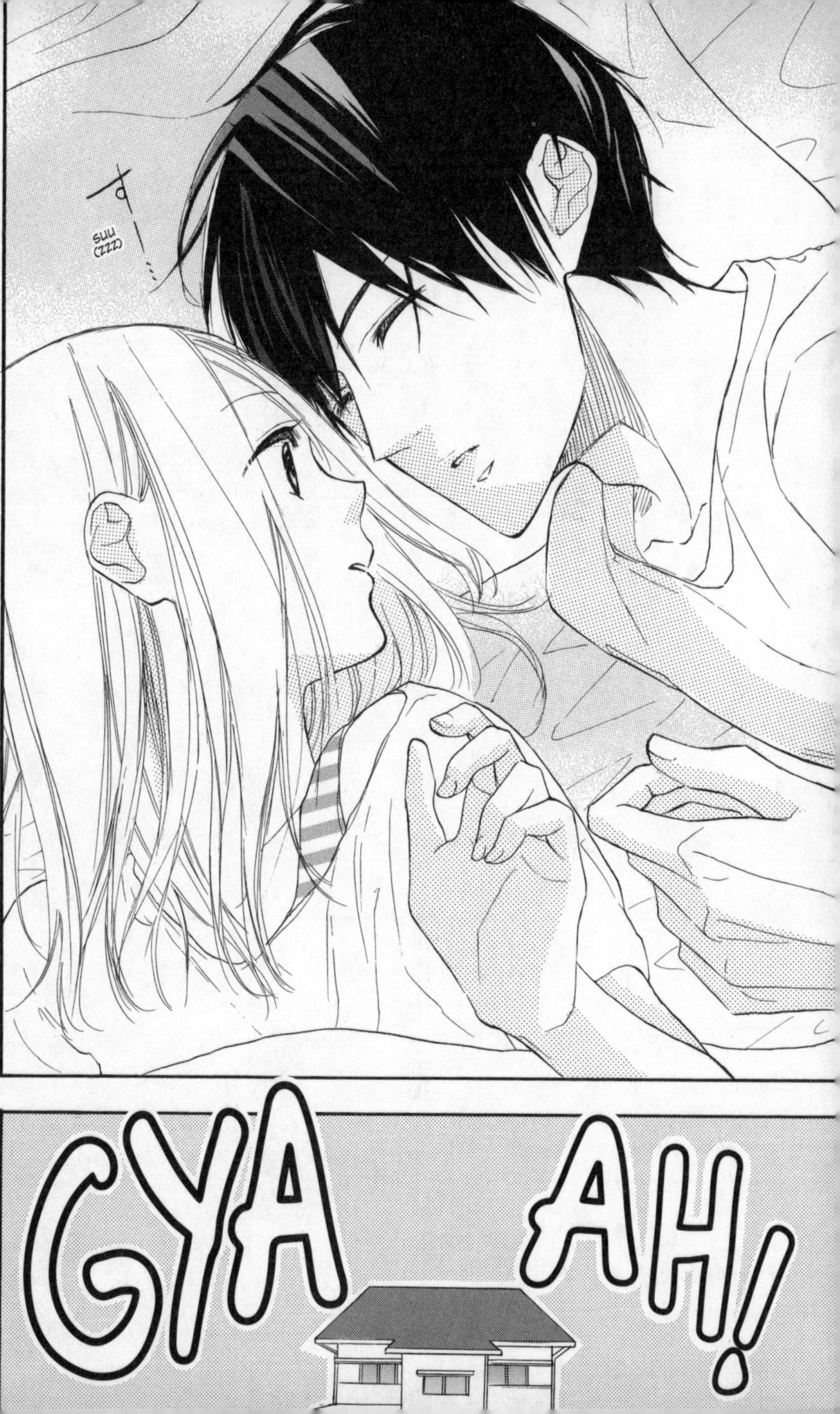

SUU (ZZZZ)
GYA AH!

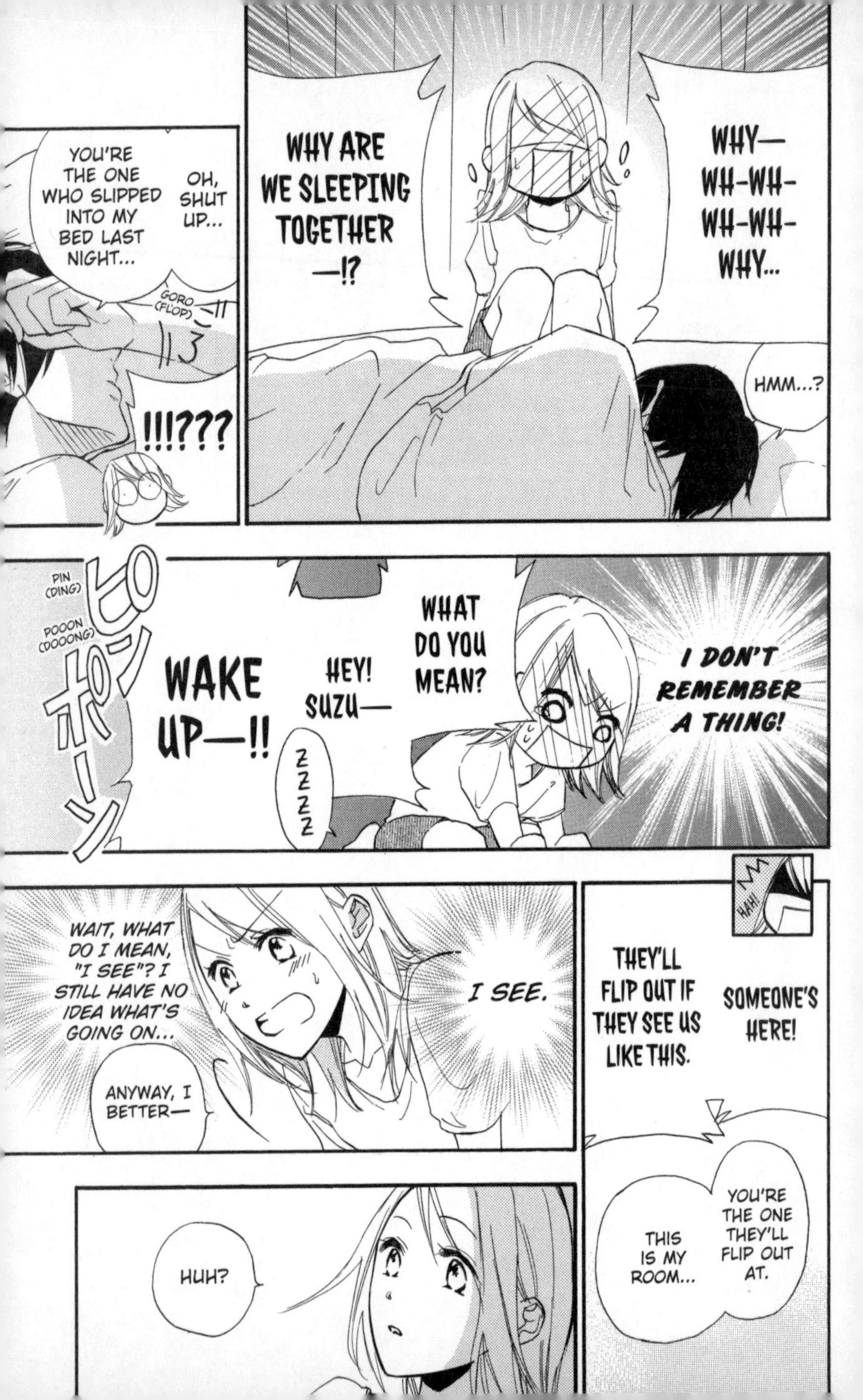
WHY— WH-WH- WH-WH- WHY...
WHY ARE WE SLEEPING TOGETHER—!?
HMM...?
OH, SHUT UP...
YOU'RE THE ONE WHO SLIPPED INTO MY BED LAST NIGHT...
GORO (FLOP)
!!!???
I DON'T REMEMBER A THING!
WHAT DO YOU MEAN?
HEY! SUZU—
ZZZZ
WAKE UP—!!
PIN (DING)
POOON (DOOONG)
HAH!
SOMEONE'S HERE!
THEY'LL FLIP OUT IF THEY SEE US LIKE THIS.
YOU'RE THE ONE THEY'LL FLIP OUT AT.
THIS IS MY ROOM...
I SEE.
WAIT, WHAT DO I MEAN, "I SEE"? I STILL HAVE NO IDEA WHAT'S GOING ON...
ANYWAY, I BETTER—
HUH?

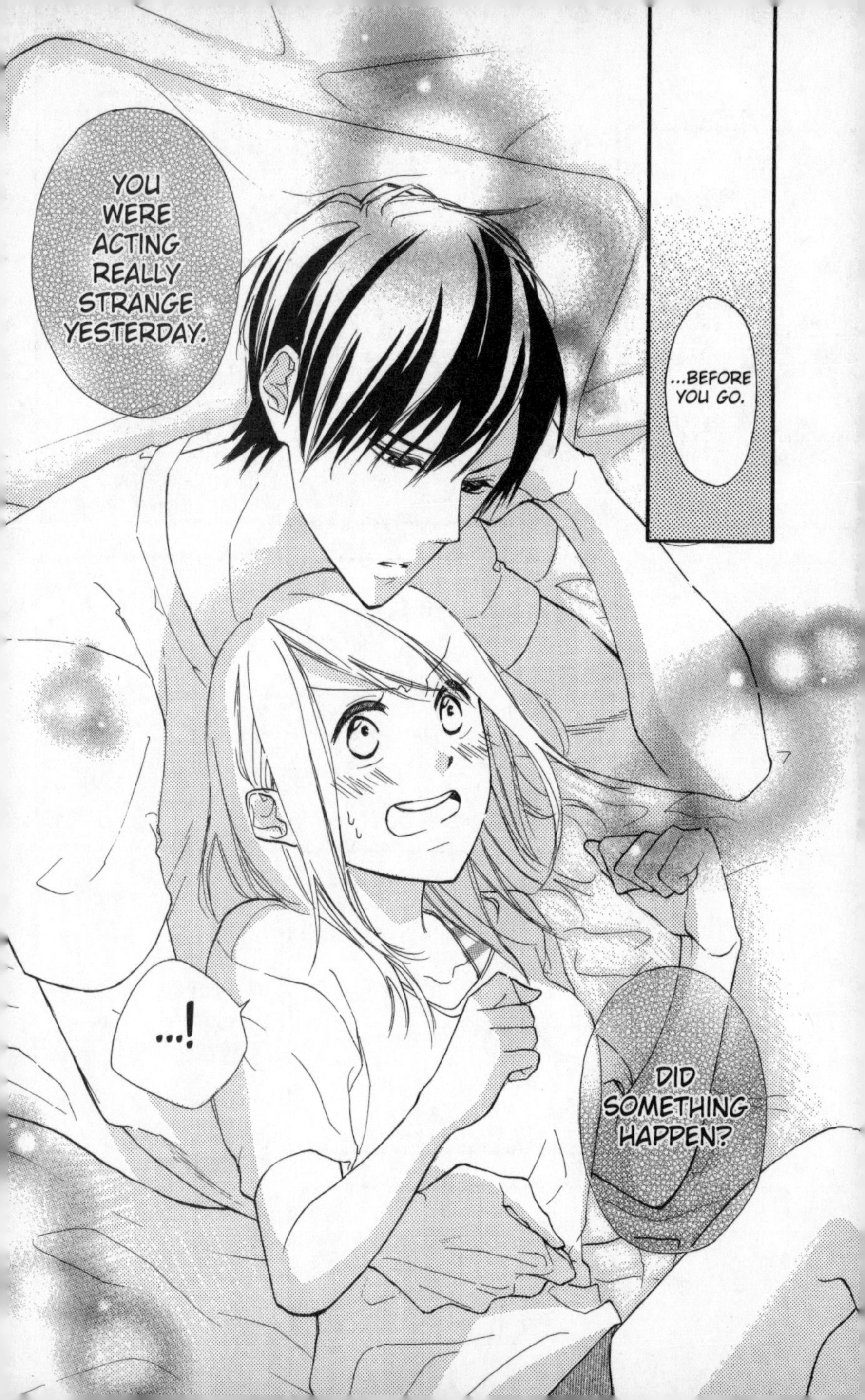
...BEFORE YOU GO.
YOU WERE ACTING REALLY STRANGE YESTERDAY.
DID SOMETHING HAPPEN?
...!

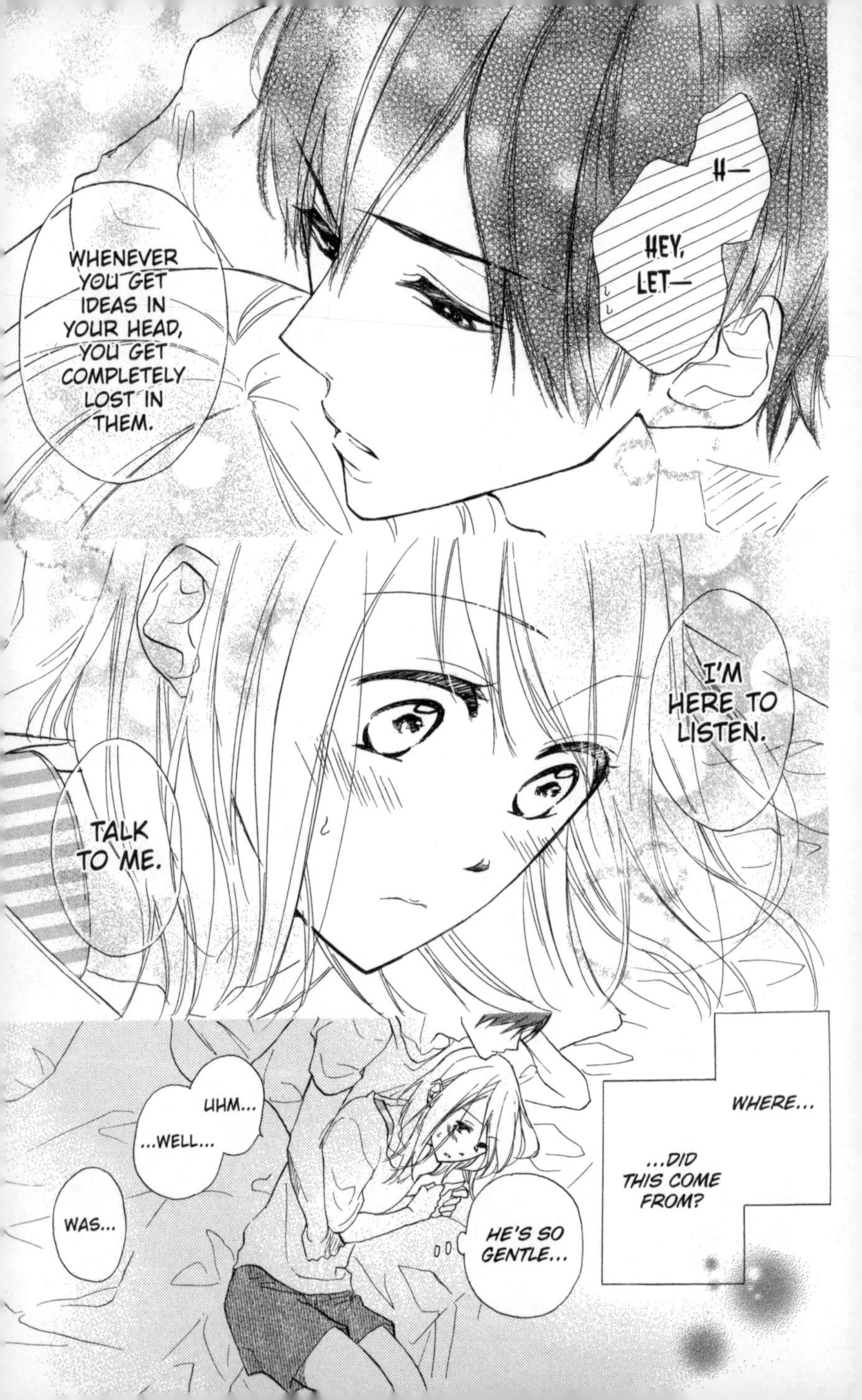
H—
HEY, LET—
WHENEVER YOU GET IDEAS IN YOUR HEAD, YOU GET COMPLETELY LOST IN THEM.
I'M HERE TO LISTEN.
TALK TO ME.
WHERE...
...DID THIS COME FROM?
HE'S SO GENTLE...
UHM... ...WELL...
WAS...

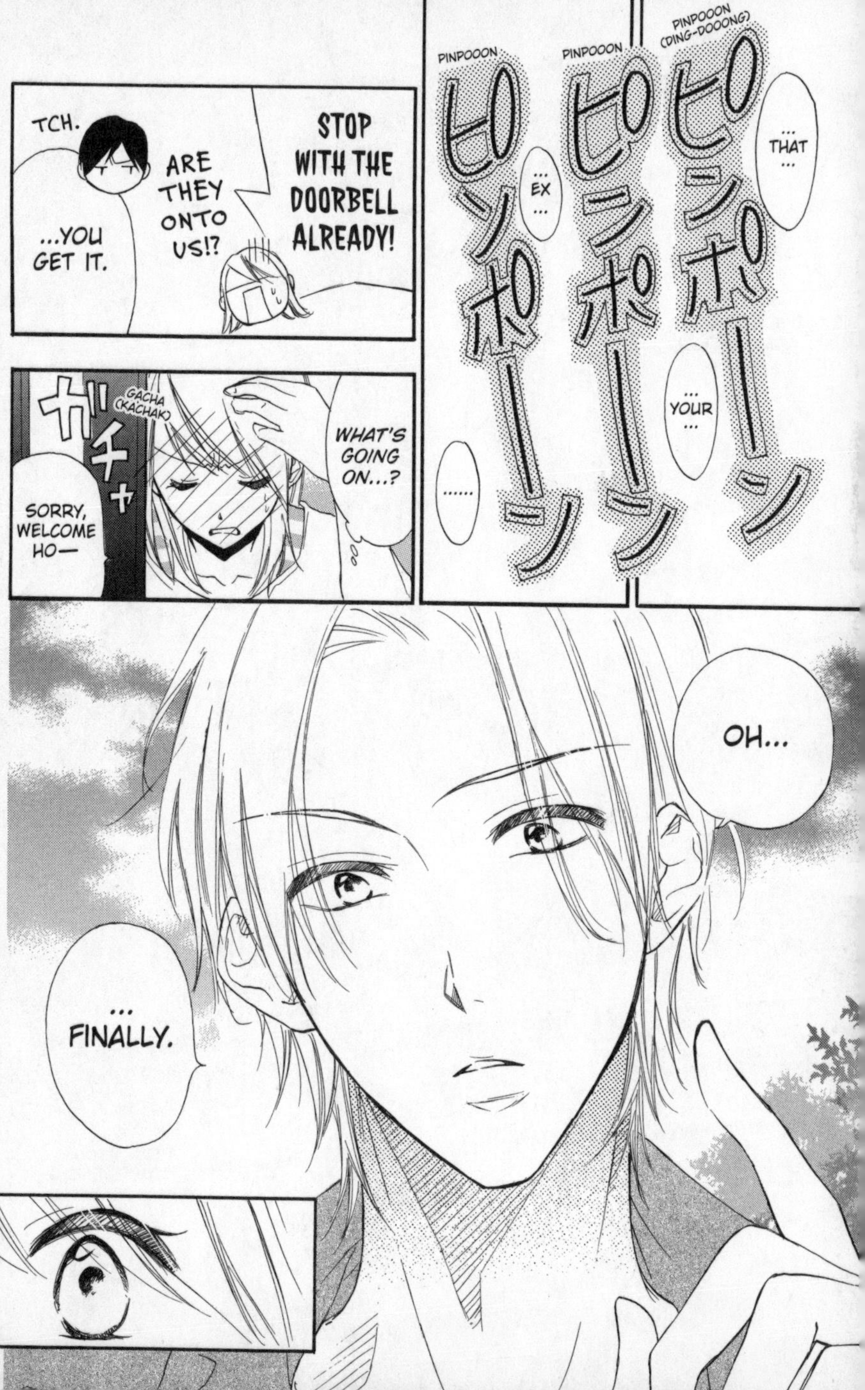
PINPOOON (DING-DOOONG)
...THAT...
...YOUR...
PINPOOON
...EX...
PINPOOON
......
STOP WITH THE DOORBELL ALREADY!
ARE THEY ONTO US!?
TCH.
...YOU GET IT.
WHAT'S GOING ON...?
GACHA (KACHAK)
SORRY, WELCOME HO—
OH...
...FINALLY.

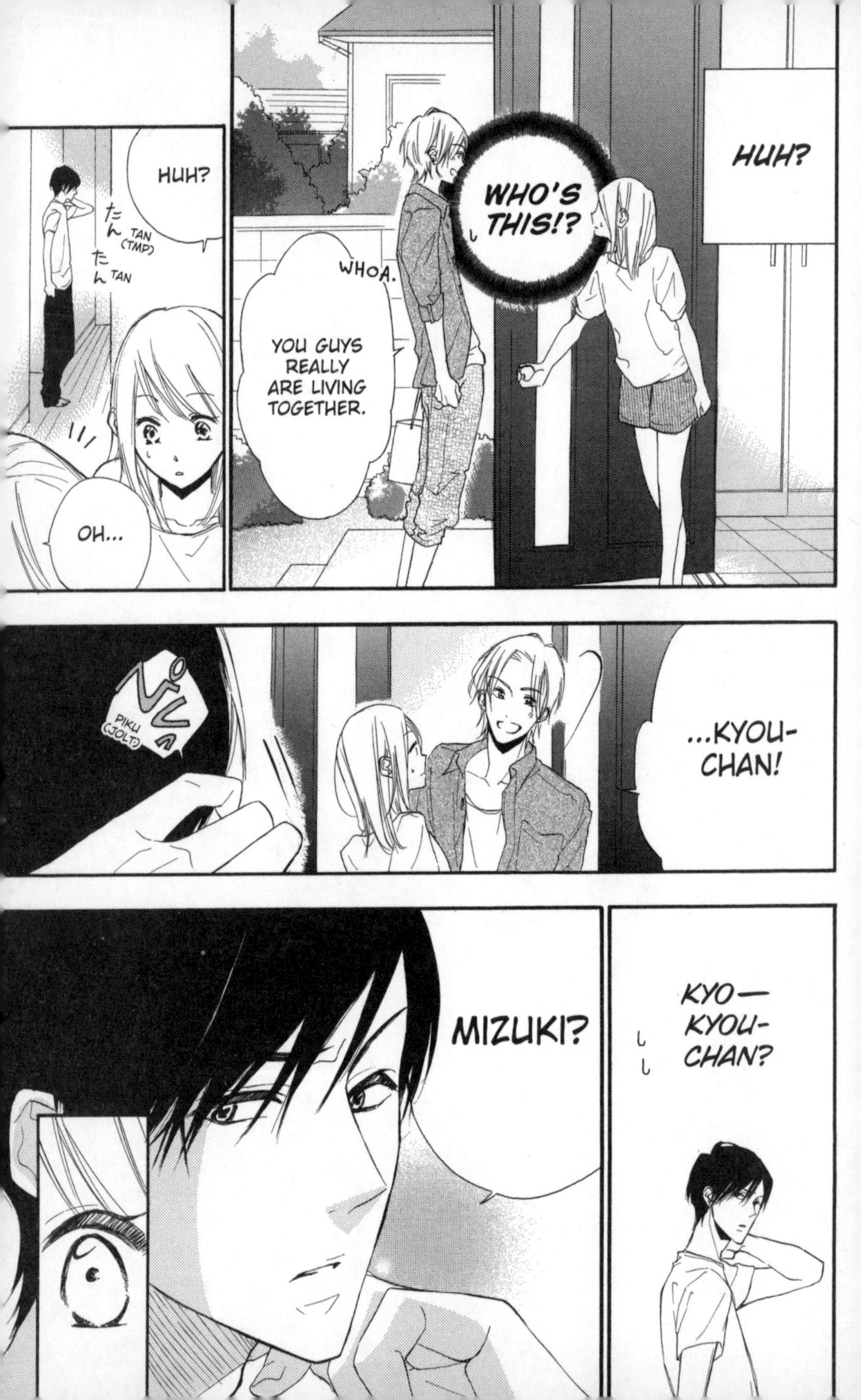
HUH?
WHO'S THIS!?
WHOA.
YOU GUYS REALLY ARE LIVING TOGETHER.
HUH?
たん TAN (TMP)
たん TAN
OH...
...KYOU-CHAN!
PIKU (JOLT)
KYO— KYOU-CHAN?
MIZUKI?

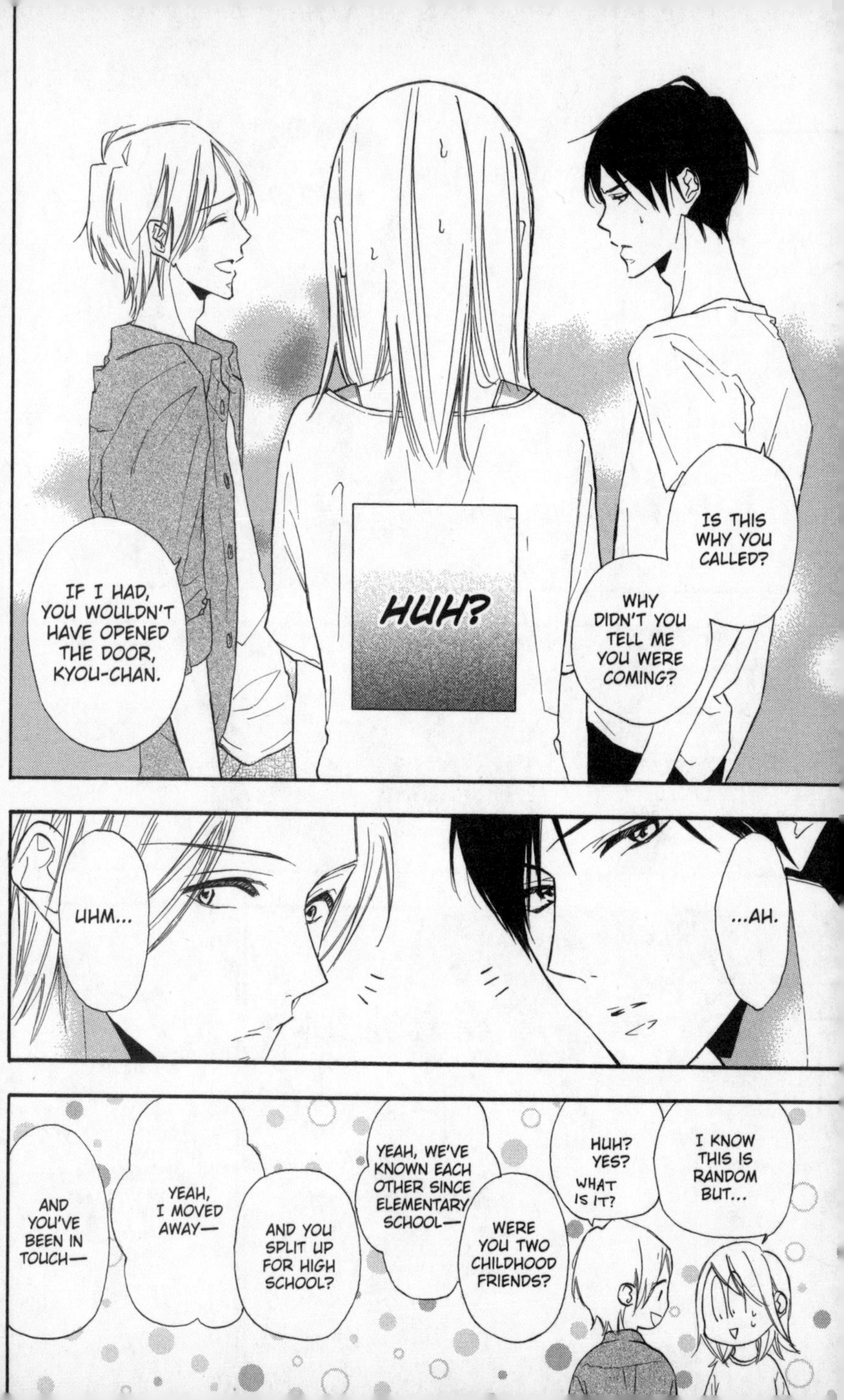
IS THIS WHY YOU CALLED?
WHY DIDN'T YOU TELL ME YOU WERE COMING?
HUH?
IF I HAD, YOU WOULDN'T HAVE OPENED THE DOOR, KYOU-CHAN.
...AH.
UHM...
I KNOW THIS IS RANDOM BUT...
HUH? YES?
WHAT IS IT?
WERE YOU TWO CHILDHOOD FRIENDS?
YEAH, WE'VE KNOWN EACH OTHER SINCE ELEMENTARY SCHOOL—
AND YOU SPLIT UP FOR HIGH SCHOOL?
YEAH, I MOVED AWAY—
AND YOU'VE BEEN IN TOUCH—

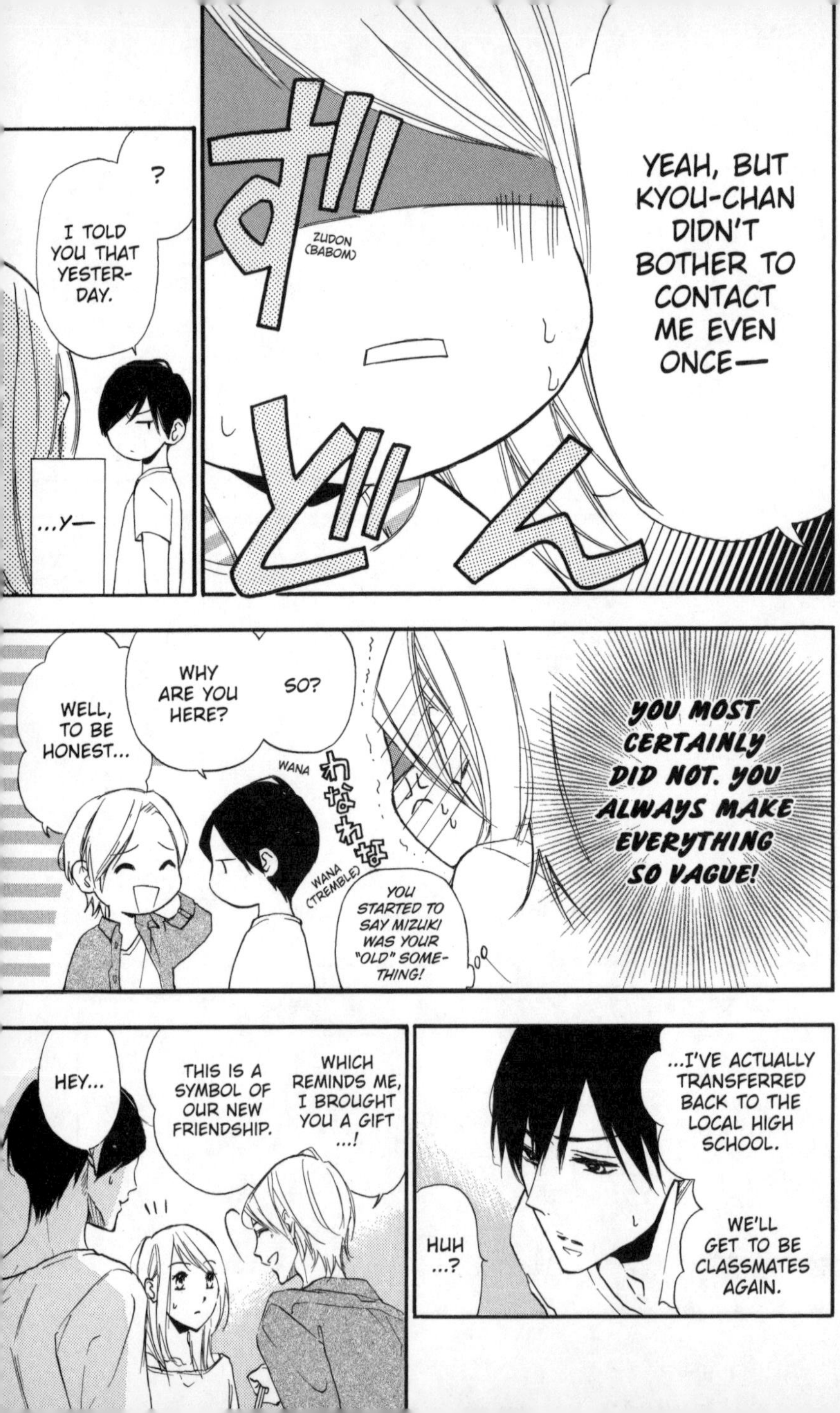
YEAH, BUT KYOU-CHAN DIDN'T BOTHER TO CONTACT ME EVEN ONCE—
ZUDON (BABOM)
?
I TOLD YOU THAT YESTER-DAY.
...Y—
YOU MOST CERTAINLY DID NOT. YOU ALWAYS MAKE EVERYTHING SO VAGUE!
WANA WANA (TREMBLE)
YOU STARTED TO SAY MIZUKI WAS YOUR "OLD" SOME-THING!
SO?
WHY ARE YOU HERE?
WELL, TO BE HONEST...
...I'VE ACTUALLY TRANSFERRED BACK TO THE LOCAL HIGH SCHOOL.
WE'LL GET TO BE CLASSMATES AGAIN.
HUH ...?
WHICH REMINDS ME, I BROUGHT YOU A GIFT ...!
THIS IS A SYMBOL OF OUR NEW FRIENDSHIP.
HEY...

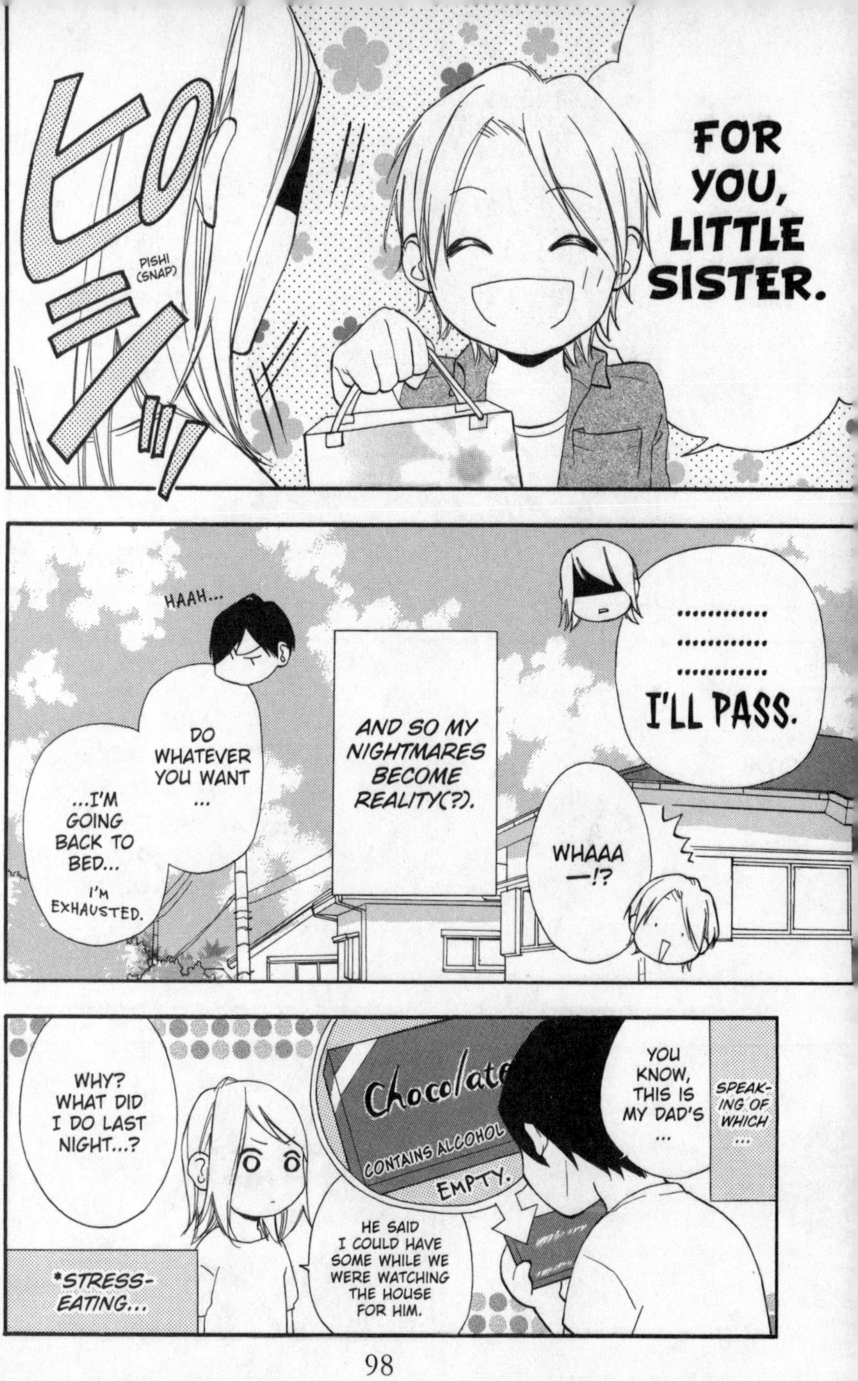
FOR YOU, LITTLE SISTER.
PISHI (SNAP)
....
....
....
I'LL PASS.
WHAAA—!?
AND SO MY NIGHTMARES BECOME REALITY(?).
HAAH...
DO WHATEVER YOU WANT ...
...I'M GOING BACK TO BED...
I'M EXHAUSTED.
SPEAKING OF WHICH ...
YOU KNOW, THIS IS MY DAD'S ...
HE SAID I COULD HAVE SOME WHILE WE WERE WATCHING THE HOUSE FOR HIM.
Chocolate
CONTAINS ALCOHOL
EMPTY.
WHY? WHAT DID I DO LAST NIGHT...?
*STRESS-EATING...

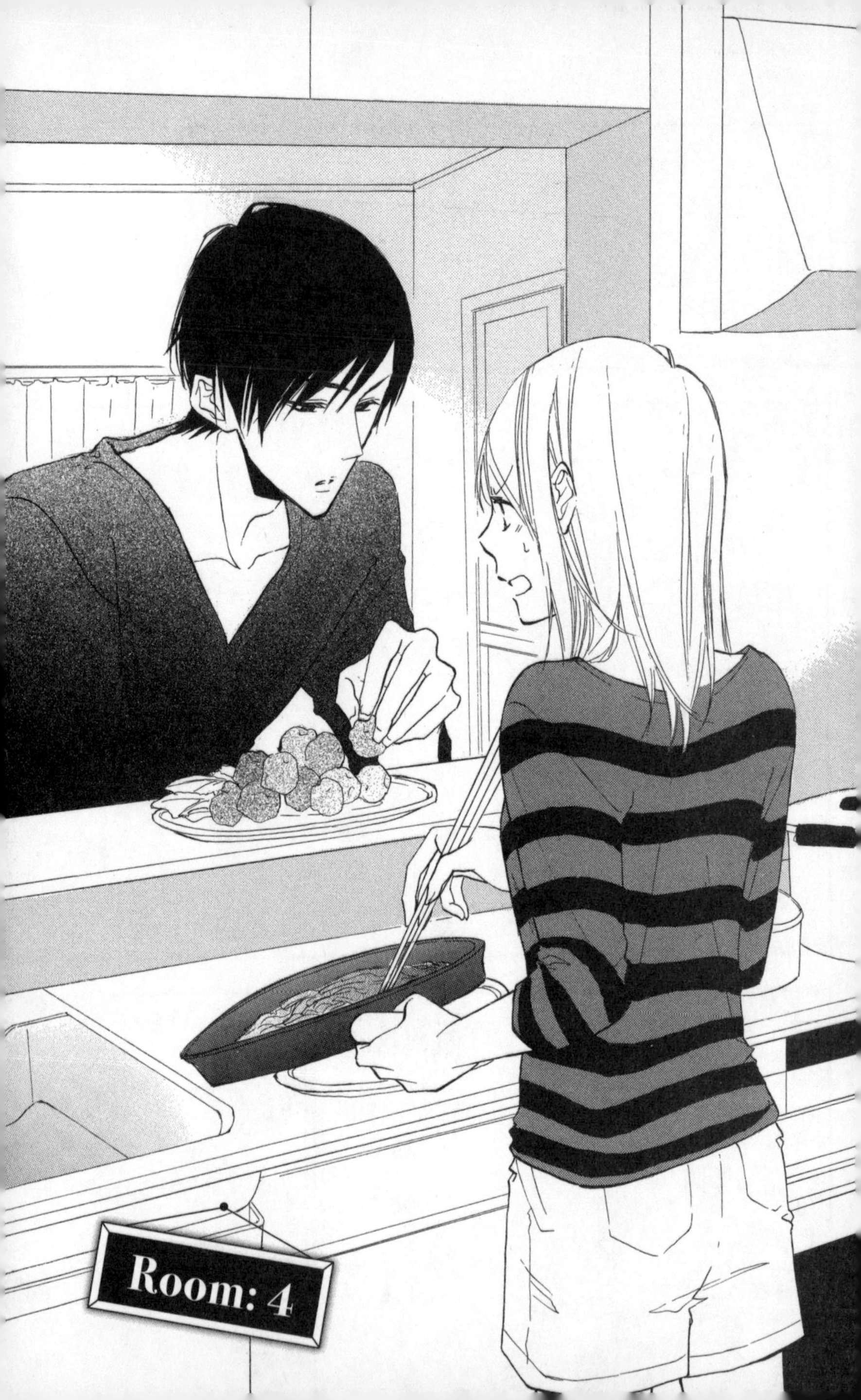
Room: 4

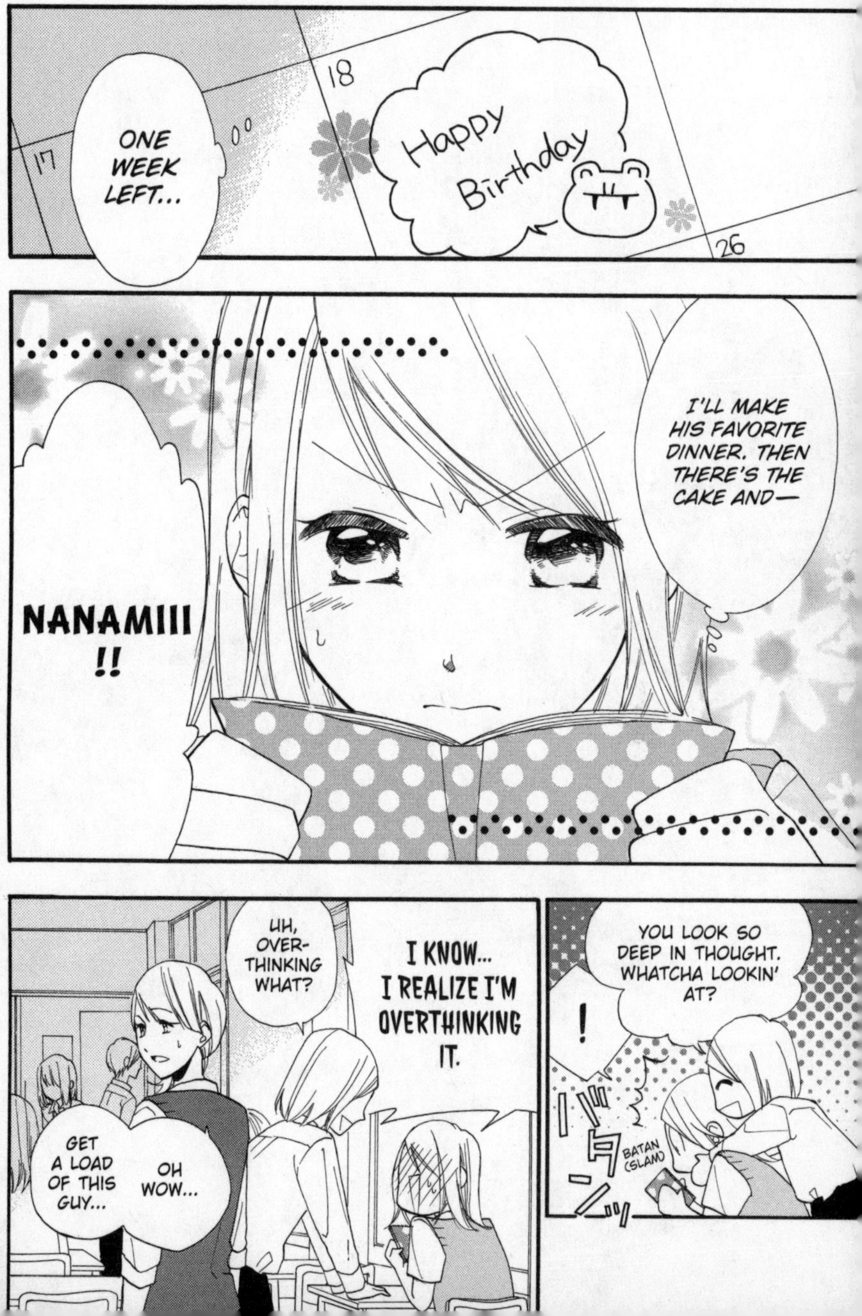
Happy Birthday
26
18
ONE WEEK LEFT...
17
I'LL MAKE HIS FAVORITE DINNER. THEN THERE'S THE CAKE AND—
NANAMIII !!
YOU LOOK SO DEEP IN THOUGHT. WHATCHA LOOKIN' AT?
!
BATAN (SLAM)
I KNOW... I REALIZE I'M OVERTHINKING IT.
UH, OVER-THINKING WHAT?
OH WOW...
GET A LOAD OF THIS GUY...

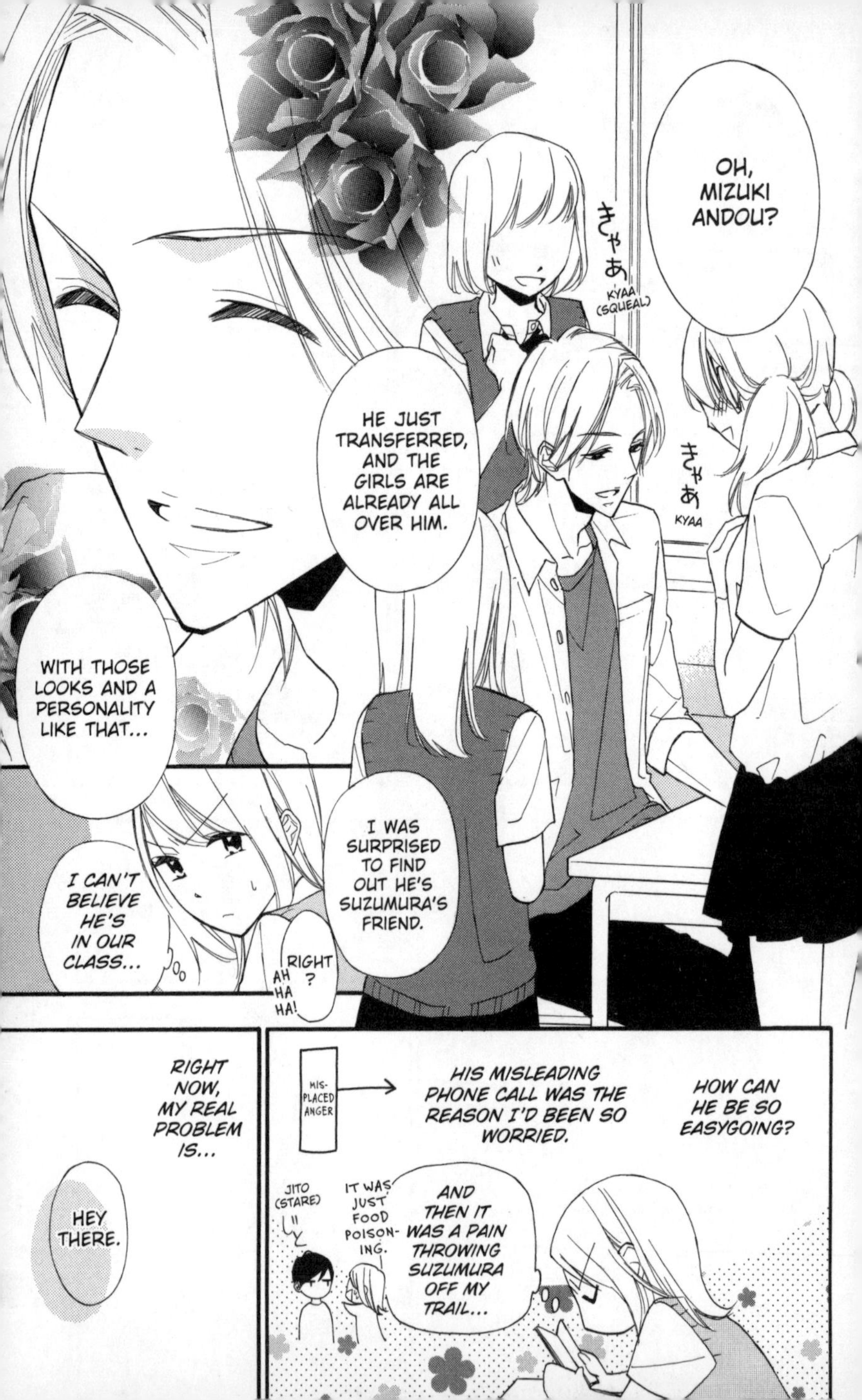
OH, MIZUKI ANDOU?
きゃあ
KYAA (SQUEAL)
きゃあ
KYAA
HE JUST TRANSFERRED, AND THE GIRLS ARE ALREADY ALL OVER HIM.
WITH THOSE LOOKS AND A PERSONALITY LIKE THAT...
I WAS SURPRISED TO FIND OUT HE'S SUZUMURA'S FRIEND.
I CAN'T BELIEVE HE'S IN OUR CLASS...
RIGHT?
AH HA HA HA!
HOW CAN HE BE SO EASYGOING?
HIS MISLEADING PHONE CALL WAS THE REASON I'D BEEN SO WORRIED.
MIS-PLACED ANGER
AND THEN IT WAS A PAIN THROWING SUZUMURA OFF MY TRAIL...
IT WAS JUST FOOD POISON-ING.
JITO (STARE)
RIGHT NOW, MY REAL PROBLEM IS...
HEY THERE.

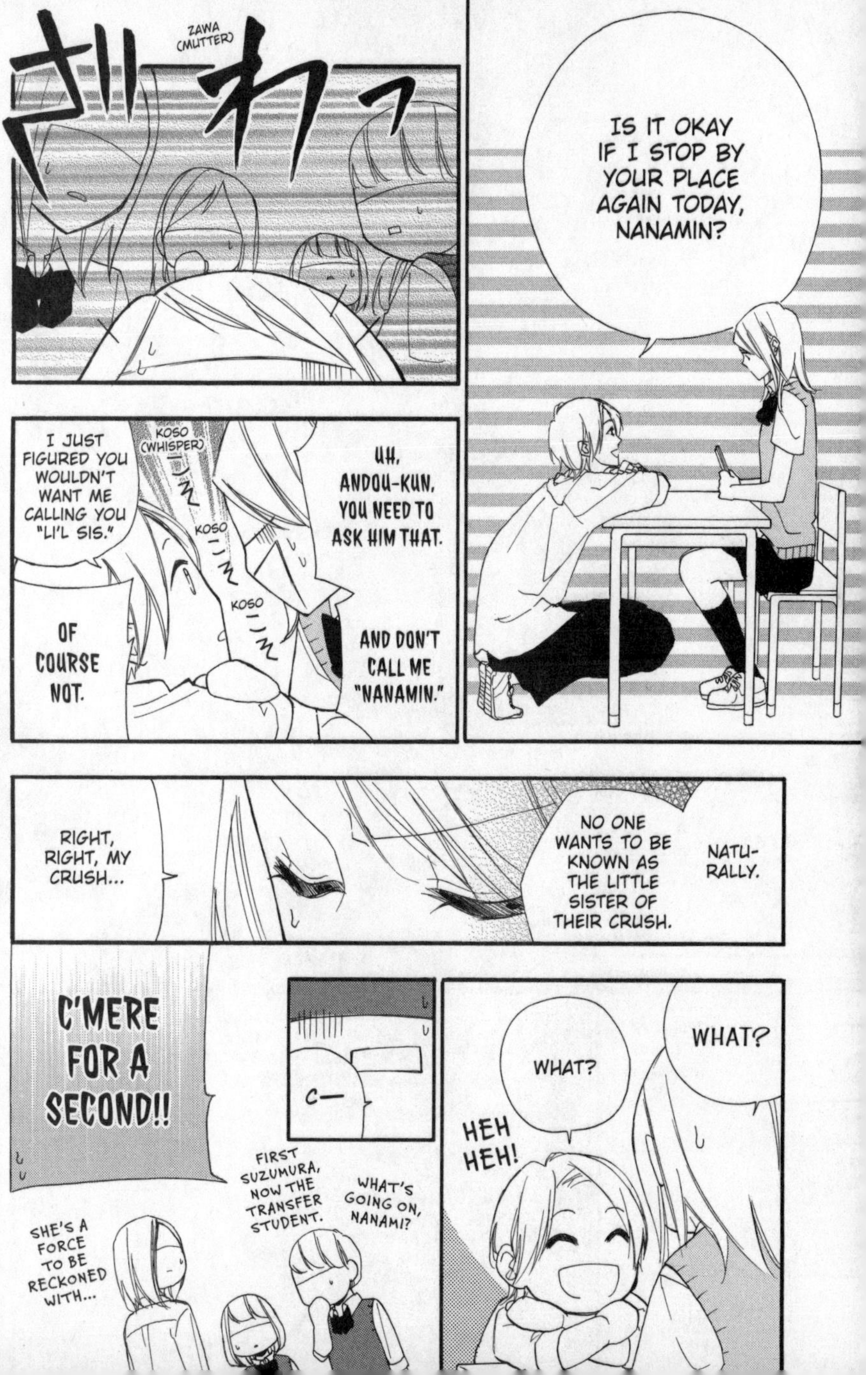
IS IT OKAY IF I STOP BY YOUR PLACE AGAIN TODAY, NANAMIN?
ZAWA (MUTTER)
UH, ANDOU-KUN, YOU NEED TO ASK HIM THAT.
AND DON'T CALL ME "NANAMIN."
KOSO (WHISPER)
KOSO
KOSO
I JUST FIGURED YOU WOULDN'T WANT ME CALLING YOU "LI'L SIS."
OF COURSE NOT.
NATU-RALLY.
NO ONE WANTS TO BE KNOWN AS THE LITTLE SISTER OF THEIR CRUSH.
RIGHT, RIGHT, MY CRUSH...
WHAT?
WHAT?
HEH HEH!
C—
C'MERE FOR A SECOND!!
WHAT'S GOING ON, NANAMI?
FIRST SUZUMURA, NOW THE TRANSFER STUDENT.
SHE'S A FORCE TO BE RECKONED WITH...

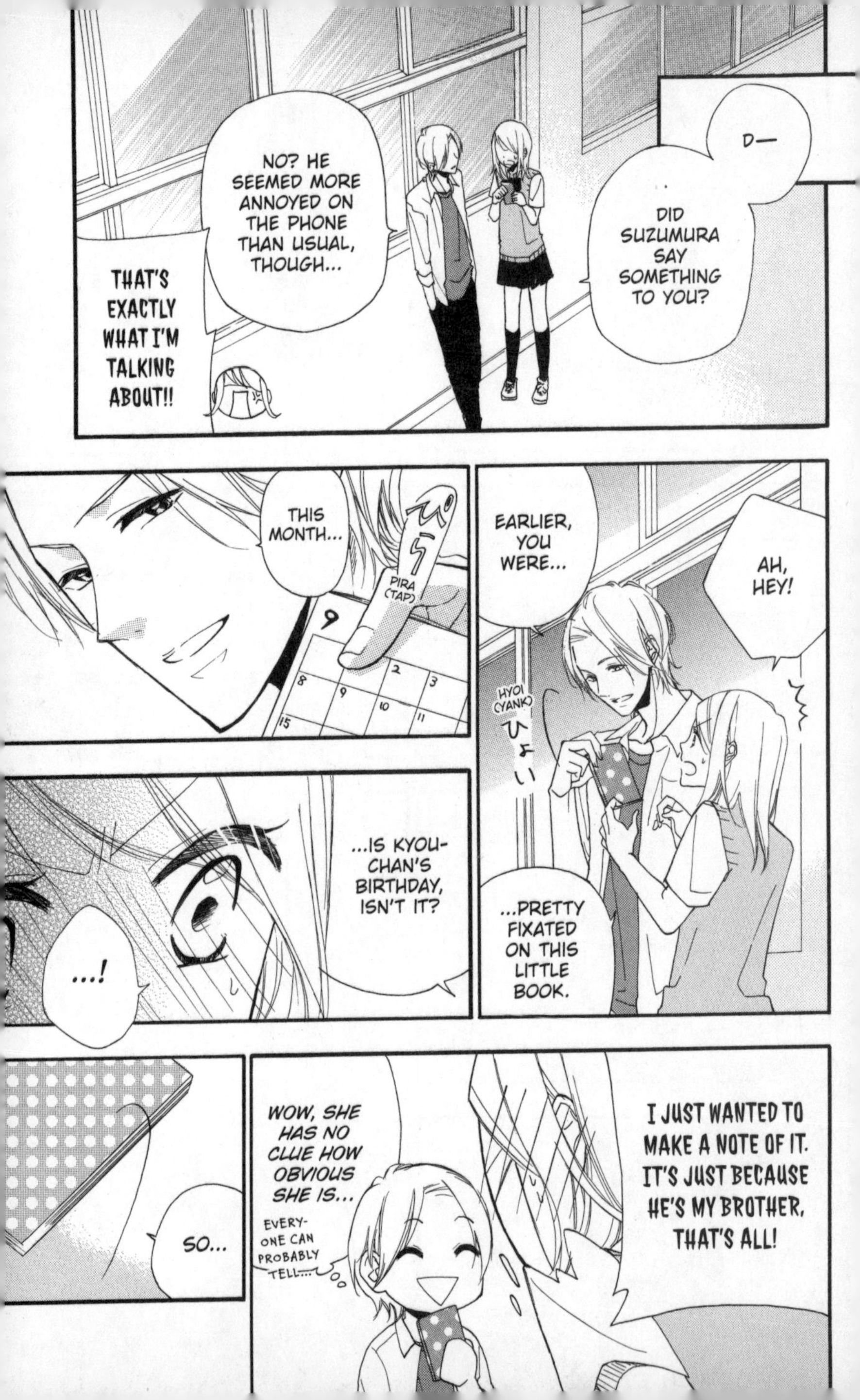
D—
DID SUZUMURA SAY SOMETHING TO YOU?
NO? HE SEEMED MORE ANNOYED ON THE PHONE THAN USUAL, THOUGH...
THAT'S EXACTLY WHAT I'M TALKING ABOUT!!
AH, HEY!
EARLIER, YOU WERE...
HYOI (YANK)
...PRETTY FIXATED ON THIS LITTLE BOOK.
THIS MONTH...
PIRA (TAP)
...IS KYOU-CHAN'S BIRTHDAY, ISN'T IT?
...!
I JUST WANTED TO MAKE A NOTE OF IT. IT'S JUST BECAUSE HE'S MY BROTHER, THAT'S ALL!
WOW, SHE HAS NO CLUE HOW OBVIOUS SHE IS...
EVERYONE CAN PROBABLY TELL...
SO...

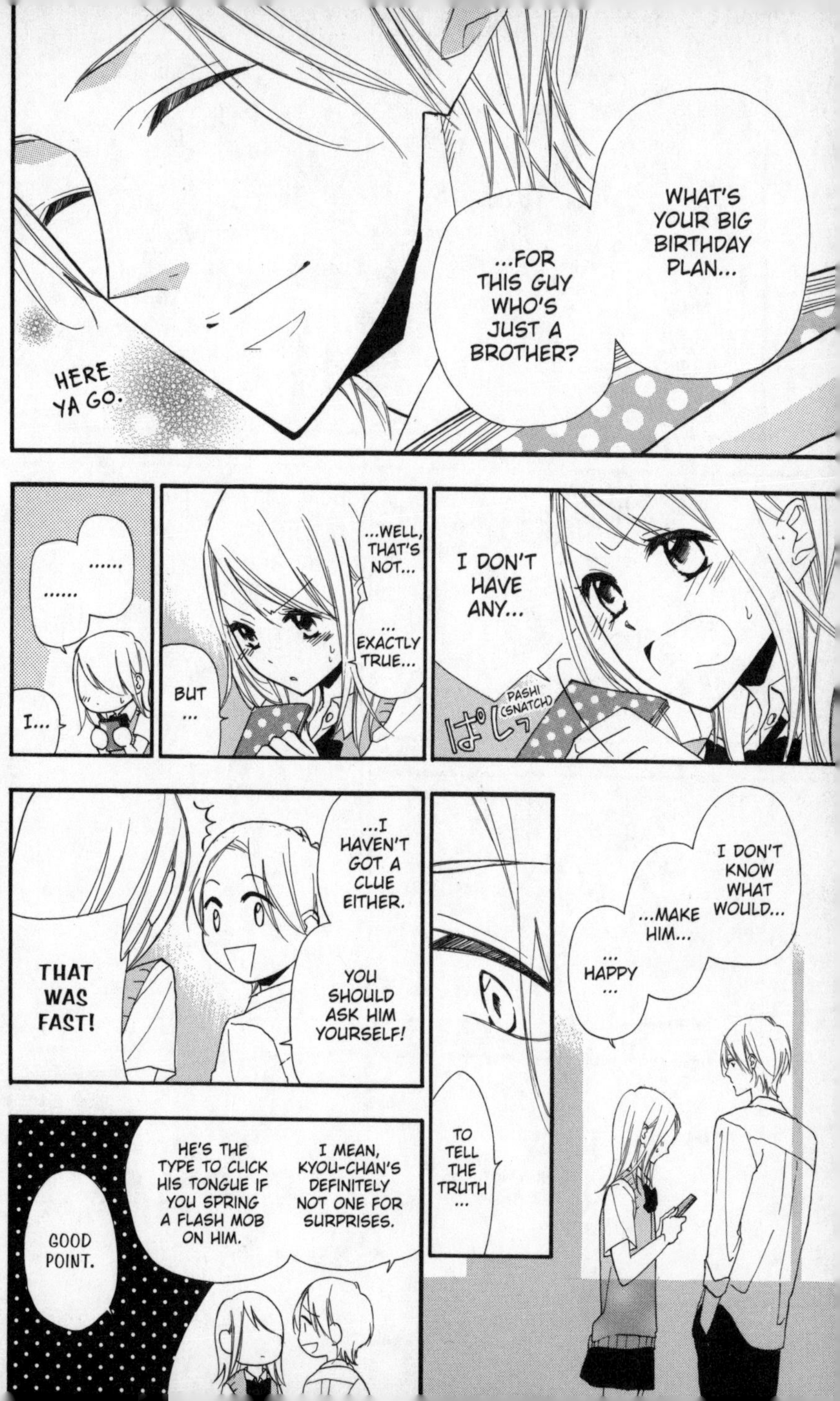

WHAT'S YOUR BIG BIRTHDAY PLAN...
...FOR THIS GUY WHO'S JUST A BROTHER?
HERE YA GO.
I DON'T HAVE ANY...
PASHI (SNATCH)
...WELL, THAT'S NOT...
...EXACTLY TRUE...
BUT...
......
......
I...
I DON'T KNOW WHAT WOULD...
...MAKE HIM...
...HAPPY...
TO TELL THE TRUTH...
...I HAVEN'T GOT A CLUE EITHER.
YOU SHOULD ASK HIM YOURSELF!
THAT WAS FAST!
I MEAN, KYOU-CHAN'S DEFINITELY NOT ONE FOR SURPRISES.
HE'S THE TYPE TO CLICK HIS TONGUE IF YOU SPRING A FLASH MOB ON HIM.
GOOD POINT.

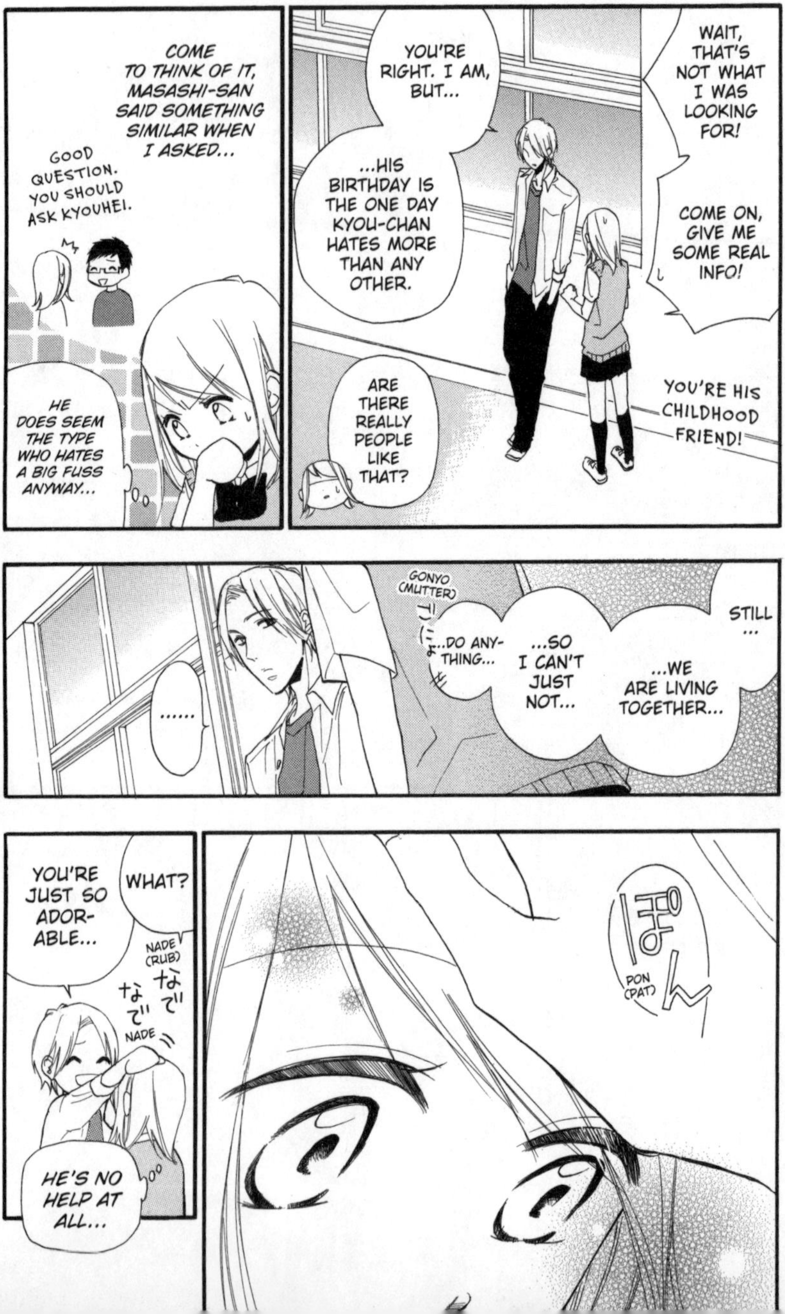
WAIT, THAT'S NOT WHAT I WAS LOOKING FOR!
COME ON, GIVE ME SOME REAL INFO!
YOU'RE HIS CHILDHOOD FRIEND!
YOU'RE RIGHT. I AM, BUT...
...HIS BIRTHDAY IS THE ONE DAY KYOU-CHAN HATES MORE THAN ANY OTHER.
ARE THERE REALLY PEOPLE LIKE THAT?
COME TO THINK OF IT, MASASHI-SAN SAID SOMETHING SIMILAR WHEN I ASKED...
GOOD QUESTION. YOU SHOULD ASK KYOUHEI.
HE DOES SEEM THE TYPE WHO HATES A BIG FUSS ANYWAY...
STILL...
...WE ARE LIVING TOGETHER...
...SO I CAN'T JUST NOT...
...DO ANYTHING...
GONYO (MUTTER)
ごにょ
......
ぽん
PON (PAT)
WHAT?
YOU'RE JUST SO ADORABLE...
NADE (RUB)
なでなで
NADE
HE'S NO HELP AT ALL...

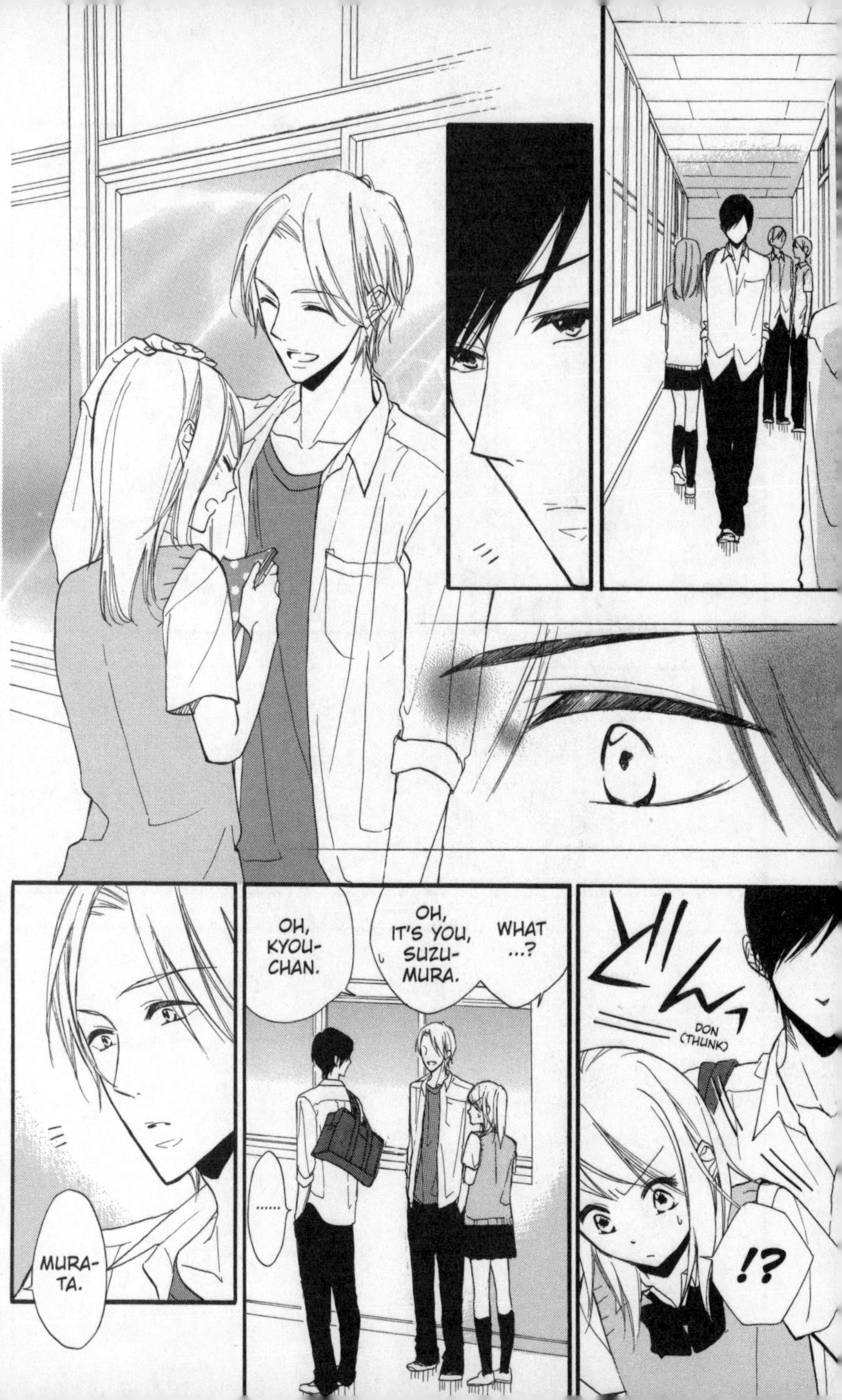
DON (THUNK)
!?
WHAT ...?
OH, IT'S YOU, SUZU-MURA.
OH, KYOU-CHAN.
......
MURA-TA.

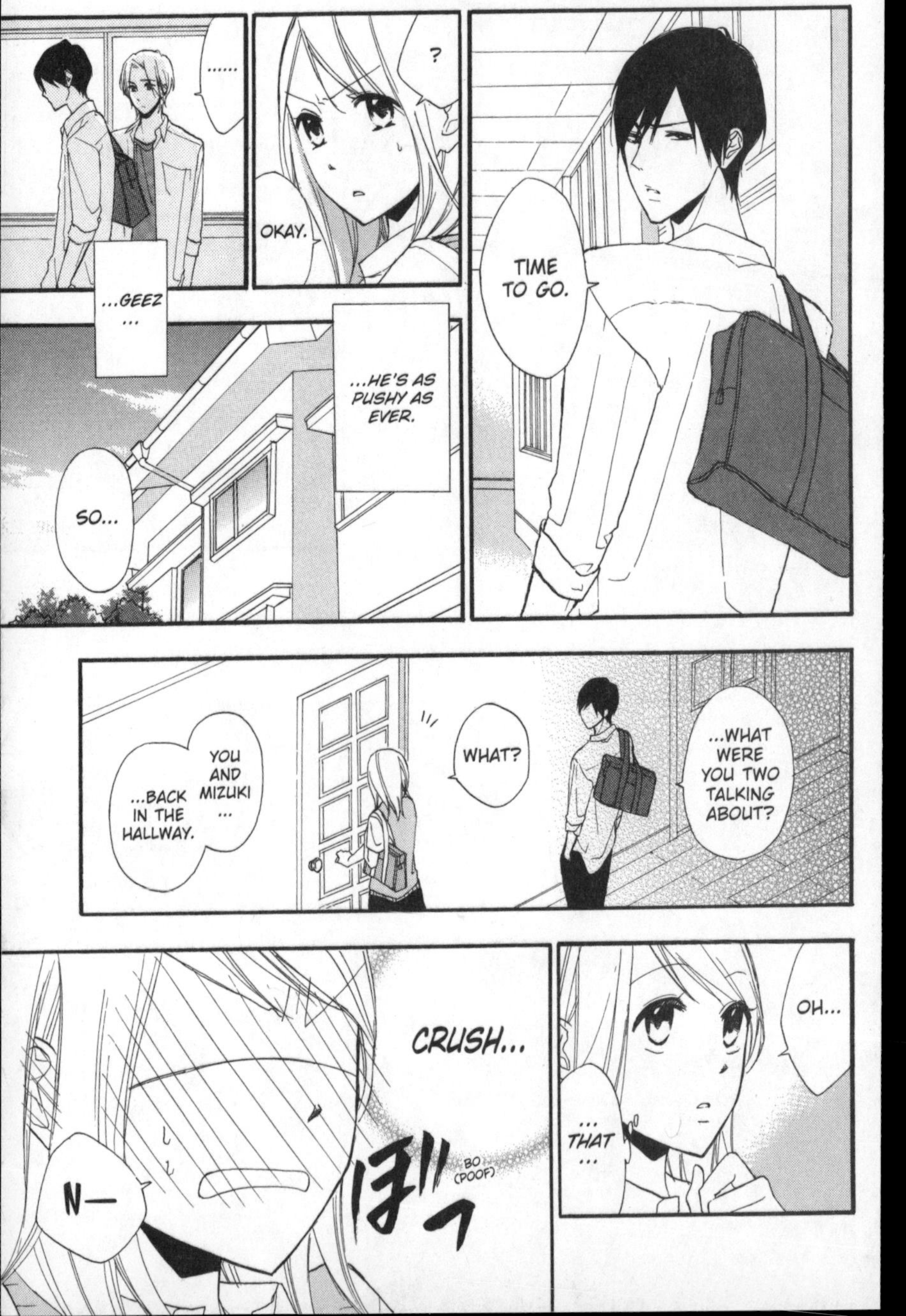
TIME TO GO.
?
OKAY.
......
...GEEZ ...
...HE'S AS PUSHY AS EVER.
SO...
...WHAT WERE YOU TWO TALKING ABOUT?
WHAT?
YOU AND MIZUKI ... ...BACK IN THE HALLWAY.
OH...
...THAT ...
CRUSH...
BO (POOF)
N—

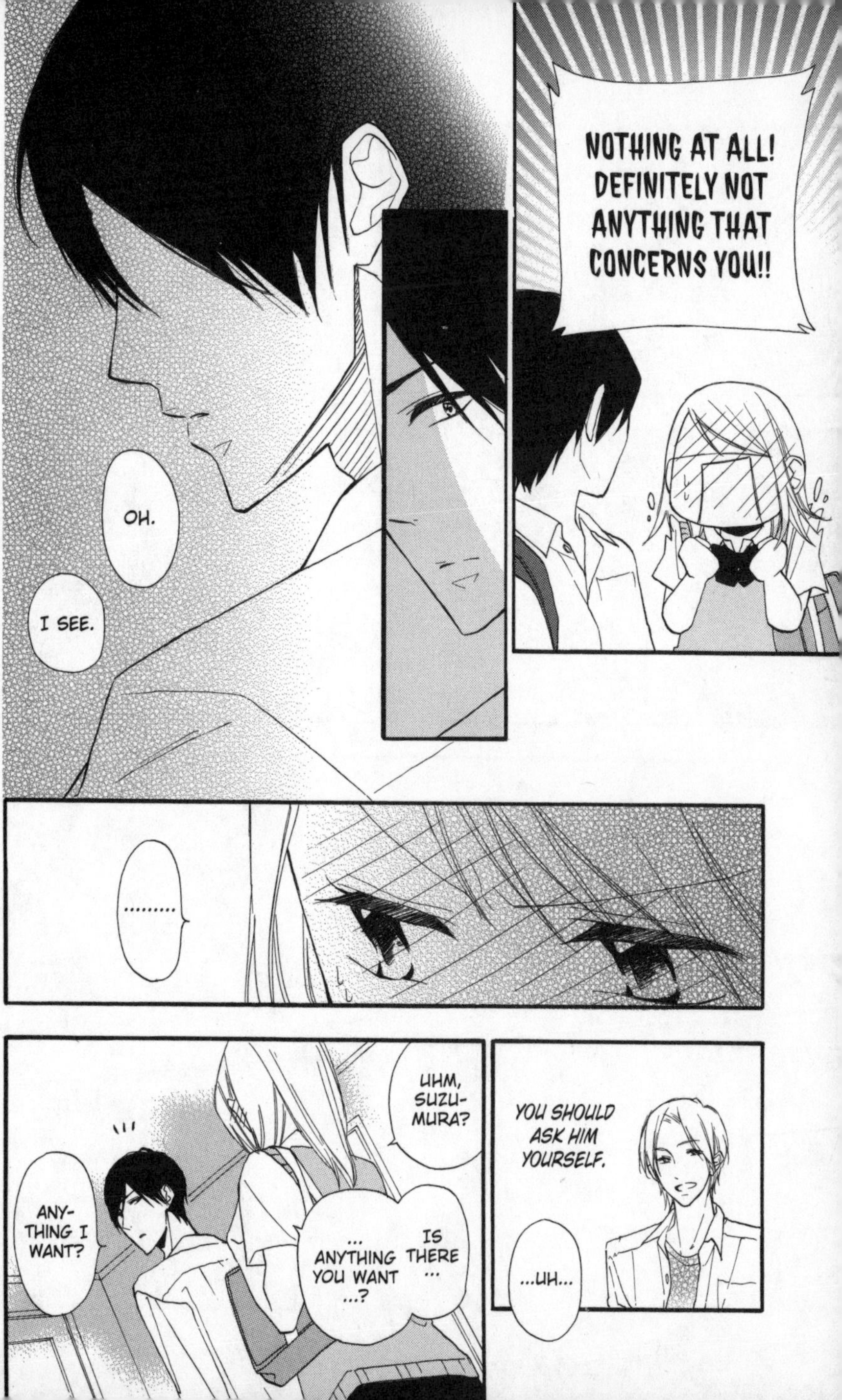
NOTHING AT ALL! DEFINITELY NOT ANYTHING THAT CONCERNS YOU!!
OH.
I SEE.
....
YOU SHOULD ASK HIM YOURSELF.
...UH...
UHM, SUZUMURA?
IS THERE ... ... ANYTHING YOU WANT ...?
ANYTHING I WANT?

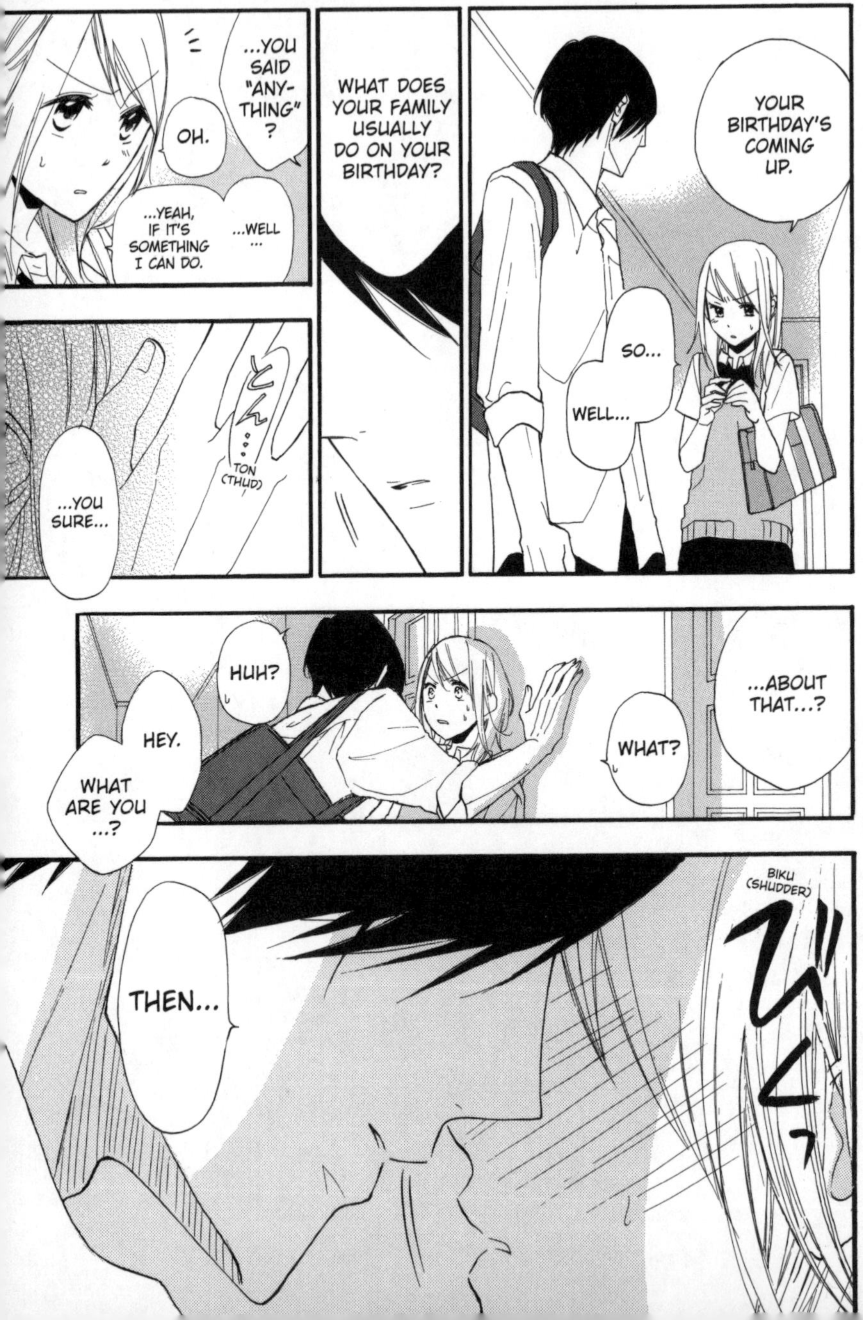
YOUR BIRTHDAY'S COMING UP.
SO... WELL...
WHAT DOES YOUR FAMILY USUALLY DO ON YOUR BIRTHDAY?
...YOU SAID "ANY-THING"?
OH.
...WELL ...
...YEAH, IF IT'S SOMETHING I CAN DO.
とん...
TON (THUD)
...YOU SURE...
...ABOUT THAT...?
WHAT?
HUH?
HEY.
WHAT ARE YOU ...?
BIKU (SHUDDER)
THEN...

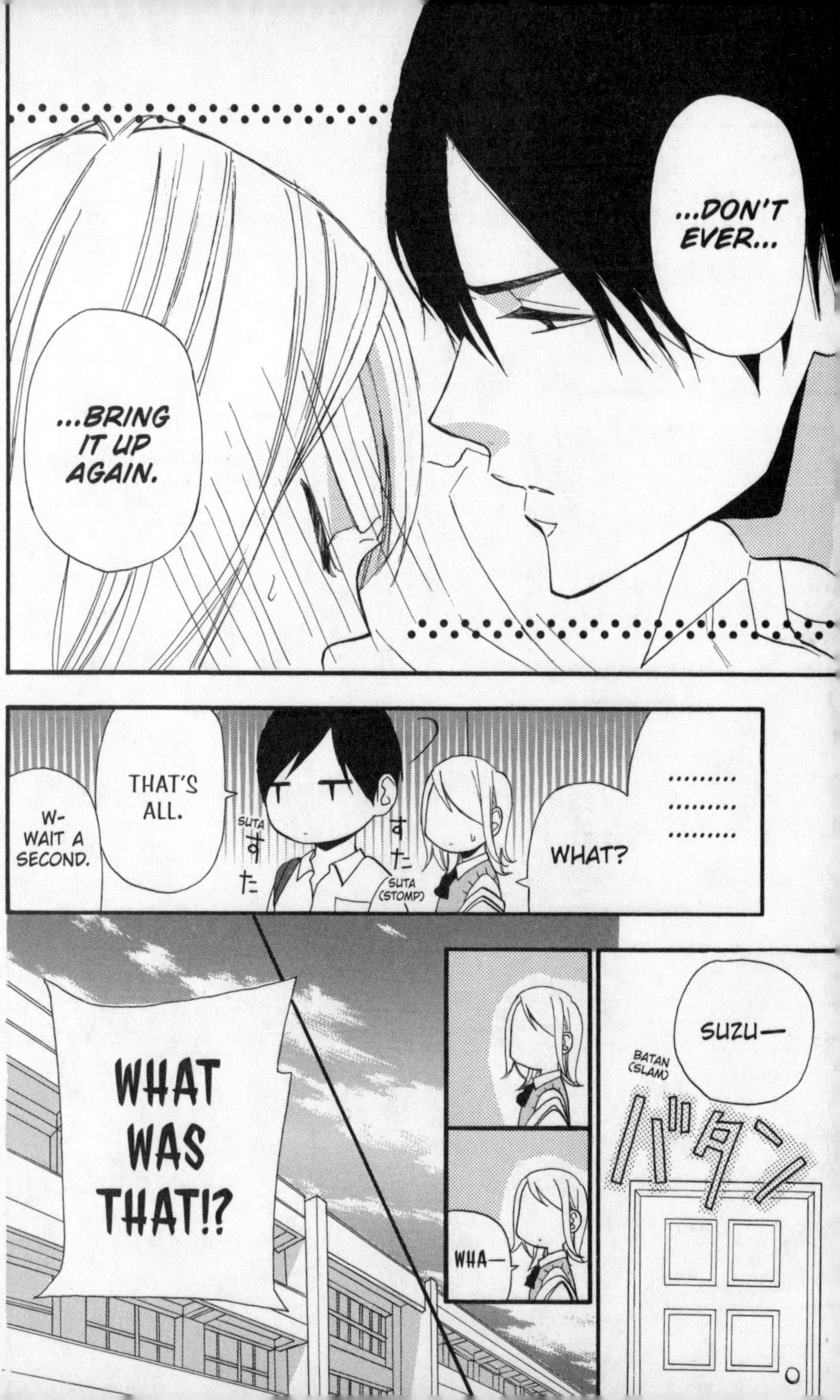
...DON'T EVER...
...BRING IT UP AGAIN.
....
....
....
WHAT?
すた
SUTA (STOMP)
すた
SUTA
THAT'S ALL.
W-WAIT A SECOND.
SUZU—
バタン
BATAN (SLAM)
WHA—
WHAT WAS THAT!?

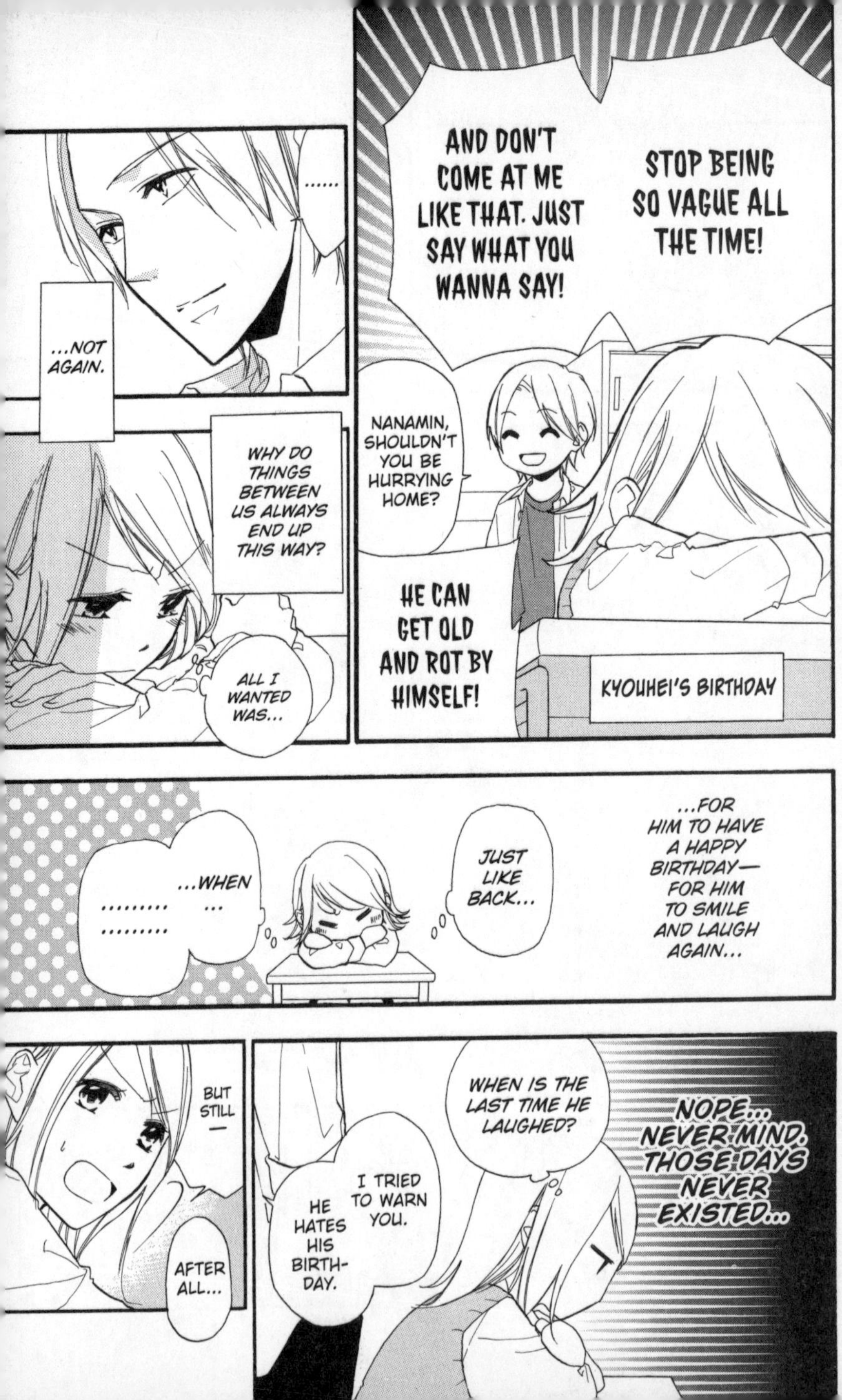
STOP BEING SO VAGUE ALL THE TIME!
AND DON'T COME AT ME LIKE THAT. JUST SAY WHAT YOU WANNA SAY!
NANAMIN, SHOULDN'T YOU BE HURRYING HOME?
HE CAN GET OLD AND ROT BY HIMSELF!
KYOUHEI'S BIRTHDAY
......
...NOT AGAIN.
WHY DO THINGS BETWEEN US ALWAYS END UP THIS WAY?
ALL I WANTED WAS...
...FOR HIM TO HAVE A HAPPY BIRTHDAY— FOR HIM TO SMILE AND LAUGH AGAIN...
JUST LIKE BACK...
...WHEN ...
....
NOPE... NEVER MIND. THOSE DAYS NEVER EXISTED...
WHEN IS THE LAST TIME HE LAUGHED?
I TRIED TO WARN YOU.
HE HATES HIS BIRTH-DAY.
BUT STILL—
AFTER ALL...

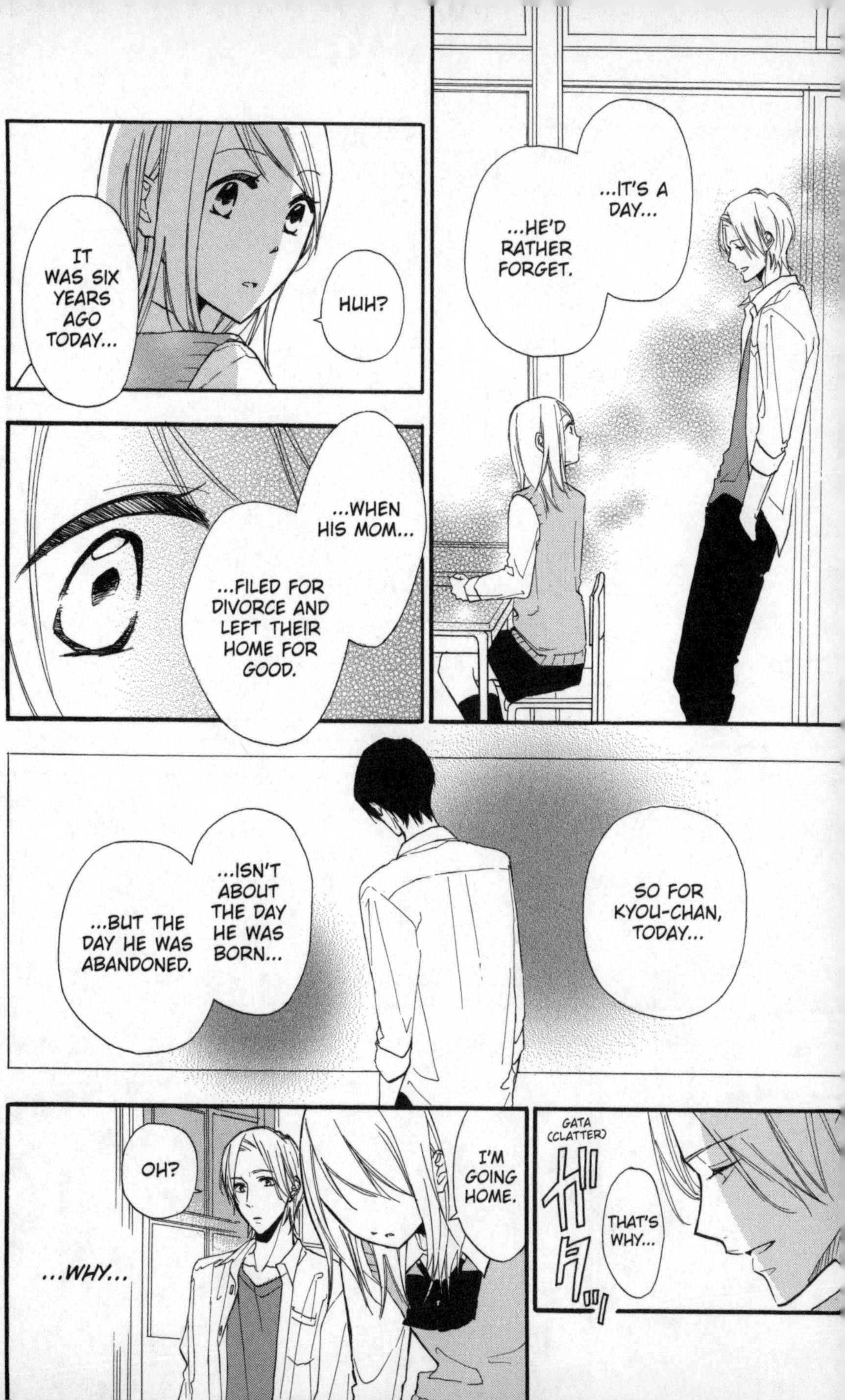
...IT'S A DAY...
...HE'D RATHER FORGET.
HUH?
IT WAS SIX YEARS AGO TODAY...
...WHEN HIS MOM...
...FILED FOR DIVORCE AND LEFT THEIR HOME FOR GOOD.
SO FOR KYOU-CHAN, TODAY...
...ISN'T ABOUT THE DAY HE WAS BORN...
...BUT THE DAY HE WAS ABANDONED.
GATA (CLATTER)
THAT'S WHY...
I'M GOING HOME.
OH?
...WHY...

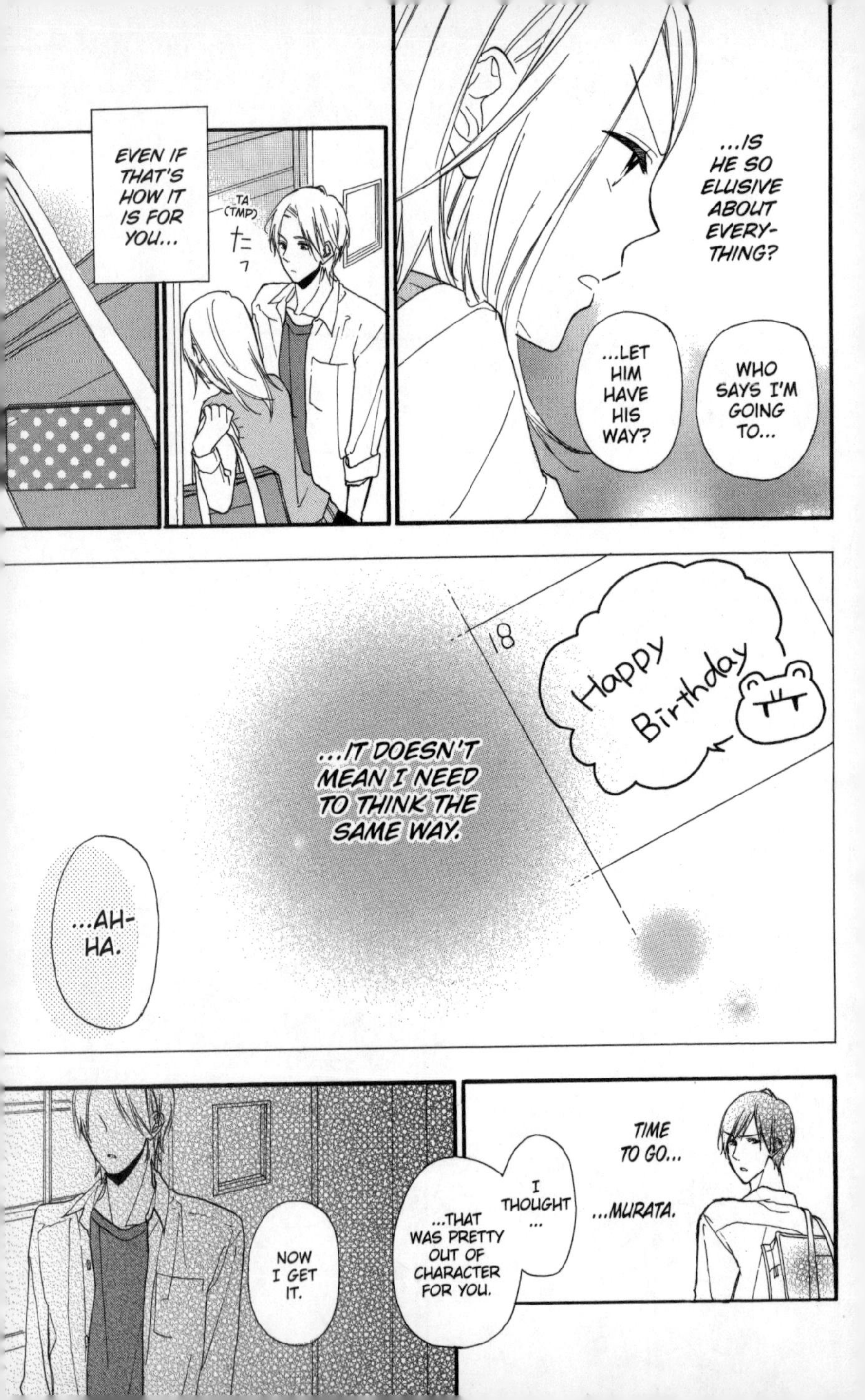
...IS HE SO ELUSIVE ABOUT EVERYTHING?
WHO SAYS I'M GOING TO...
...LET HIM HAVE HIS WAY?
EVEN IF THAT'S HOW IT IS FOR YOU...
TA (TMP)
...IT DOESN'T MEAN I NEED TO THINK THE SAME WAY.
18
Happy Birthday
...AH-HA.
TIME TO GO...
...MURATA.
I THOUGHT...
...THAT WAS PRETTY OUT OF CHARACTER FOR YOU.
NOW I GET IT.

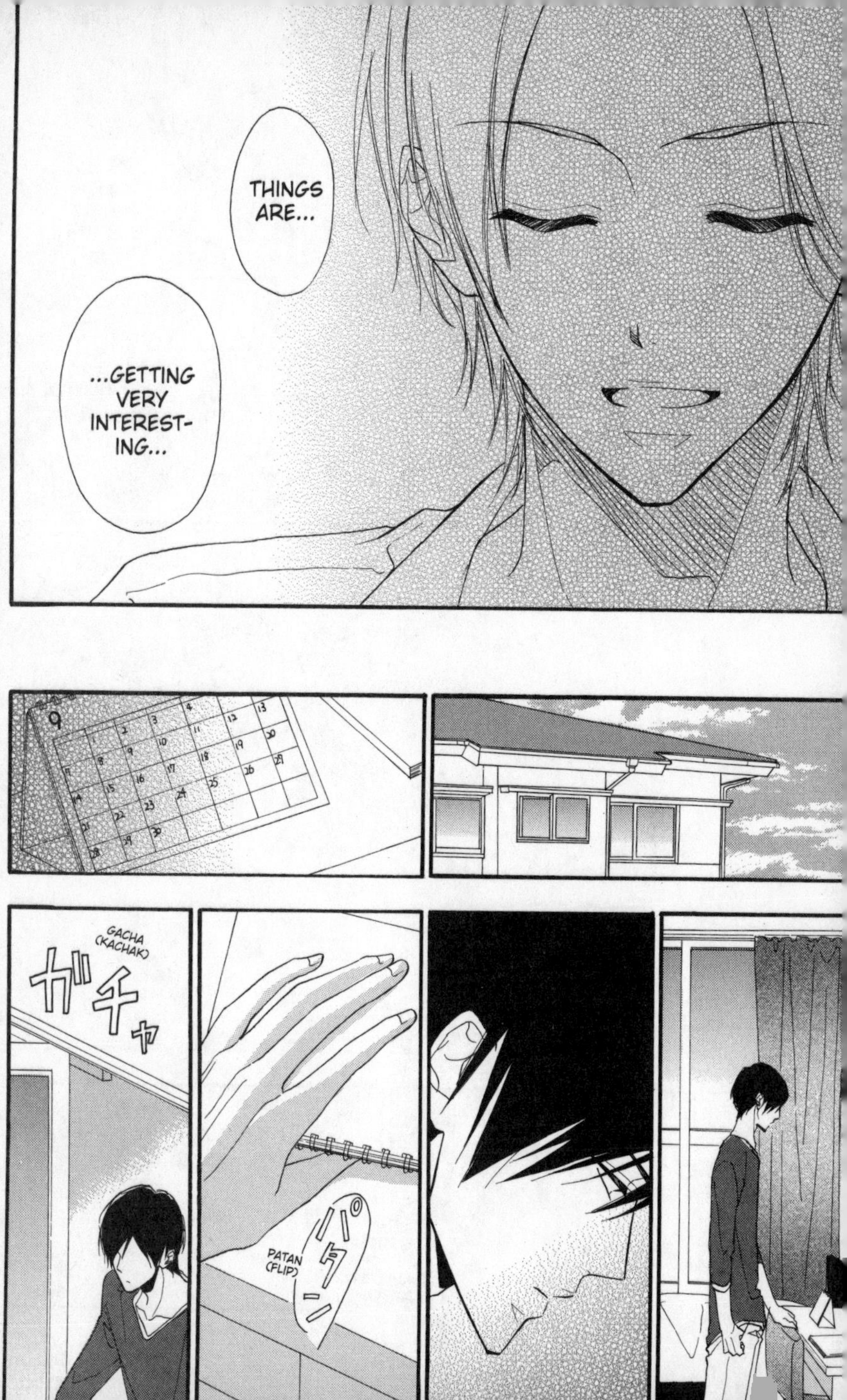
THINGS ARE...
...GETTING VERY INTEREST-ING...
パターン
PATAN (FLIP)
ガチャ
GACHA (KACHAK)

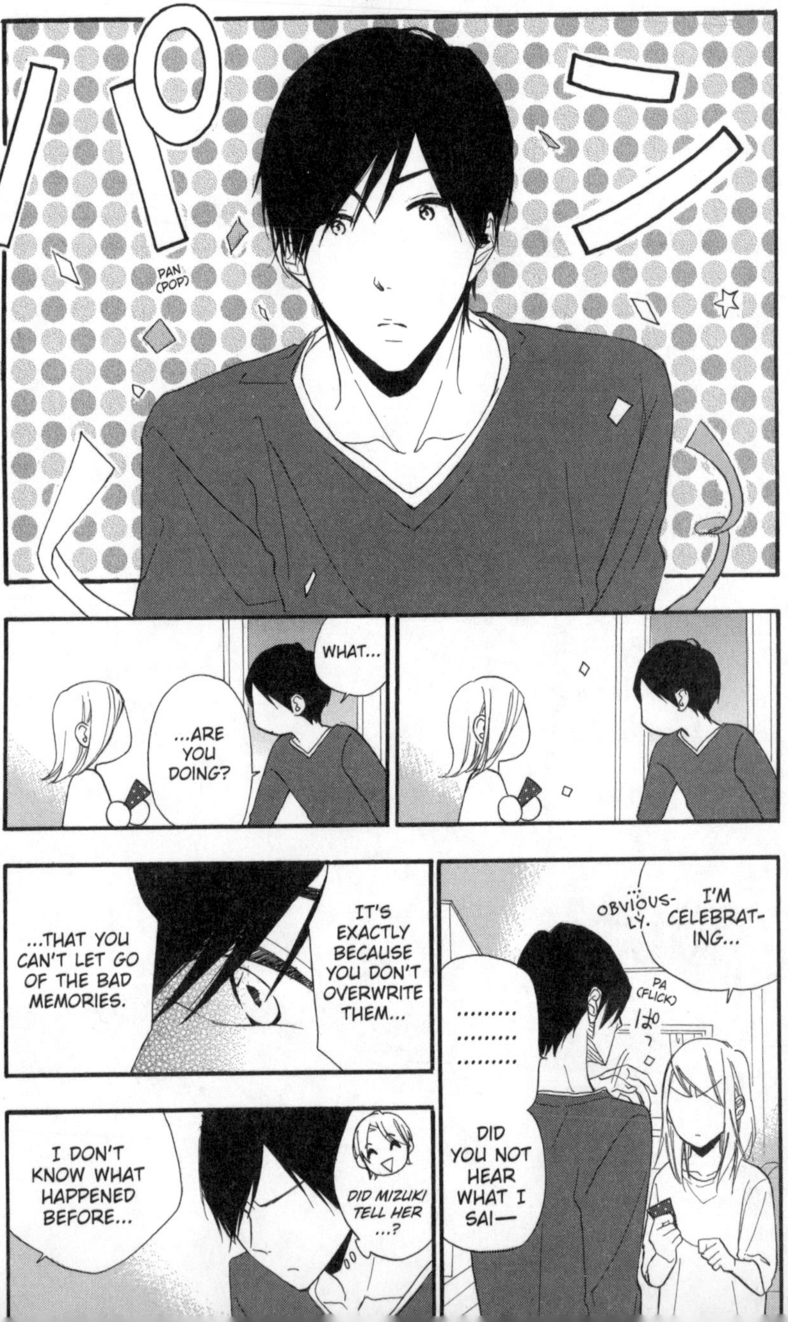
PAN (POP)
WHAT...
...ARE YOU DOING?
I'M CELEBRATING...
...OBVIOUSLY.
PA (FLICK)
....
....
....
DID YOU NOT HEAR WHAT I SAI—
IT'S EXACTLY BECAUSE YOU DON'T OVERWRITE THEM...
...THAT YOU CAN'T LET GO OF THE BAD MEMORIES.
DID MIZUKI TELL HER ...?
I DON'T KNOW WHAT HAPPENED BEFORE...

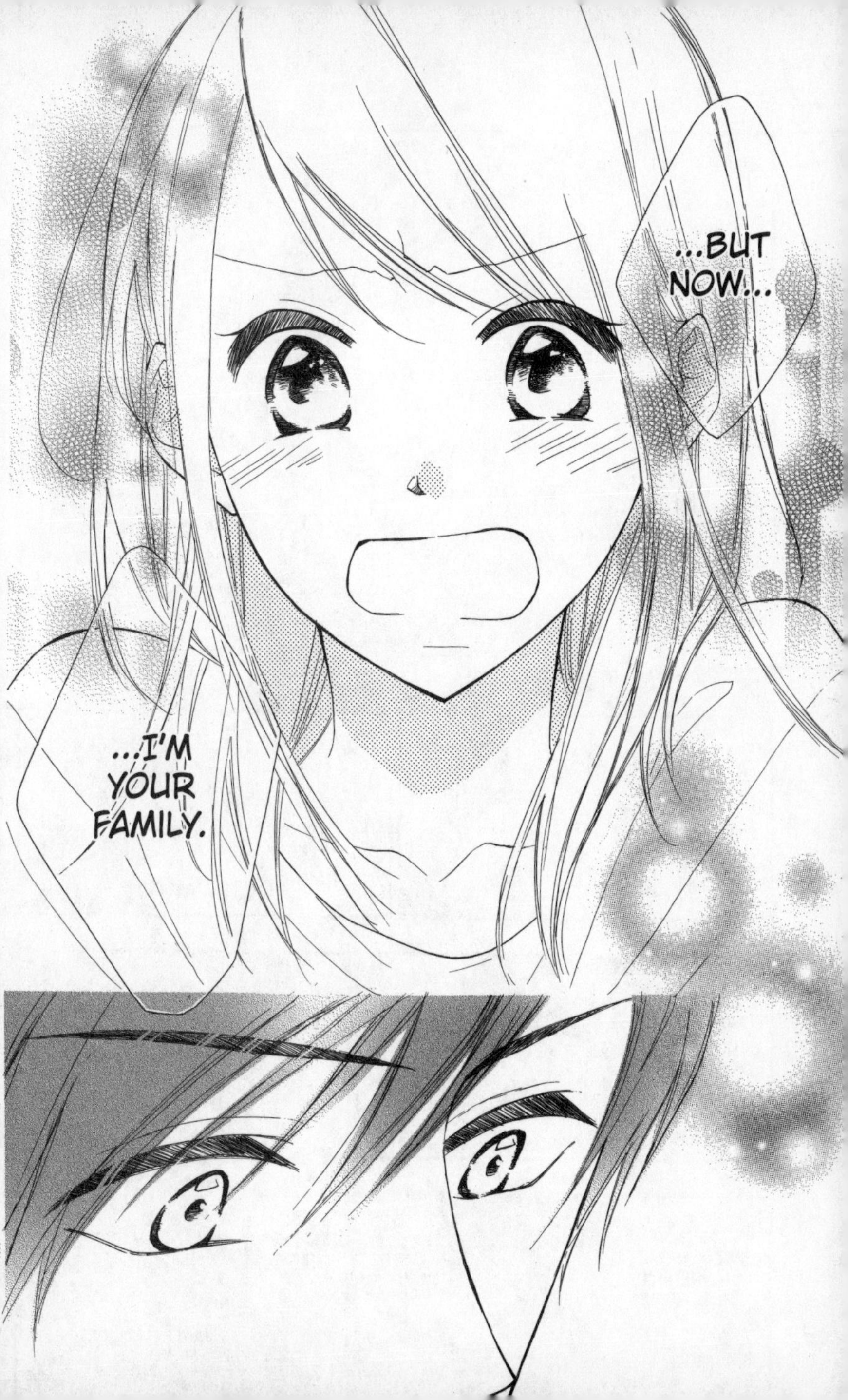
...BUT NOW...
...I'M YOUR FAMILY.

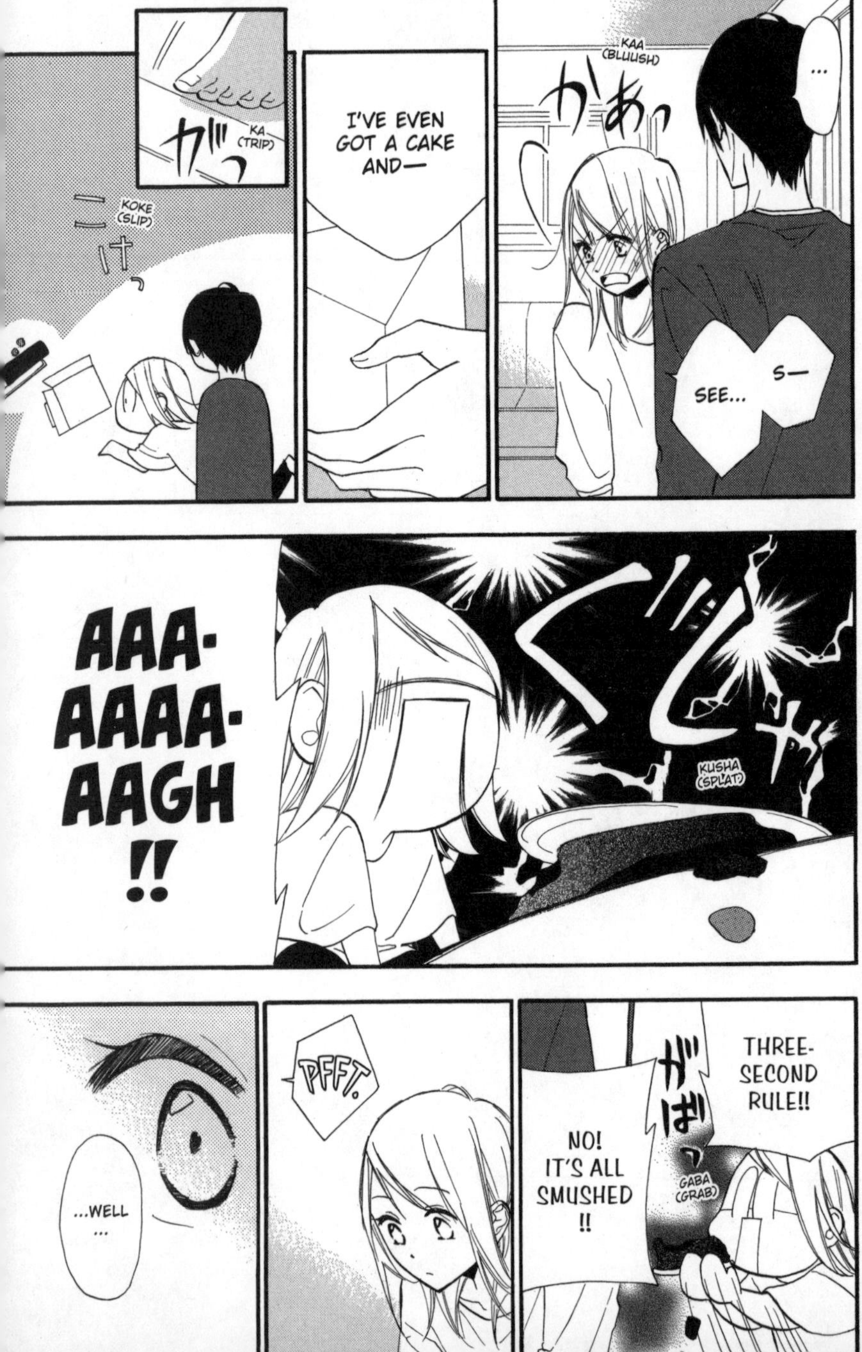
...
S—
SEE...
KAA (BLUUSH)
I'VE EVEN GOT A CAKE AND—
KA (TRIP)
KOKE (SLIP)
KUSHA (SPLAT)
AAA-AAAA-AAGH!!
THREE-SECOND RULE!!
GABA (GRAB)
NO! IT'S ALL SMUSHED !!
PFFT.
...WELL ...

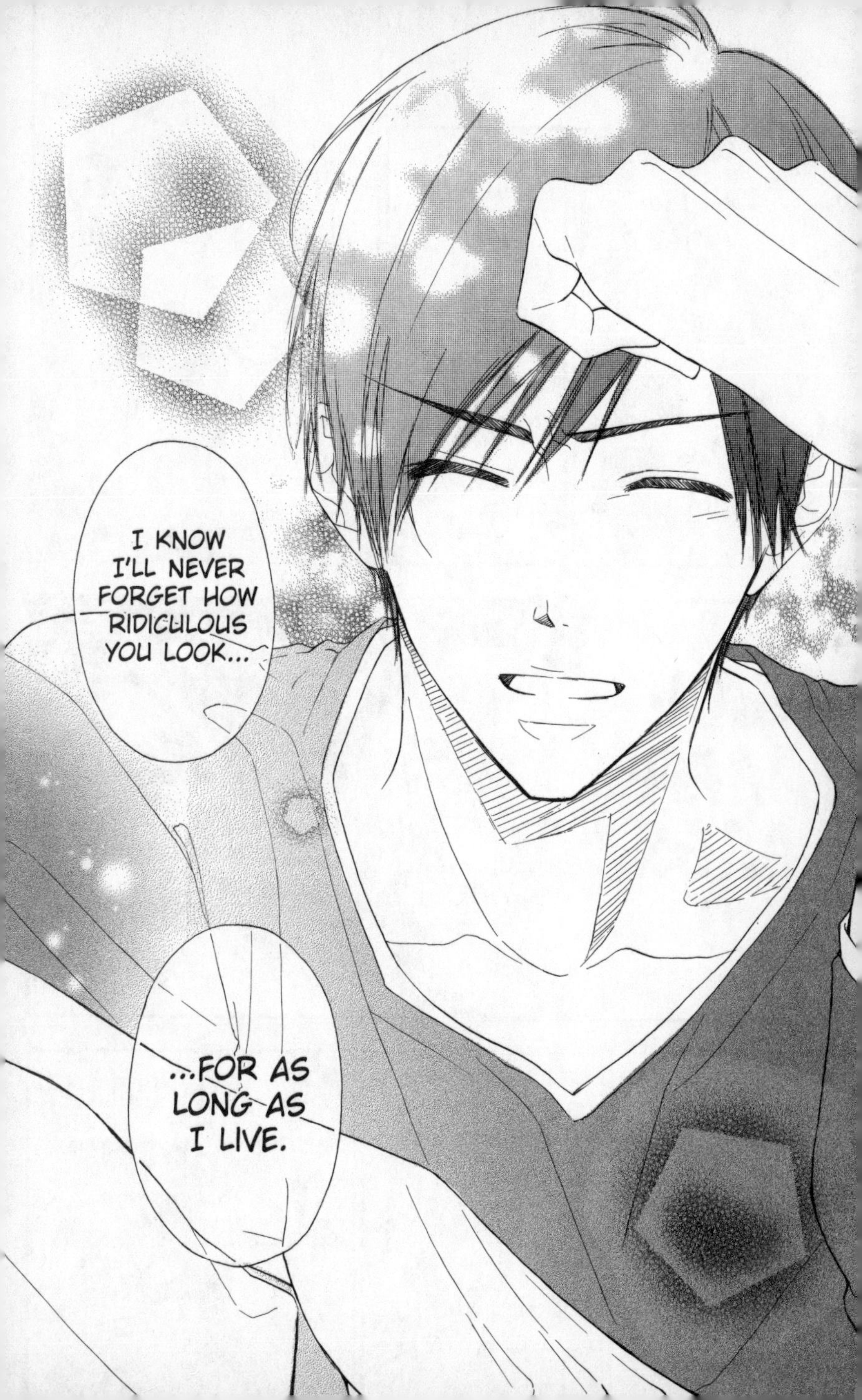
I KNOW I'LL NEVER FORGET HOW RIDICULOUS YOU LOOK...
...FOR AS LONG AS I LIVE.

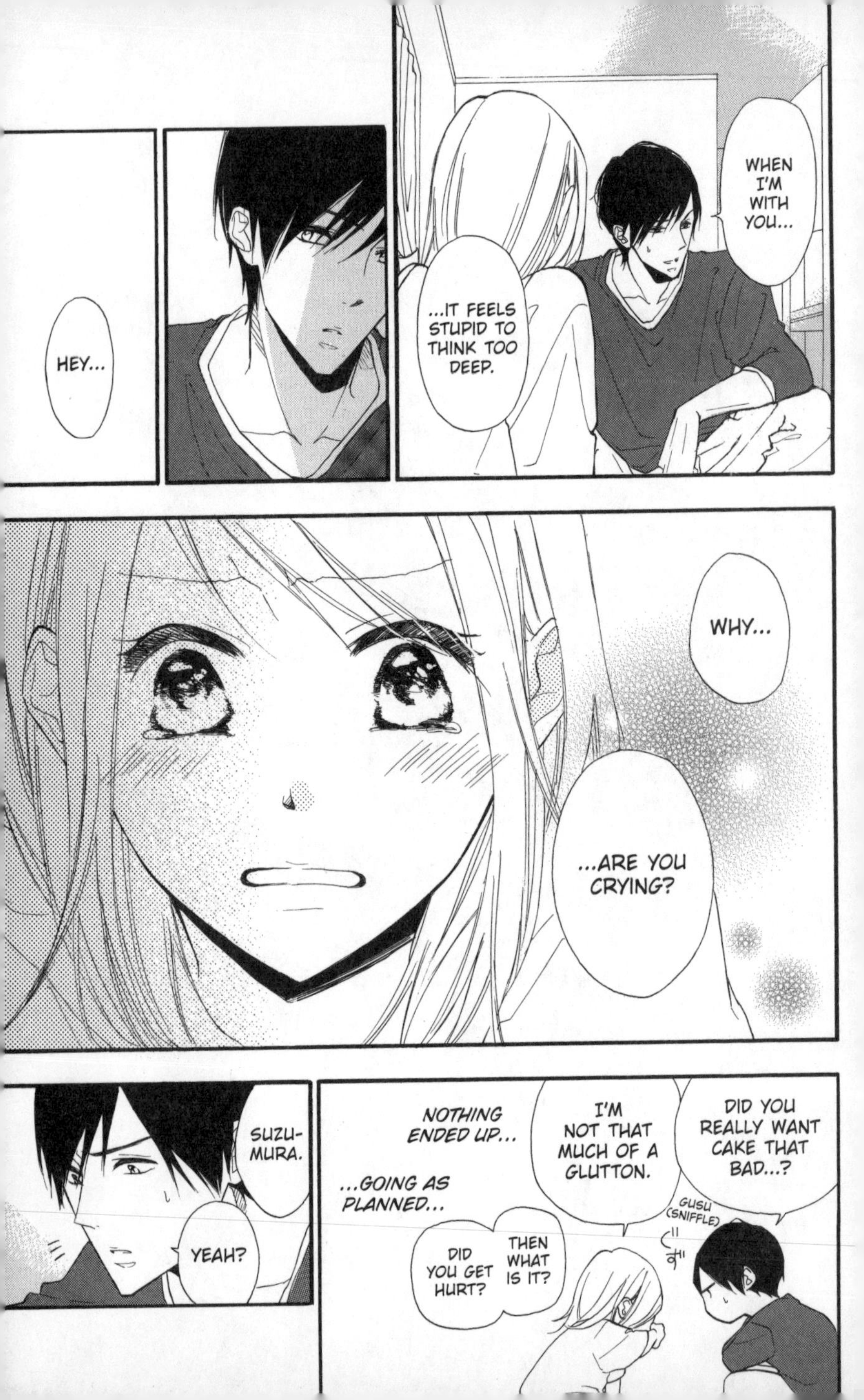
WHEN I'M WITH YOU...
...IT FEELS STUPID TO THINK TOO DEEP.
HEY...
WHY...
...ARE YOU CRYING?
DID YOU REALLY WANT CAKE THAT BAD...?
I'M NOT THAT MUCH OF A GLUTTON.
NOTHING ENDED UP...
...GOING AS PLANNED...
GUSU (SNIFFLE)
THEN WHAT IS IT?
DID YOU GET HURT?
SUZU-MURA.
YEAH?

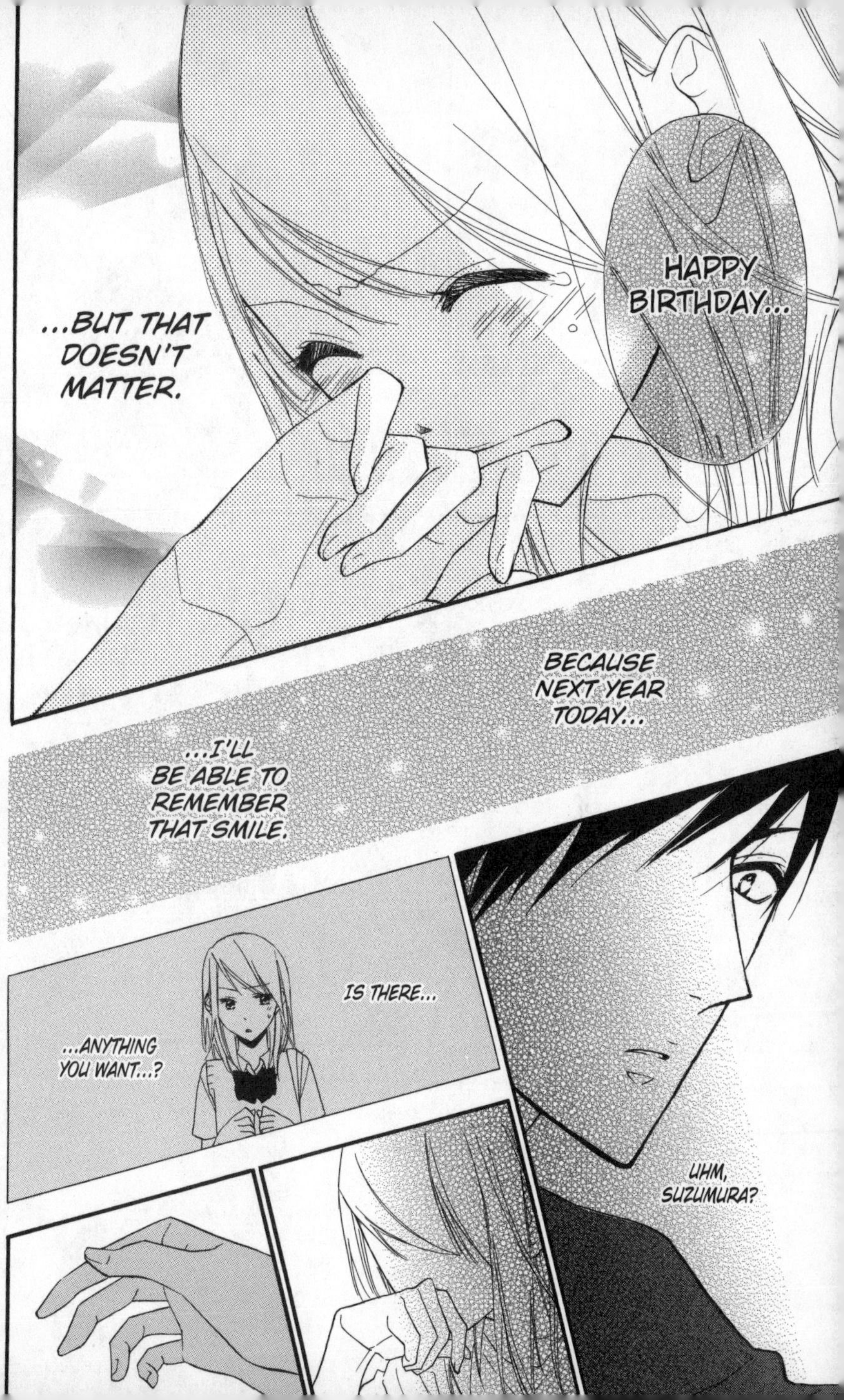
HAPPY BIRTHDAY...
...BUT THAT DOESN'T MATTER.
BECAUSE NEXT YEAR TODAY...
...I'LL BE ABLE TO REMEMBER THAT SMILE.
IS THERE...
...ANYTHING YOU WANT...?
UHM, SUZUMURA?

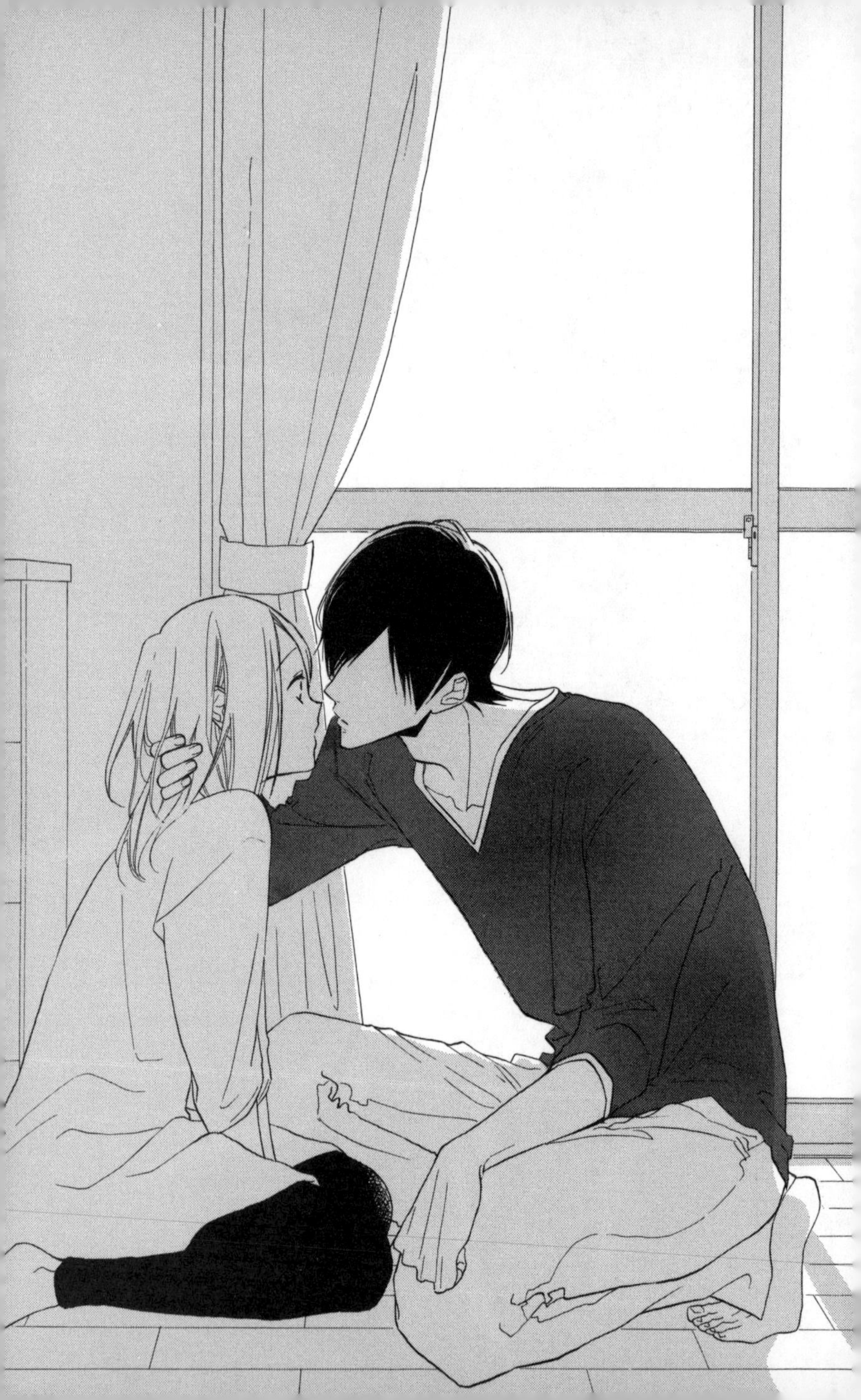

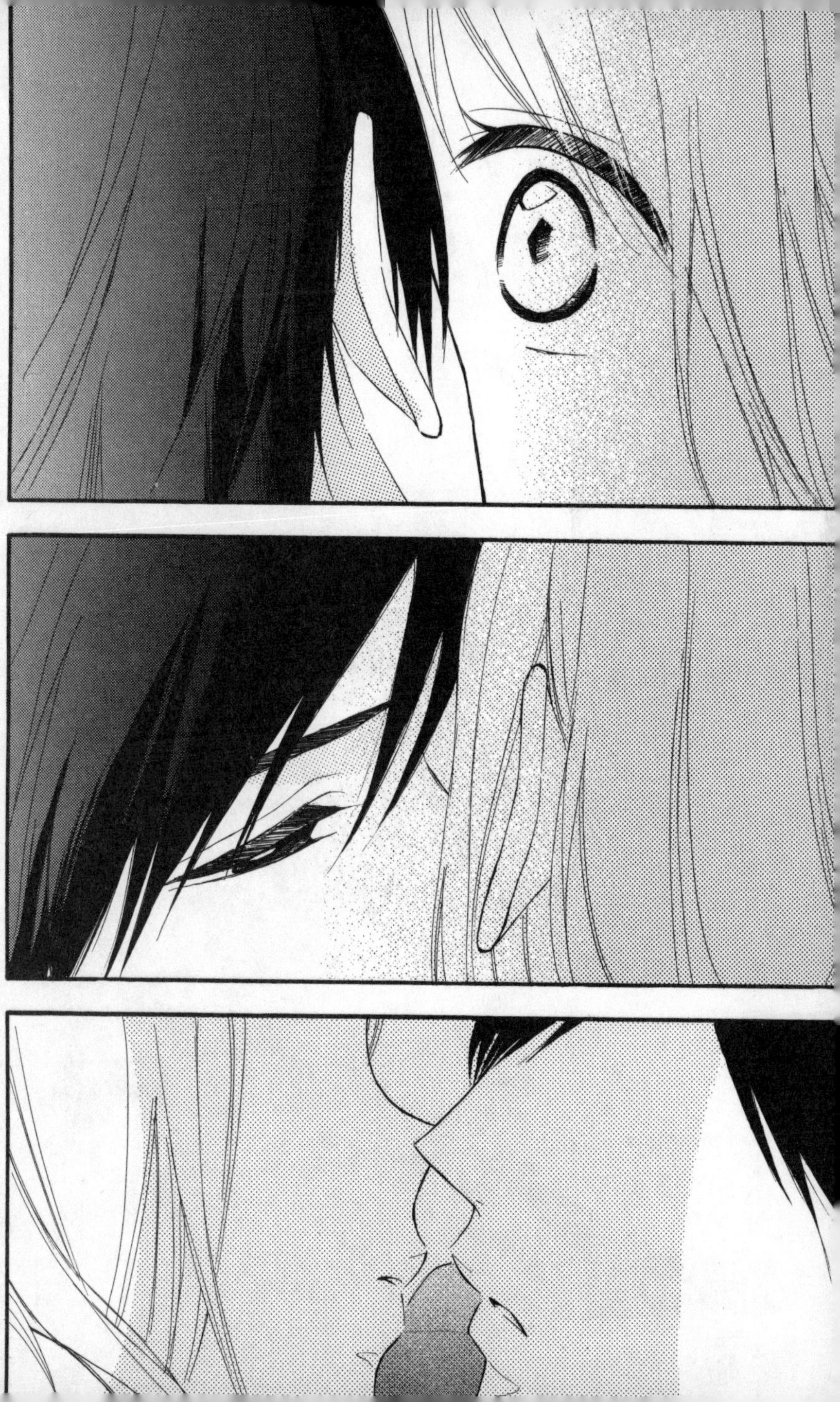

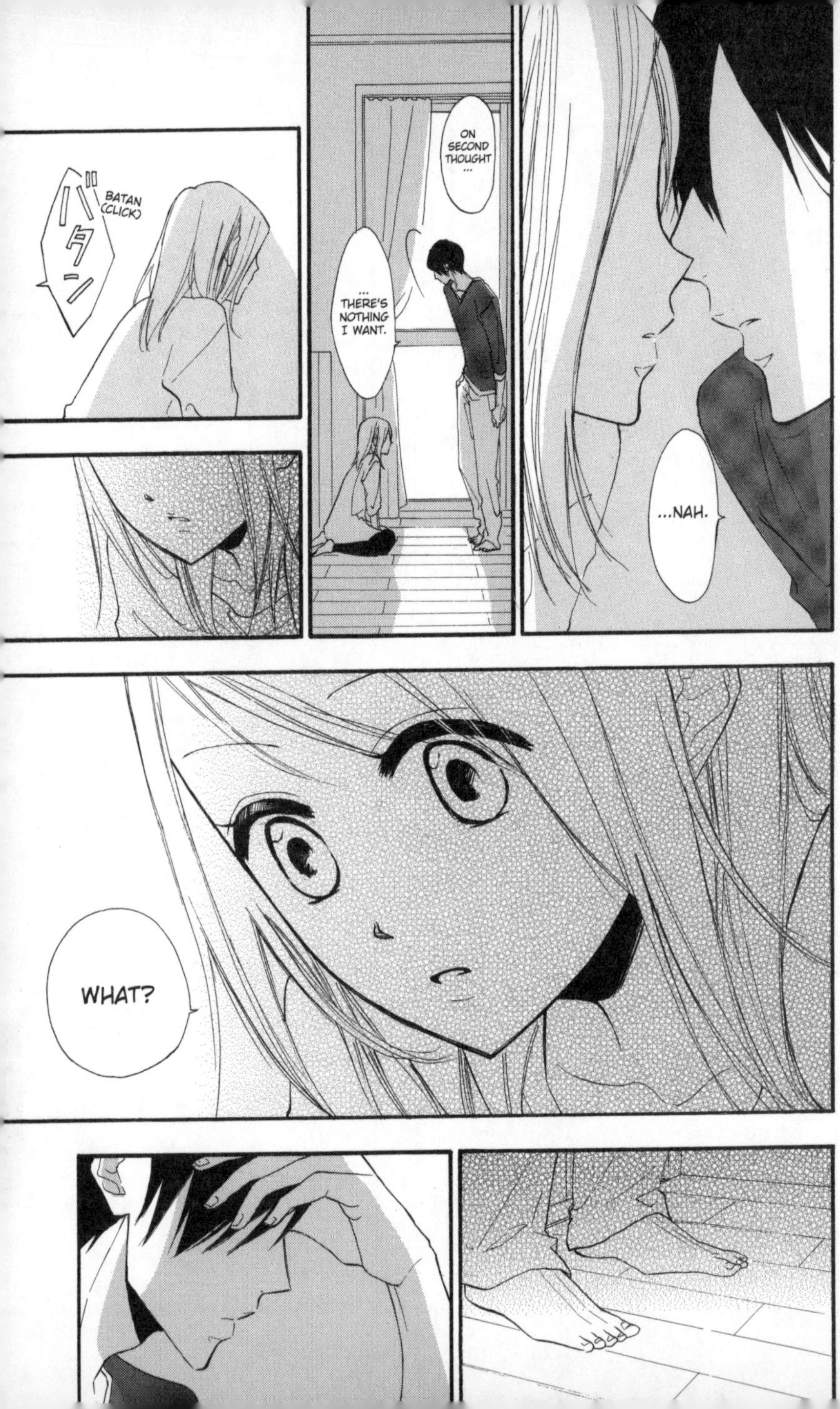
...NAH.
ON SECOND THOUGHT...
...THERE'S NOTHING I WANT.
バタン
BATAN (CLICK)
WHAT?

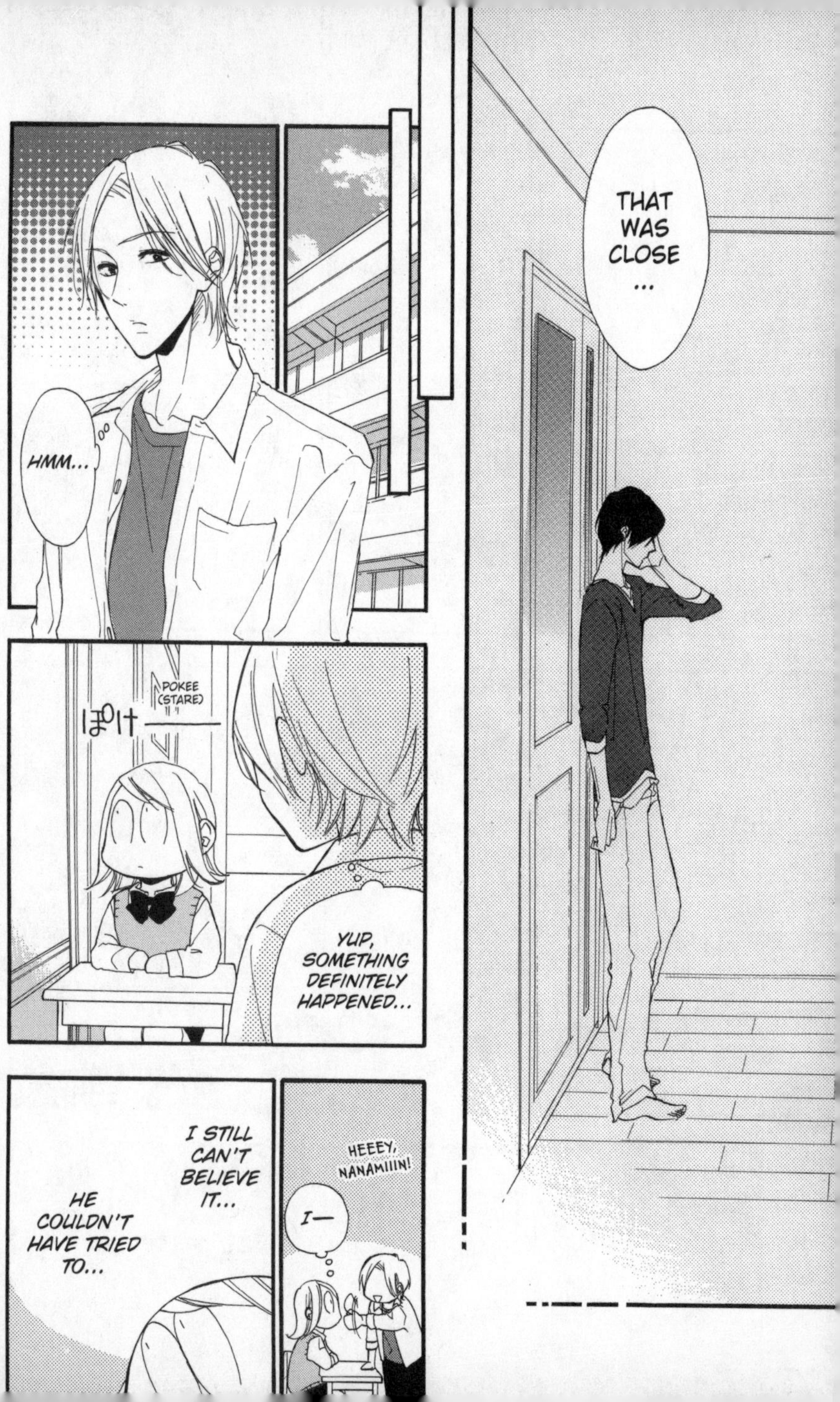
THAT WAS CLOSE ...
HMM...
ぽけ──
POKEE (STARE)
YUP, SOMETHING DEFINITELY HAPPENED...
HEEEY, NANAMIIIN!
I—
I STILL CAN'T BELIEVE IT...
HE COULDN'T HAVE TRIED TO...

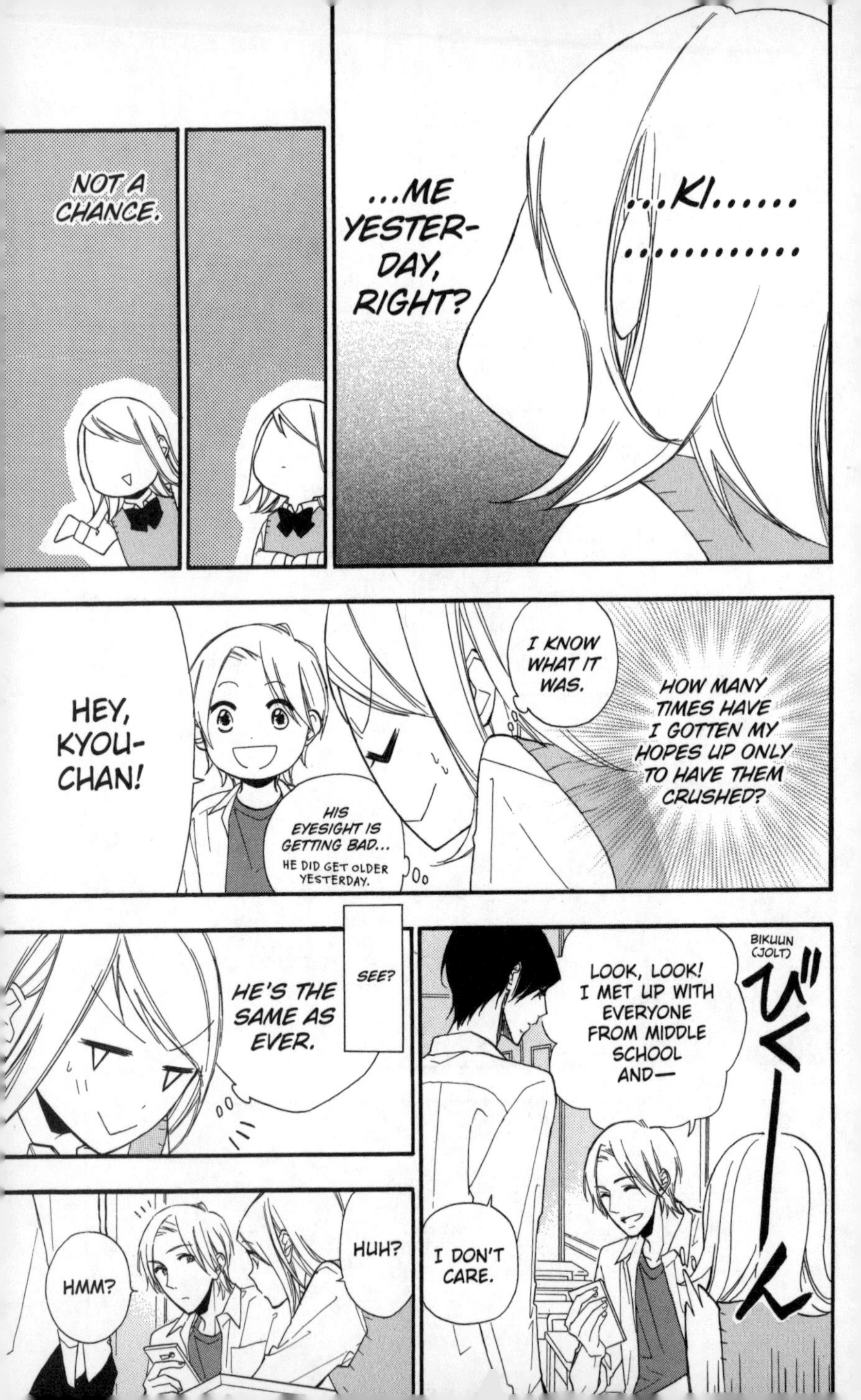
...KI......
....
...ME YESTER-DAY, RIGHT?
NOT A CHANCE.
HOW MANY TIMES HAVE I GOTTEN MY HOPES UP ONLY TO HAVE THEM CRUSHED?
I KNOW WHAT IT WAS.
HIS EYESIGHT IS GETTING BAD...
HE DID GET OLDER YESTERDAY.
HEY, KYOU-CHAN!
BIKUUN (JOLT)
びくーん
LOOK, LOOK! I MET UP WITH EVERYONE FROM MIDDLE SCHOOL AND—
I DON'T CARE.
SEE?
HE'S THE SAME AS EVER.
HUH?
HMM?

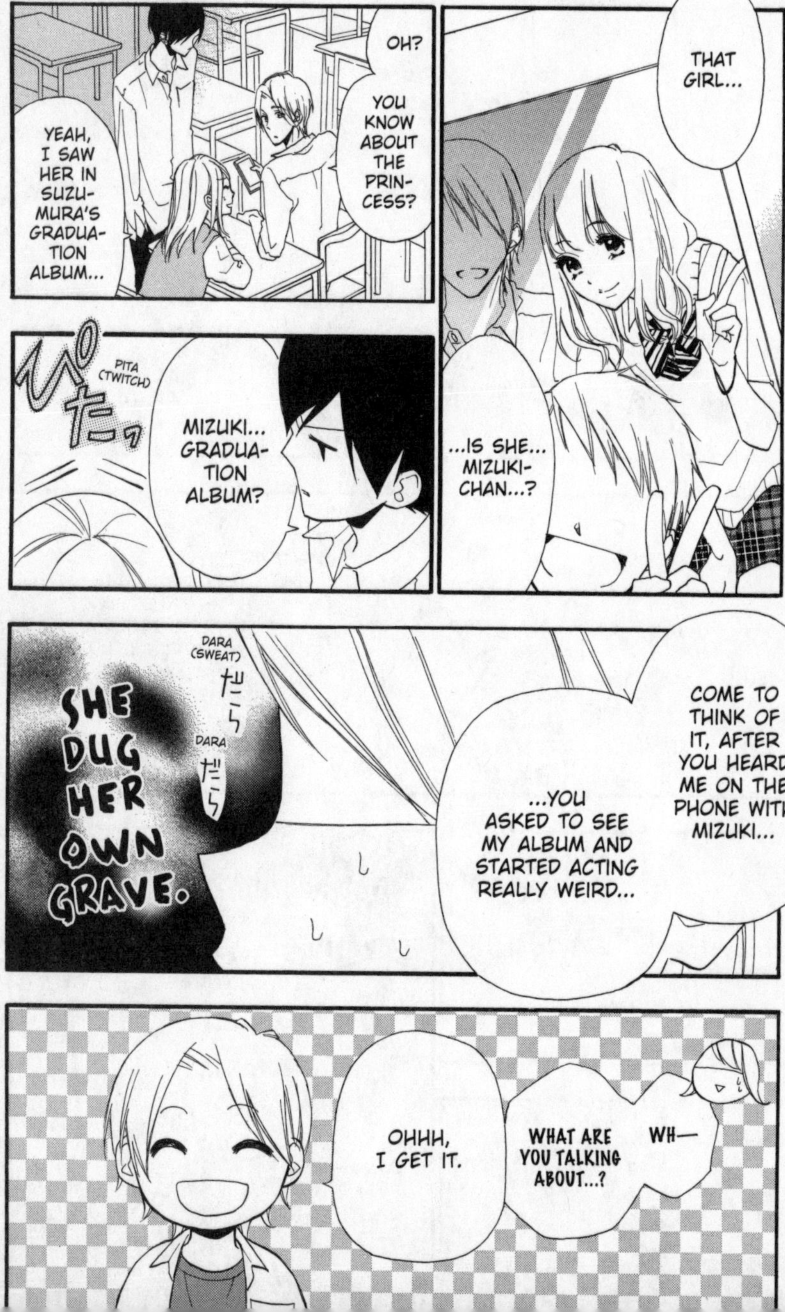
THAT GIRL...
...IS SHE... MIZUKI-CHAN...?
OH?
YOU KNOW ABOUT THE PRIN-CESS?
YEAH, I SAW HER IN SUZU-MURA'S GRADUA-TION ALBUM...
ぴたっ
PITA (TWITCH)
MIZUKI... GRADUA-TION ALBUM?
COME TO THINK OF IT, AFTER YOU HEARD ME ON THE PHONE WITH MIZUKI...
...YOU ASKED TO SEE MY ALBUM AND STARTED ACTING REALLY WEIRD...
だら
DARA (SWEAT)
だら
DARA
SHE DUG HER OWN GRAVE.
WH—
WHAT ARE YOU TALKING ABOUT...?
OHHH, I GET IT.

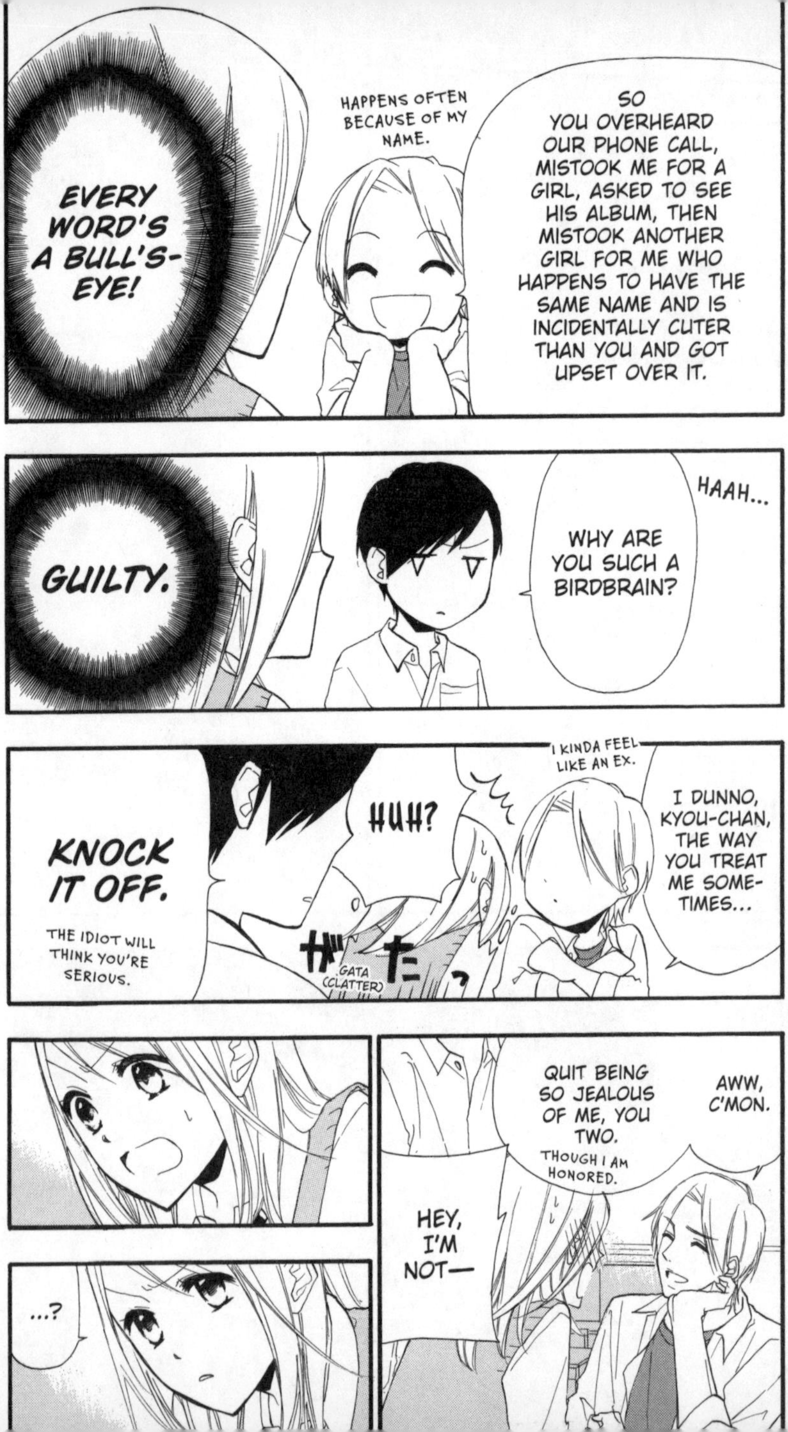
SO YOU OVERHEARD OUR PHONE CALL, MISTOOK ME FOR A GIRL, ASKED TO SEE HIS ALBUM, THEN MISTOOK ANOTHER GIRL FOR ME WHO HAPPENS TO HAVE THE SAME NAME AND IS INCIDENTALLY CUTER THAN YOU AND GOT UPSET OVER IT.
HAPPENS OFTEN BECAUSE OF MY NAME.
EVERY WORD'S A BULL'S-EYE!
HAAH...
WHY ARE YOU SUCH A BIRDBRAIN?
GUILTY.
I DUNNO, KYOU-CHAN, THE WAY YOU TREAT ME SOME-TIMES...
I KINDA FEEL LIKE AN EX.
HUH?
GATA (CLATTER)
KNOCK IT OFF.
THE IDIOT WILL THINK YOU'RE SERIOUS.
AWW, C'MON.
QUIT BEING SO JEALOUS OF ME, YOU TWO.
THOUGH I AM HONORED.
HEY, I'M NOT—
...?

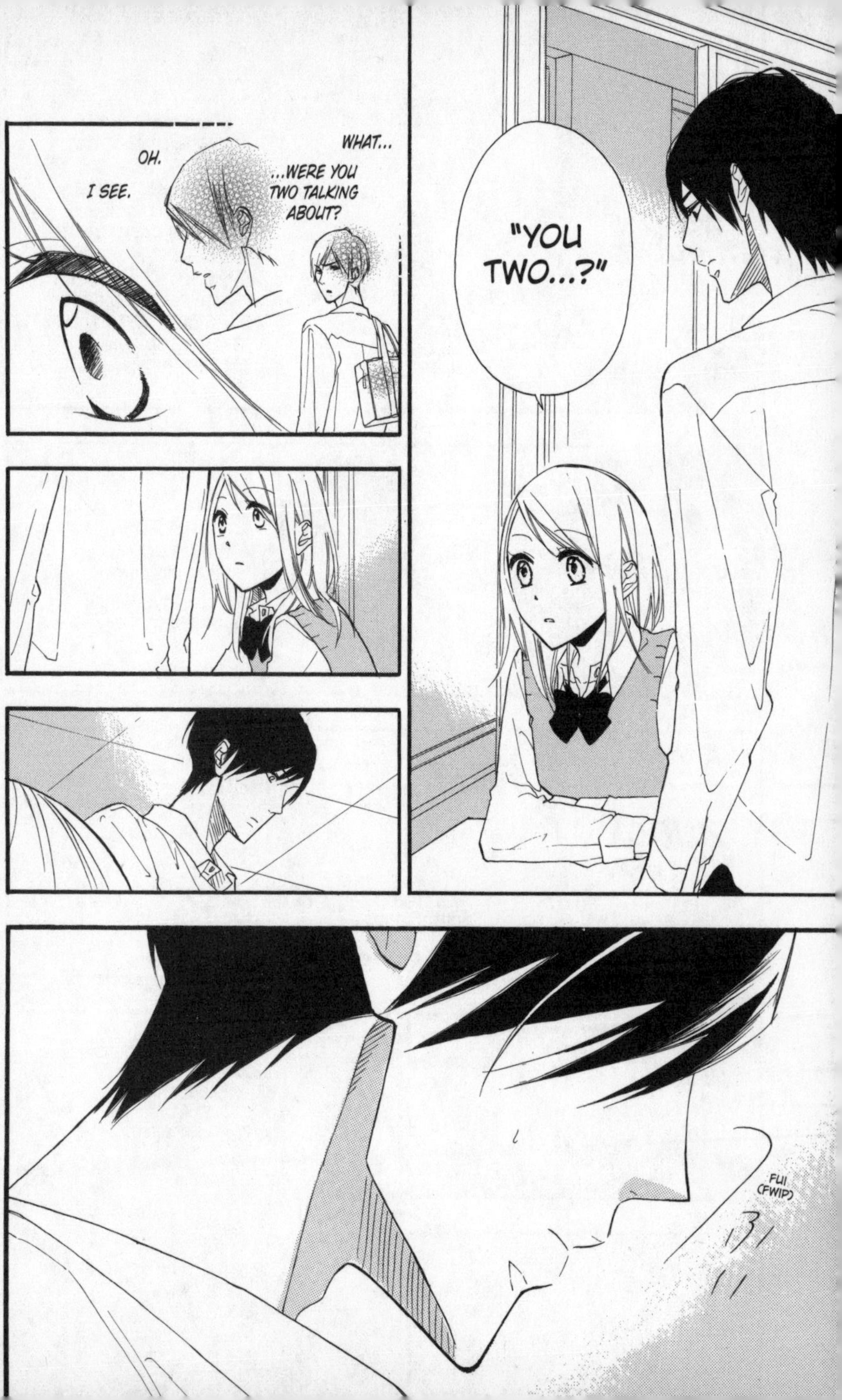
"YOU TWO...?"
WHAT...
...WERE YOU TWO TALKING ABOUT?
OH.
I SEE.
FUI (FWIP)

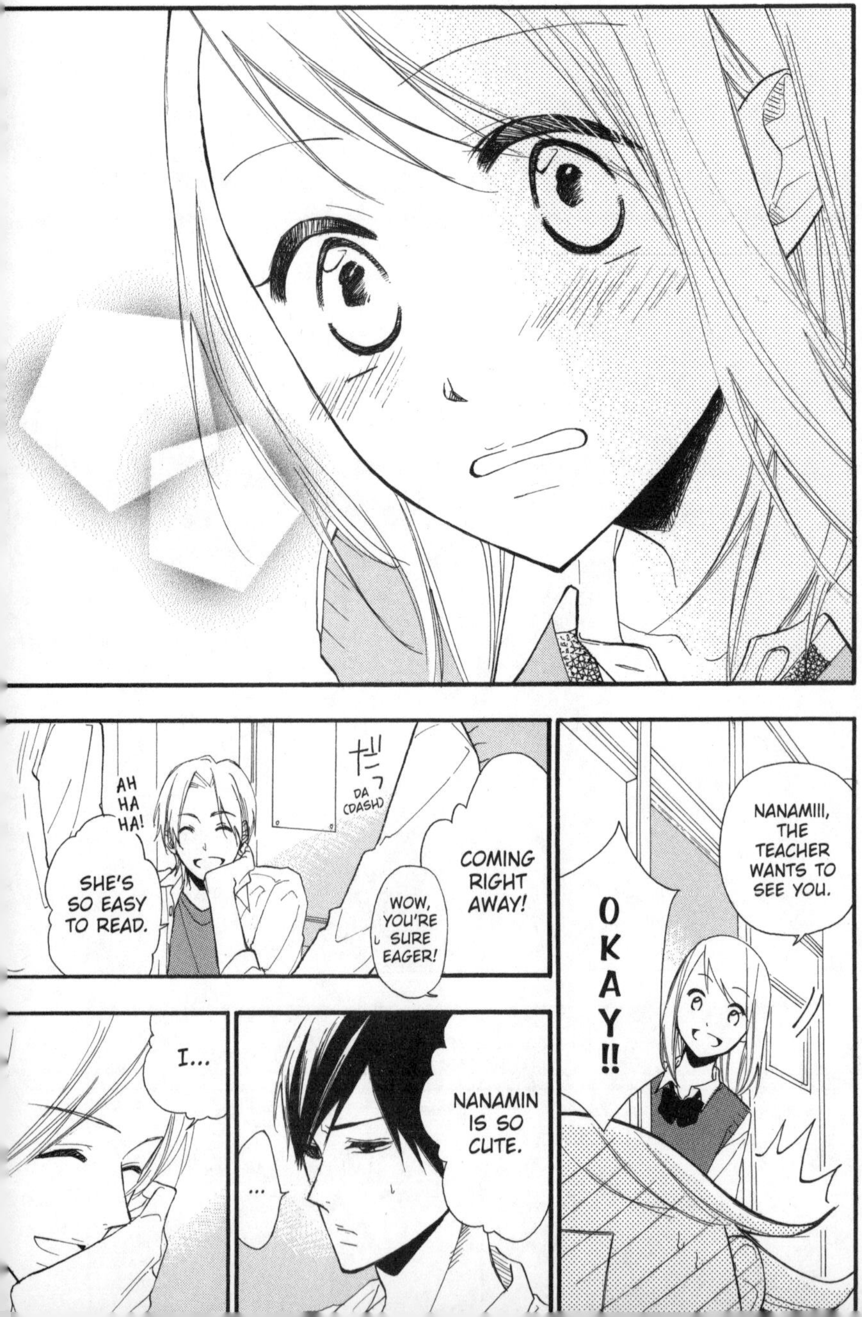
NANAMIII, THE TEACHER WANTS TO SEE YOU.
OKAY!!
COMING RIGHT AWAY!
WOW, YOU'RE SURE EAGER!
だっ
DA (DASH)
AH HA HA!
SHE'S SO EASY TO READ.
NANAMIN IS SO CUTE.
...
I...

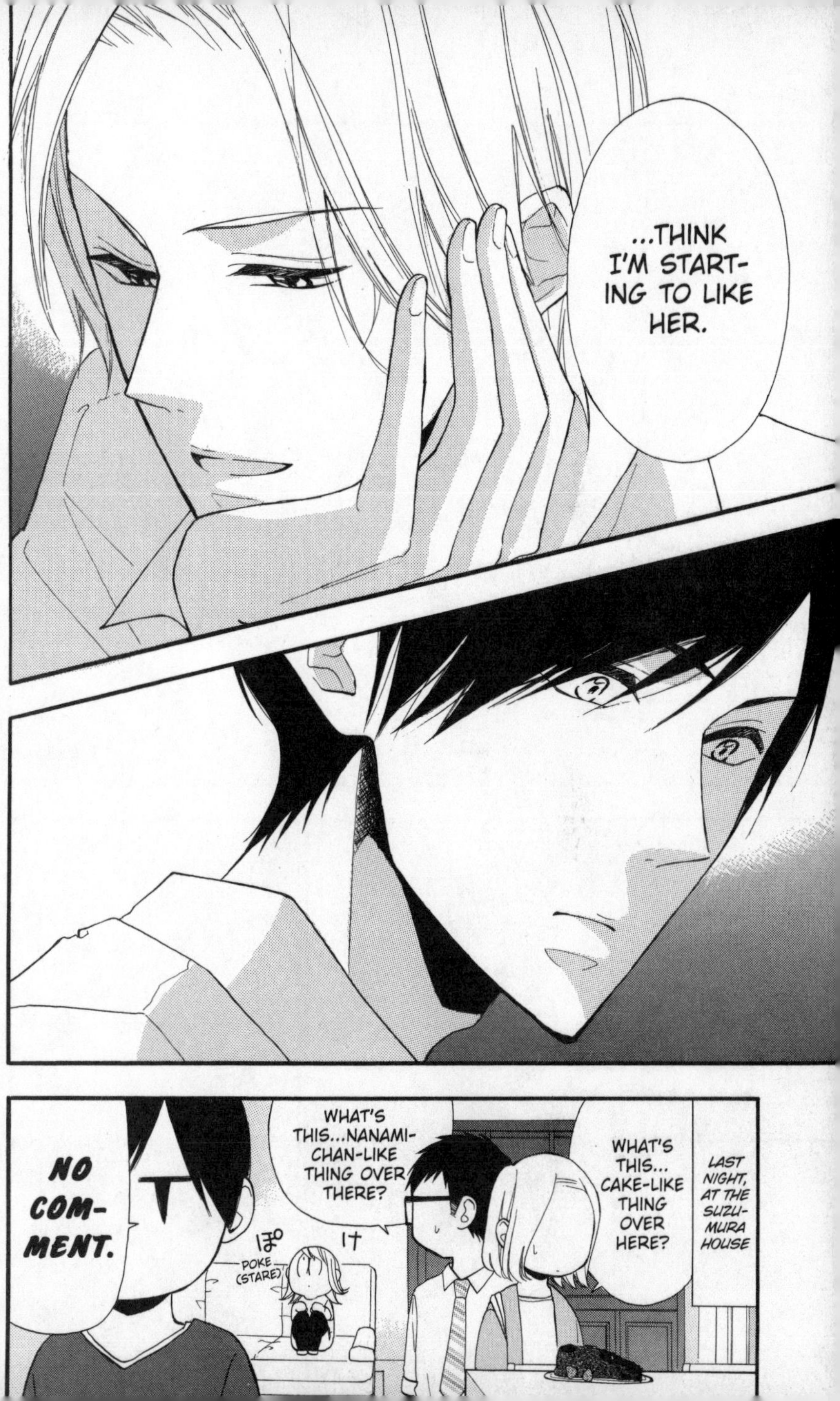
...THINK I'M START-ING TO LIKE HER.
LAST NIGHT, AT THE SUZU-MURA HOUSE
WHAT'S THIS... CAKE-LIKE THING OVER HERE?
WHAT'S THIS...NANAMI-CHAN-LIKE THING OVER THERE?
ぽけ
POKE (STARE)
NO COM-MENT.

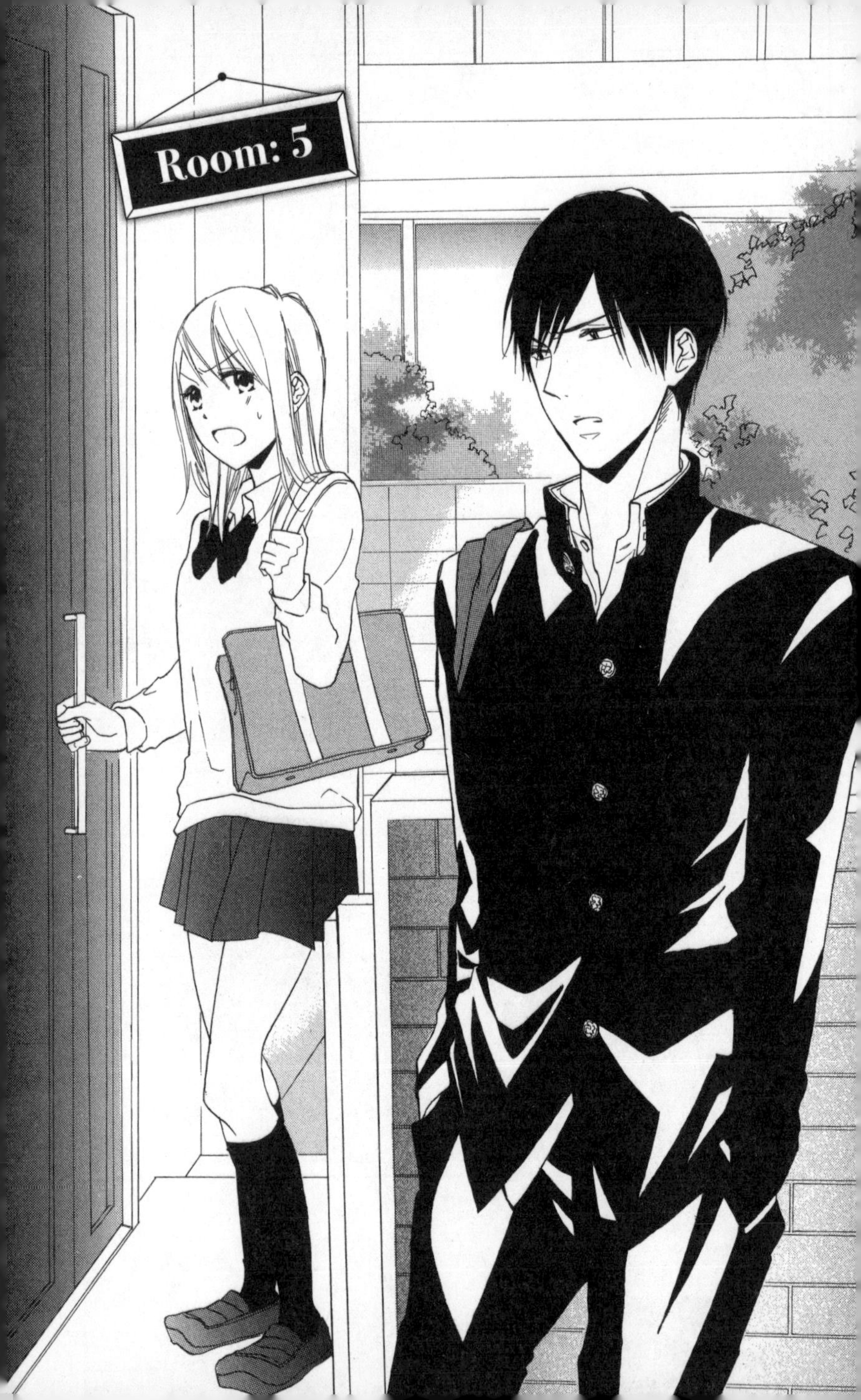
Room: 5

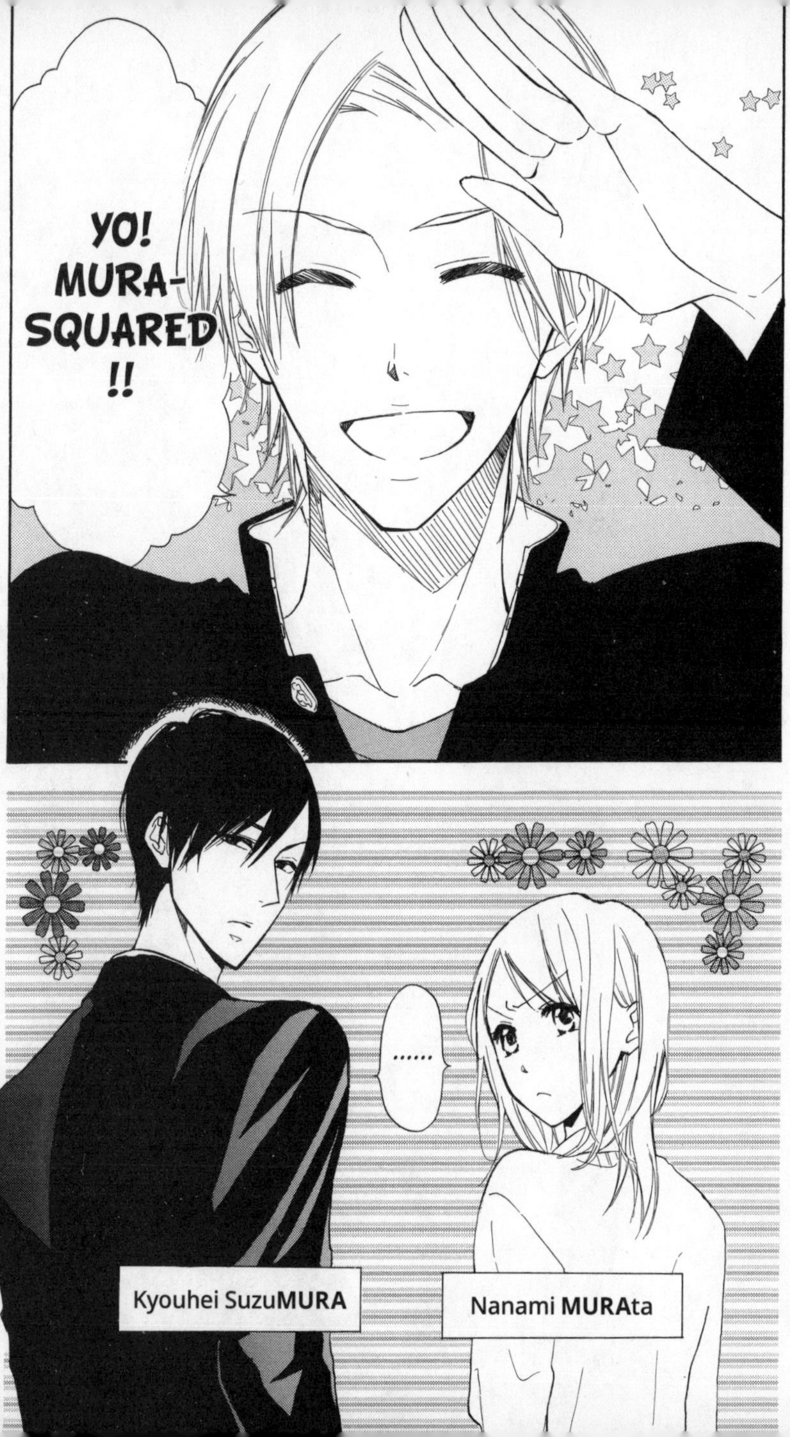
YO! MURA-SQUARED!!
......
Nanami MURAta
Kyouhei SuzuMURA

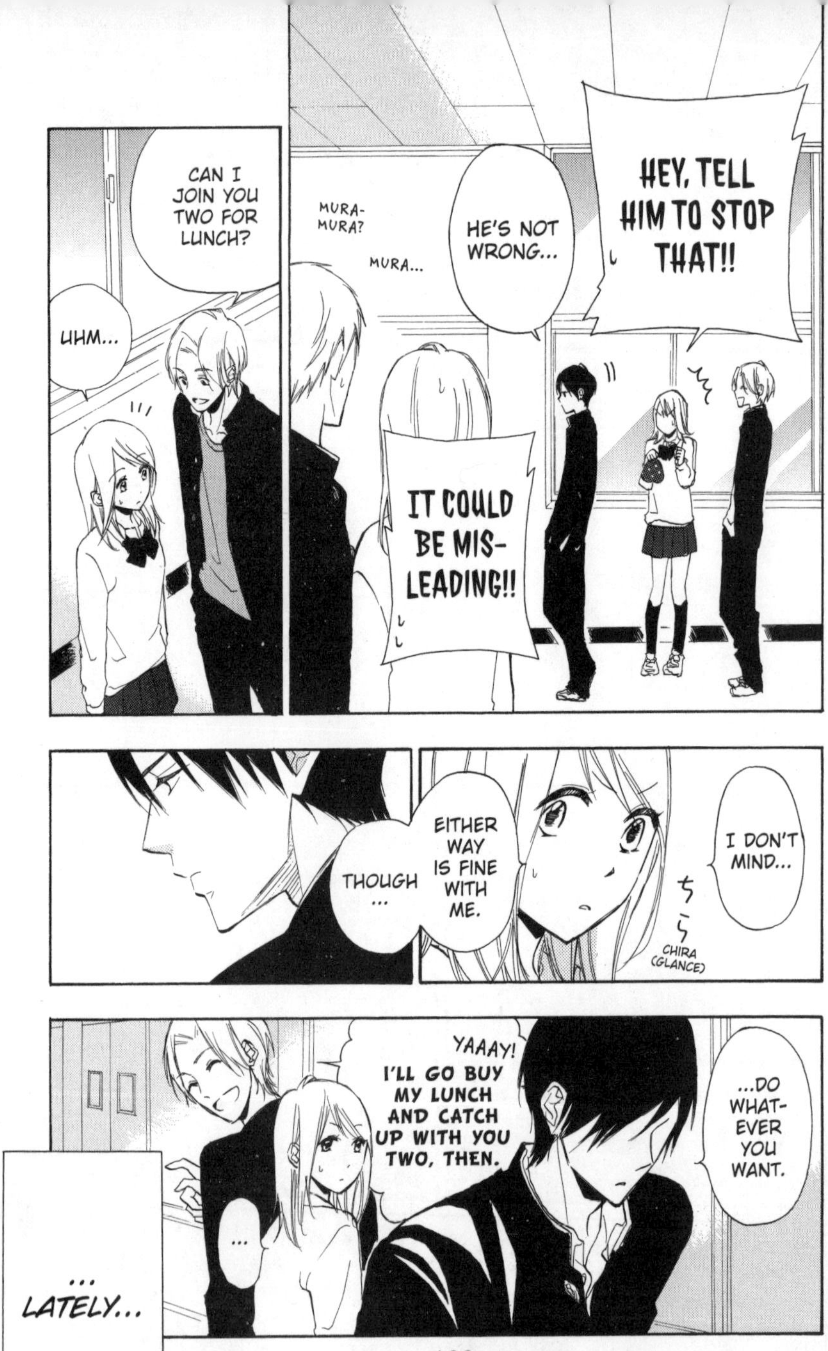
HEY, TELL HIM TO STOP THAT!!
HE'S NOT WRONG...
MURA-MURA?
MURA...
IT COULD BE MIS-LEADING!!
CAN I JOIN YOU TWO FOR LUNCH?
UHM...
I DON'T MIND...
ちら
CHIRA (GLANCE)
EITHER WAY IS FINE WITH ME.
THOUGH...
...DO WHAT-EVER YOU WANT.
YAAAY! I'LL GO BUY MY LUNCH AND CATCH UP WITH YOU TWO, THEN.
...
... LATELY...

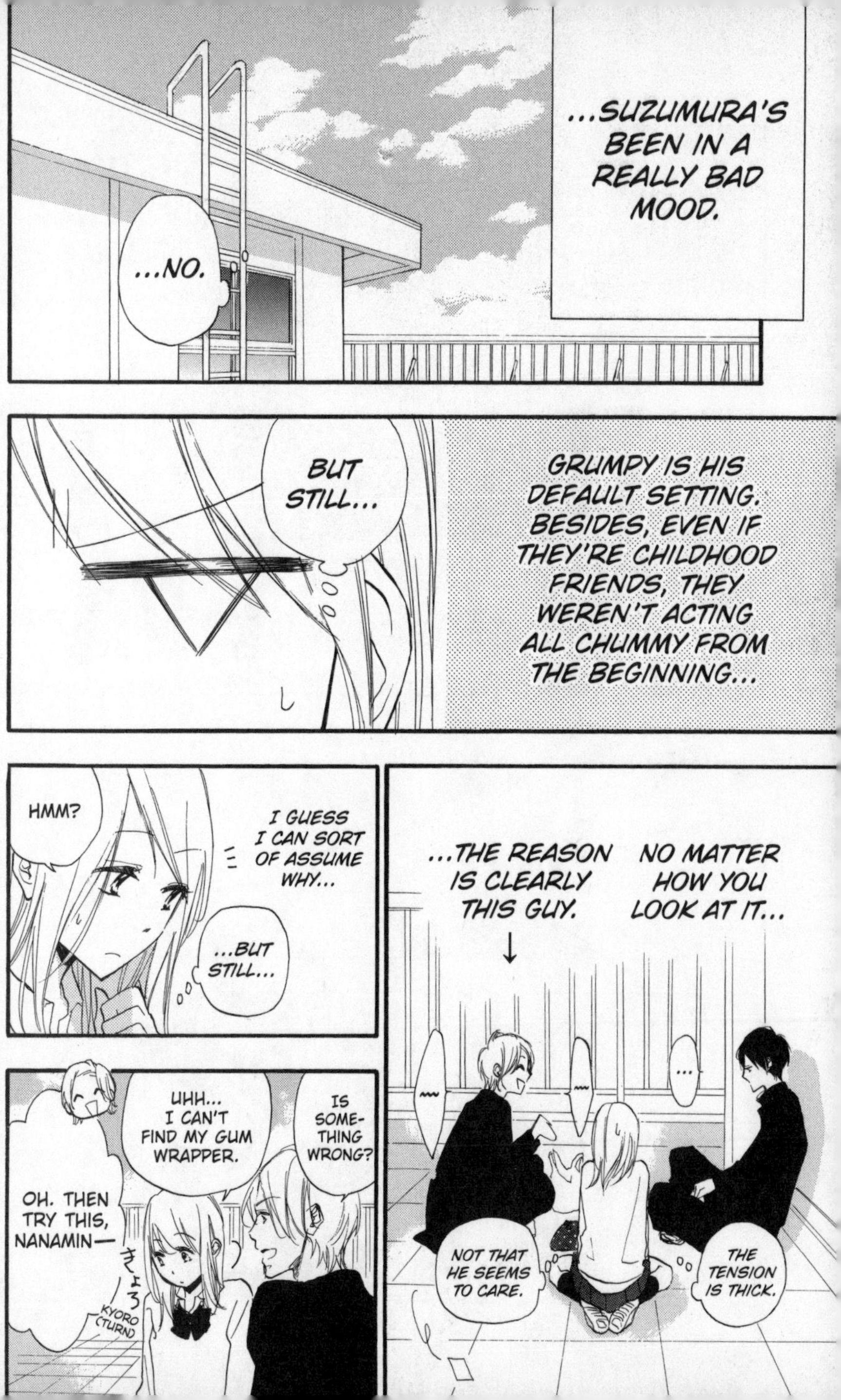
...SUZUMURA'S BEEN IN A REALLY BAD MOOD.
...NO.
GRUMPY IS HIS DEFAULT SETTING. BESIDES, EVEN IF THEY'RE CHILDHOOD FRIENDS, THEY WEREN'T ACTING ALL CHUMMY FROM THE BEGINNING...
BUT STILL...
NO MATTER HOW YOU LOOK AT IT...
...THE REASON IS CLEARLY THIS GUY.
...
THE TENSION IS THICK.
NOT THAT HE SEEMS TO CARE.
I GUESS I CAN SORT OF ASSUME WHY...
HMM?
...BUT STILL...
IS SOMETHING WRONG?
UHH... I CAN'T FIND MY GUM WRAPPER.
きょろ
KYORO (TURN)
OH. THEN TRY THIS, NANAMIN—

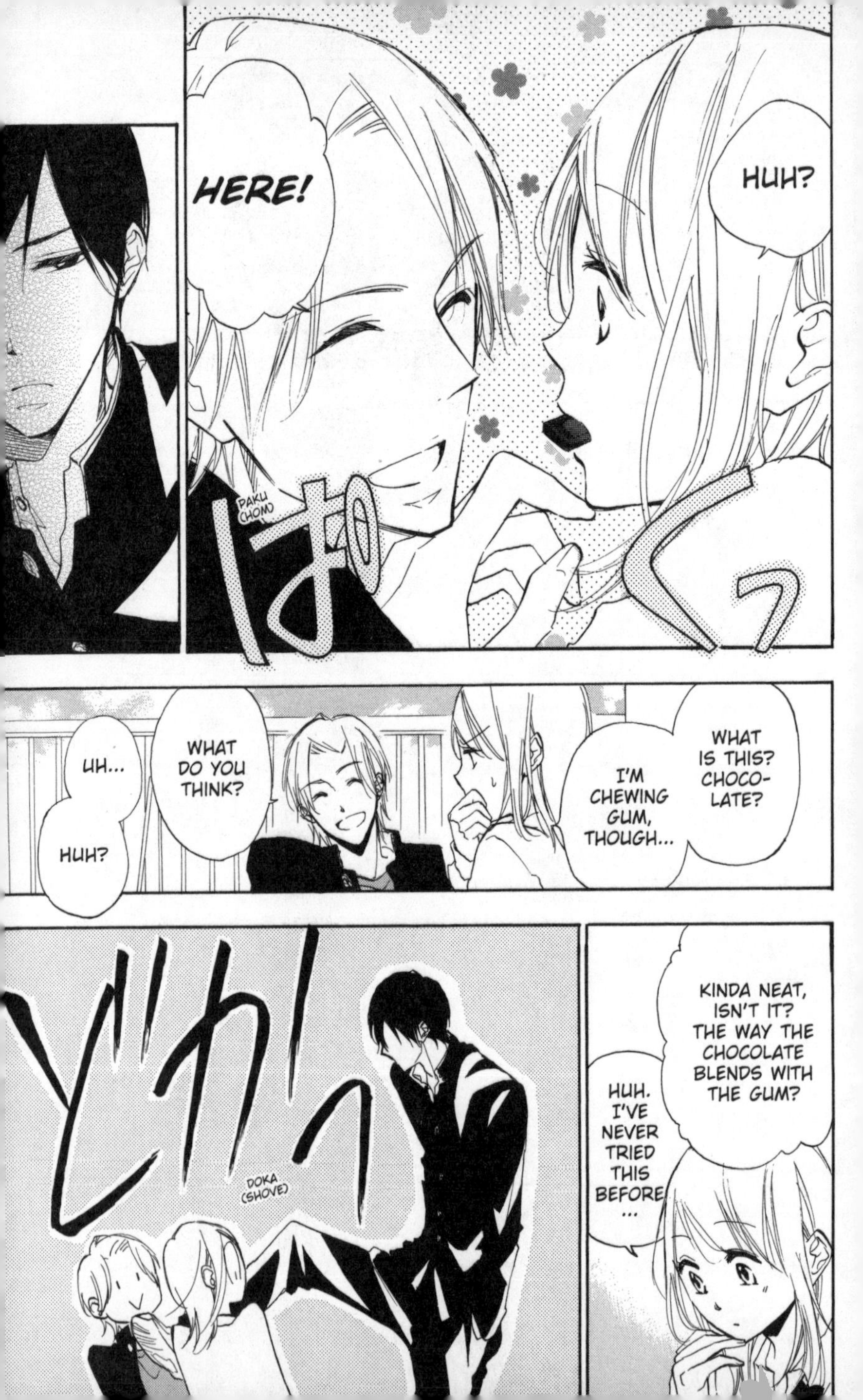
HUH?
HERE!
PAKU (CHOM)
WHAT IS THIS? CHOCO-LATE?
I'M CHEWING GUM, THOUGH...
WHAT DO YOU THINK?
UH...
HUH?
KINDA NEAT, ISN'T IT? THE WAY THE CHOCOLATE BLENDS WITH THE GUM?
HUH. I'VE NEVER TRIED THIS BEFORE...
DOKA (SHOVE)

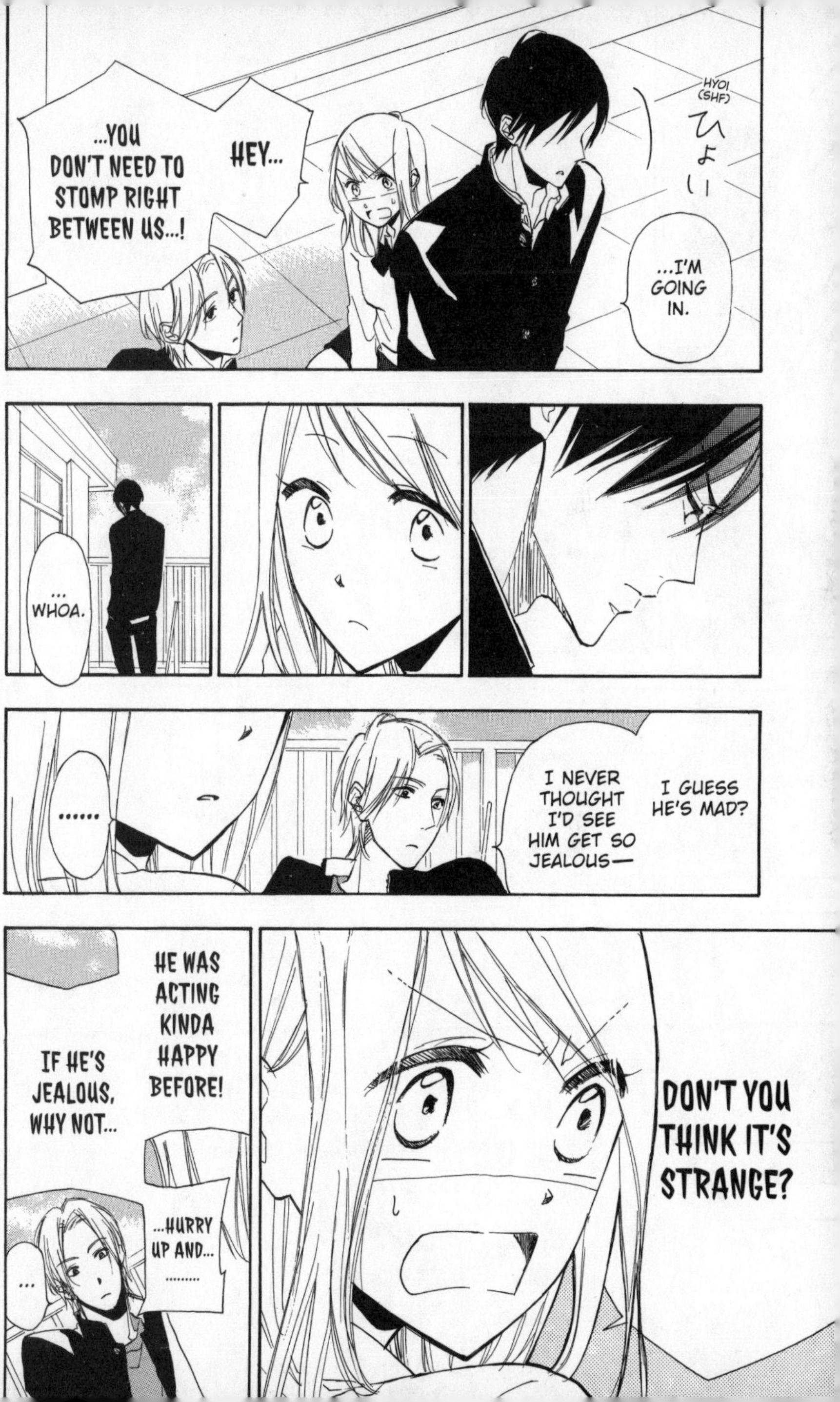
HYOI (SHF)
ひょい
...I'M GOING IN.
HEY...
...YOU DON'T NEED TO STOMP RIGHT BETWEEN US...!
... WHOA.
I GUESS HE'S MAD?
I NEVER THOUGHT I'D SEE HIM GET SO JEALOUS—
......
DON'T YOU THINK IT'S STRANGE?
HE WAS ACTING KINDA HAPPY BEFORE!
IF HE'S JEALOUS, WHY NOT...
...HURRY UP AND... ....
...

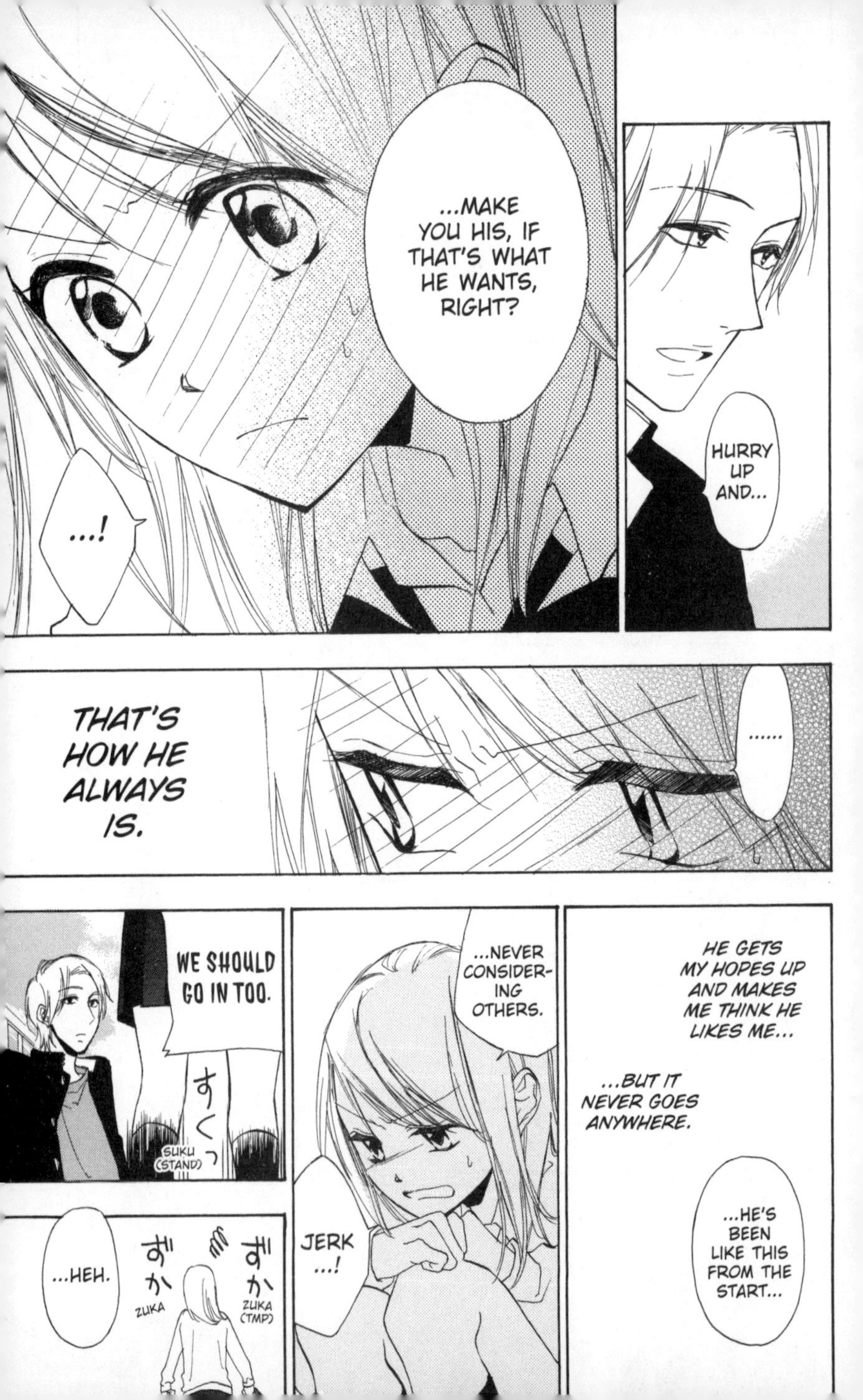
HURRY UP AND...
...MAKE YOU HIS, IF THAT'S WHAT HE WANTS, RIGHT?
...!
......
THAT'S HOW HE ALWAYS IS.
HE GETS MY HOPES UP AND MAKES ME THINK HE LIKES ME...
...BUT IT NEVER GOES ANYWHERE.
...HE'S BEEN LIKE THIS FROM THE START...
...NEVER CONSIDER-ING OTHERS.
JERK ...!
WE SHOULD GO IN TOO.
すくっ
SUKU (STAND)
ずか
ZUKA (TMP)
ずか
ZUKA
...HEH.

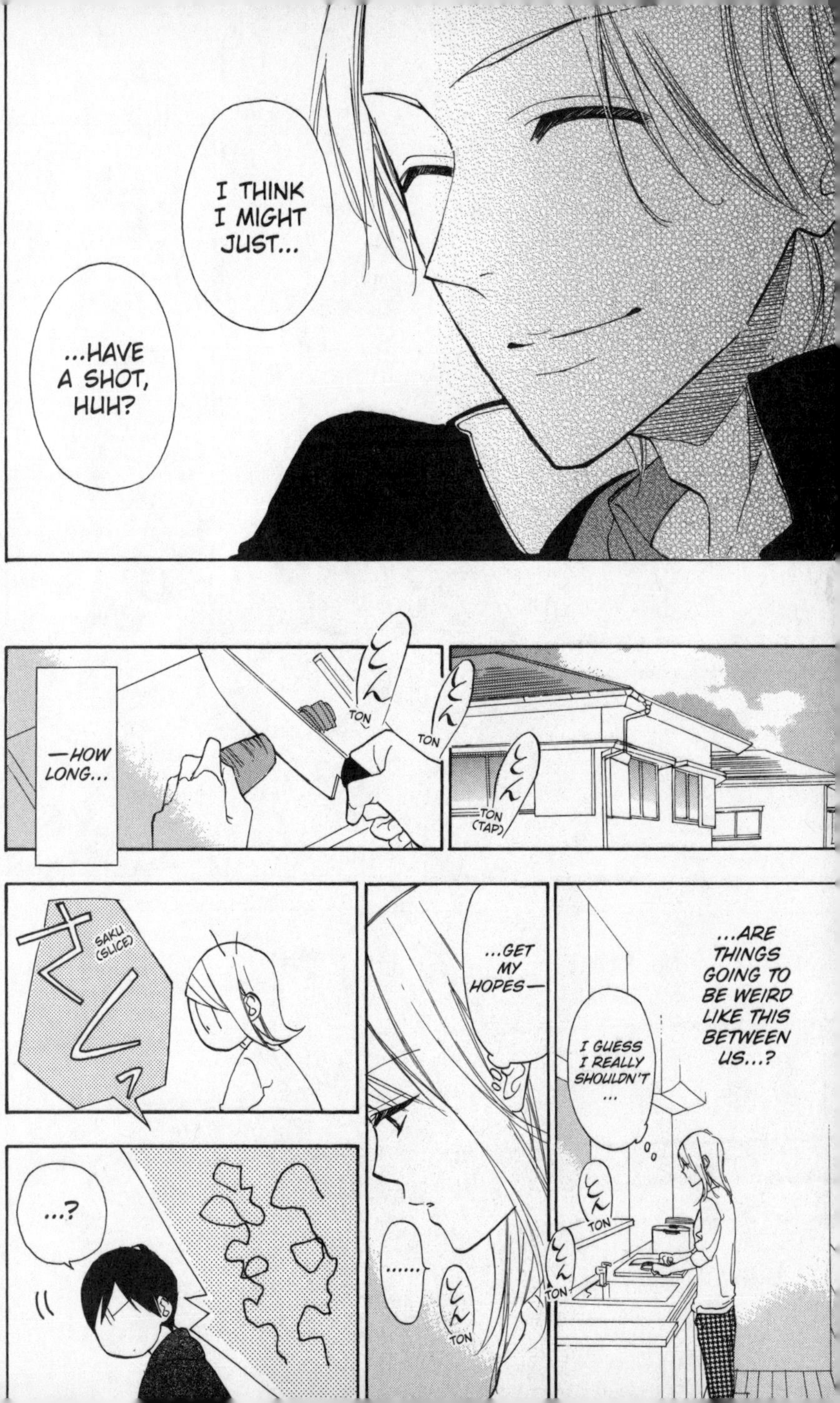
I THINK I MIGHT JUST...
...HAVE A SHOT, HUH?
とん
TON (TAP)
とん
TON
とん
TON
—HOW LONG...
...ARE THINGS GOING TO BE WEIRD LIKE THIS BETWEEN US...?
I GUESS I REALLY SHOULDN'T ...
とん
TON
とん
TON
...GET MY HOPES—
......
とん
TON
さくっ
SAKU (SLICE)
...?

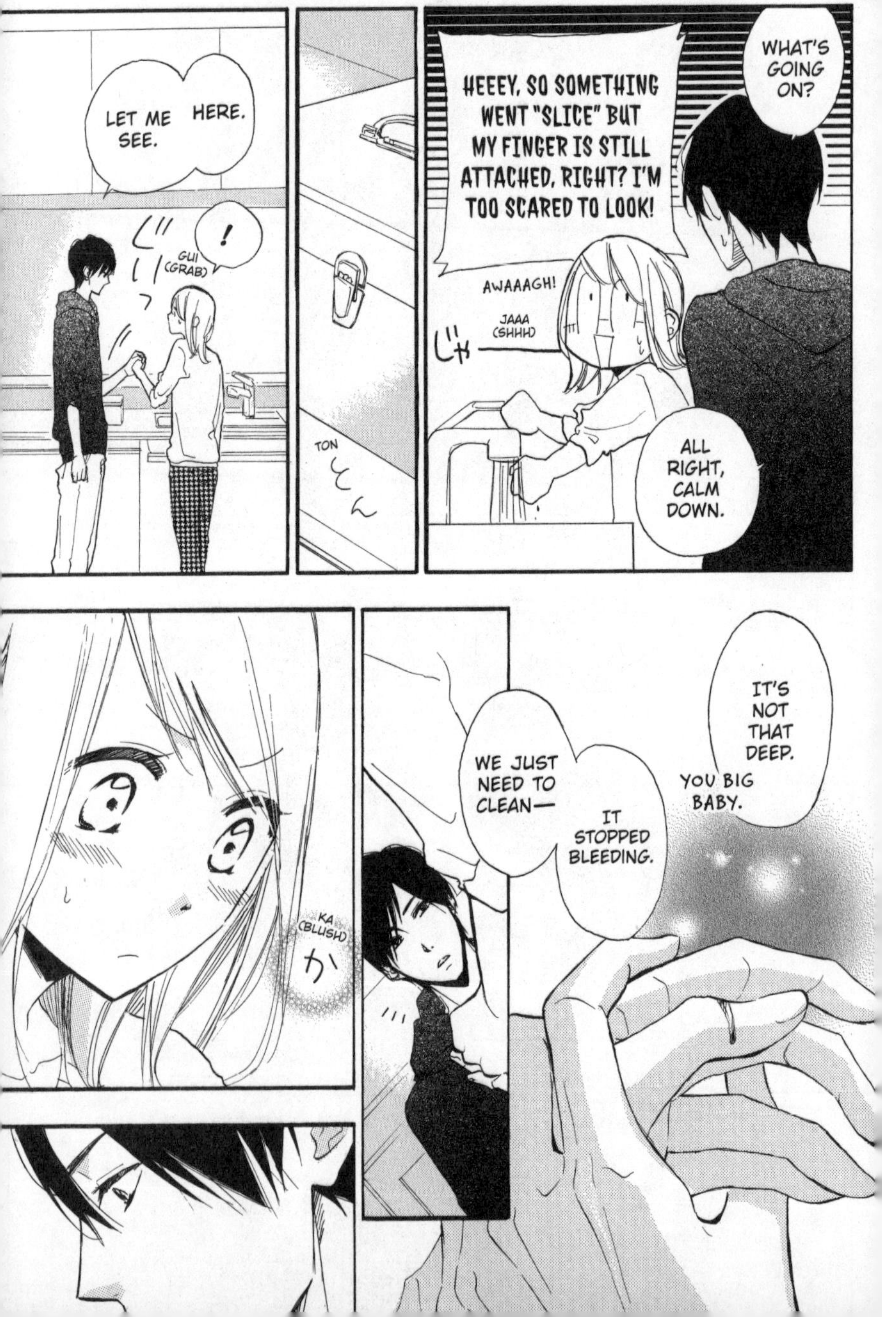
WHAT'S GOING ON?
HEEEY, SO SOMETHING WENT "SLICE" BUT MY FINGER IS STILL ATTACHED, RIGHT? I'M TOO SCARED TO LOOK!
AWAAAGH!
JAAA (SHHH)
じゃ
ALL RIGHT, CALM DOWN.
TON
とん
HERE.
LET ME SEE.
GUI (GRAB)
!
IT'S NOT THAT DEEP.
YOU BIG BABY.
IT STOPPED BLEEDING.
WE JUST NEED TO CLEAN—
KA (BLUSH)
か

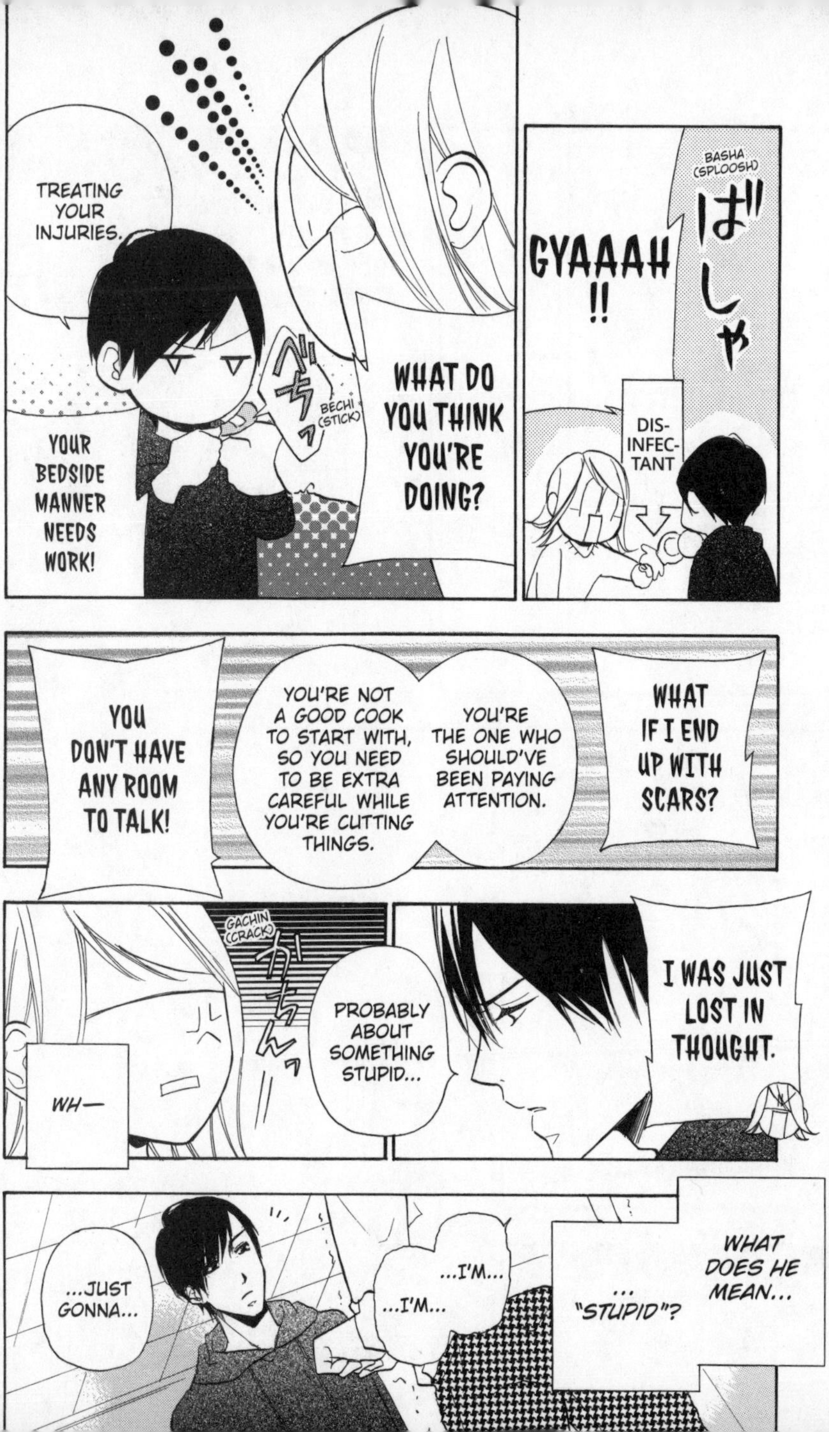
BASHA (SPLOOSH)
ばしゃ
GYAAAH!!
DIS-INFECTANT
WHAT DO YOU THINK YOU'RE DOING?
BECHI (STICK)
べちっ
TREATING YOUR INJURIES.
YOUR BEDSIDE MANNER NEEDS WORK!
WHAT IF I END UP WITH SCARS?
YOU'RE THE ONE WHO SHOULD'VE BEEN PAYING ATTENTION.
YOU'RE NOT A GOOD COOK TO START WITH, SO YOU NEED TO BE EXTRA CAREFUL WHILE YOU'RE CUTTING THINGS.
YOU DON'T HAVE ANY ROOM TO TALK!
I WAS JUST LOST IN THOUGHT.
PROBABLY ABOUT SOMETHING STUPID...
GACHIN (CRACK)
がちんっ
WH—
WHAT DOES HE MEAN...
..."STUPID"?
...I'M...
...I'M...
...JUST GONNA...

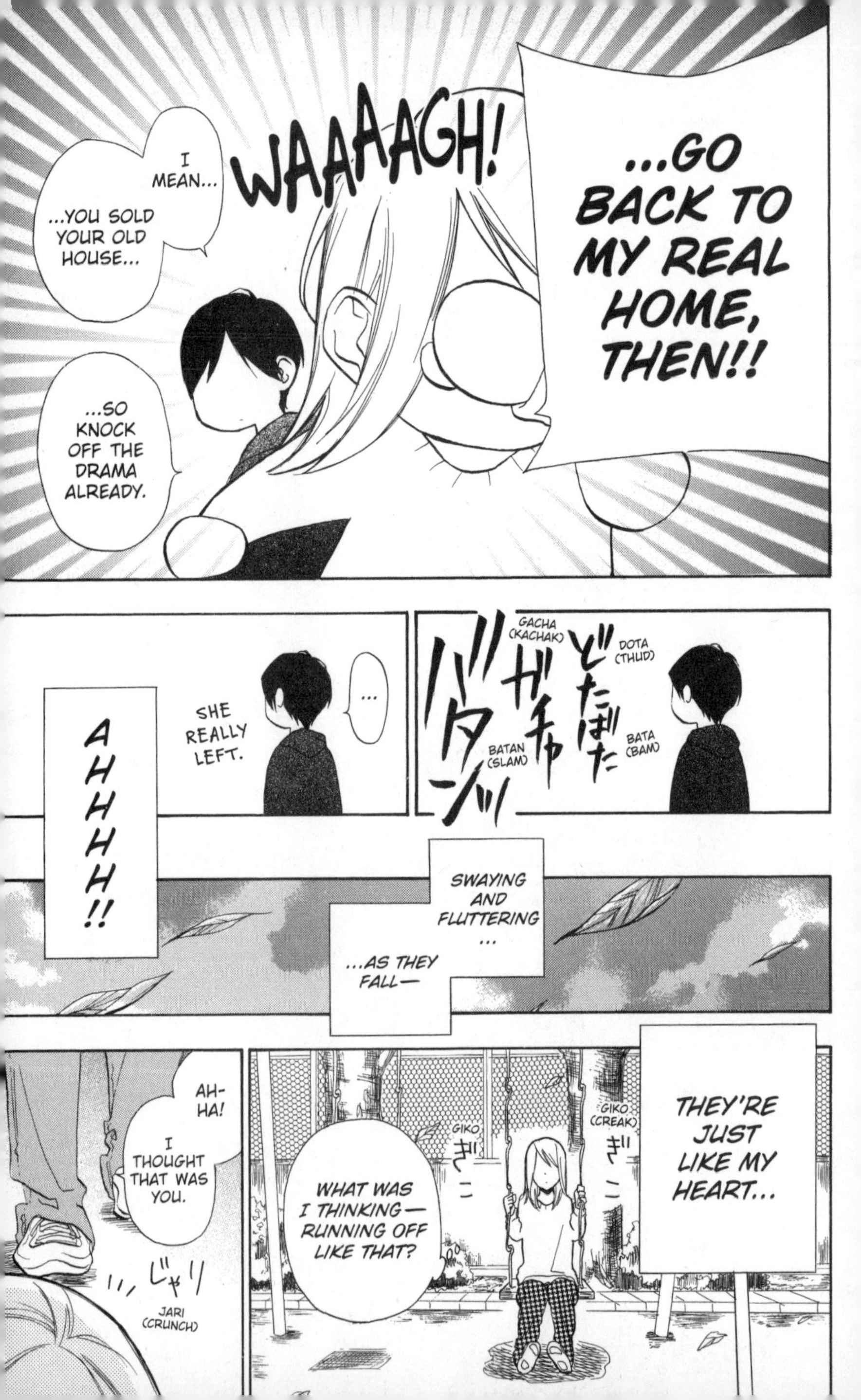
...GO BACK TO MY REAL HOME, THEN!!
WAAAAGH!
I MEAN...
...YOU SOLD YOUR OLD HOUSE...
...SO KNOCK OFF THE DRAMA ALREADY.
どたばた
DOTA (THUD)
BATA (BAM)
ガチャ
GACHA (KACHAK)
バターンッ
BATAN (SLAM)
...
SHE REALLY LEFT.
AHHHHH!!
SWAYING AND FLUTTERING ...
...AS THEY FALL—
THEY'RE JUST LIKE MY HEART...
ぎこ
GIKO (CREAK)
ぎこ
GIKO
WHAT WAS I THINKING— RUNNING OFF LIKE THAT?
AH-HA! I THOUGHT THAT WAS YOU.
じゃり
JARI (CRUNCH)

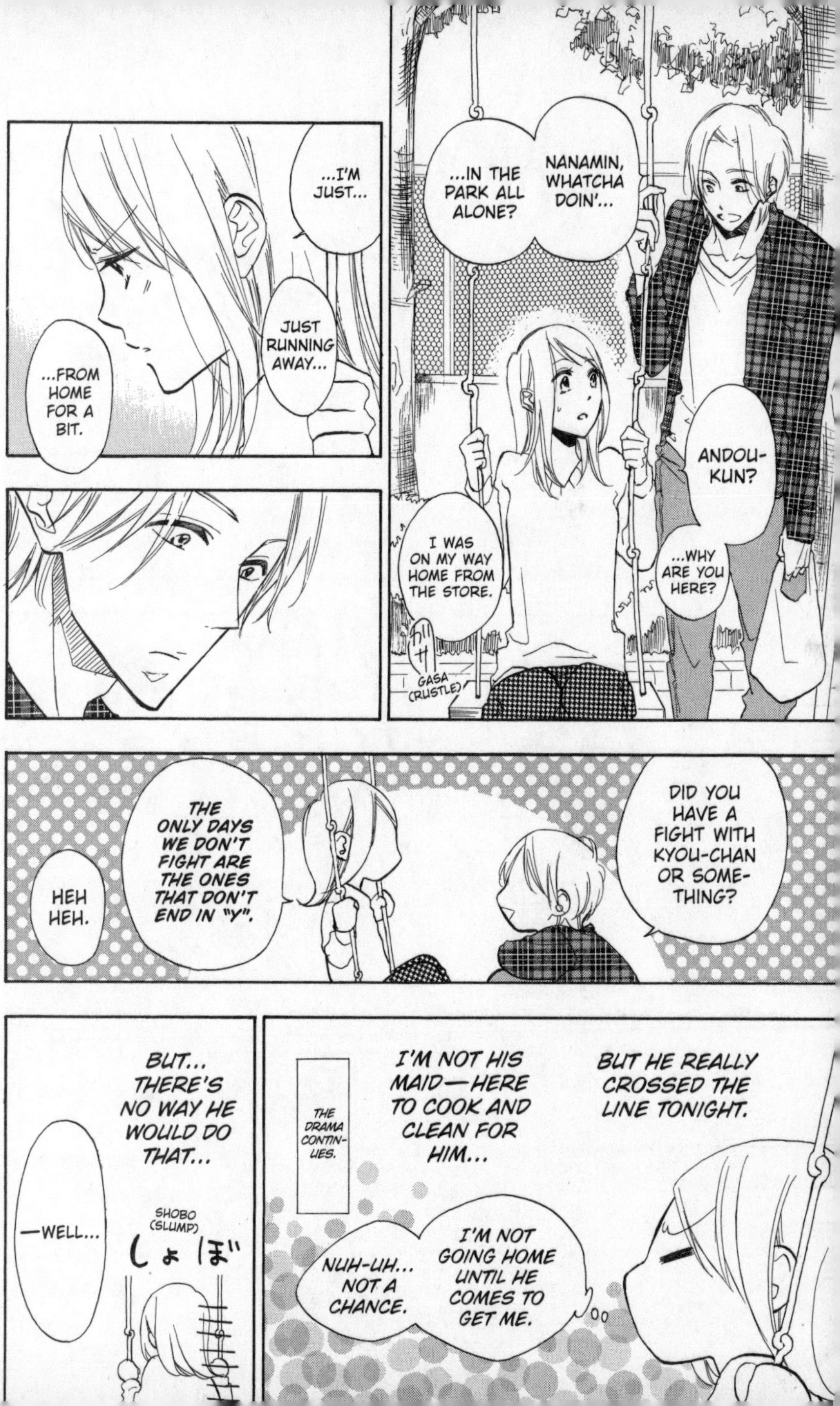
NANAMIN, WHATCHA DOIN'...
...IN THE PARK ALL ALONE?
ANDOU-KUN?
...WHY ARE YOU HERE?
I WAS ON MY WAY HOME FROM THE STORE.
カサ
GASA (RUSTLE)
...I'M JUST...
JUST RUNNING AWAY...
...FROM HOME FOR A BIT.
DID YOU HAVE A FIGHT WITH KYOU-CHAN OR SOME-THING?
THE ONLY DAYS WE DON'T FIGHT ARE THE ONES THAT DON'T END IN "Y".
HEH HEH.
BUT HE REALLY CROSSED THE LINE TONIGHT.
I'M NOT HIS MAID—HERE TO COOK AND CLEAN FOR HIM...
THE DRAMA CONTIN-UES.
I'M NOT GOING HOME UNTIL HE COMES TO GET ME.
NUH-UH... NOT A CHANCE.
BUT... THERE'S NO WAY HE WOULD DO THAT...
—WELL...
SHOBO (SLUMP)
しょぼ

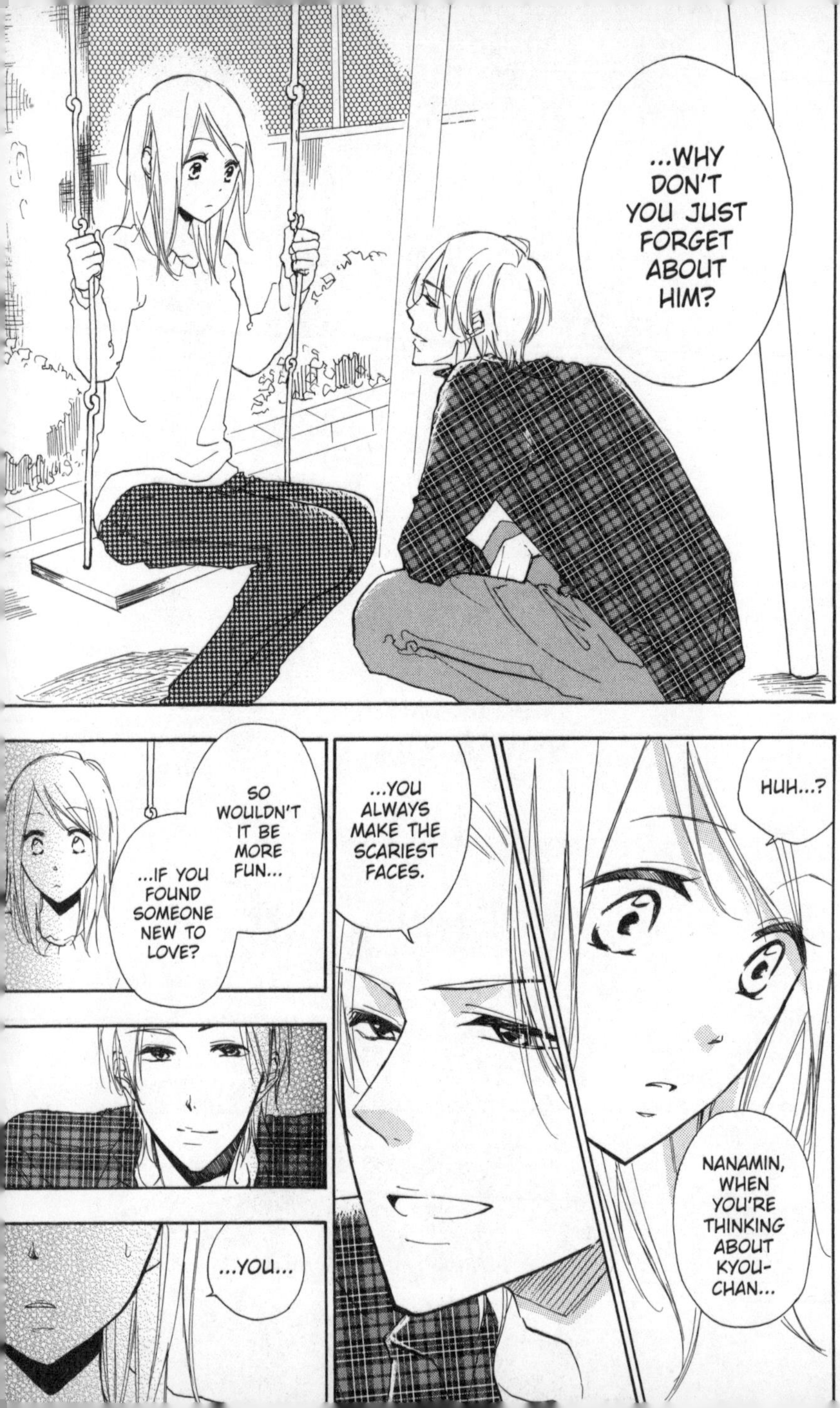
...WHY DON'T YOU JUST FORGET ABOUT HIM?
HUH...?
NANAMIN, WHEN YOU'RE THINKING ABOUT KYOU-CHAN...
...YOU ALWAYS MAKE THE SCARIEST FACES.
SO WOULDN'T IT BE MORE FUN...
...IF YOU FOUND SOMEONE NEW TO LOVE?
...YOU...

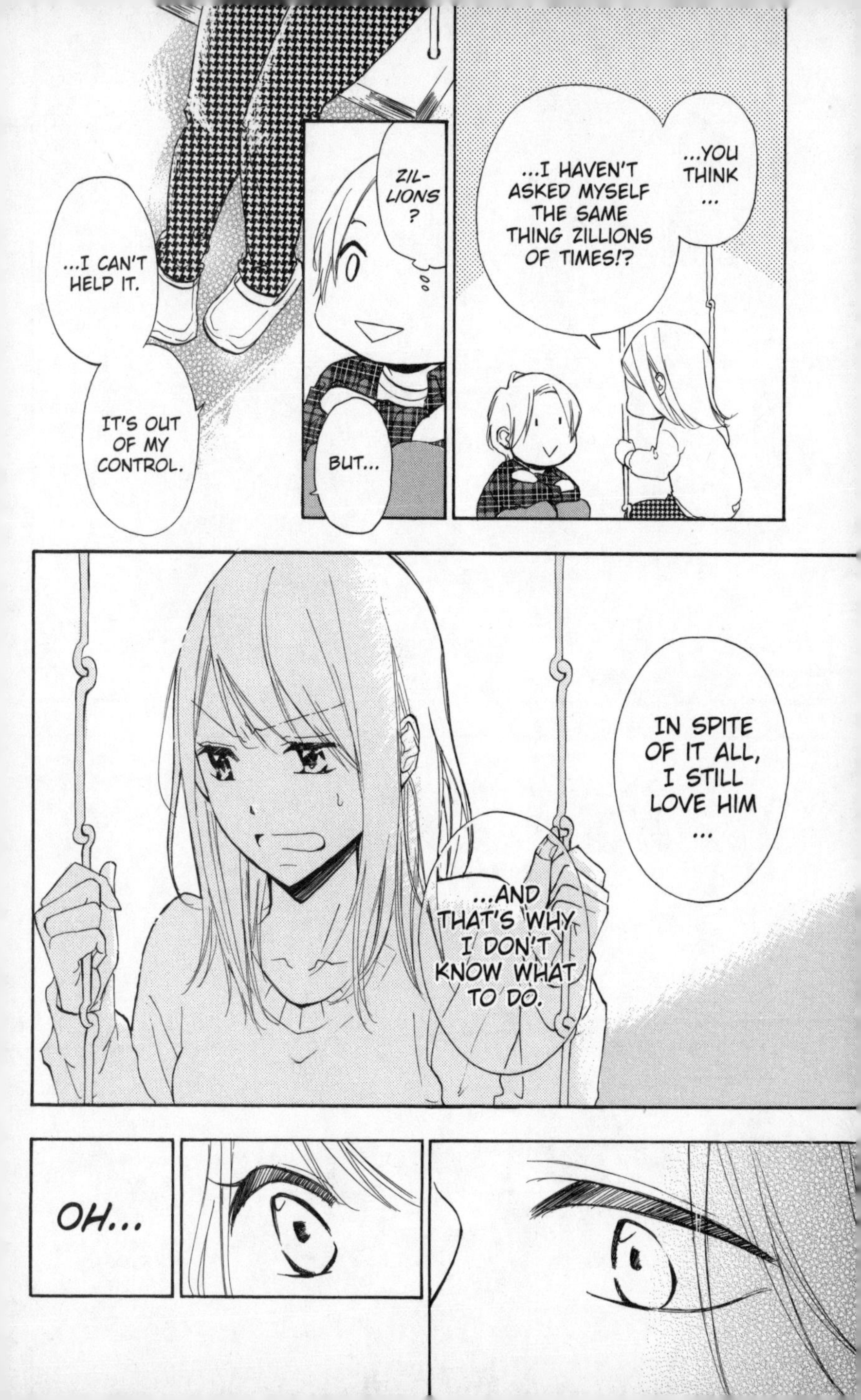
...YOU THINK...
...I HAVEN'T ASKED MYSELF THE SAME THING ZILLIONS OF TIMES!?
ZIL-LIONS?
BUT...
...I CAN'T HELP IT.
IT'S OUT OF MY CONTROL.
IN SPITE OF IT ALL, I STILL LOVE HIM...
...AND THAT'S WHY I DON'T KNOW WHAT TO DO.
OH...

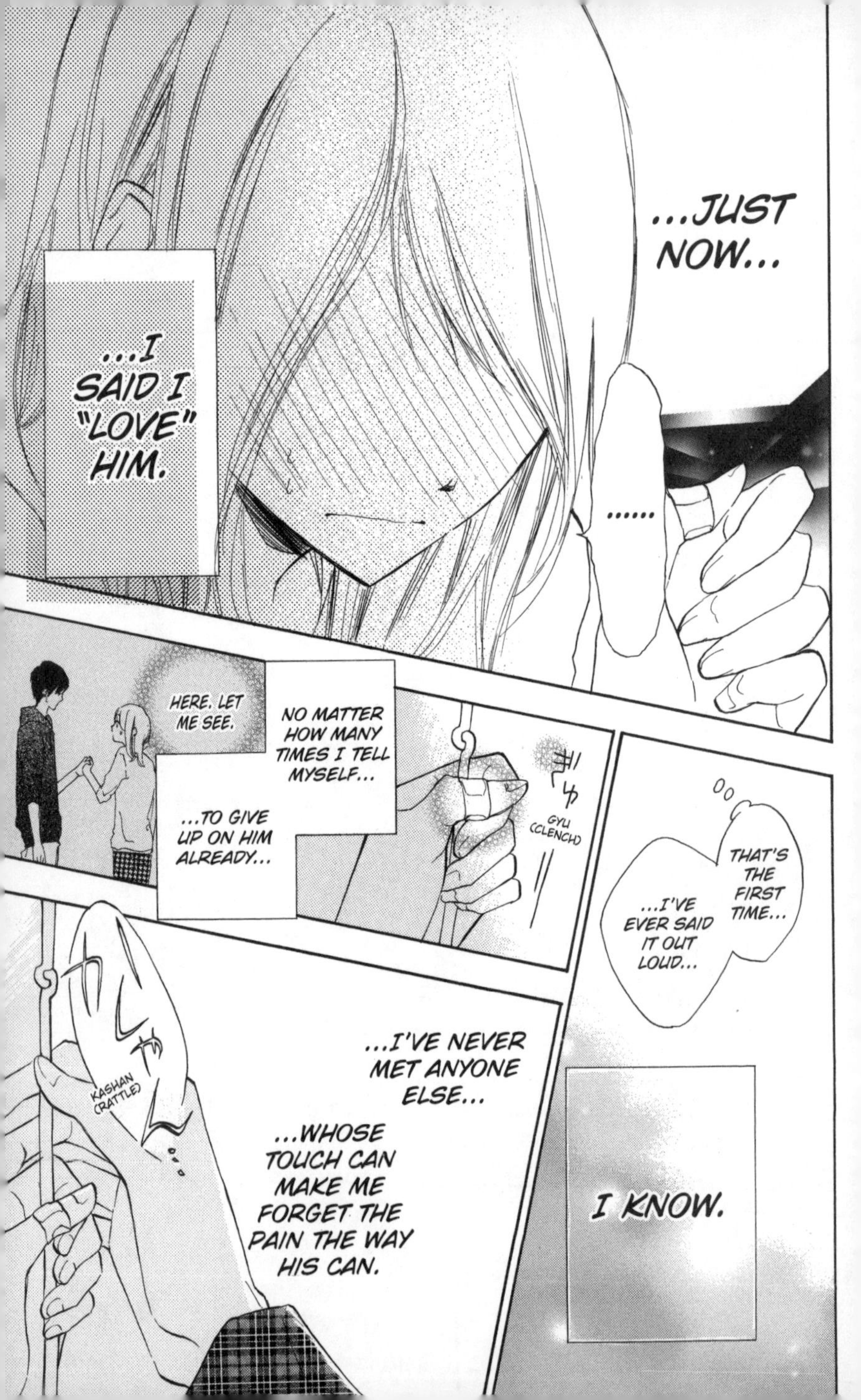
...JUST NOW...
...I SAID I "LOVE" HIM.
......
THAT'S THE FIRST TIME...
...I'VE EVER SAID IT OUT LOUD...
I KNOW.
GYU (CLENCH)
HERE. LET ME SEE.
NO MATTER HOW MANY TIMES I TELL MYSELF...
...TO GIVE UP ON HIM ALREADY...
KASHAN (RATTLE)
...I'VE NEVER MET ANYONE ELSE...
...WHOSE TOUCH CAN MAKE ME FORGET THE PAIN THE WAY HIS CAN.

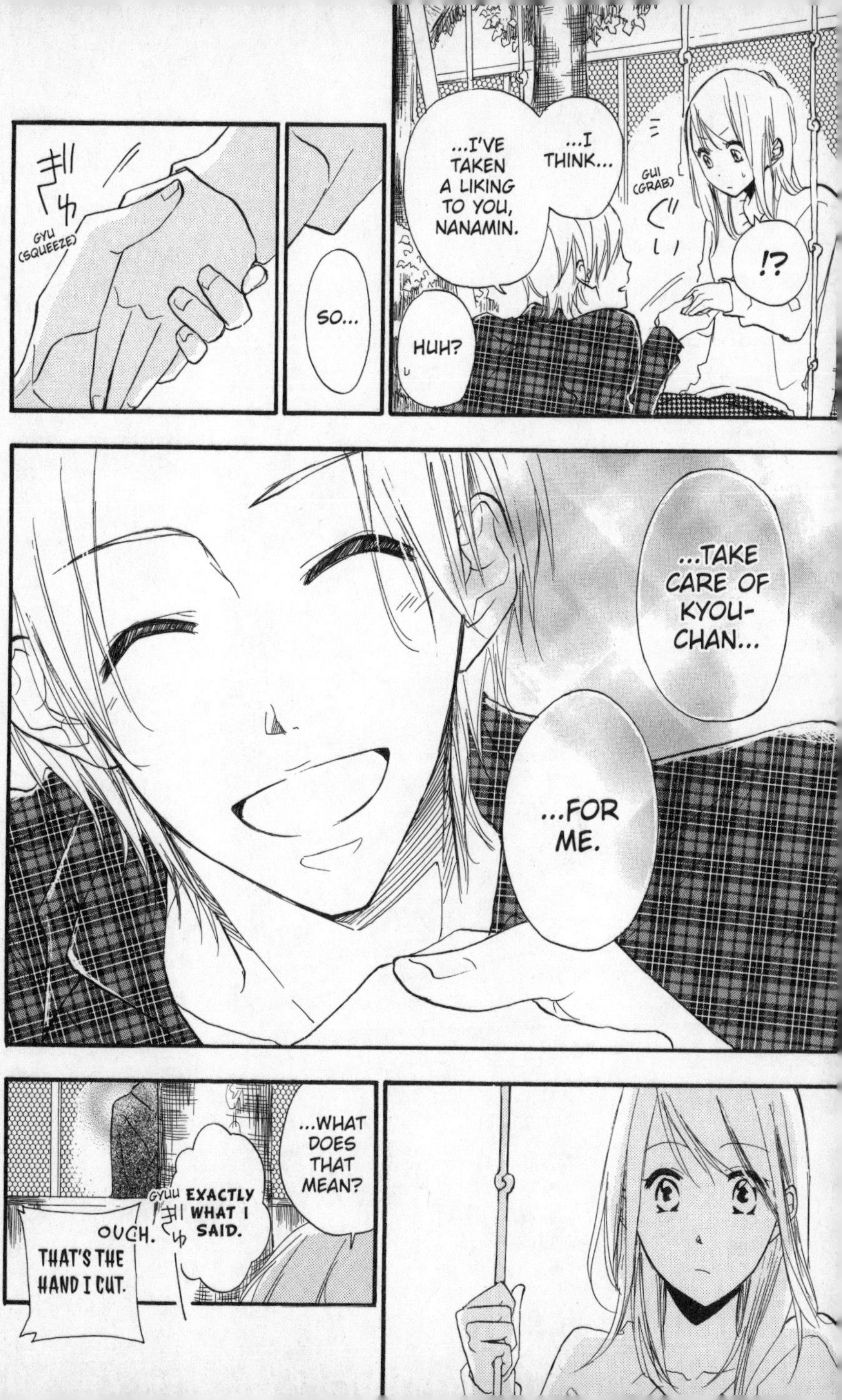
!?
GUI (GRAB)
...I THINK...
...I'VE TAKEN A LIKING TO YOU, NANAMIN.
HUH?
SO...
GYU (SQUEEZE)
...TAKE CARE OF KYOU-CHAN...
...FOR ME.
...WHAT DOES THAT MEAN?
EXACTLY WHAT I SAID.
GYUU
OUCH.
THAT'S THE HAND I CUT.

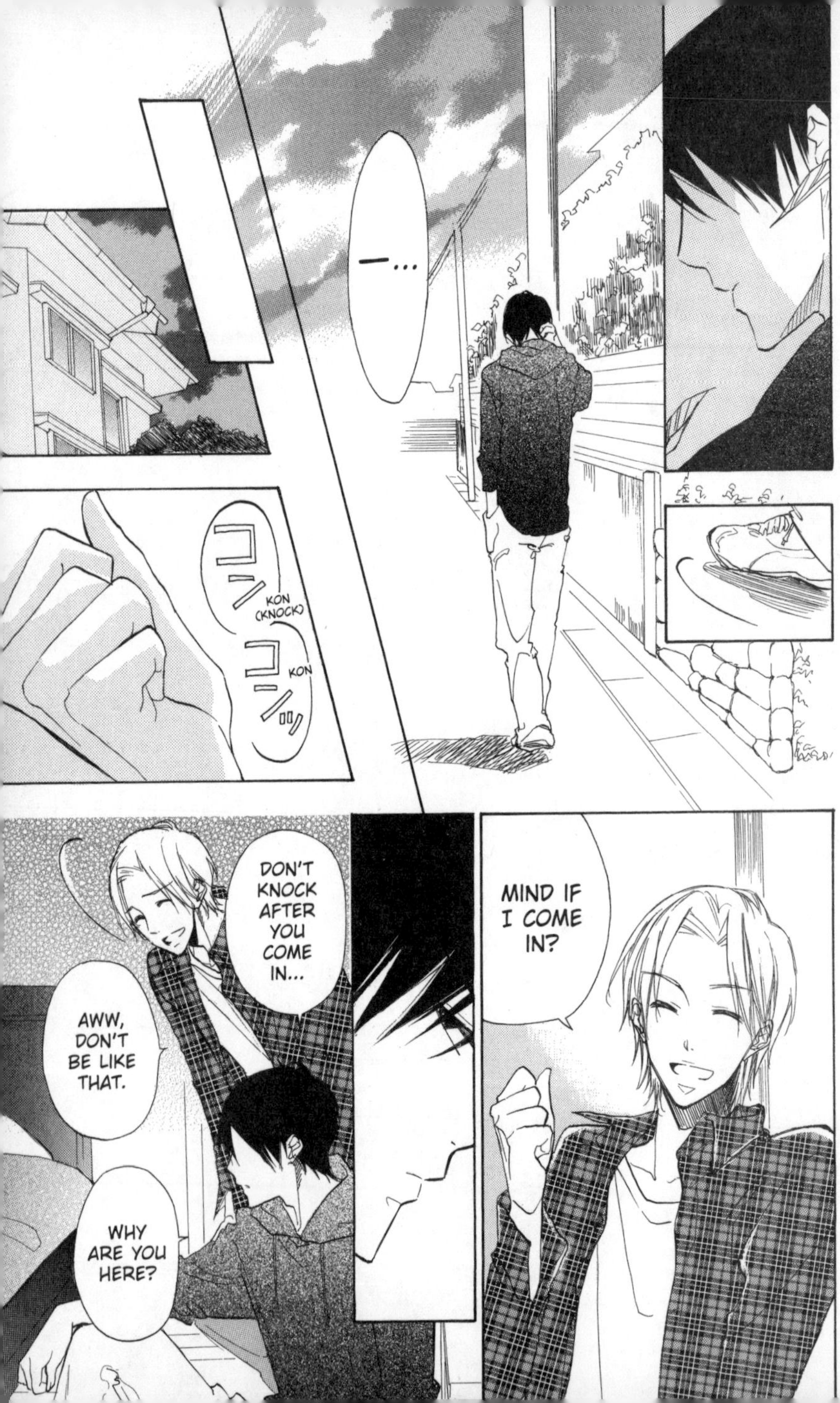
—...
コン
KON (KNOCK)
コンッ
KON
MIND IF I COME IN?
DON'T KNOCK AFTER YOU COME IN...
AWW, DON'T BE LIKE THAT.
WHY ARE YOU HERE?

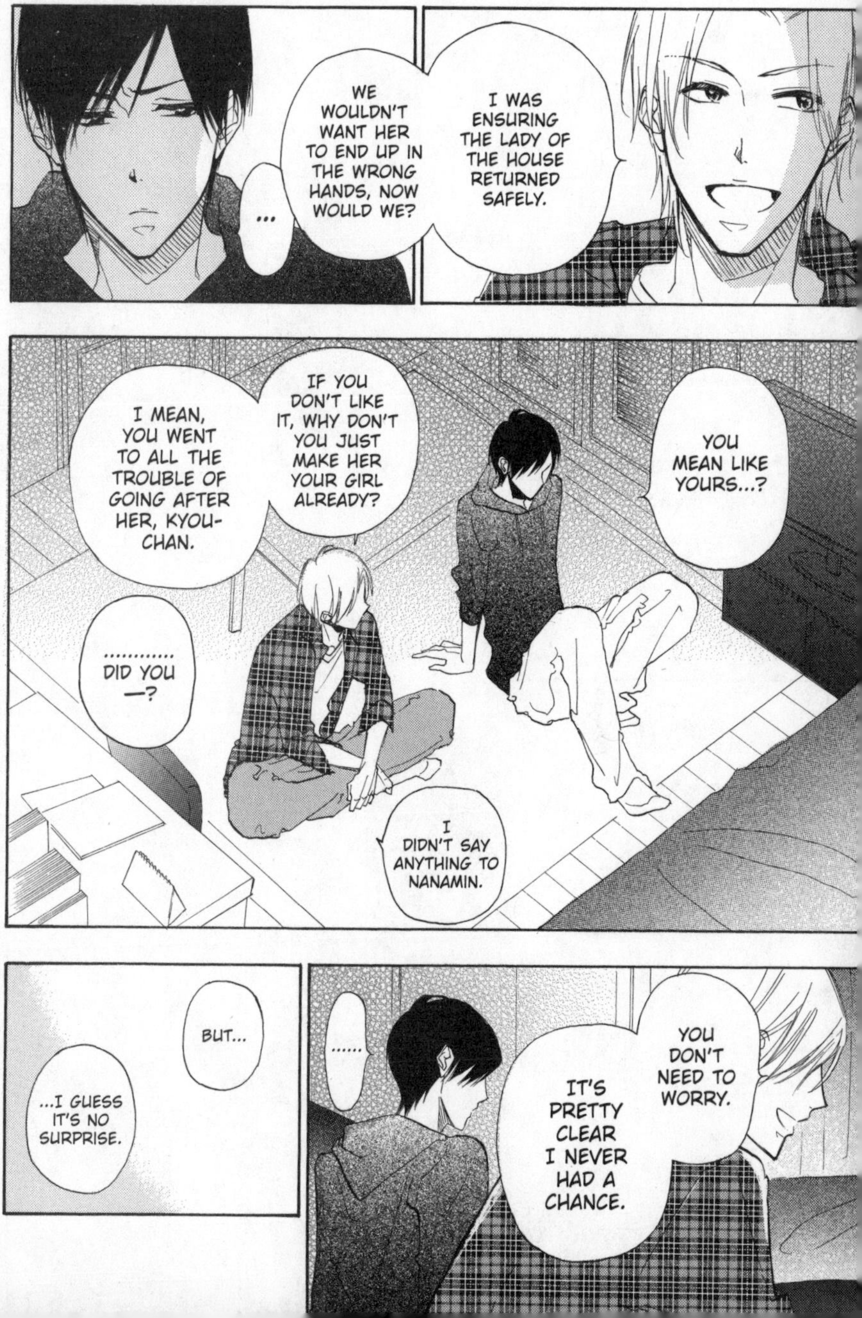
I WAS ENSURING THE LADY OF THE HOUSE RETURNED SAFELY.
WE WOULDN'T WANT HER TO END UP IN THE WRONG HANDS, NOW WOULD WE?
...
YOU MEAN LIKE YOURS...?
IF YOU DON'T LIKE IT, WHY DON'T YOU JUST MAKE HER YOUR GIRL ALREADY?
I MEAN, YOU WENT TO ALL THE TROUBLE OF GOING AFTER HER, KYOU-CHAN.
.... DID YOU —?
I DIDN'T SAY ANYTHING TO NANAMIN.
YOU DON'T NEED TO WORRY.
IT'S PRETTY CLEAR I NEVER HAD A CHANCE.
......
BUT...
...I GUESS IT'S NO SURPRISE.

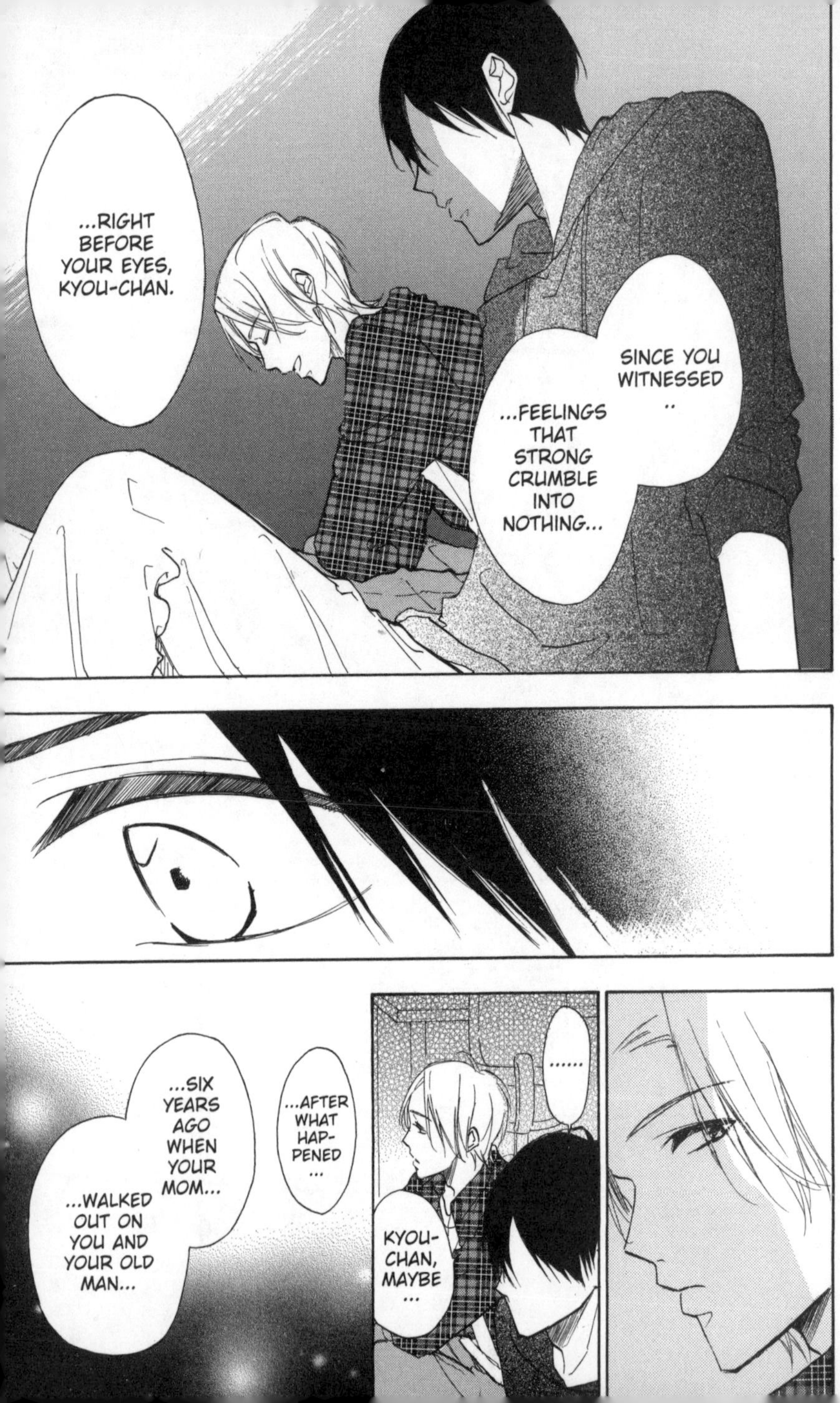
SINCE YOU WITNESSED ..
...FEELINGS THAT STRONG CRUMBLE INTO NOTHING...
...RIGHT BEFORE YOUR EYES, KYOU-CHAN.
......
KYOU-CHAN, MAYBE ...
...AFTER WHAT HAP-PENED ...
...SIX YEARS AGO WHEN YOUR MOM...
...WALKED OUT ON YOU AND YOUR OLD MAN...

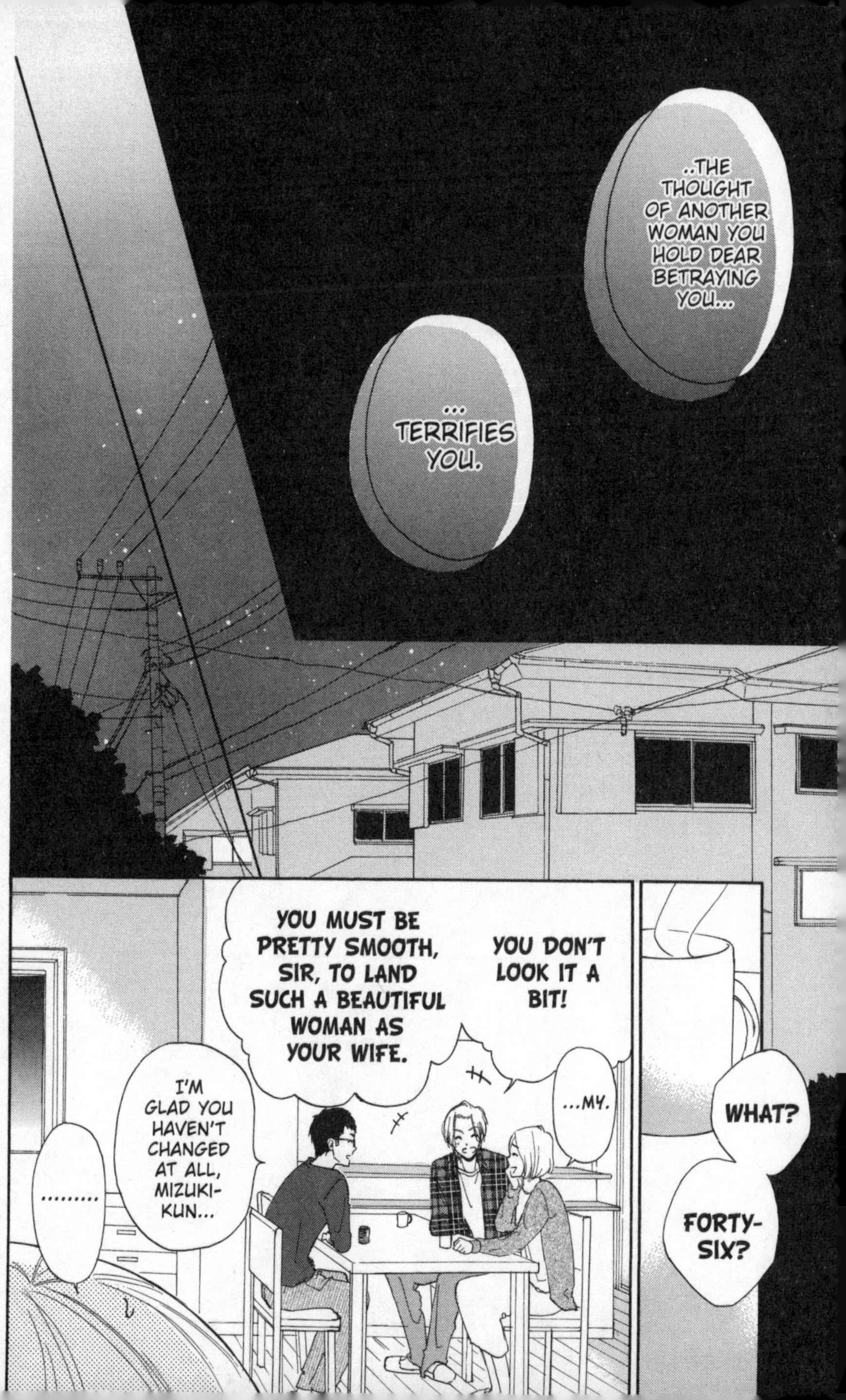
..THE THOUGHT OF ANOTHER WOMAN YOU HOLD DEAR BETRAYING YOU...
...TERRIFIES YOU.
WHAT?
FORTY-SIX?
YOU DON'T LOOK IT A BIT!
YOU MUST BE PRETTY SMOOTH, SIR, TO LAND SUCH A BEAUTIFUL WOMAN AS YOUR WIFE.
...MY.
I'M GLAD YOU HAVEN'T CHANGED AT ALL, MIZUKI-KUN...
....

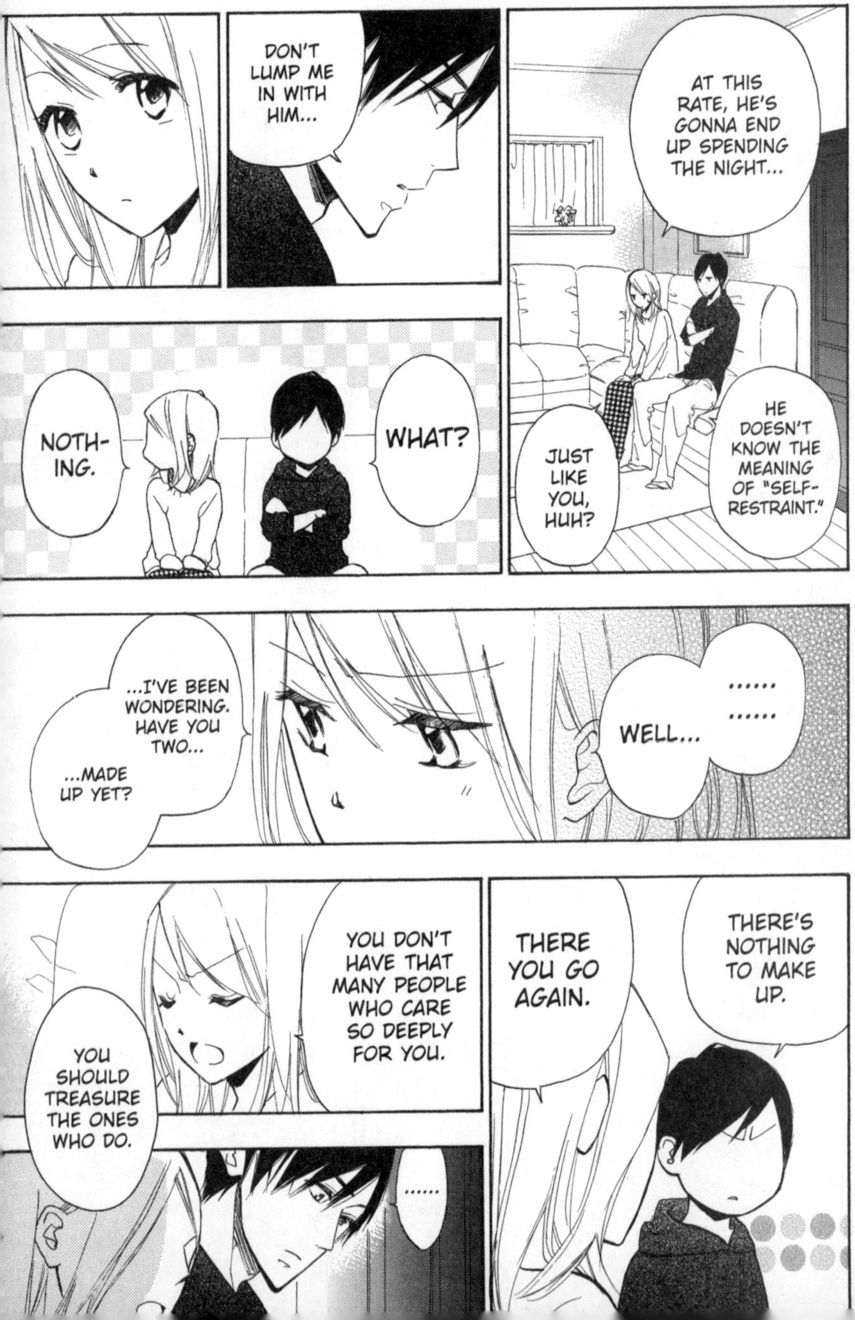
AT THIS RATE, HE'S GONNA END UP SPENDING THE NIGHT...
HE DOESN'T KNOW THE MEANING OF "SELF-RESTRAINT."
JUST LIKE YOU, HUH?
DON'T LUMP ME IN WITH HIM...
WHAT?
NOTH-ING.
....
WELL...
...I'VE BEEN WONDERING. HAVE YOU TWO...
...MADE UP YET?
THERE'S NOTHING TO MAKE UP.
THERE YOU GO AGAIN.
YOU DON'T HAVE THAT MANY PEOPLE WHO CARE SO DEEPLY FOR YOU.
YOU SHOULD TREASURE THE ONES WHO DO.
......

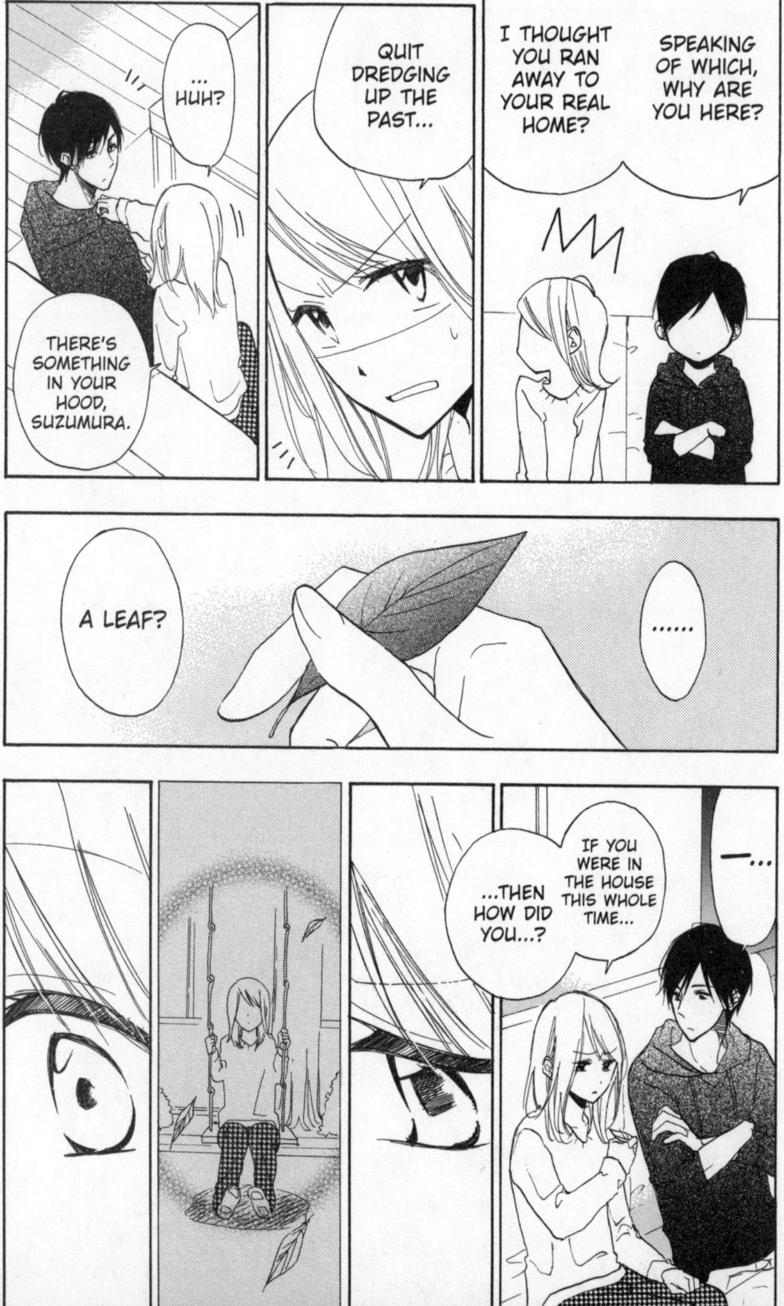
SPEAKING OF WHICH, WHY ARE YOU HERE?
I THOUGHT YOU RAN AWAY TO YOUR REAL HOME?
QUIT DREDGING UP THE PAST...
... HUH?
THERE'S SOMETHING IN YOUR HOOD, SUZUMURA.
......
A LEAF?
—...
IF YOU WERE IN THE HOUSE THIS WHOLE TIME...
...THEN HOW DID YOU...?

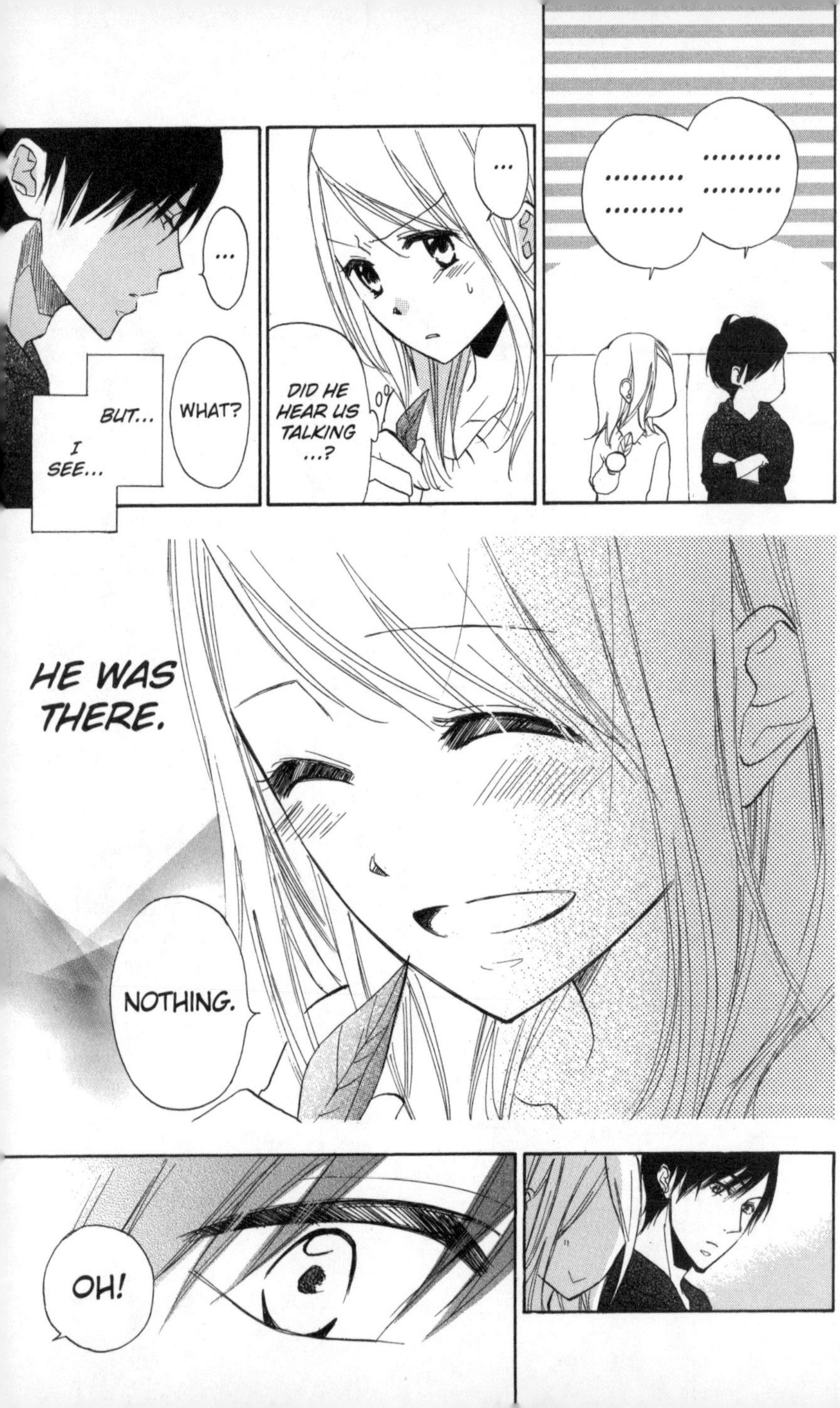

....
....
....
....
...
DID HE HEAR US TALKING ...?
...
WHAT?
BUT...
I SEE...
HE WAS THERE.
NOTHING.
OH!

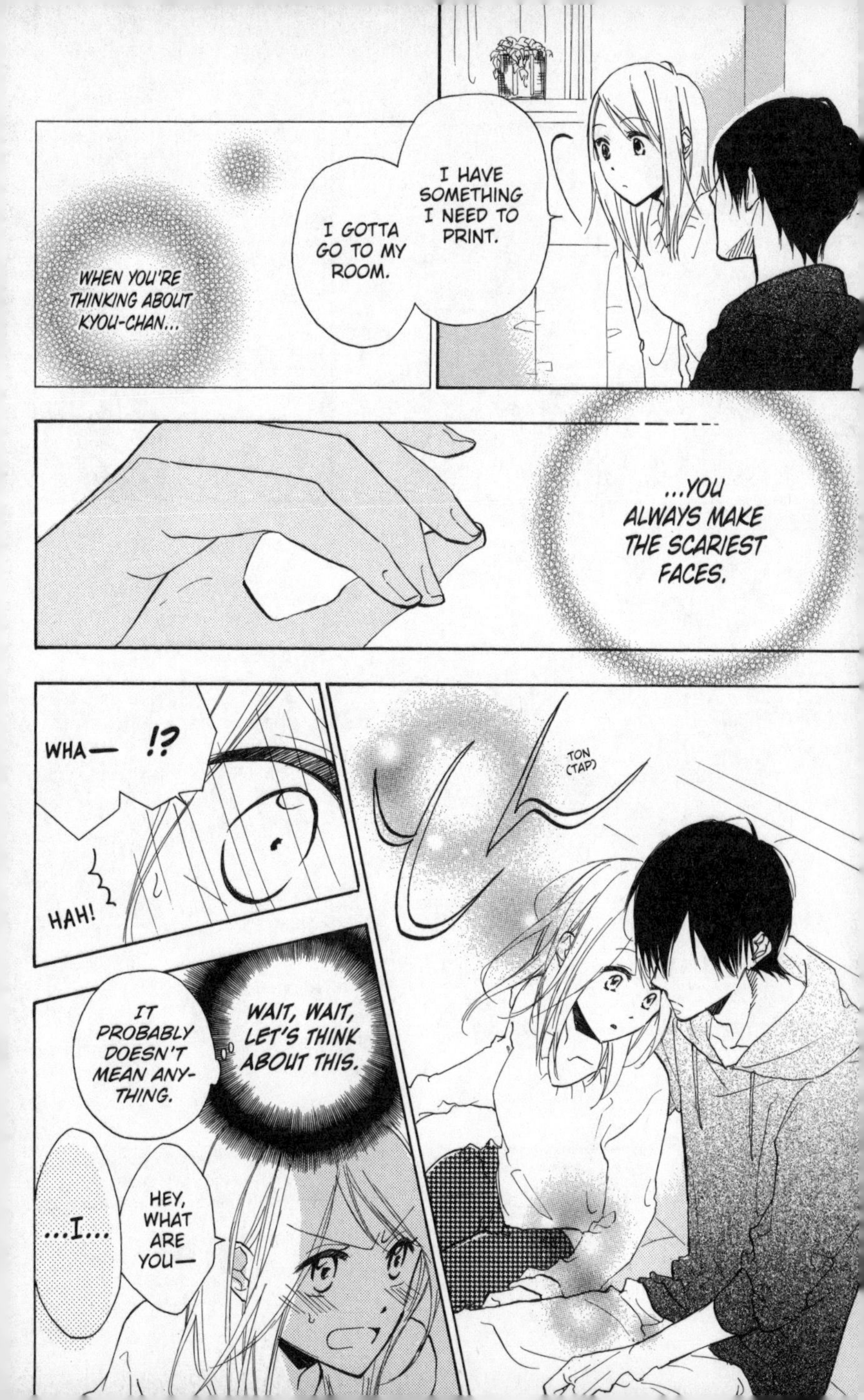
I HAVE SOMETHING I NEED TO PRINT.
I GOTTA GO TO MY ROOM.
WHEN YOU'RE THINKING ABOUT KYOU-CHAN...
...YOU ALWAYS MAKE THE SCARIEST FACES.
TON (TAP)
WHA— !?
HAH!
WAIT, WAIT, LET'S THINK ABOUT THIS.
IT PROBABLY DOESN'T MEAN ANY-THING.
HEY, WHAT ARE YOU—
...I...

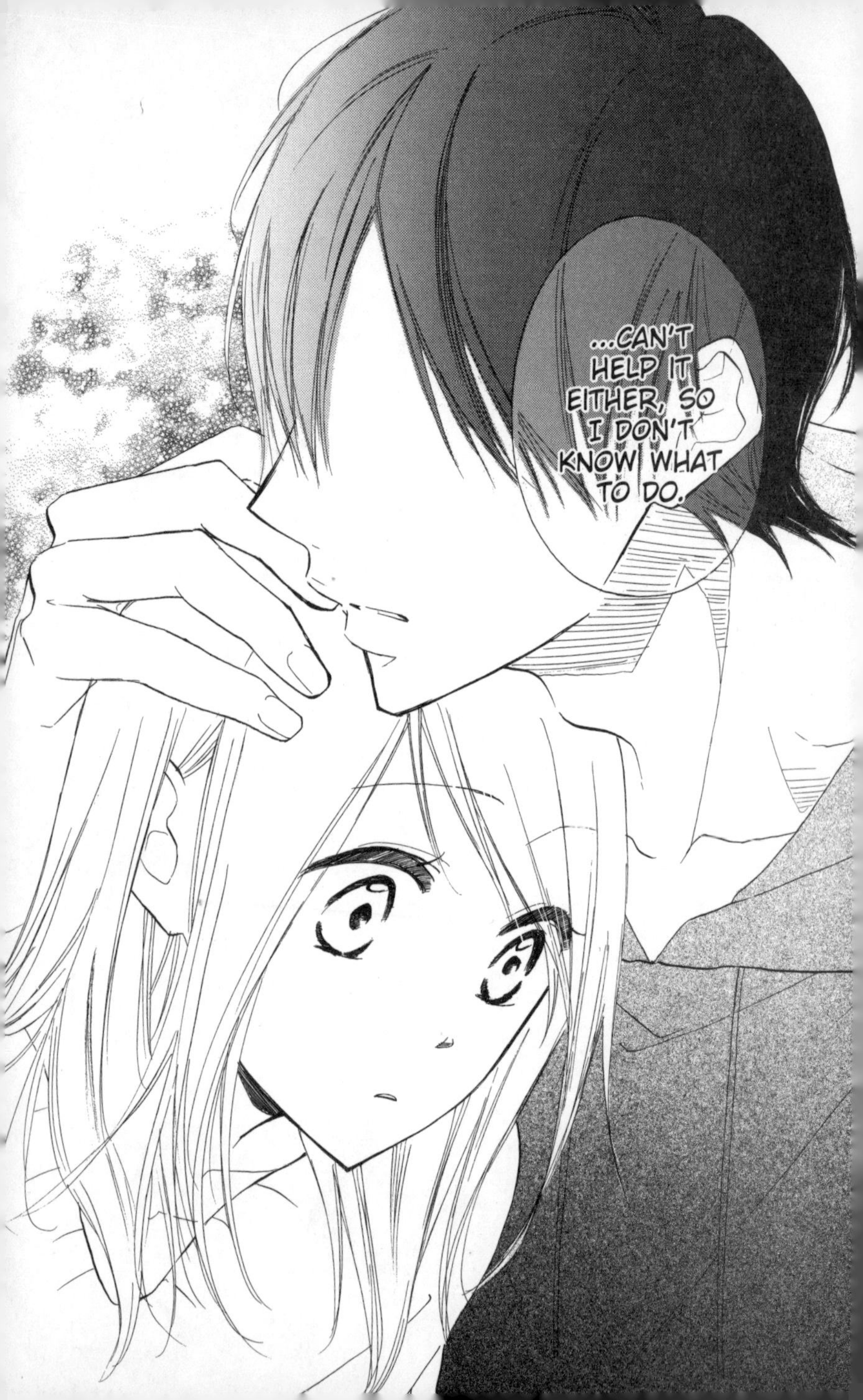
...CAN'T HELP IT EITHER, SO I DON'T KNOW WHAT TO DO.

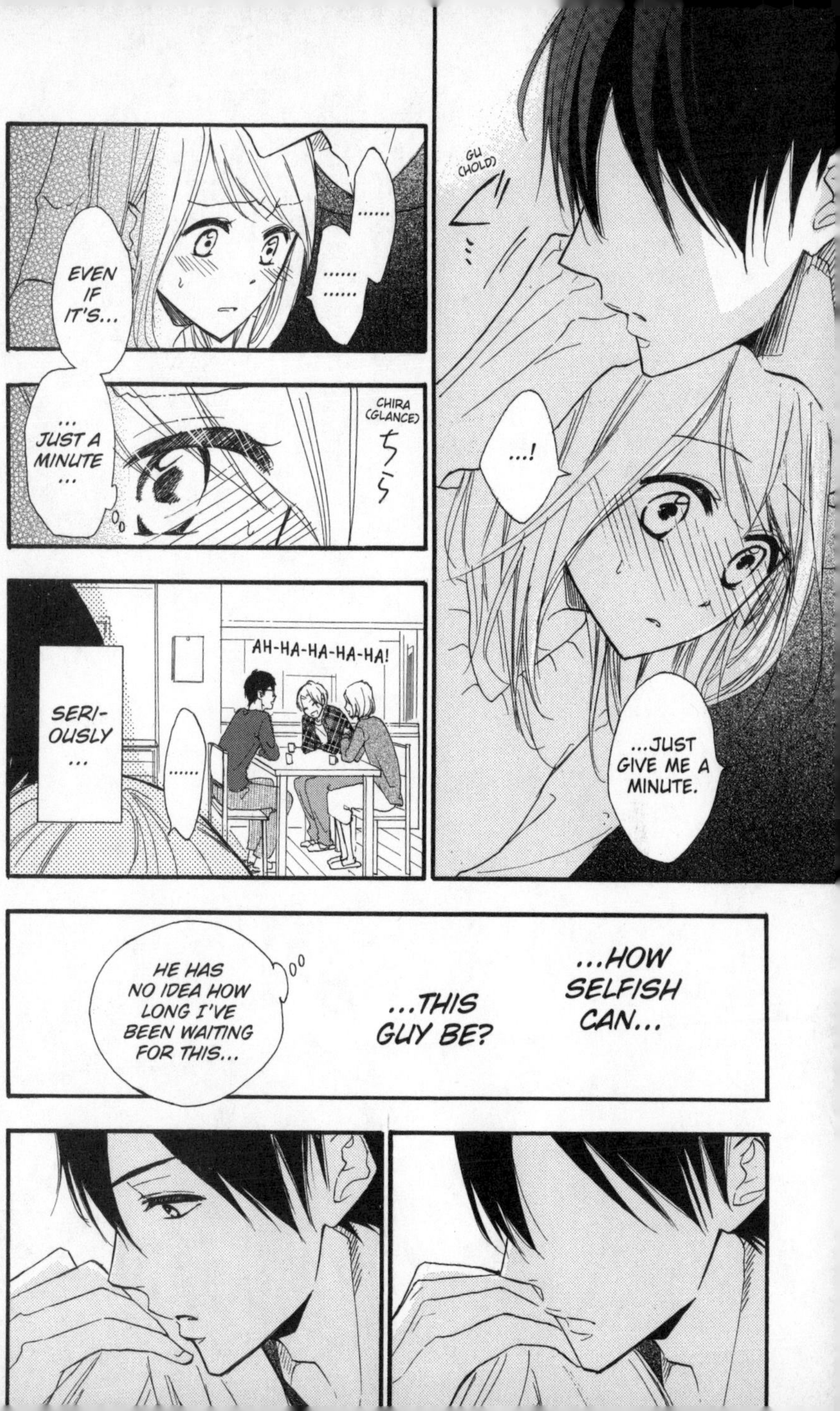
GU (HOLD)
...!
...JUST GIVE ME A MINUTE.
......
......
......
EVEN IF IT'S...
CHIRA (GLANCE)
ちら
...JUST A MINUTE...
AH-HA-HA-HA-HA!
......
SERI-OUSLY...
...HOW SELFISH CAN...
...THIS GUY BE?
HE HAS NO IDEA HOW LONG I'VE BEEN WAITING FOR THIS...

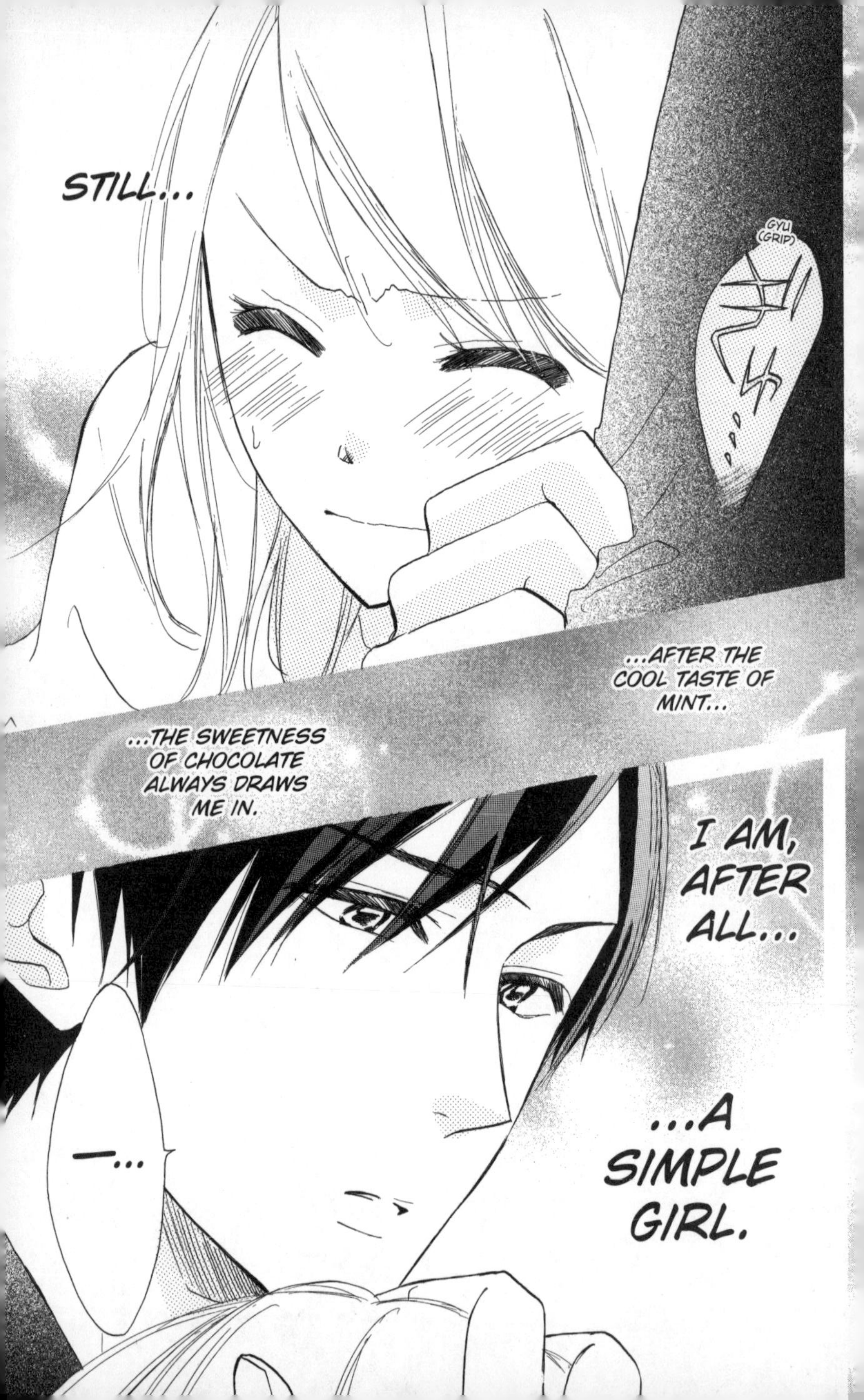
STILL...
GYU (GRIP)
...AFTER THE COOL TASTE OF MINT...
...THE SWEETNESS OF CHOCOLATE ALWAYS DRAWS ME IN.
I AM, AFTER ALL...
...A SIMPLE GIRL.
—...

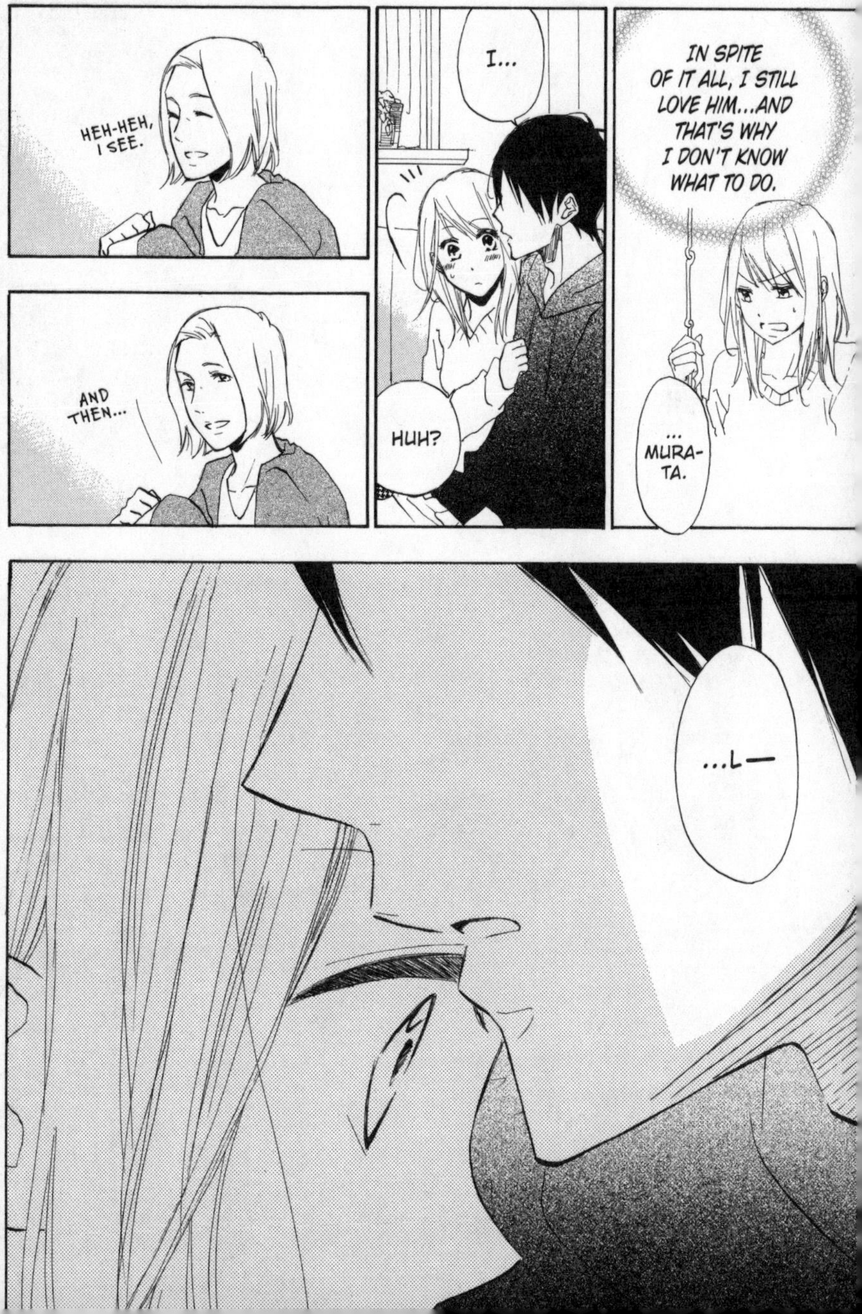
IN SPITE OF IT ALL, I STILL LOVE HIM...AND THAT'S WHY I DON'T KNOW WHAT TO DO.
... MURATA.
I...
HUH?
HEH-HEH, I SEE.
AND THEN...
...L—

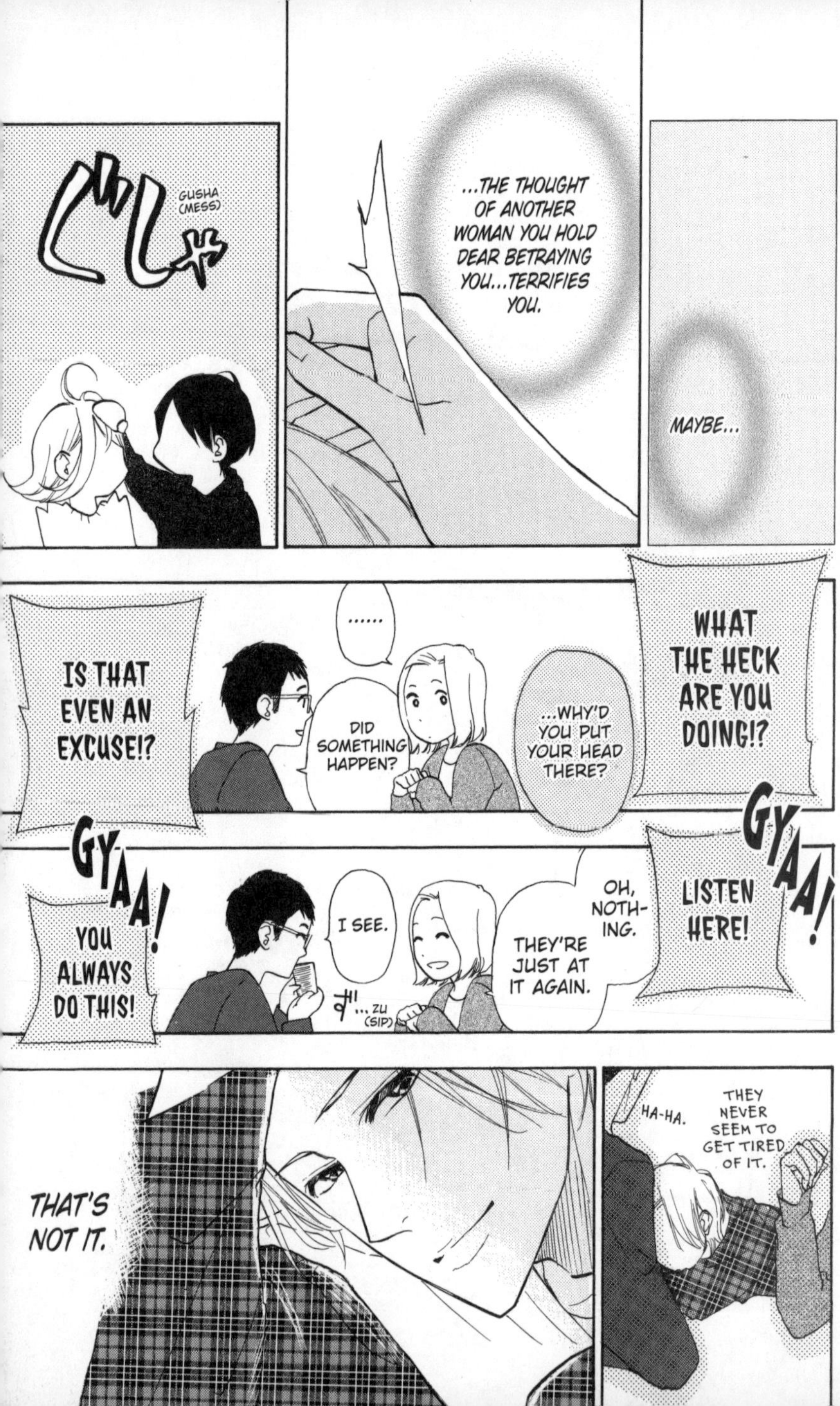
MAYBE...
...THE THOUGHT OF ANOTHER WOMAN YOU HOLD DEAR BETRAYING YOU...TERRIFIES YOU.
ぐしゃ
GUSHA (MESS)
WHAT THE HECK ARE YOU DOING!?
...WHY'D YOU PUT YOUR HEAD THERE?
......
DID SOMETHING HAPPEN?
IS THAT EVEN AN EXCUSE!?
GYAA!
LISTEN HERE!
OH, NOTHING.
THEY'RE JUST AT IT AGAIN.
I SEE.
ずっ... ZU (SIP)
GYAA!
YOU ALWAYS DO THIS!
THEY NEVER SEEM TO GET TIRED OF IT.
HA-HA.
THAT'S NOT IT.

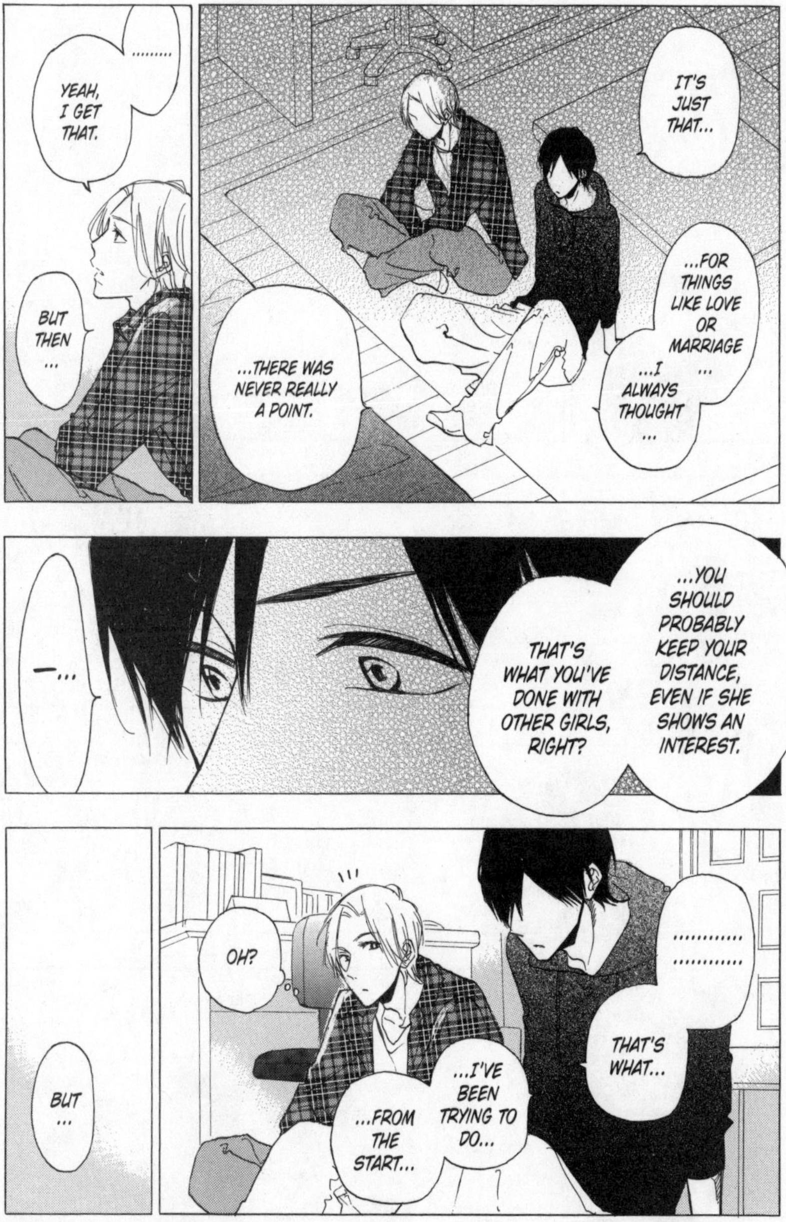
IT'S JUST THAT...
...FOR THINGS LIKE LOVE OR MARRIAGE...
...I ALWAYS THOUGHT...
...THERE WAS NEVER REALLY A POINT.
....
YEAH, I GET THAT.
BUT THEN ...
...YOU SHOULD PROBABLY KEEP YOUR DISTANCE, EVEN IF SHE SHOWS AN INTEREST.
THAT'S WHAT YOU'VE DONE WITH OTHER GIRLS, RIGHT?
—...
....
THAT'S WHAT...
...I'VE BEEN TRYING TO DO...
...FROM THE START...
OH?
BUT ...

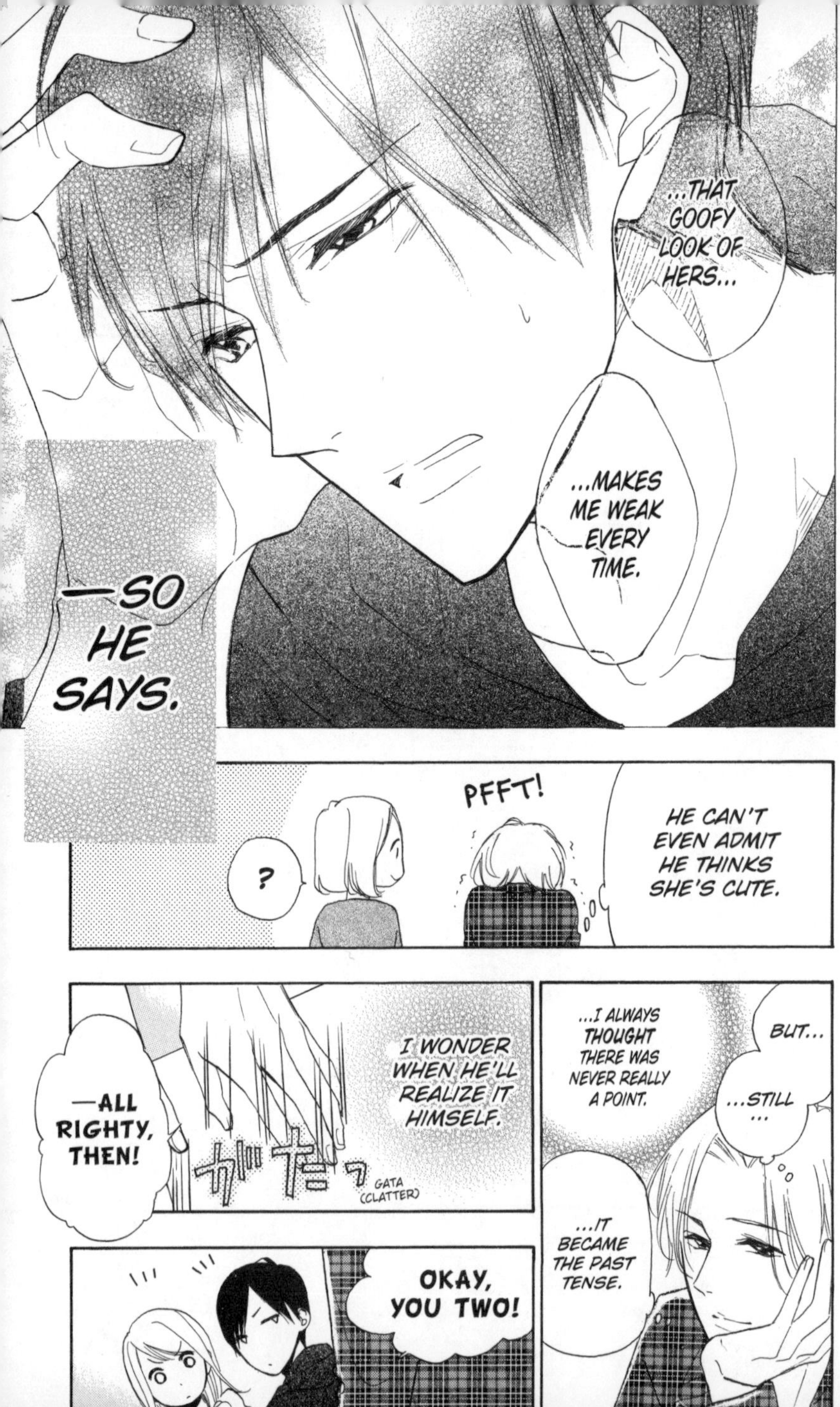
...THAT GOOFY LOOK OF HERS...
...MAKES ME WEAK EVERY TIME.
—SO HE SAYS.
HE CAN'T EVEN ADMIT HE THINKS SHE'S CUTE.
PFFT!
?
BUT...
...I ALWAYS THOUGHT THERE WAS NEVER REALLY A POINT.
...STILL...
...IT BECAME THE PAST TENSE.
I WONDER WHEN HE'LL REALIZE IT HIMSELF.
—ALL RIGHTY, THEN!
ガタッ
GATA (CLATTER)
OKAY, YOU TWO!

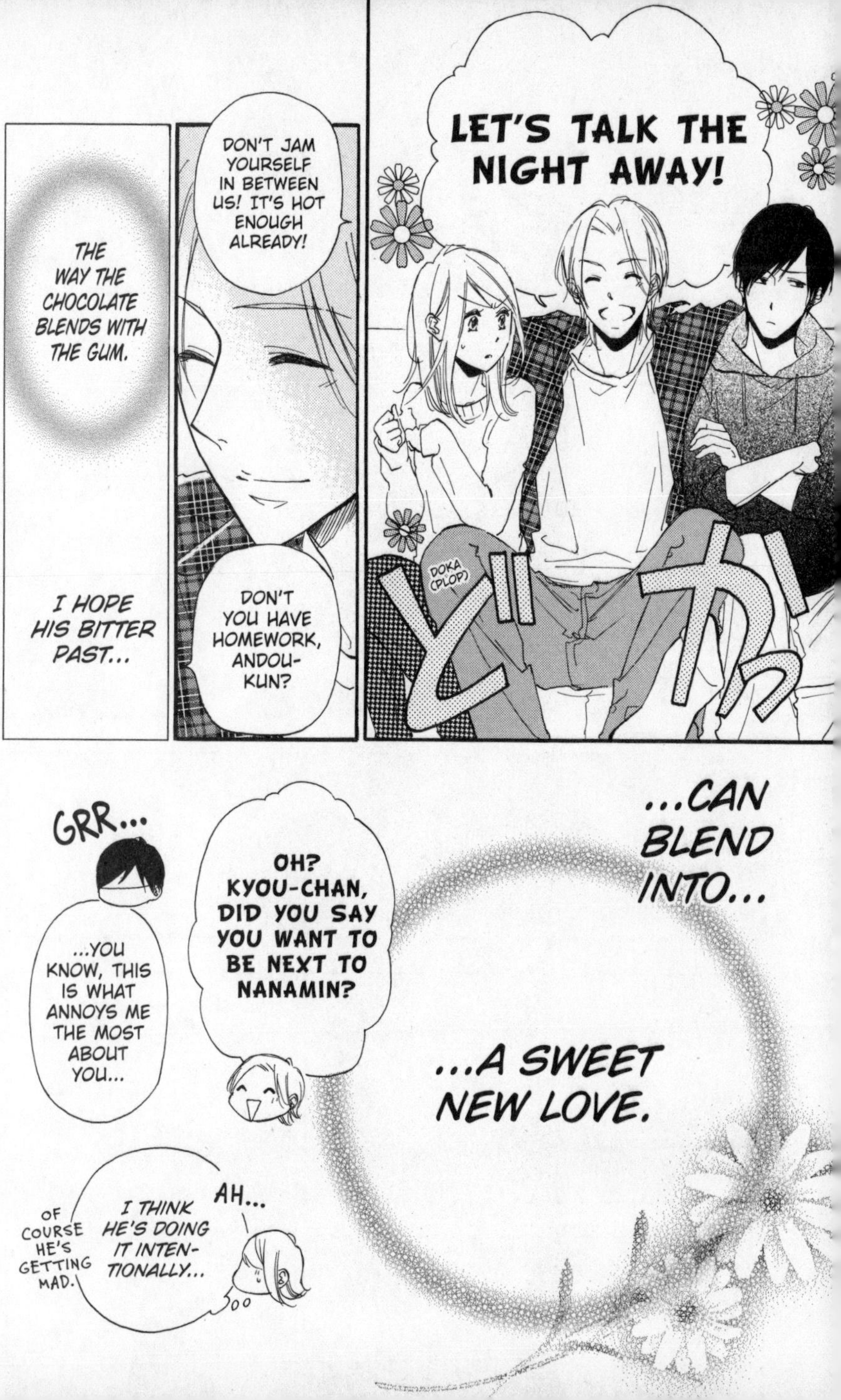
LET'S TALK THE NIGHT AWAY!
DOKA (PLOP)
DON'T JAM YOURSELF IN BETWEEN US! IT'S HOT ENOUGH ALREADY!
DON'T YOU HAVE HOMEWORK, ANDOU-KUN?
THE WAY THE CHOCOLATE BLENDS WITH THE GUM.
I HOPE HIS BITTER PAST...
...CAN BLEND INTO...
...A SWEET NEW LOVE.
OH? KYOU-CHAN, DID YOU SAY YOU WANT TO BE NEXT TO NANAMIN?
GRR...
...YOU KNOW, THIS IS WHAT ANNOYS ME THE MOST ABOUT YOU...
AH...
I THINK HE'S DOING IT INTENTIONALLY...
OF COURSE HE'S GETTING MAD.

Room: 6

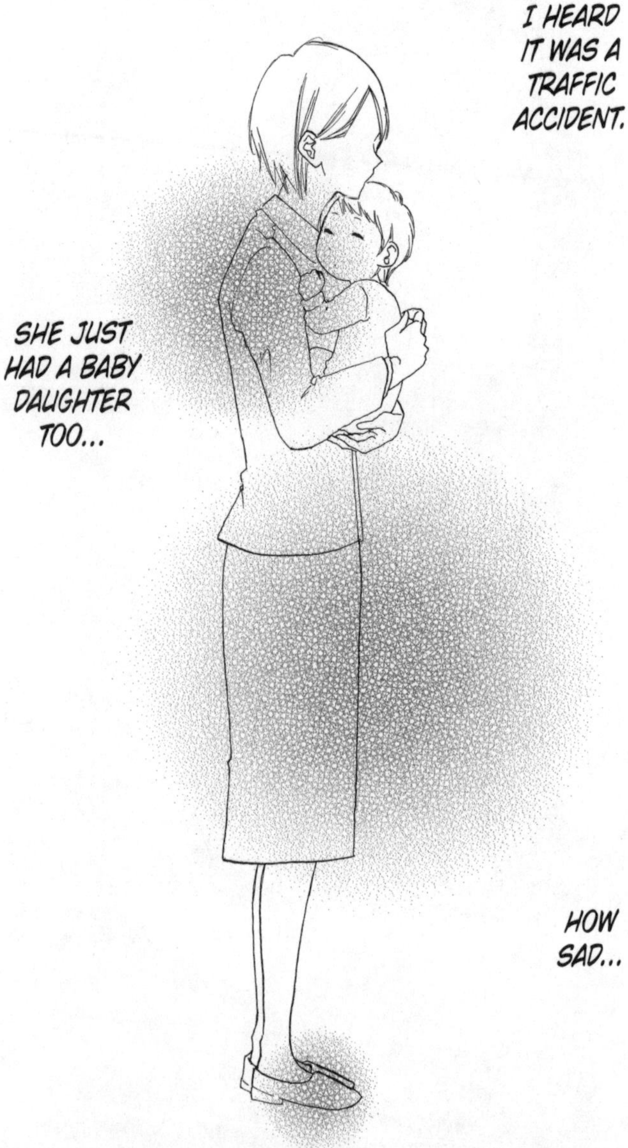
I HEARD IT WAS A TRAFFIC ACCIDENT.
SHE JUST HAD A BABY DAUGHTER TOO...
HOW SAD...

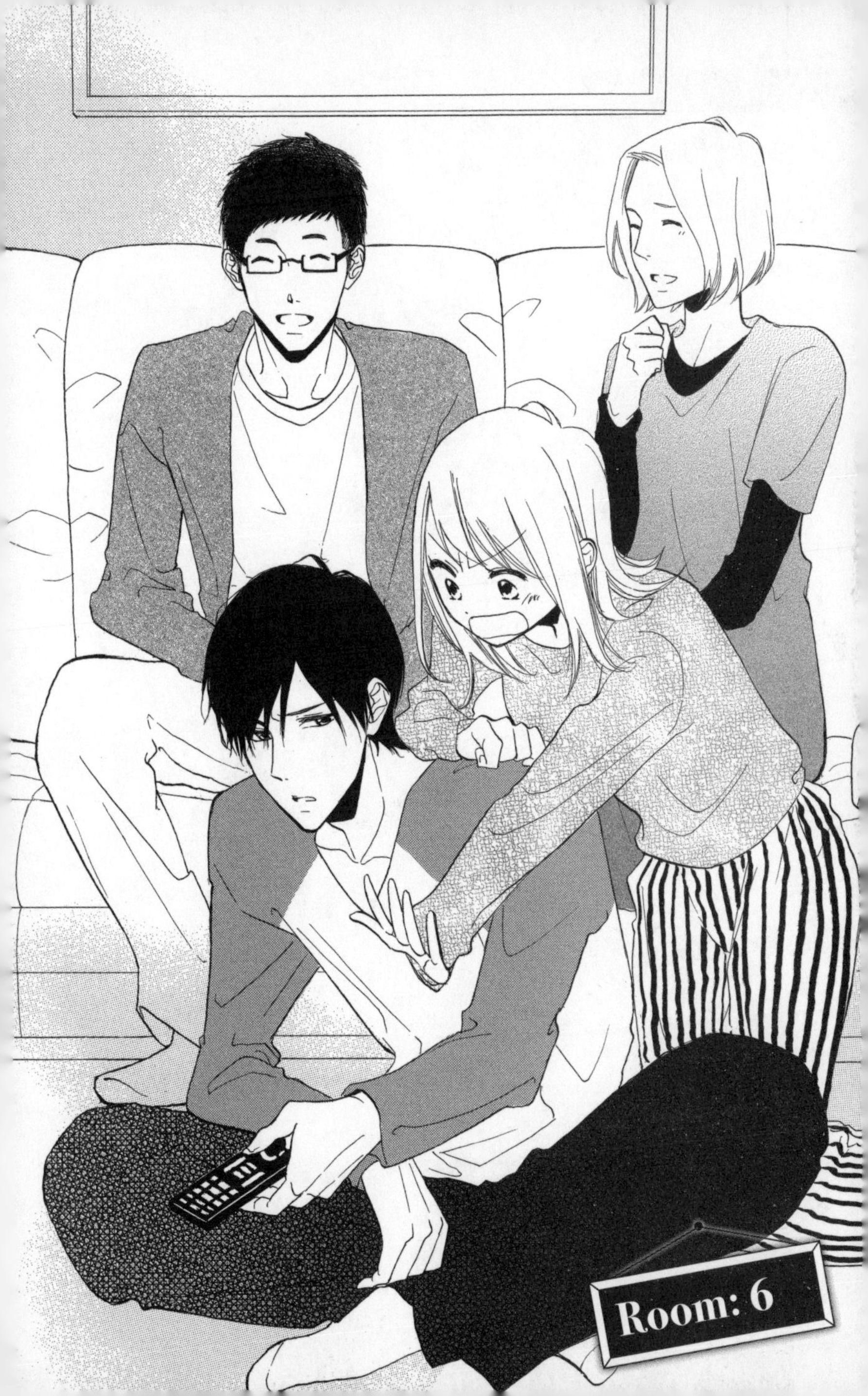
Room: 6

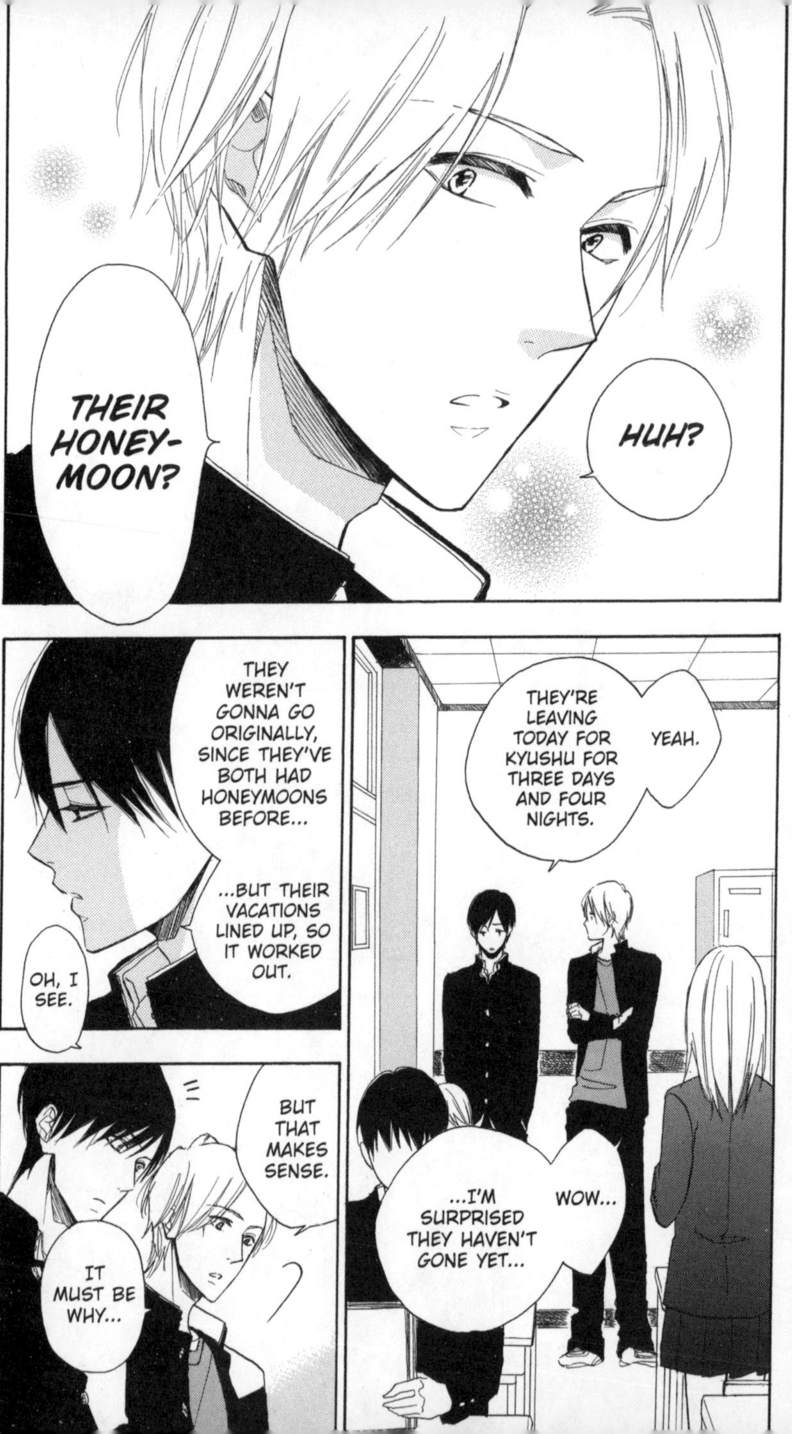
HUH?
THEIR HONEY-MOON?
YEAH.
THEY'RE LEAVING TODAY FOR KYUSHU FOR THREE DAYS AND FOUR NIGHTS.
WOW...
...I'M SURPRISED THEY HAVEN'T GONE YET...
THEY WEREN'T GONNA GO ORIGINALLY, SINCE THEY'VE BOTH HAD HONEYMOONS BEFORE...
...BUT THEIR VACATIONS LINED UP, SO IT WORKED OUT.
OH, I SEE.
BUT THAT MAKES SENSE.
IT MUST BE WHY...

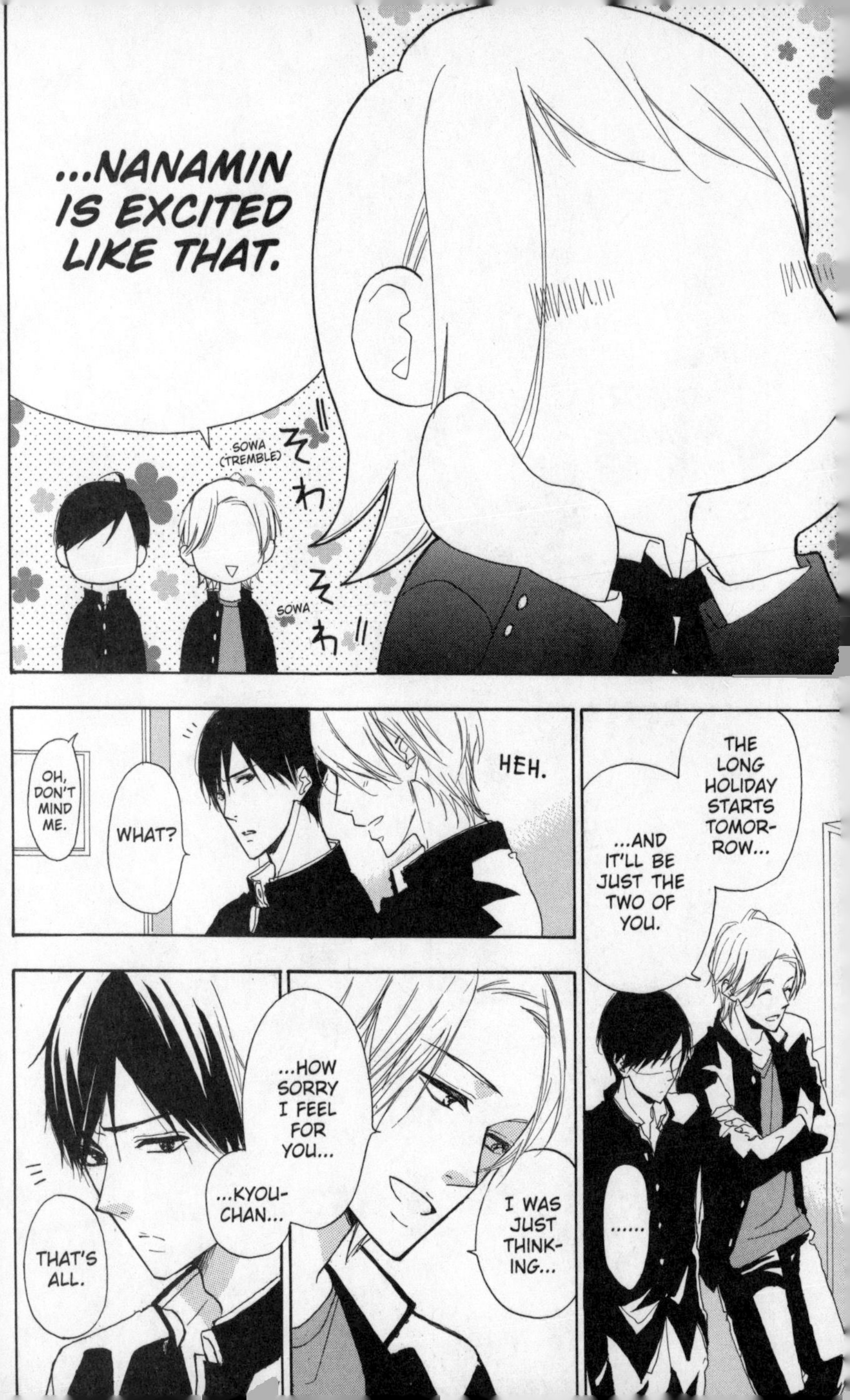
...NANAMIN IS EXCITED LIKE THAT.
SOWA (TREMBLE)
SOWA
THE LONG HOLIDAY STARTS TOMORROW...
...AND IT'LL BE JUST THE TWO OF YOU.
......
HEH.
WHAT?
OH, DON'T MIND ME.
I WAS JUST THINKING...
...HOW SORRY I FEEL FOR YOU...
...KYOU-CHAN...
THAT'S ALL.

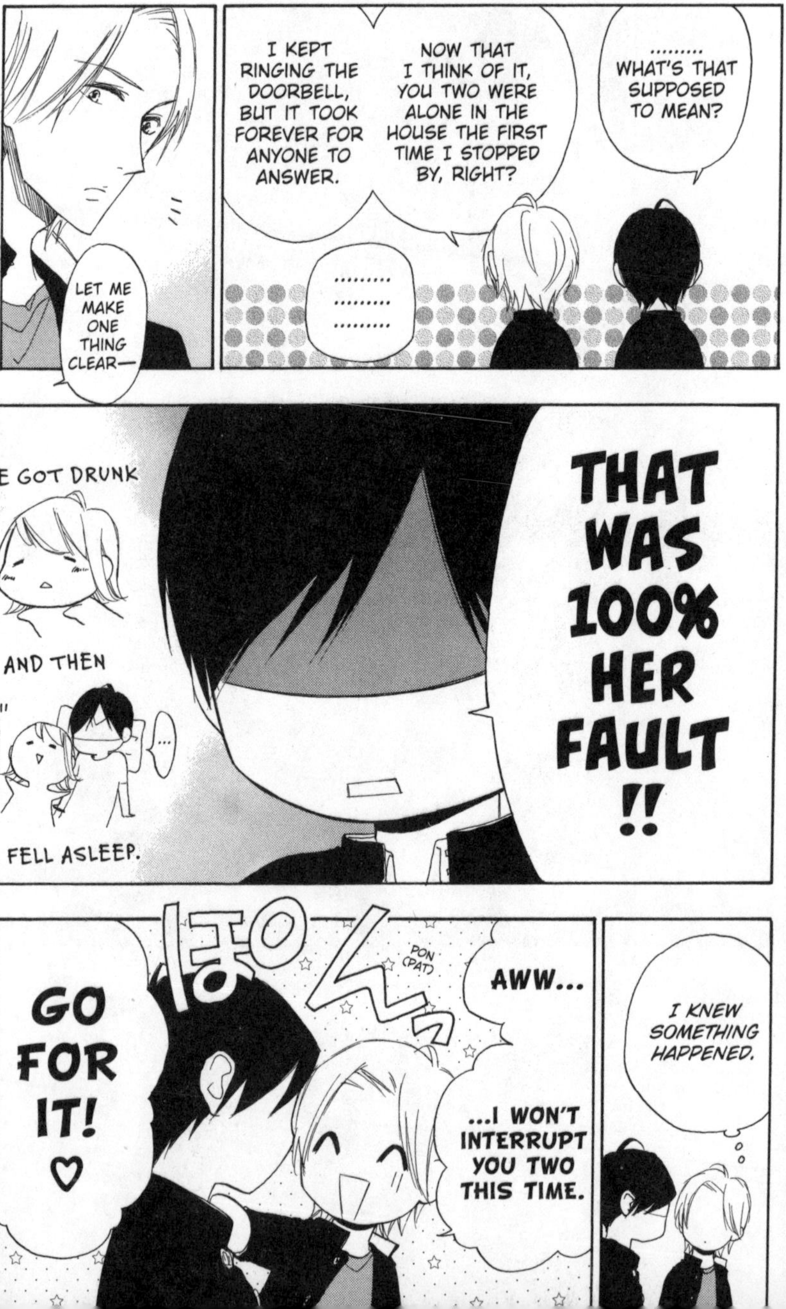
....
WHAT'S THAT SUPPOSED TO MEAN?
NOW THAT I THINK OF IT, YOU TWO WERE ALONE IN THE HOUSE THE FIRST TIME I STOPPED BY, RIGHT?
I KEPT RINGING THE DOORBELL, BUT IT TOOK FOREVER FOR ANYONE TO ANSWER.
....
LET ME MAKE ONE THING CLEAR—
THAT WAS 100% HER FAULT!!
SHE GOT DRUNK
AND THEN
GUU (ZZZ)
...
FELL ASLEEP.
I KNEW SOMETHING HAPPENED.
AWW...
PON (PAT)
...I WON'T INTERRUPT YOU TWO THIS TIME.
GO FOR IT! ♡

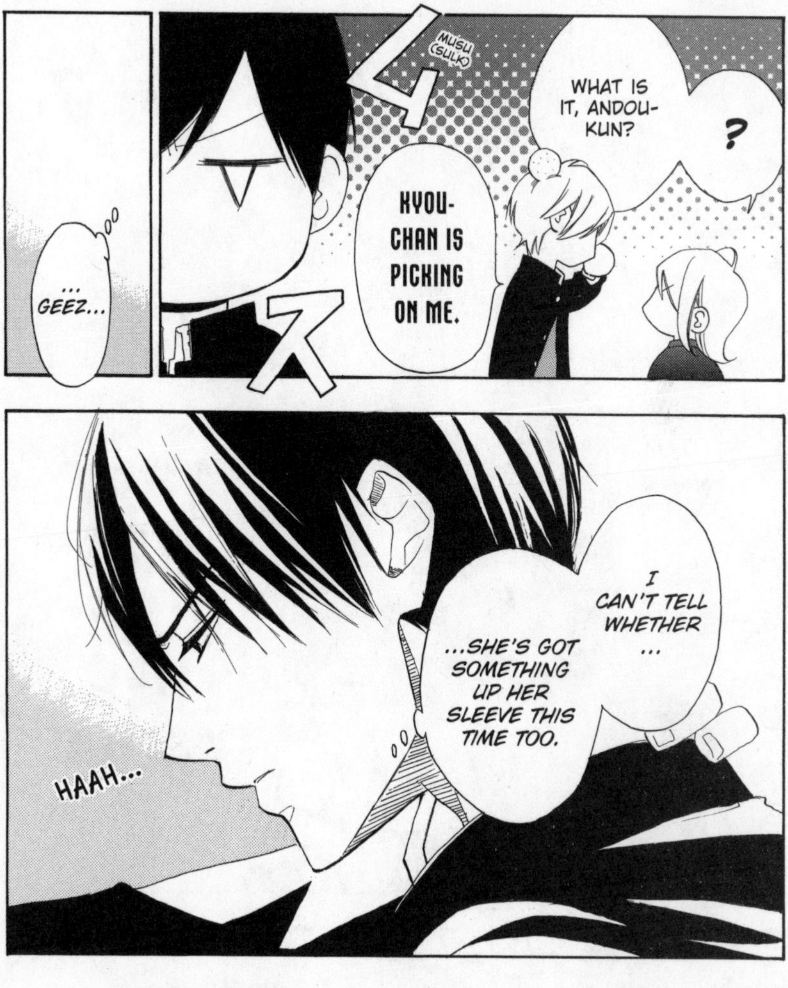
WHAT IS IT, ANDOU-KUN?
?
MUSU (SULK)
KYOU-CHAN IS PICKING ON ME.
... GEEZ...
I CAN'T TELL WHETHER ...
...SHE'S GOT SOMETHING UP HER SLEEVE THIS TIME TOO.
HAAH...
I DUNNO WHAT HAPPENED, BUT YOU SHOULD APOLOGIZE!
YEAH, WHAT SHE SAID.
YOU GUYS ARE SUCH A PAIN.

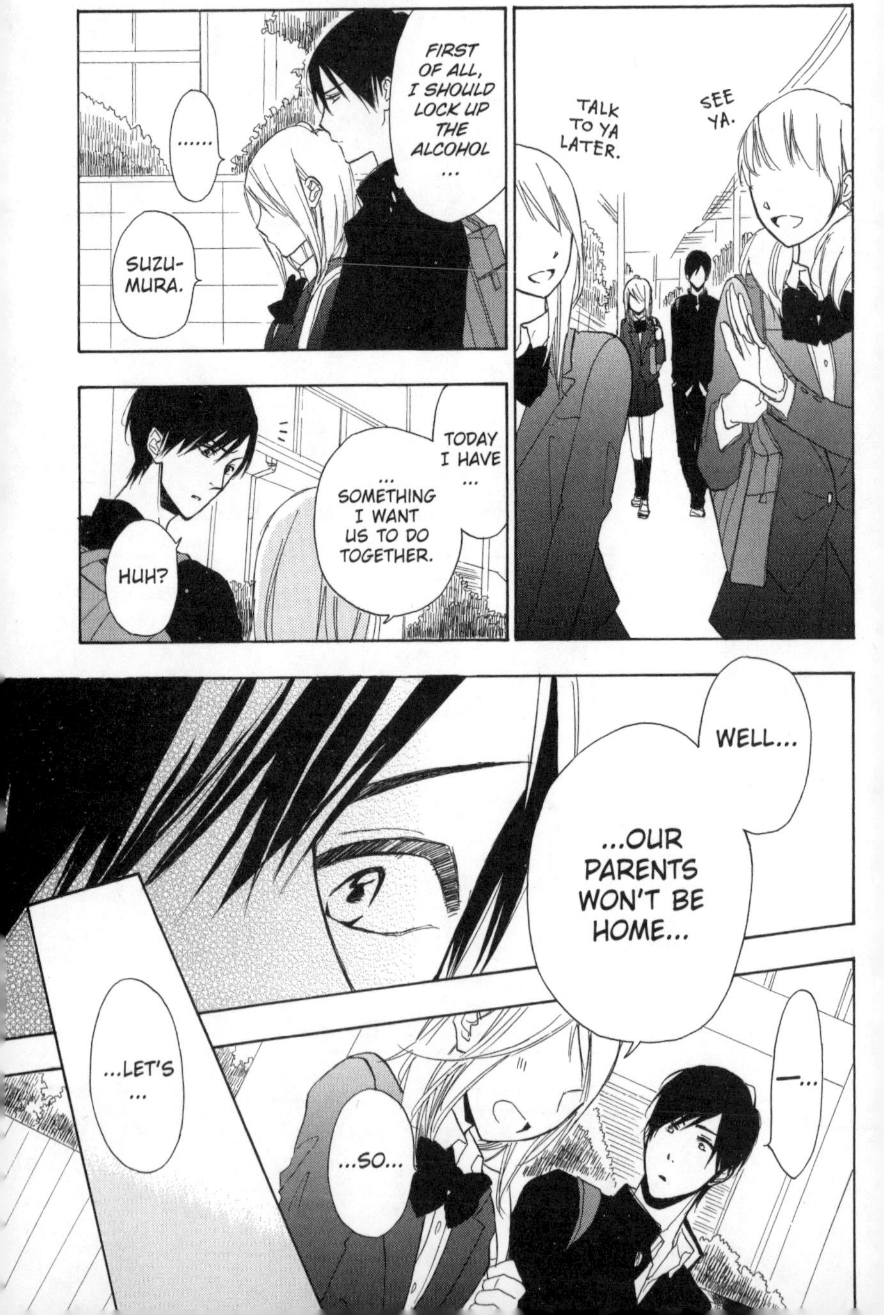
SEE YA.
TALK TO YA LATER.
FIRST OF ALL, I SHOULD LOCK UP THE ALCOHOL ...
......
SUZU-MURA.
TODAY I HAVE ...
... SOMETHING I WANT US TO DO TOGETHER.
HUH?
WELL...
...OUR PARENTS WON'T BE HOME...
—...
...SO...
...LET'S ...

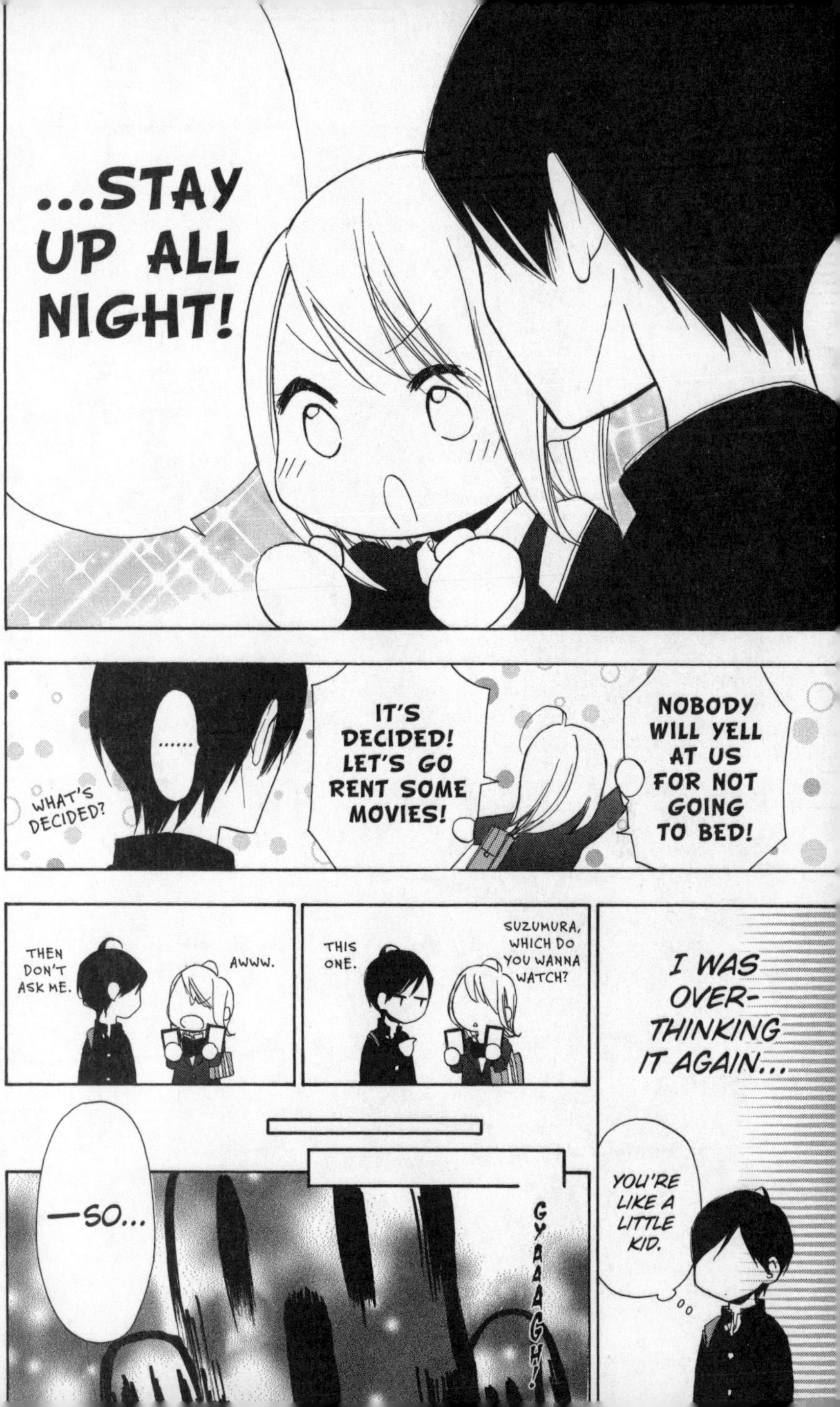
...STAY UP ALL NIGHT!
NOBODY WILL YELL AT US FOR NOT GOING TO BED!
IT'S DECIDED! LET'S GO RENT SOME MOVIES!
......
WHAT'S DECIDED?
I WAS OVER-THINKING IT AGAIN...
YOU'RE LIKE A LITTLE KID.
SUZUMURA, WHICH DO YOU WANNA WATCH?
THIS ONE.
AWWW.
THEN DON'T ASK ME.
GYAAAAGH!
—SO...

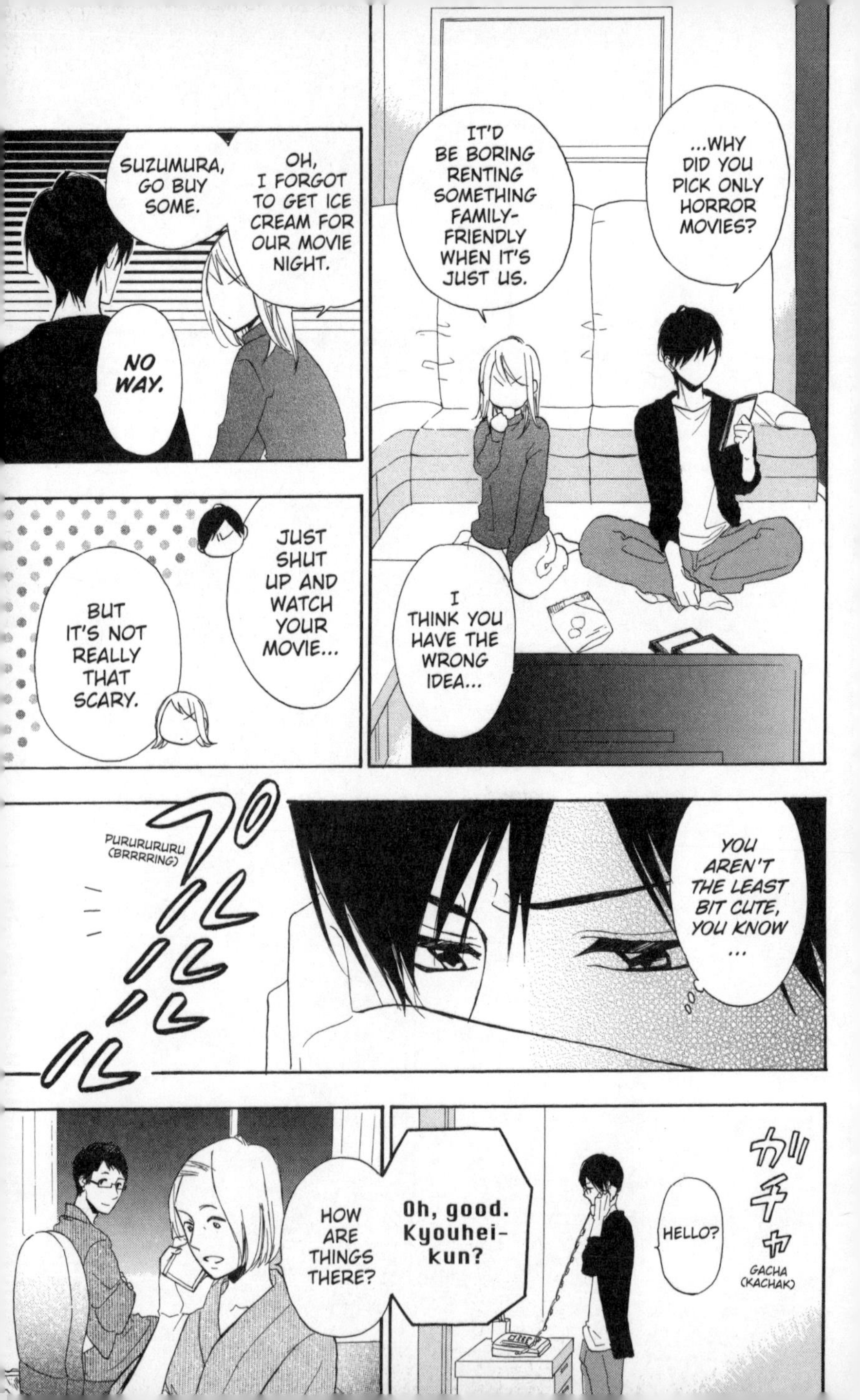

...WHY DID YOU PICK ONLY HORROR MOVIES?
IT'D BE BORING RENTING SOMETHING FAMILY-FRIENDLY WHEN IT'S JUST US.
I THINK YOU HAVE THE WRONG IDEA...
OH, I FORGOT TO GET ICE CREAM FOR OUR MOVIE NIGHT.
SUZUMURA, GO BUY SOME.
NO WAY.
JUST SHUT UP AND WATCH YOUR MOVIE...
BUT IT'S NOT REALLY THAT SCARY.
YOU AREN'T THE LEAST BIT CUTE, YOU KNOW ...
プルルルル
PURURURURU (BRRRRING)
ガチャ
GACHA (KACHAK)
HELLO?
Oh, good. Kyouhei-kun?
HOW ARE THINGS THERE?

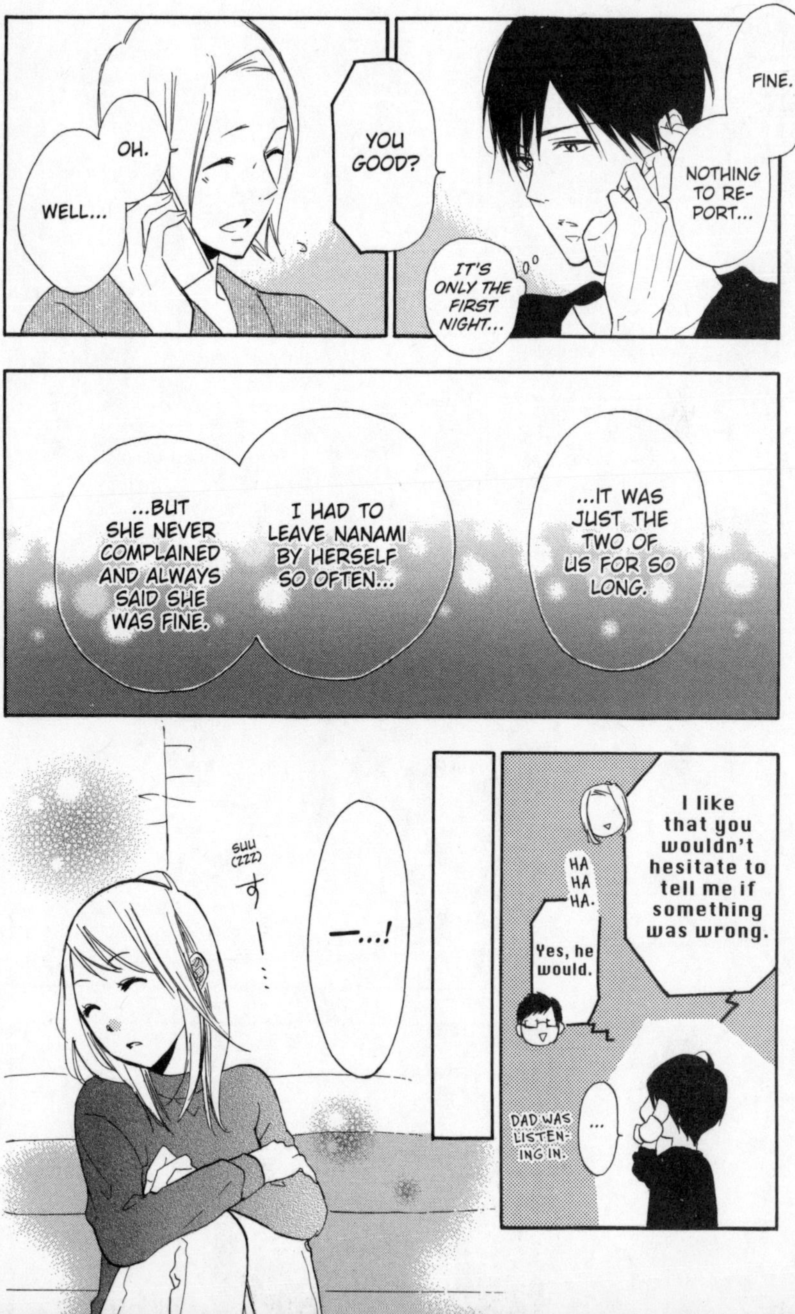
FINE.
NOTHING TO RE-PORT...
IT'S ONLY THE FIRST NIGHT...
YOU GOOD?
OH.
WELL...
...IT WAS JUST THE TWO OF US FOR SO LONG.
I HAD TO LEAVE NANAMI BY HERSELF SO OFTEN...
...BUT SHE NEVER COMPLAINED AND ALWAYS SAID SHE WAS FINE.
I like that you wouldn't hesitate to tell me if something was wrong.
HA HA HA.
Yes, he would.
...
DAD WAS LISTEN-ING IN.
—...!
SUU (ZZZ)
すー…

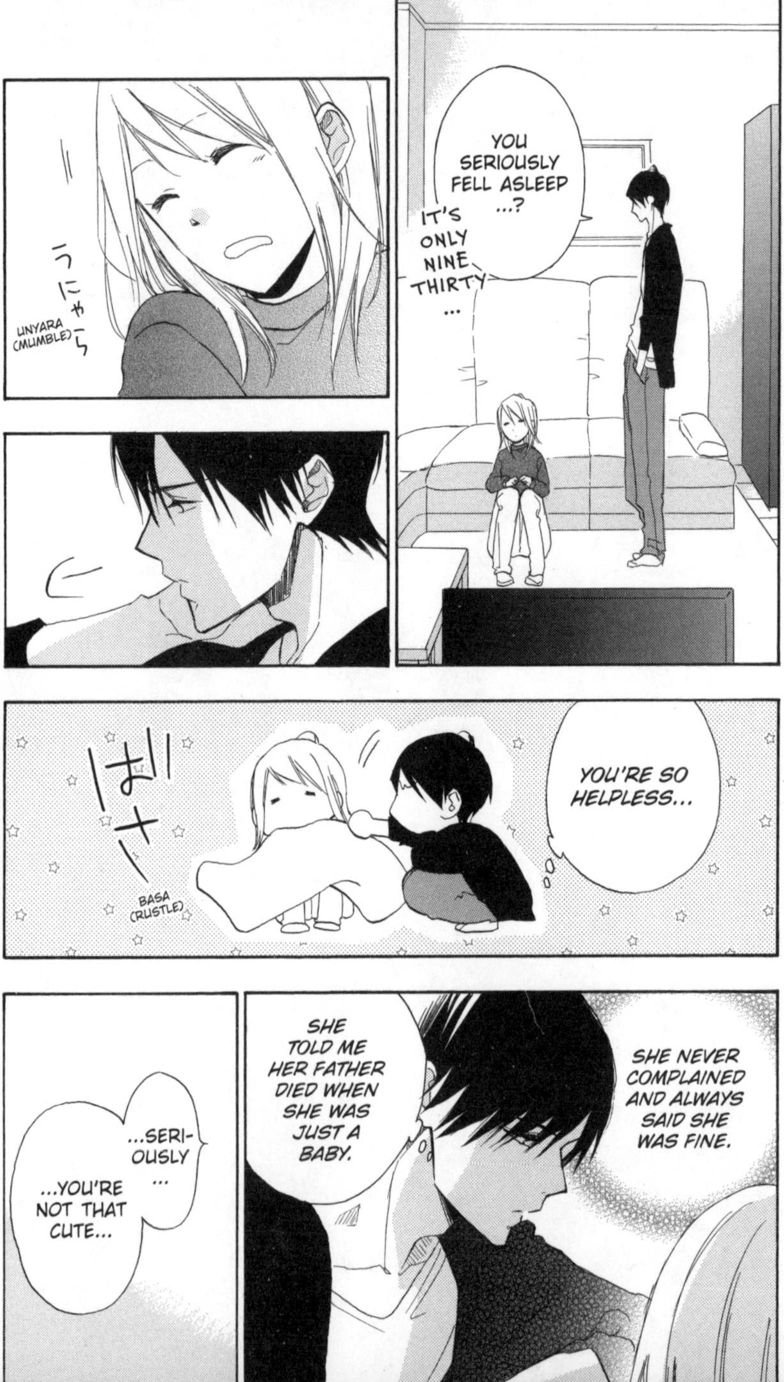
YOU SERIOUSLY FELL ASLEEP ...?
IT'S ONLY NINE THIRTY ...
うにゃら
UNYARA (MUMBLE)
YOU'RE SO HELPLESS...
ばさ
BASA (RUSTLE)
SHE NEVER COMPLAINED AND ALWAYS SAID SHE WAS FINE.
SHE TOLD ME HER FATHER DIED WHEN SHE WAS JUST A BABY.
...SERIOUSLY ...
...YOU'RE NOT THAT CUTE...

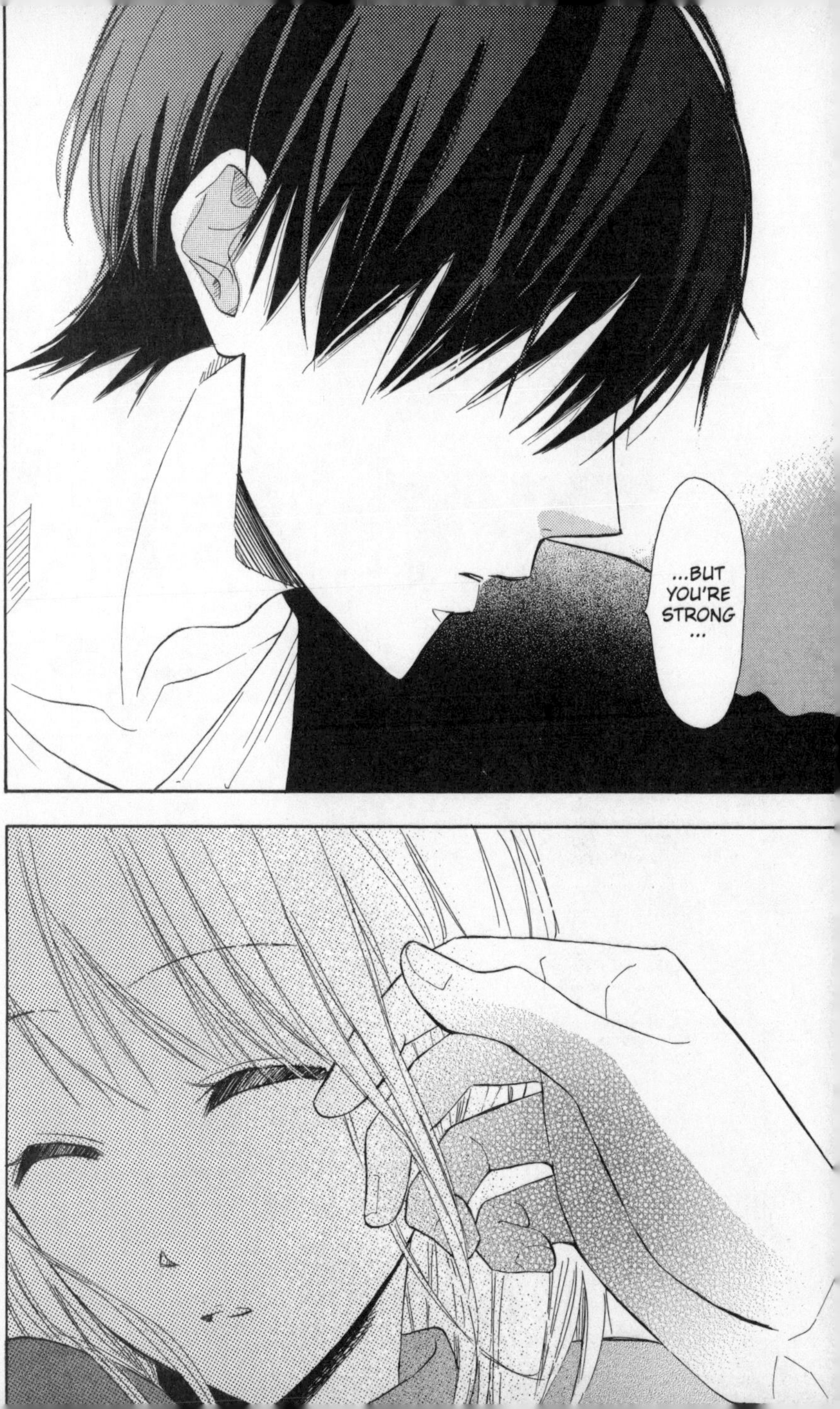
...BUT YOU'RE STRONG ...

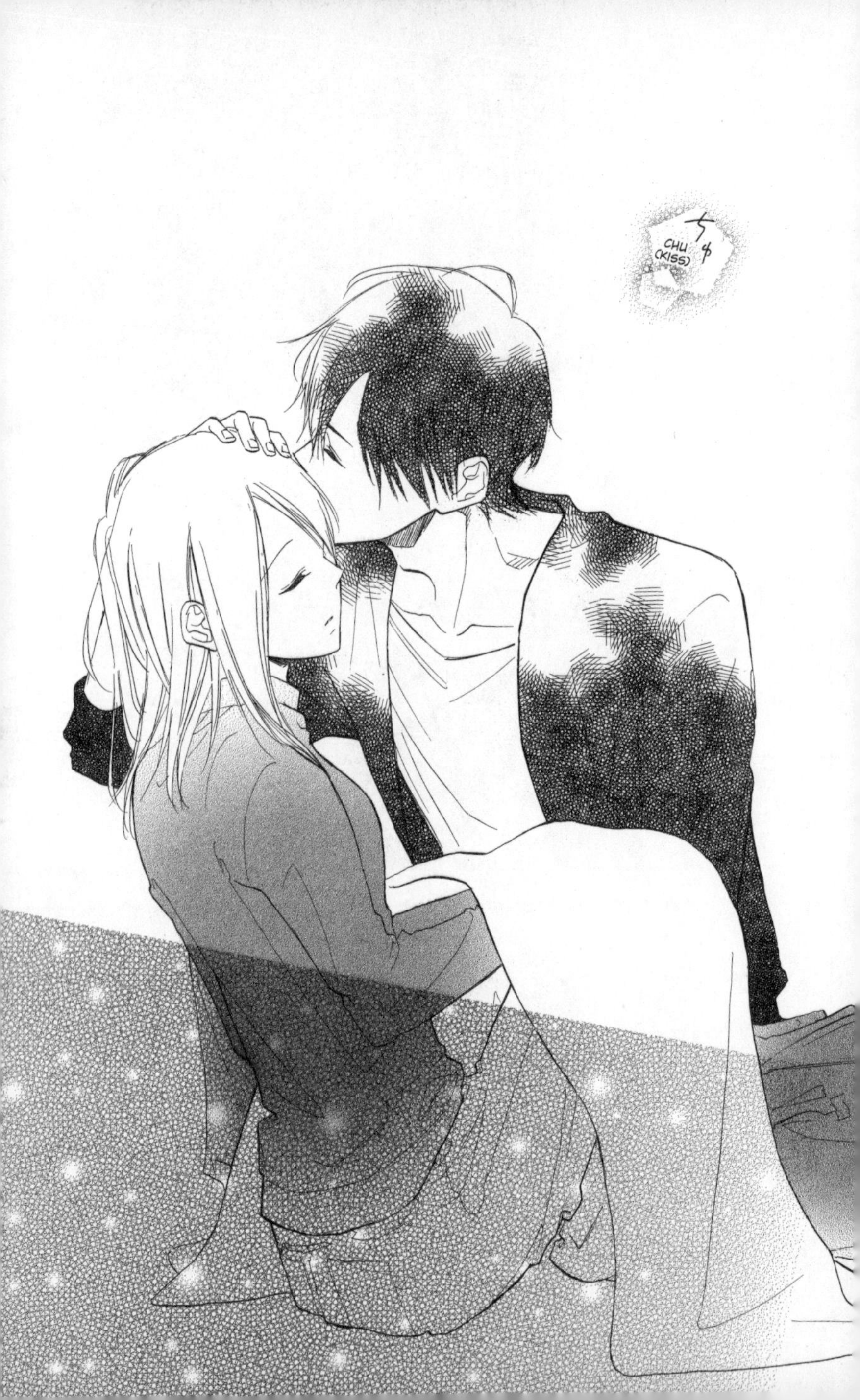
ちゅ
CHU (KISS)

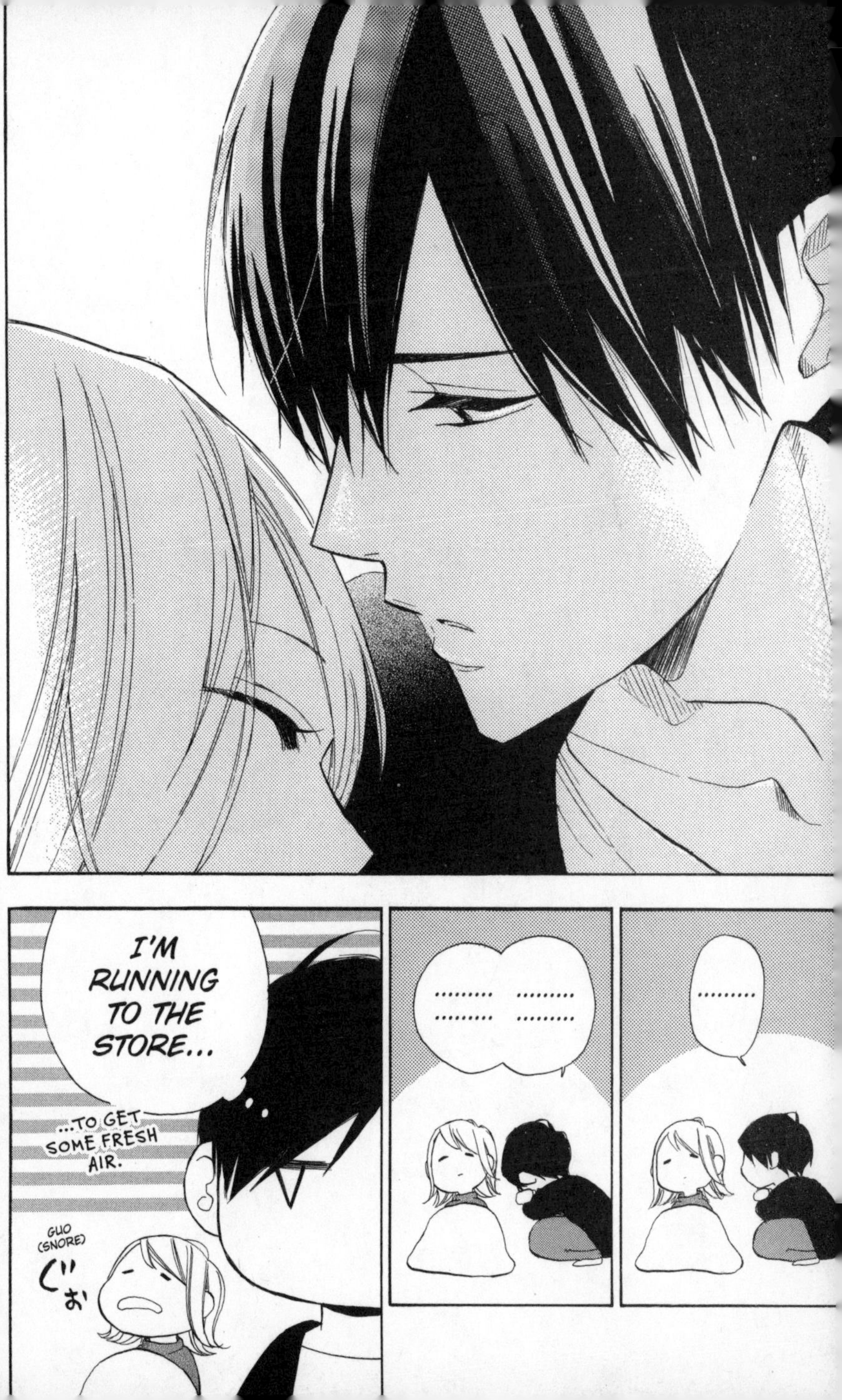
....
....
....
I'M RUNNING TO THE STORE...
...TO GET SOME FRESH AIR.
GUO (SNORE)
ぐぉ

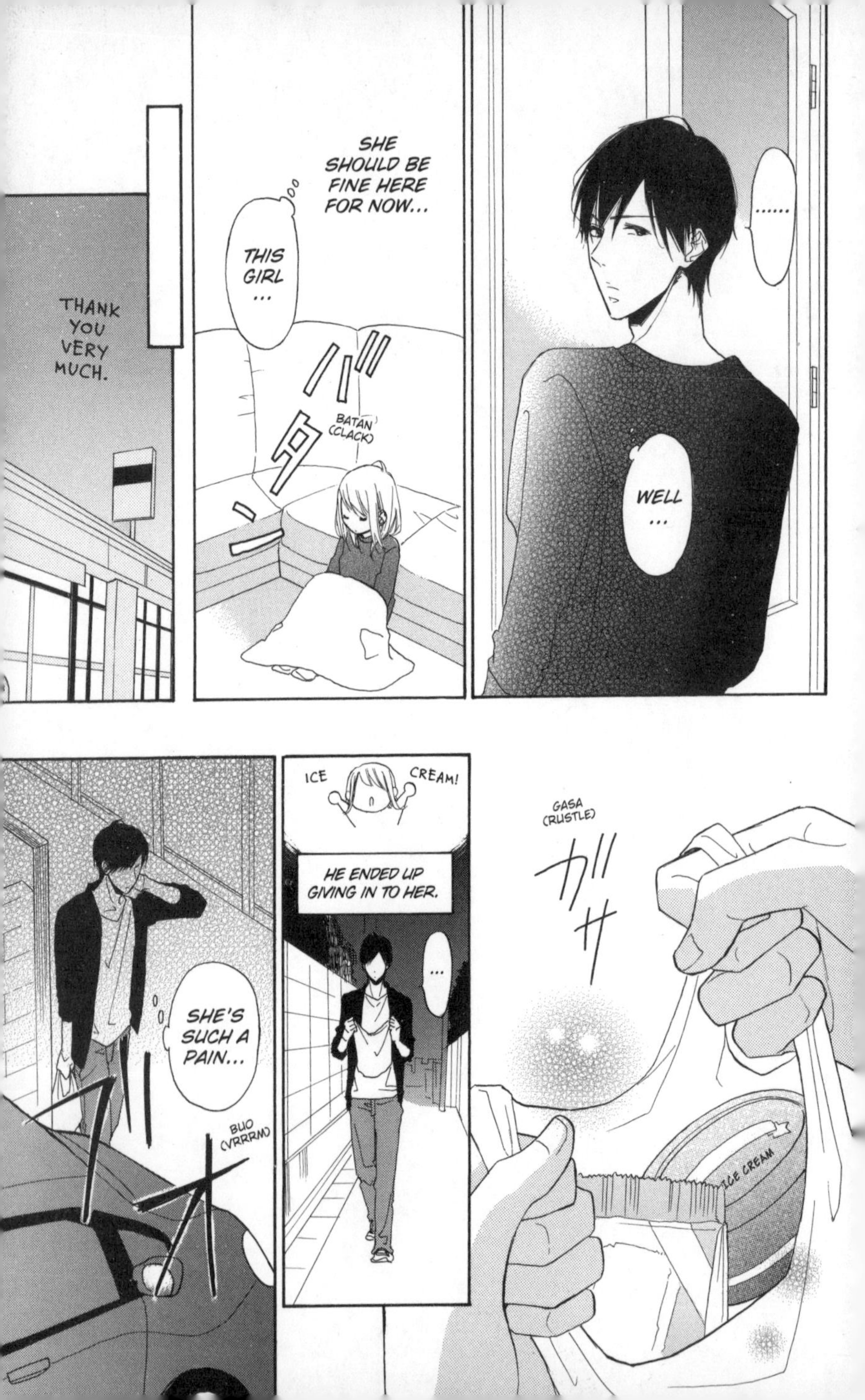
......
WELL ...
SHE SHOULD BE FINE HERE FOR NOW...
THIS GIRL ...
BATAN (CLACK)
THANK YOU VERY MUCH.
GASA (RUSTLE)
ICE CREAM
ICE CREAM!
HE ENDED UP GIVING IN TO HER.
...
SHE'S SUCH A PAIN...
BUO (VRRRM)

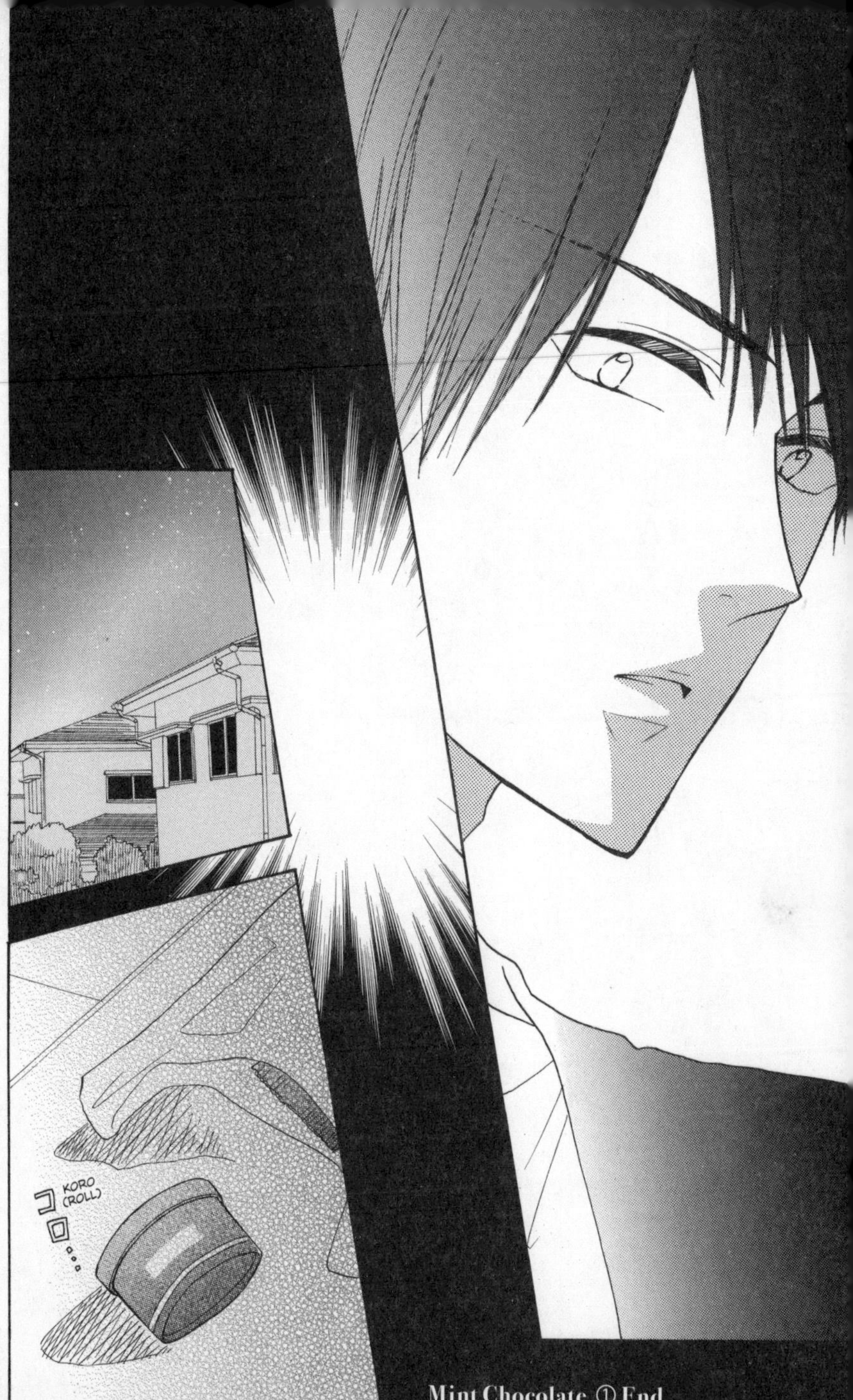

コロ...
KORO (ROLL)

Mint Chocolate ① End

Bonus Chapter

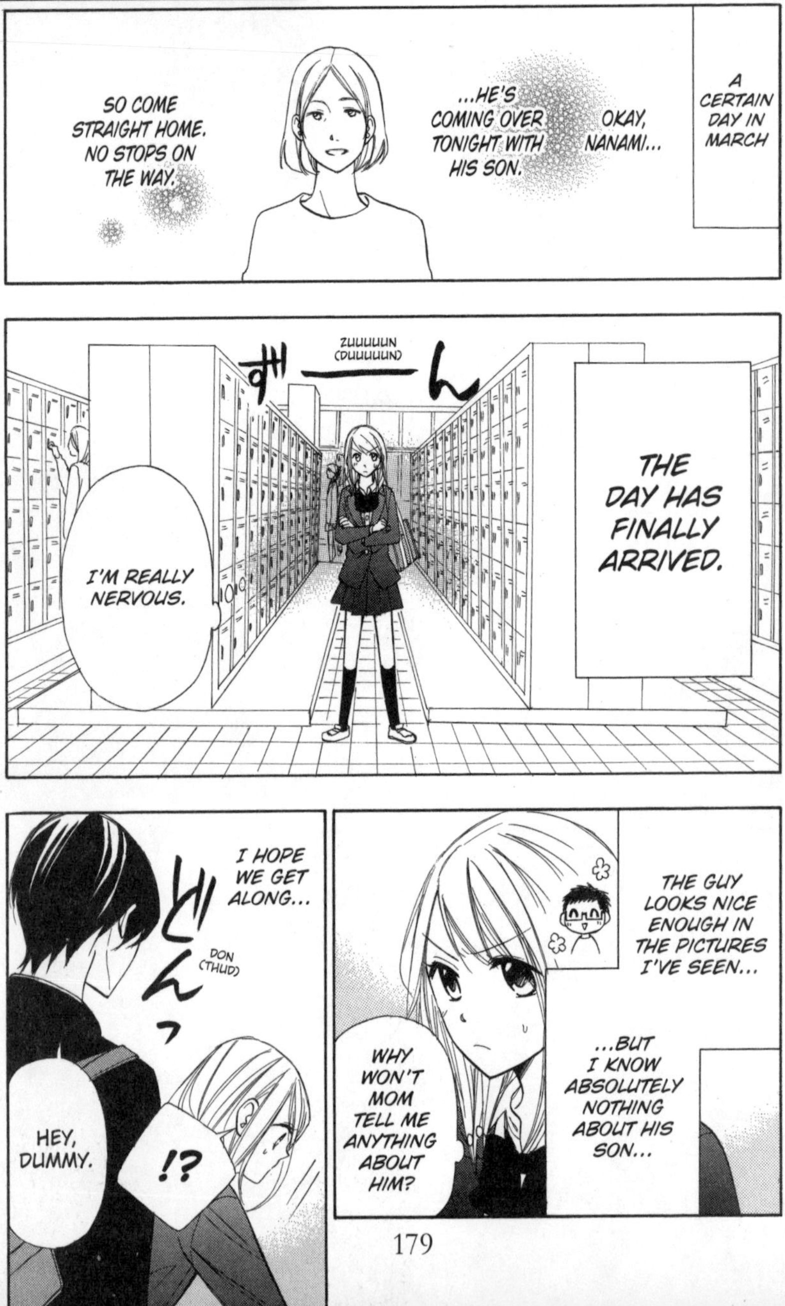
A CERTAIN DAY IN MARCH
OKAY, NANAMI...
...HE'S COMING OVER TONIGHT WITH HIS SON.
SO COME STRAIGHT HOME. NO STOPS ON THE WAY.
THE DAY HAS FINALLY ARRIVED.
ZUUUUUN (DUUUUUN)
I'M REALLY NERVOUS.
THE GUY LOOKS NICE ENOUGH IN THE PICTURES I'VE SEEN...
...BUT I KNOW ABSOLUTELY NOTHING ABOUT HIS SON...
WHY WON'T MOM TELL ME ANYTHING ABOUT HIM?
I HOPE WE GET ALONG...
DON (THUD)
!?
HEY, DUMMY.

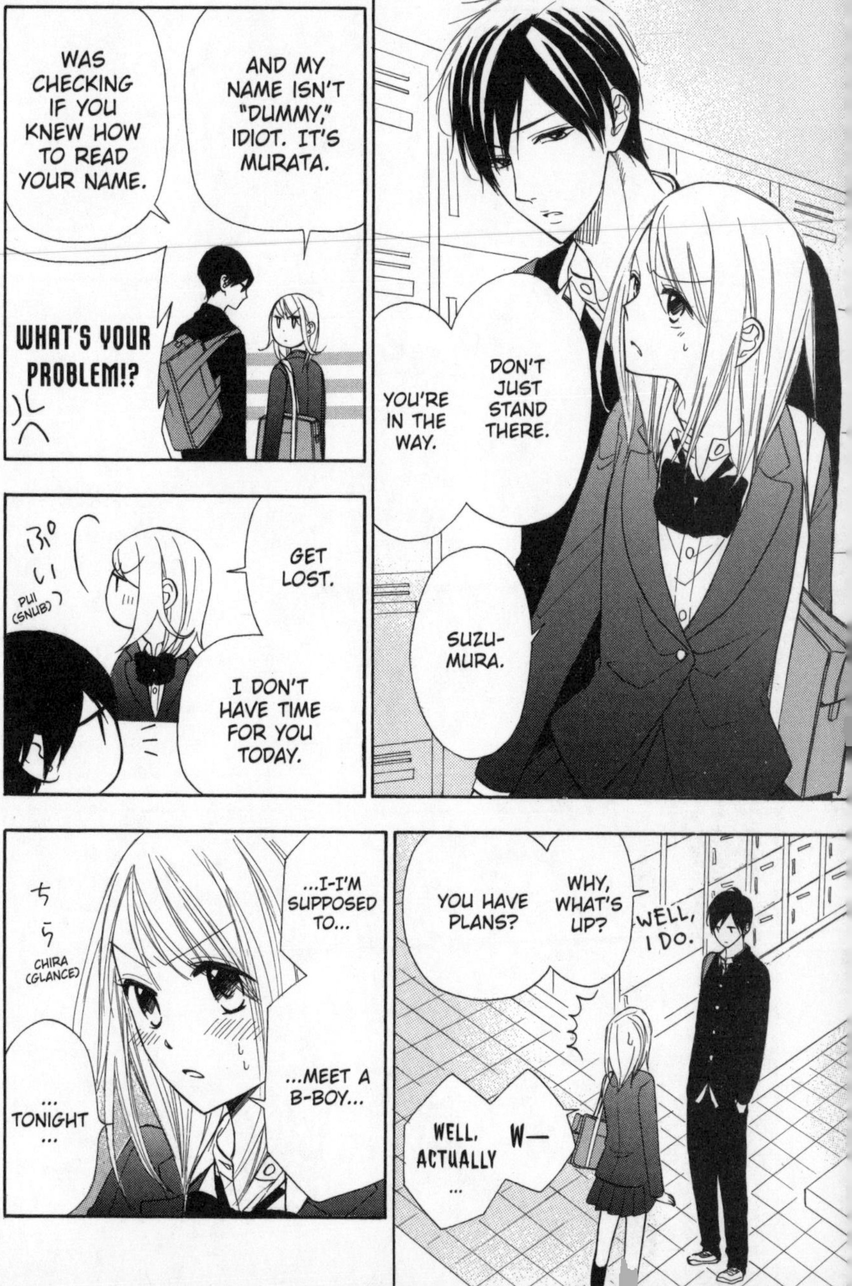

DON'T JUST STAND THERE.
YOU'RE IN THE WAY.
SUZU-MURA.
AND MY NAME ISN'T "DUMMY," IDIOT. IT'S MURATA.
WAS CHECKING IF YOU KNEW HOW TO READ YOUR NAME.
WHAT'S YOUR PROBLEM!?
GET LOST.
ぷい
PUI (SNUB)
I DON'T HAVE TIME FOR YOU TODAY.
WHY, WHAT'S UP?
YOU HAVE PLANS?
WELL, I DO.
W—
WELL, ACTUALLY ...
...I-I'M SUPPOSED TO...
ちら
CHIRA (GLANCE)
...MEET A B-BOY...
... TONIGHT ...

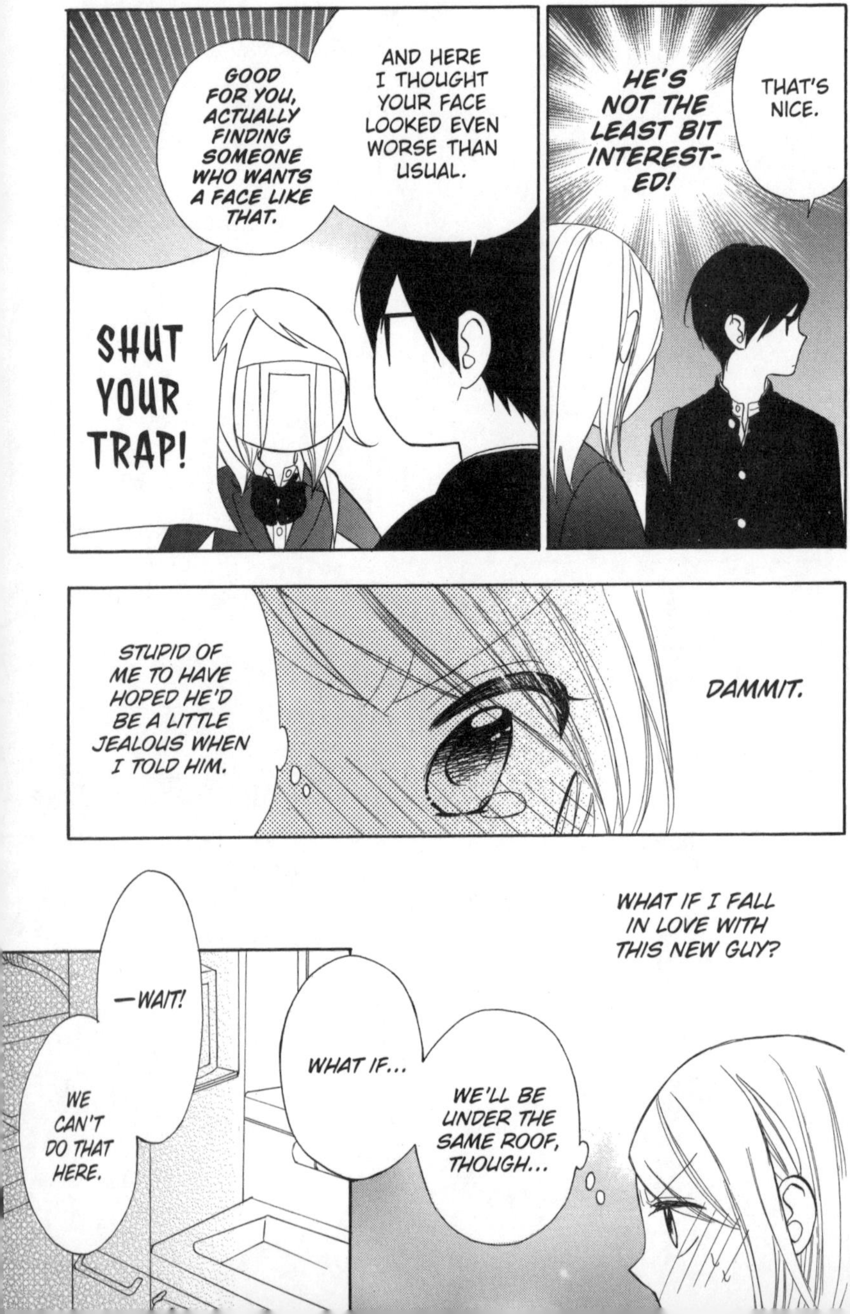
THAT'S NICE.
HE'S NOT THE LEAST BIT INTEREST-ED!
AND HERE I THOUGHT YOUR FACE LOOKED EVEN WORSE THAN USUAL.
GOOD FOR YOU, ACTUALLY FINDING SOMEONE WHO WANTS A FACE LIKE THAT.
SHUT YOUR TRAP!
DAMMIT.
STUPID OF ME TO HAVE HOPED HE'D BE A LITTLE JEALOUS WHEN I TOLD HIM.
WHAT IF I FALL IN LOVE WITH THIS NEW GUY?
WE'LL BE UNDER THE SAME ROOF, THOUGH...
WHAT IF...
—WAIT!
WE CAN'T DO THAT HERE.

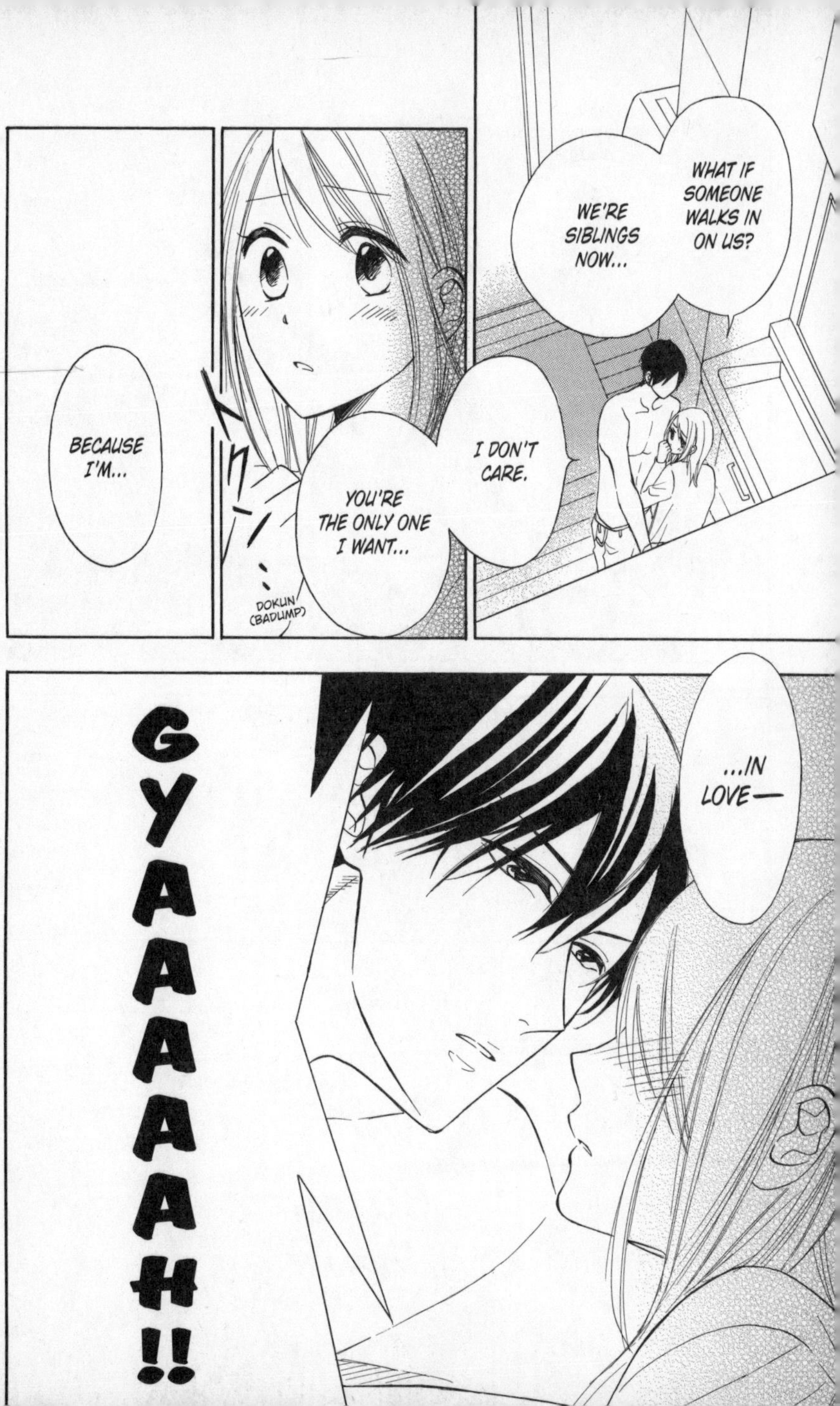

WHAT IF SOMEONE WALKS IN ON US?
WE'RE SIBLINGS NOW...
I DON'T CARE.
YOU'RE THE ONLY ONE I WANT...
DOKUN (BADUMP)
BECAUSE I'M...
...IN LOVE—
GYAAAAAH!!

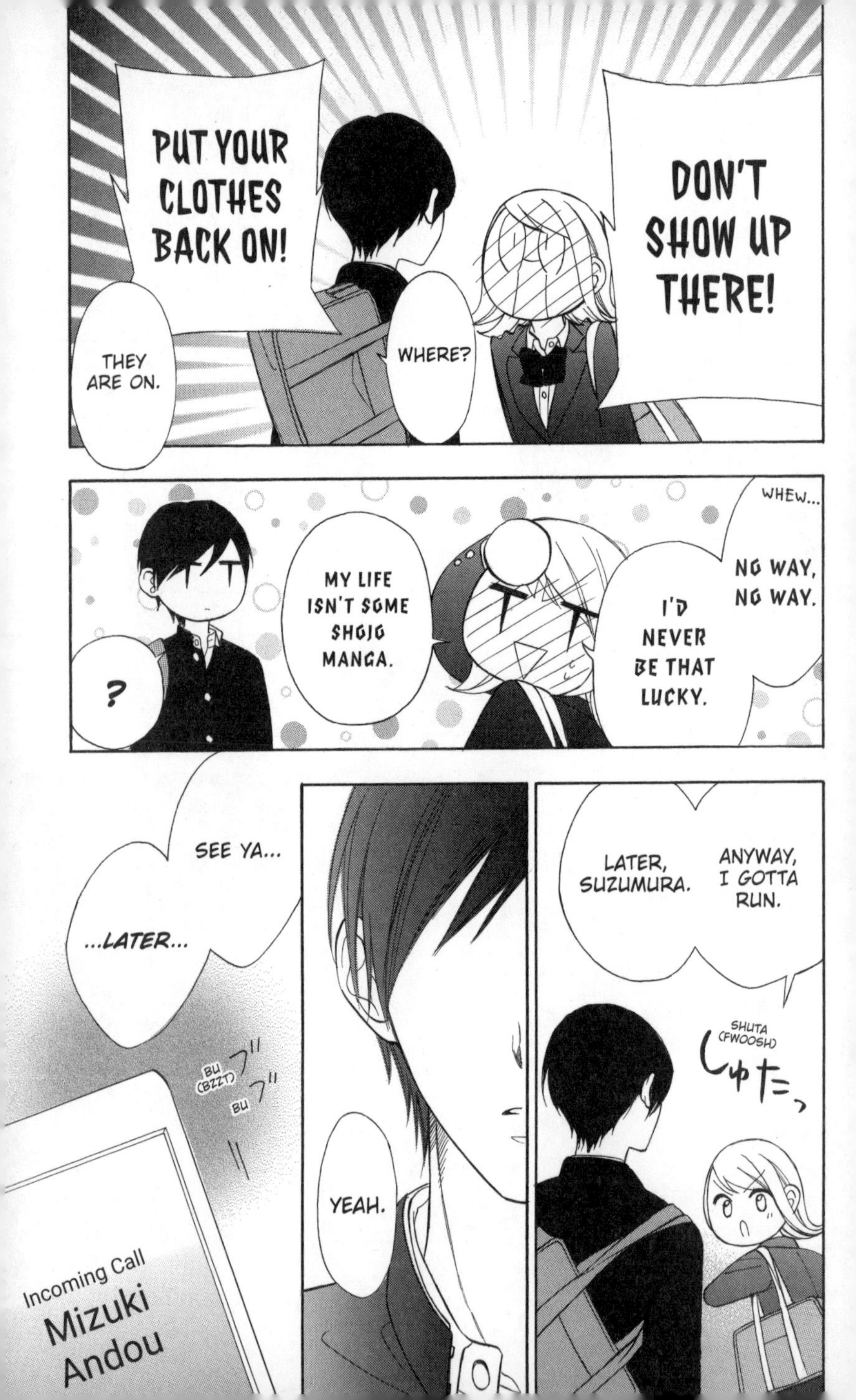
DON'T SHOW UP THERE!
WHERE?
PUT YOUR CLOTHES BACK ON!
THEY ARE ON.
WHEW...
NO WAY, NO WAY.
I'D NEVER BE THAT LUCKY.
MY LIFE ISN'T SOME SHOJO MANGA.
?
ANYWAY, I GOTTA RUN.
LATER, SUZUMURA.
SHUTA (FWOOSH)
しゅたっ
YEAH.
SEE YA...
...LATER...
BU (BZZT) ブ
BU ブ
Incoming Call
Mizuki Andou

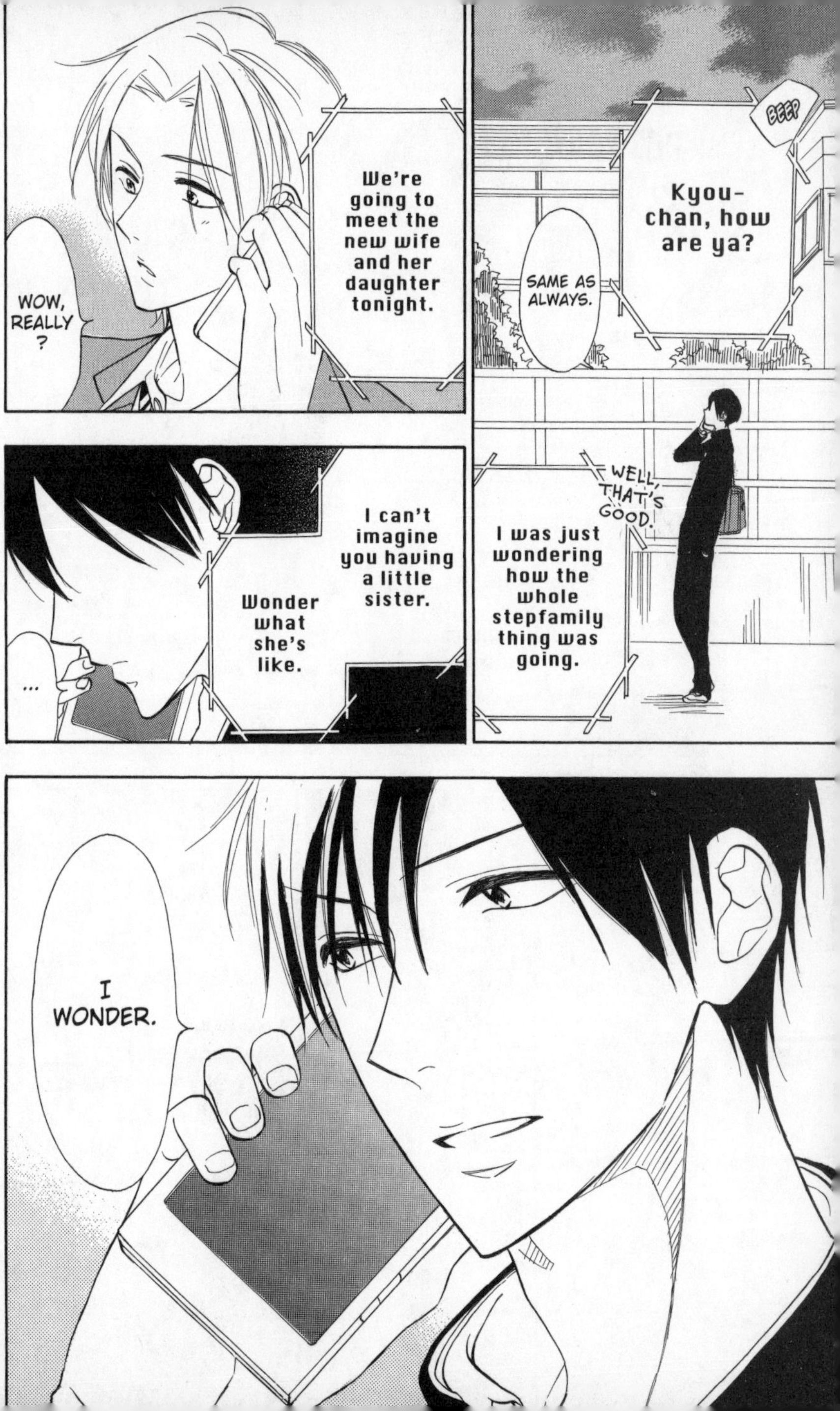
BEEP
Kyou-chan, how are ya?
SAME AS ALWAYS.
WELL, THAT'S GOOD!
I was just wondering how the whole stepfamily thing was going.
We're going to meet the new wife and her daughter tonight.
WOW, REALLY?
I can't imagine you having a little sister.
Wonder what she's like.
...
I WONDER.

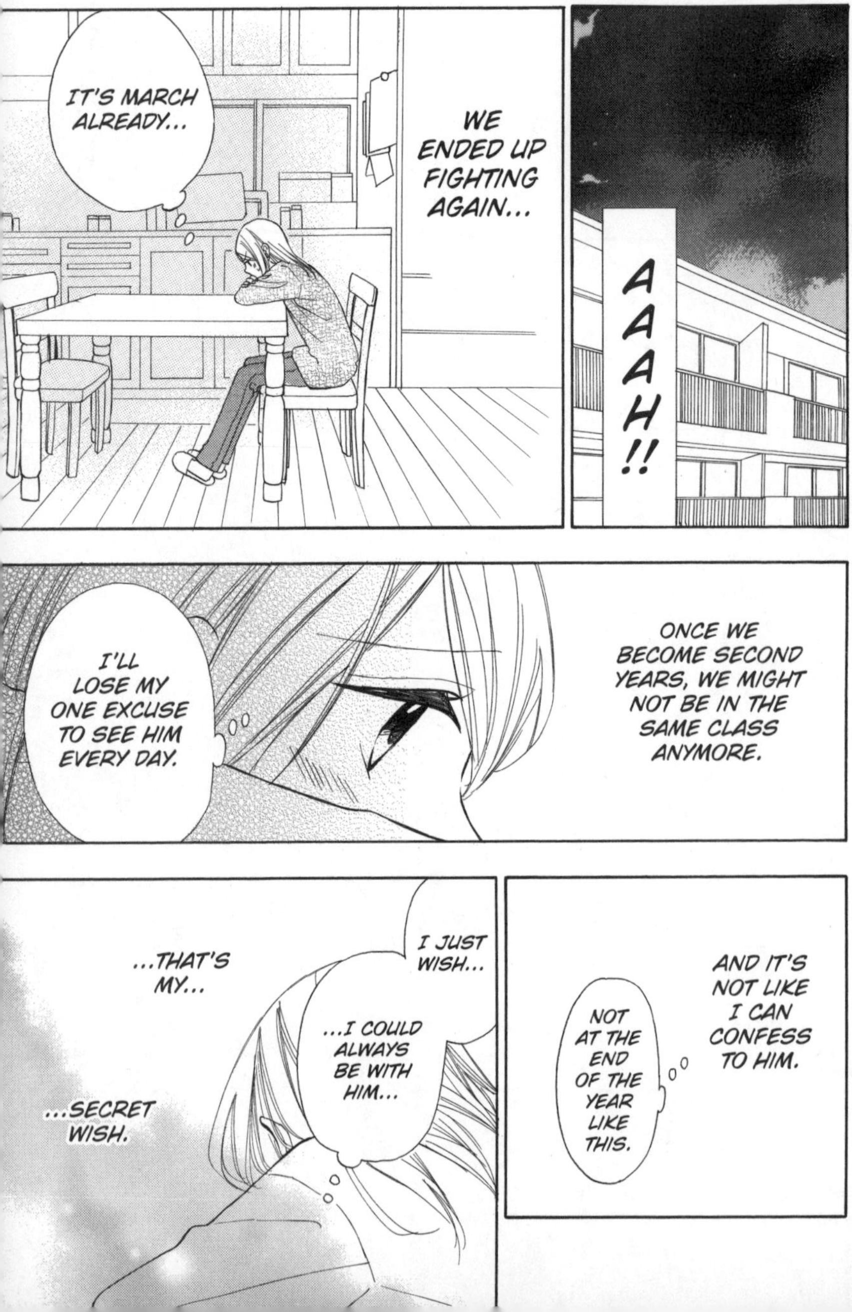
AAAAH!!
WE ENDED UP FIGHTING AGAIN...
IT'S MARCH ALREADY...
ONCE WE BECOME SECOND YEARS, WE MIGHT NOT BE IN THE SAME CLASS ANYMORE.
I'LL LOSE MY ONE EXCUSE TO SEE HIM EVERY DAY.
AND IT'S NOT LIKE I CAN CONFESS TO HIM.
NOT AT THE END OF THE YEAR LIKE THIS.
I JUST WISH...
...I COULD ALWAYS BE WITH HIM...
...THAT'S MY...
...SECRET WISH.

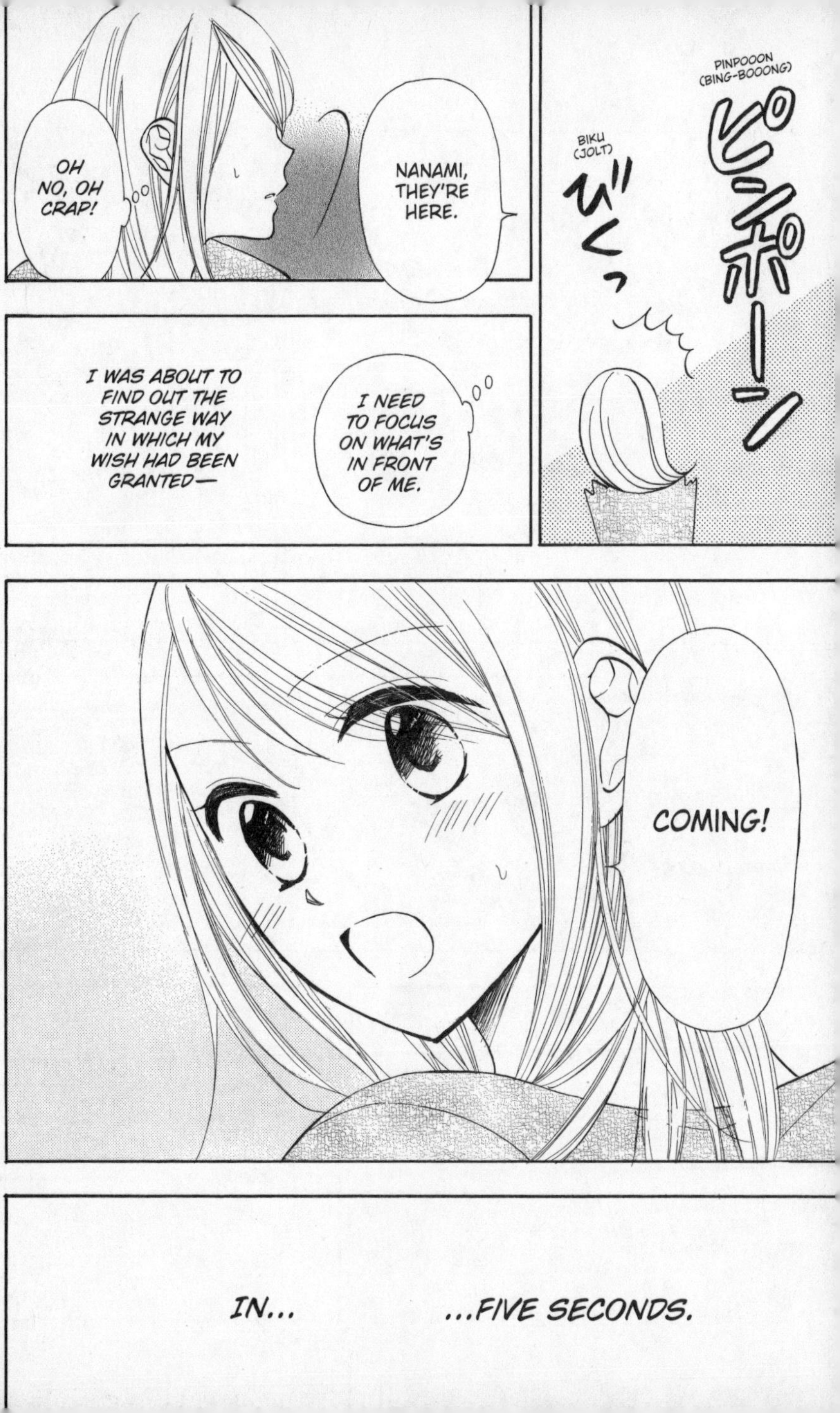
PINPOOON (BING-BOOONG)
ピンポーン
BIKU (JOLT)
びくっ
NANAMI, THEY'RE HERE.
OH NO, OH CRAP!
I NEED TO FOCUS ON WHAT'S IN FRONT OF ME.
I WAS ABOUT TO FIND OUT THE STRANGE WAY IN WHICH MY WISH HAD BEEN GRANTED—
COMING!
IN...
...FIVE SECONDS.

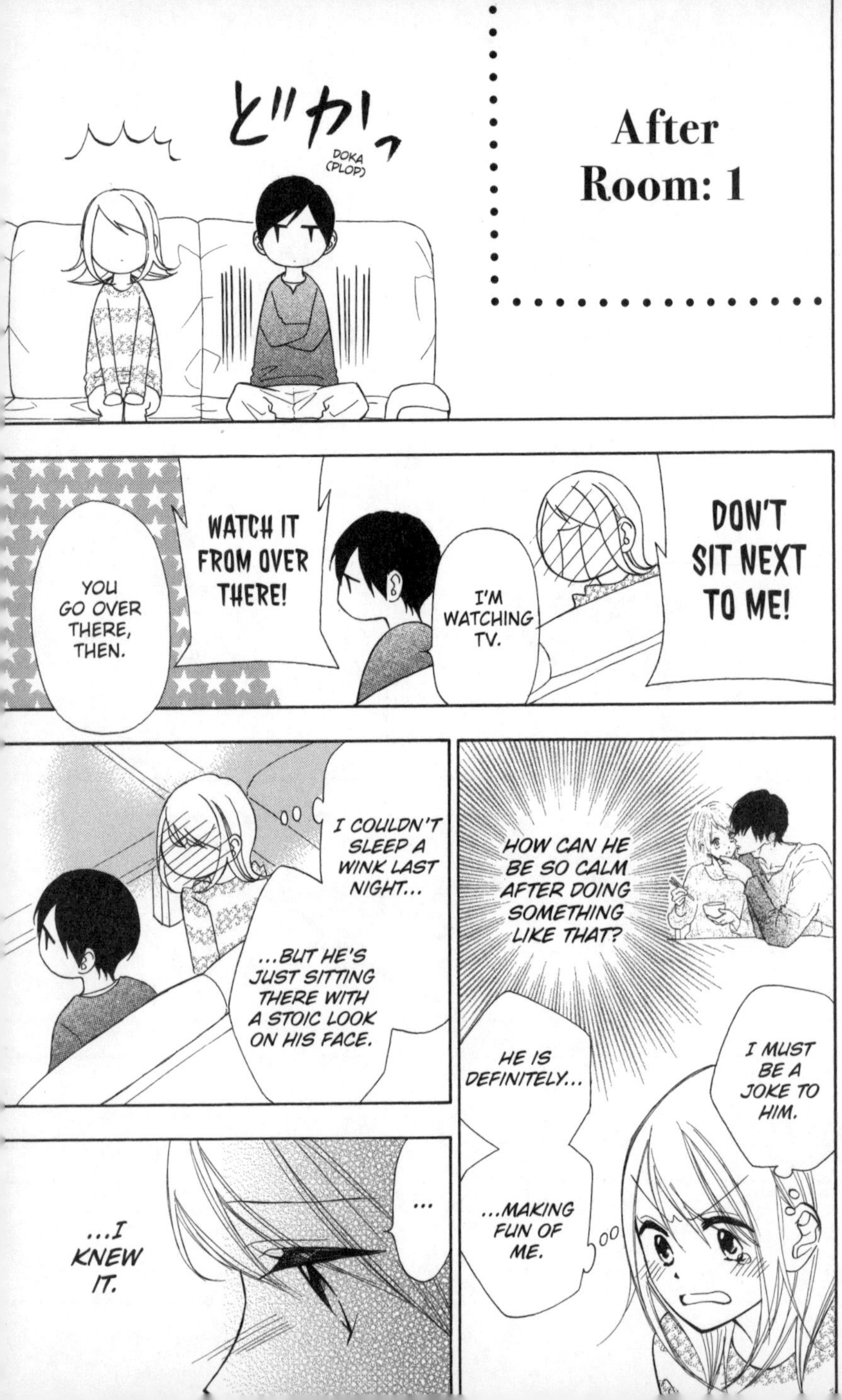
After Room: 1
どかっ
DOKA (PLOP)
DON'T SIT NEXT TO ME!
I'M WATCHING TV.
WATCH IT FROM OVER THERE!
YOU GO OVER THERE, THEN.
HOW CAN HE BE SO CALM AFTER DOING SOMETHING LIKE THAT?
I MUST BE A JOKE TO HIM.
HE IS DEFINITELY...
...MAKING FUN OF ME.
I COULDN'T SLEEP A WINK LAST NIGHT...
...BUT HE'S JUST SITTING THERE WITH A STOIC LOOK ON HIS FACE.
...
...I KNEW IT.

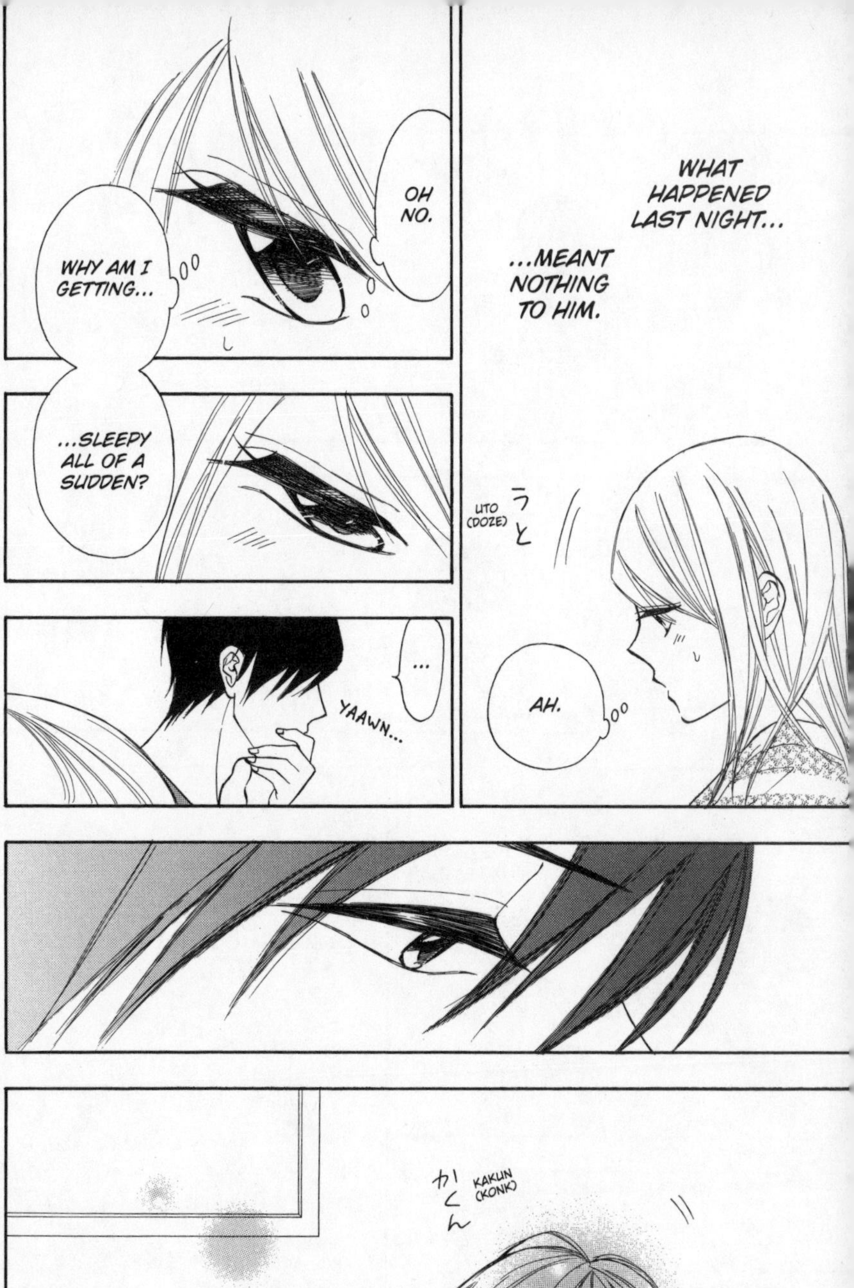
WHAT HAPPENED LAST NIGHT...
...MEANT NOTHING TO HIM.
UTO (DOZE)
AH.
OH NO.
WHY AM I GETTING...
...SLEEPY ALL OF A SUDDEN?
...
YAAWN...
KAKUN (KONK)

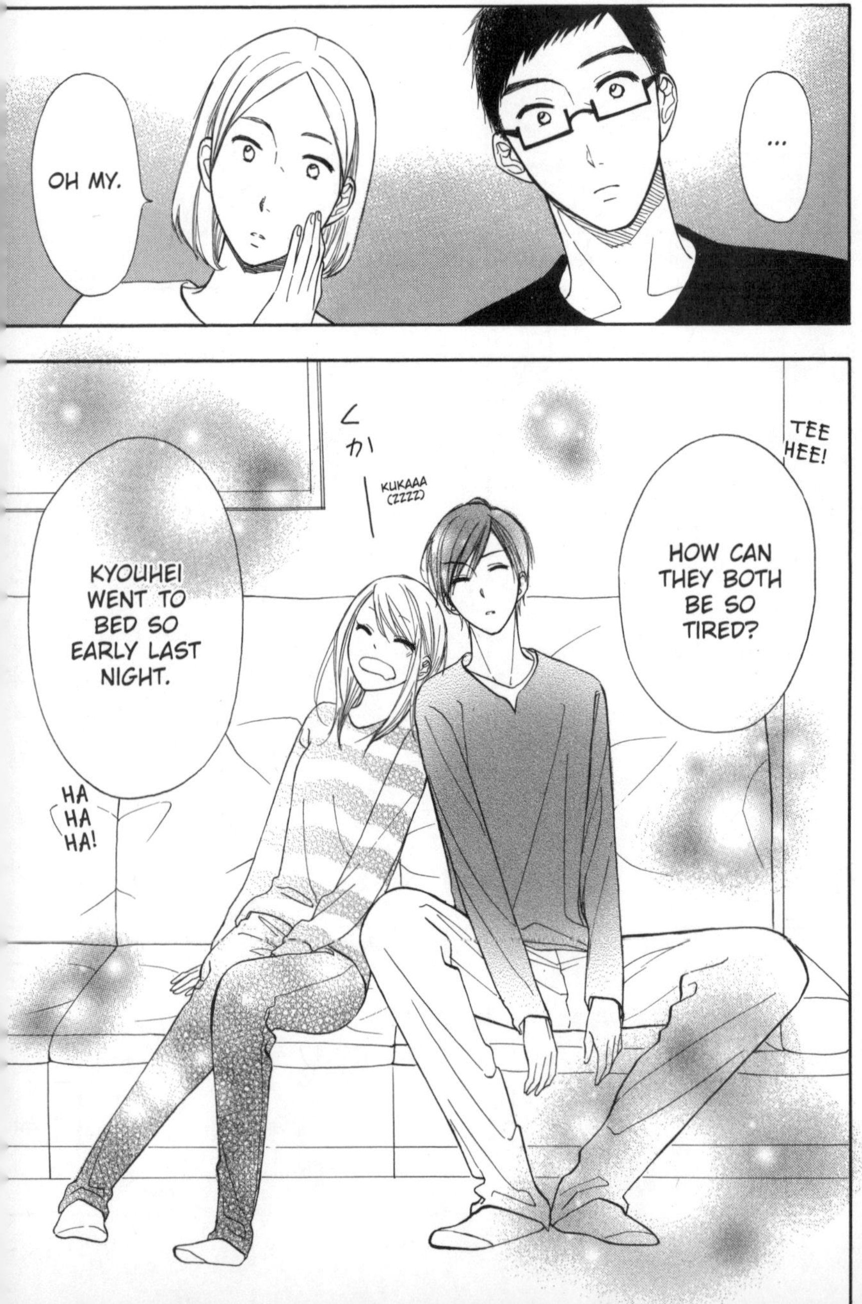
...
OH MY.
TEE HEE!
HOW CAN THEY BOTH BE SO TIRED?
くか
KUKAAA (ZZZZ)
KYOUHEI WENT TO BED SO EARLY LAST NIGHT.
HA HA HA!

NEW LAST NAME

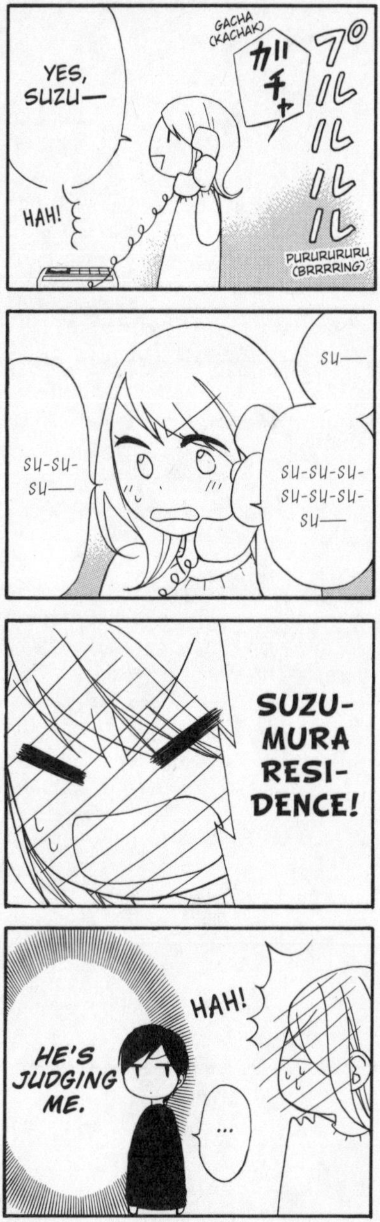
プルルルル
PURURURURU (BRRRRING)
ガチャ
GACHA (KACHAK)
YES, SUZU—
HAH!
SU—
SU-SU-SU-SU-SU-SU-SU—
SU-SU-SU—
SUZUMURA RESIDENCE!
HAH!
HE'S JUDGING ME.
...

MENU MAYHEM

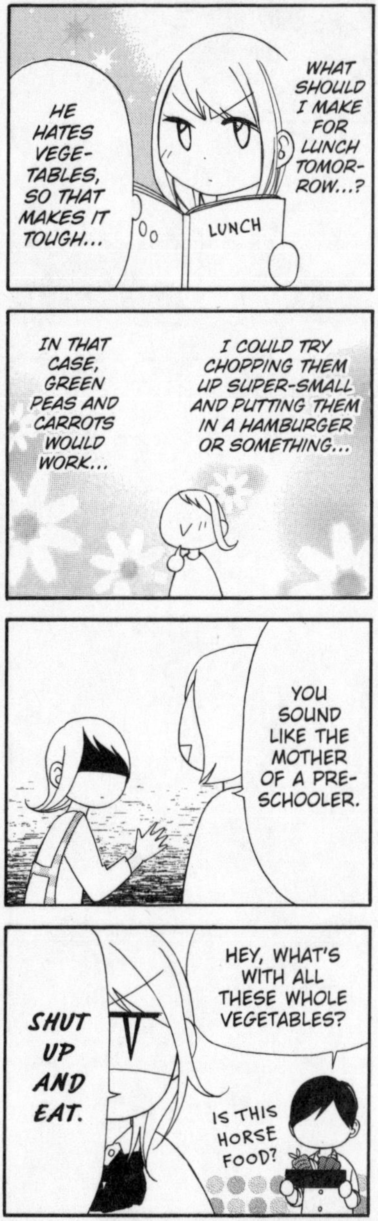
WHAT SHOULD I MAKE FOR LUNCH TOMORROW...?
LUNCH
HE HATES VEGETABLES, SO THAT MAKES IT TOUGH...
I COULD TRY CHOPPING THEM UP SUPER-SMALL AND PUTTING THEM IN A HAMBURGER OR SOMETHING...
IN THAT CASE, GREEN PEAS AND CARROTS WOULD WORK...
YOU SOUND LIKE THE MOTHER OF A PRESCHOOLER.
HEY, WHAT'S WITH ALL THESE WHOLE VEGETABLES?
IS THIS HORSE FOOD?
SHUT UP AND EAT.

Bonus Chapter End

TRANSLATION NOTES

Common Honorifics

-san: The Japanese equivalent of Mr./Mrs./Miss. If a situation calls for politeness, this is the fail-safe honorific.

-kun: Used most often when referring to boys, this indicates affection or familiarity. Occasionally used by older men among their peers, but it may also be used by anyone referring to a person of lower standing.

-chan: An affectionate honorific indicating familiarity used mostly in reference to girls; also used in reference to cute persons or animals of either gender.

no honorific: Indicates familiarity or closeness; if used without permission or reason, addressing someone in this manner would constitute an insult.

Page 11
Class duty: In Japanese high schools, students are expected to assist in cleaning classrooms and helping teachers prepare for their next lessons by running errands and setting up equipment.

Page 34
High school grades: High school in Japan starts in tenth grade and runs through twelfth. Therefore, the first year of high school is equivalent to tenth grade in the United States, second year to eleventh, and third to twelfth.

Page 185
High school year: A typical Japanese school year starts in April and ends in March. The holiday break schedule is divided more similarly to year-round schools in the United States than the typical September to June schedule.

MINT CHOCOLATE

1

MAMI ORIKASA

Translation: Amber Tamosaitis | Lettering: Sara Linsley

This book is a work of fiction. Names, characters, places, and incidents are the product of the author's imagination or are used fictitiously. Any resemblance to actual events, locales, or persons, living or dead, is coincidental.

MINT CHOCOLATE by Mami Orikasa
© Mami Orikasa 2018
All rights reserved.
First published in Japan in 2018 by HAKUSENSHA, Inc., Tokyo.
English language translation rights in U.S.A., Canada and U.K. arranged with
HAKUSENSHA, Inc., Tokyo through Tuttle-Mori Agency, Inc., Tokyo.

English translation © 2021 by Yen Press, LLC

Yen Press
150 West 30th Street, 19th Floor
New York, NY 10001

Visit us at yenpress.com ♥ facebook.com/yenpress ♥ twitter.com/yenpress
yenpress.tumblr.com ♥ instagram.com/yenpress

First Yen Press Edition: January 2021

Yen Press is an imprint of Yen Press, LLC.
The Yen Press name and logo are trademarks of Yen Press, LLC.

The publisher is not responsible for websites (or their content) that are not owned by the publisher.

Library of Congress Control Number: 2020949568

ISBNs: 978-1-9753-2026-3 (paperback)
978-1-9753-2027-0 (ebook)

10 9 8 7 6 5 4 3 2 1

WOR

Printed in the United States of America